EUROPE UN
17

EUROPE UNDER NAPOLEON 1799–1815

MICHAEL BROERS

Lecturer in History, University of Leeds

A member of the Hodder Headline Group
LONDON • NEW YORK • SYDNEY • AUCKLAND

First published in Great Britain in 1996 by
Arnold, a member of the Hodder Headline Group,
338 Euston Road, London NW1 3BH
175 Fifth Avenue, New York, NY 10010

Distributed exclusively in the USA by
St Martin's Press, Inc.
175 Fifth Avenue, New York, NY 10010

British Library Cataloguing in Publication Data
A catalogue record for this book is available from the British Library

Library of Congress Cataloging-in-Publication Data
A catalog record for this book is available from the Library of Congress

ISBN 0 340 66265 4 (hb)
ISBN 0 340 66264 6 (pb)

Typeset in 10/12pt Sabon by
Anneset, Weston-super-Mare, Somerset
Printed and bound in Great Britain by
J W Arrowsmith Ltd, Bristol

à Richard Cobb,
Légion d'Honneur,
'His presence on the field made a difference of 40,000 men.'

and to Sue Broers,
'...une nuit à Paris...'

Contents

List of maps

Preface

This book has known many incarnations, and it has taken a long time to write. The thanks I owe to others in this task may well become almost as long as the apologies and explanations I will incur for its errors and follies. Its faults are still to be exposed, but the debts are already with me.

In the north of England, I have had the good fortune to have access to two of the finest university libraries in Europe, the John Rylands in Manchester and the truly glorious Brotherton in Leeds. I cannot thank or praise their staffs, founders and benefactors enough. To Neil Plummer, of the Brotherton, my thanks and admiration. The staff of the British Library have been unfailing in their patience and reliability as the work has progressed.

Much of the work and, indeed, the writing of this work took place – appropriately enough, – in Paris, and I owe a great deal to my many friends and colleagues there. To M. Michel Fleury and Madame Auffrey, of the Institut de la Francophonie, where these words are written, whose generosity and very practical support have been my mainstay. To the staff of the Bibliothèque Nationale and the Archives Nationales de Paris, in particular my old friends Claire and Philippe Béchu, Jacky Plaut, Pierre Portet and Gérard Hérmisse, who have provided both professional knowledge and deep comradeship for many years, for although archival sources may not dominate the pages of this book directly, they have exercised a powerful influence on it at every stage. To my oldest friends, Hélène and Jean-Michel Chevet, simply for listening and always being there. In each of these cases, it is impossible to separate the personal from the professional, and so it should be. For many years, M. and Madame Charles Bonis provided the best *état-majeur* imaginable.

Professors Jean Tulard and Louis Bergeron have encouraged me from the very outset in the study of the Napoleonic period, as have many closer at hand: Alan Forrest, Jim McMillan, Colin Lucas, Geoffrey Ellis and Clive Emsley. Among my own cohort, Charles Esdaile and Mike Heffernan have rendered invaluable professional assistance and, above all, the camaraderie so needed when so much work has been done in real isolation, away from

Paris. In Leeds, where I teach, my head of department, Bill Speck, has been a constant source of support, both in securing me leave at a crucial point in the work for this book, and as a friend in times of need.

Finally, I have four outstanding debts to acknowledge. The deepest of all to Christopher Wheeler, at Arnold, who had faith in the project. To Tim Blanning, who read every word, and without whom it would all have been for nought. To Sue, my wife, and the most loyal *bonapartiste* I have ever known! I hope she will endure the criticisms of *l'Empereur* in these pages with as much goodwill as she has the long, hard-fought campaign that produced them! This book is her Spanish Ulcer, the guerrilla behind every rock. Thanks to her, at no point in its writing did I ever identify with Napoleon, for no one could be better loved than I am.

Odd as it will seem to those who knew him, this book belongs, above all, to the late Richard Cobb, *mon maître*. It tries to see the Napoleonic era through the eyes of those on the ground, those who endured it, and in so doing, to be loyal to the truths he shared with me. If this book has kept within its gaze the soldiers, the peasants, the local officials, who bore the brunt of the lunacies of masters and ideas, it is thanks to his influence. I write these words in the city, indeed in the neighbourhood, he taught me to love. Richard would have been appalled to be compared to Napoleon, but his presence and his passing have left as indelible a mark as any man can make, within his own empire. I'm sorry he won't be here to curse me.

Paris 4e   January 1996

Acknowledgements

The author and publishers are grateful to the authors of the following books for permission to base some of the maps drawn for this book on their work: Charles J. Esdaile, *The Wars of Napoleon* (Harlow, Langman, 1995) for maps 2(i) and 2(ii); and Alan Forrest, *Déserteurs et Insoumis* (Paris, Perrin, 1988) for maps 3(i) and 3(ii).

Introduction

Napoleon: power, genius and history

Napoleon Bonaparte is synonymous with power, so much so that the myth he spun around himself in exile sought to soften, even to obscure, that uncomfortable truth.[1] Power terrifies, it is the essence of history, not of legend, of awe rather than affection. Napoleon's success as a myth-maker was limited, but in the light of his very public career, the real surprise is that his self-advertisement made any impact at all. His chief tactic was less to deny his identification with power, than to emphasize the military exploits he achieved through its use. An all-prescient commander in the field, a magnetic leader of men, proved more interesting – and more palatable – to posterity than the image of a skilled political manipulator or, even more, of a studied master of administration. With the hindsight granted him on St Helena, Napoleon chose to emphasize personal genius, not rational calculation, as the source of his success. He wanted to obscure the real nature of his talents, and in so doing he succeeded, in part, in diminishing the importance of many of his greatest achievements. This was how Napoleon obviously preferred it, and many of his most shameless hagiographers have followed his wishes – or fallen into his trap – dwelling for the most part on his personal life and military exploits.[2]

His myth is pervasive, and in need of close surveillance, for it resembles a living organism – weeds in a cabbage patch – more than a monument that can be bulldozed. Thus, there is a continuous need to keep writing about Napoleon and his age. The myth will choke the historical reality, if left unattended. Schoolboys come first to the myth and the glory; the truth – admiring or damning – often comes too late.

Invective is a useless deterrent: power can be achieved only by the great, by people marked by genius, and to fail to recognize the link between Napoleon and genius is as gross an error as to deny he was powerful. His greatest detractors – Chateaubriand, the influential French royalist and his contemporary, Tolstoy, the Russian great novelist, and Georges Lefebvre, the Marxist historian and his finest chronicler[3] – never attempted to make him small, perhaps because they were touched by genius themselves. It is a simple task to portray him as a butcher, a warmonger, a tyrant, for he was all these things, certainly by the standards of his own times, if less arguably in the context of a later age. It is when historians – self-styled intellectuals – deny him genius, creative power and acute intelligence, that they fail in their task. It is often difficult to know if intellectuals hate Napoleon because of what he did – and they have often embraced men of far fouler character – or because he hated them in his own times, while still being more intelligent.[4]

The clearest manifestation of this is a refusal to grant him his place as the last and the greatest of the enlightened absolutists, to proclaim emphatically that he deliberately distorted the intellectual culture of the Enlightenment. This is folly. Contemporaries, friend and foe alike, were agreed that Napoleon was remarkably in tune with his times, at least until the disasters of 1812, and his unwillingness to respond to the climate of opinion in the final phase of his rule was seen as out of character at the time.[5] Thus, Napoleon regarded himself, as did those around him, as a man of the Enlightenment. More to the point, so did his civil servants. A mass of evidence shouts this at the observer from the actions, policies and discourse of the regime. Napoleon led his troops by personal magnitude, perhaps; he worked well with his bureaucracts because they shared a common ideology, a particular perception of the Enlightenment.

Georges Lefebvre interpreted the inner strength of the regime in terms of class: Napoleon's genius hinged on his ability to discern the central place of the bourgeoisie in society, and to base his rule on it. This is at once too sweeping and too narrow an evaluation of his sources of support, based on an inaccurate configuration of European society in the early nineteenth century. Nevertheless, Lefebvre's classic Marxism has a great merit, for it places the regime and its leader in the wider context of their times, treating them as a natural product of those times and, above all, it acknowledges the lasting impact of Napoleonic rule on European history. The conclusions of the Marxist approach are, at the very least, debatable, but the instincts are true, especially in the hands of Lefebvre. In this interpretation, Napoleon was not a boorish, ham-fisted general; he was no mere military dictator,[6] but the harbinger of change, the catalyst of the capitalist order of the nineteenth century. Lefebvre condemned Napoleon, but he acknowledged the need to understand him, because his political achievements were seminal. Lefebvre set Napoleon firmly in the wider context of his times, and in so doing wrote the finest single book on the period. Nevertheless, his antipathy to Napoleon narrowed his range of enquiry in crucial ways. It is a deadly error to dismiss the regime as a military dictatorship, unworthy of serious political analysis.

Antipathy is no barrier to great history, as Lefebvre proved. It also drives the only comprehensive study of Napoleon to rival Lefebvre's. The masterly life of Napoleon written by Jean Tulard[7] appeared almost a generation after Lefebvre's book. Its greatness lies in a sureness of touch, a refusal to be drawn into the powerful currents of Napoleonic hagiography so prevalent in French writing on the subject and, in common with Lefebvre, an approach determined to set the man in the context of his times, a goal pursued in his other general study of the period, *Le Grand Empire*.[8] Tulard's life of Napoleon is subtitled 'The Myth of the Saviour'. This signals, on the one hand, its critical approach to the subject, a positive strength. Yet, it also hints at the Francocentric character of Tulard's interests, for the 'myth of the saviour', initiated by Napoleon, is a specifically French aspect of the Napoleonic heritage. The image of Napoleon as the founder of a potent myth in French political culture – that only a strong, autocratic hand could save the French from themselves – is an incisive, dynamic theme at the centre of Tulard's work, but it illuminates only the French aspects of that legacy.[9] The recent volumes by Martin Lyons and, especially, by Geoffrey Ellis, set excellent standards for the historiography of the period, in any language. However, they too are decidedly Francocentric, each devoting no more than a chapter to the non-French bulk of the Empire.[10] The work of Louis Bergeron is a model of scholarship, but limits itself to France, and particularly to the social and economic aspects of the period; within its confines, a classic, it lacks a European dimension.[11] The two finest studies of Napoleon remain those of Tulard and Lefebvre, and they are the work of his opponents, perhaps a lasting tribute to the abilities of all three men concerned.

However, there is a form of hagiography that is misleading and dangerous when it turns its attention to Napoleon's non-military achievements. Its error lies less in attributing to Napoleon the values of the Enlightenment, than in the assumption that his advancement of them was constructive, useful or, most glaring of all in its inaccuracy, popular.[12] The nature and application of many Napoleonic reforms reveal the innate tyranny of the regime, as much as the military conquests. The common people of Europe, in their millions, hated Napoleon exactly because he espoused the Enlightenment, just as they had detested the enlightened absolutists who preceded him. The nature of this hatred among contemporaries, and the nature of its origins, are incontestable, a view which often emerges more readily in the context of specific national histories, with a long chronological range, than those specifically on the Napoleonic era.[13]

This is the major problem besetting those who attempt to set Napoleon in a genuinely European, rather than a Francocentric context. Even when it is confronted, too often the popular resistance to Napoleon has been subsumed into another great myth, 'the rise of nationalism'.[14] The popular risings against Napoleonic rule were born of hatred of enlightened reform, not of a growing belief in yet another failed, hate-filled idea conceived by nineteenth-century intellectuals.[15]

Napoleon is a European figure, as much as or even more than a part of French history, but it is only recently that attempts have been made to consider him in a European, as opposed to a national context. Napoleon exercised hegemony in Europe, he was not the ruler of an exclusively French empire. Having won these territories, he had to do something with them, and he had plans for them, but to admit this is to enter troubled waters. The Napoleonic regime had an ideology, even if it dispensed with politics, as the French revolutionaries had invented it.[16] How could such a brutal, warlike regime have any hint of intellectual sophistication? Goethe, the German poet, has a strong claim to be regarded as the finest mind of the Napoleonic age. During his meeting with Napoleon at Erfurt in 1808, they discussed his novel, *Werther*, and some of Voltaire's most politicized writings, including his play, *Mahomet*. Goethe was impressed by Napoleon, intellectually, and by his literary tastes. Those tastes were of a man of the radical Enlightenment who, like Voltaire, despised the masses, but opposed the supposed obscurantism of the old order.[17] It is difficult enough for many to admit that Napoleon read and appreciated his work, and much else besides. The life of Napoleon by Felix Markham has become a durable standard in the anglophone world; it does not mention the meeting between Napoleon and Goethe.[18] *Mahomet* praises the tolerance and culture of Islam, in the face of Catholic bigotry and backwardness. A few months after their conversation, Napoleon invaded Spain and abolished the Inquisition; the Spanish masses who rose against him did so partly in response to a folk memory derived from the *Reconquista*.[19] The military conquests may, indeed, have been driven only by a mixture of blind ambition and paranoia, but an intensely ideological civilian administration followed in their wake, and this was the essence of Napoleonic rule. Napoleon did not invade Spain because he read Voltaire, but his reading of Voltaire influenced how he chose to deal with it, once there.

Ironically, those historians who have attempted to rectify the Francocentric nature of the literature and the eschewal of ideology, notably S.J. Woolf and Charles Esdaile,[20] find it harder to confront the black side of Napoleonic rule than historians who attack him in an essentially French context. Napoleon can be castigated within the parameters of French history as the man who destroyed the political liberties of the French Revolution, as the man who put the clock back to absolute monarchy and patriarchal social values, as a blatant elitist. This is less easy to do beyond the borders of the First Republic. When historians of Napoleon, the Emperor of the West, step beyond the study of military carnage, they face a dilemma: to paint too fervent a picture of military dictatorship or reaction is, in some way, to betray the Revolution and even the Enlightenment. It is not the same to attack the ruler who abolished feudalism in Naples and Spain, as to castigate the general who virtually abolished divorce and put women back in the house. To acknowledge the regional and cultural diversity of the Napoleonic Empire is essential to any understanding of it – and the more recent studies of the Empire in Europe are long overdue in these respects; they are the long-awaited voice of common sense.

However, liberal, progressive baggage is a heavy burden, when carried beyond the natural frontiers of 1792. 'Regionalism' can, in some instances, engender a relativism that seeks to avoid what must be faced: the elitist, arrogant and oppressive nature not just of Napoleonic rule, but of the Enlightenment itself. In the wake of postmodernism, there is a growing, if still halting, will to question the value of what is coming to be termed 'the Enlightenment project'.[21] Perhaps Napoleonic rule is particularly in need of exploration in these terms, especially in its European context. It is uncomfortable to those of liberal, broadly progressive sensibilities, less painful to those inclined to shed them.

Nevertheless, historians have often found it easier to admit Napoleon as a powerful presence, than to recognize him as a genius. This is dangerous, for it denies the deep bond between genius and power, at the heart of greatness. Here, the inclination has been to concentrate on his shortcomings and the wrongheadedness of particular policies, rather than to look for a wider perspective. Another form of retreat – but one that has been the most fruitful for the historiography of the period – has been to pursue those aspects of it which have little to do with the ideology of the regime. The finest recent writings on Napoleonic France, in particular, are social and economic studies, many of them lasting contributions by gifted scholars.[22] The diplomatic history of the period has also produced excellent writing, above all in the work of Schroeder, although it also displays the dangers of approaching Napoleon's career through only one channel, for the picture that emerges is of unthinking, military conquest:[23] it is correct only as far as it goes, as are all specialist studies. The feeling remains that they are a retreat, in the context of Napoleonic history.

If the essence of the era was, indeed, Napoleon, and if the essence of Napoleon was power, wielded effectively, then the politics and ideology of his regime must be confronted, and confronted in a European perspective. So, too, must the nature of Napoleon's genius. It was far more subtle than has often been allowed, even by himself, for it had less to do with military glory or intuitive intrigue, than with the creation of a state shaped according to his ideas. He could not, and did not, do this alone. He led Europe, and he drove it. This was not the work of a crazed warlord, nor of a romantic individualist, nor of a grey bureaucrat. To dwell more on the creation than the man is not to deny his genius, but to acknowledge it, in its true form. The assessment of Goethe seems the most realistic and far-sighted: Napoleon was a genius, and if he was a dark genius, it was because he incarnated a dark age. He is not to be belittled, but treated as all greatness should: with a mixture of caution, detachment and respect.

Napoleon's genius was for seeing where power lay, and drawing it to himself. Napoleon was both a brute and a methodical clerk, for both are essential to autocracy, but they were not his essence, nor that of his regime. He seized authority in difficult circumstances, when few wanted the challenge, transformed that authority into power with consummate skill and wielded it for 15 years, in ever-changing circumstances, with a remarkable degree of competence in the face of widespread opposition and resentment. That anything durable should emerge from the maelstrom of his career is the genuinely astounding part of his story, if the least glamorous.

The political inheritance: France and Europe, 1789–1799

Napoleon received a triple inheritance from the regimes of revolutionary France. He was heir to a series of fundamental institutional reforms, most of them dating from the early years of the Revolution, 1789–91, which gave him the foundations of a state apparatus more centralized, unchallenged and potentially powerful than that possessed by any other major pro-revolutionary European state. However, beside this, was the troubled political heritage of the Revolution: he led a country divided between the small, largely urban, determined section of the propertied classes (a minority even within their narrow ranks) and the vast, if unorganized mass of counter-revolutionary opposition – a seething, if ultimately impotent countryside, besieging an archipelago of pro-revolutionary urban islands. Added to this were the bitter divisions within the ranks of the revolutionaries themselves: the period 1792–94 had seen a series of bitter purges at the heart of the government, in Paris, but they also had wide repercussions throughout the provinces. Finally, he inherited a major European war, which was in its seventh year when he took power in 1799.

The inheritance of the 1790s was mixed, at best; on balance, the survival of the new order created after 1789 was hardly assured at the moment Napoleon ceased to be a general and became a political leader. Had the circumstances been favourable to those in power in the autumn of 1799, they would not have meddled with a political system of their own recent making, or turned for leadership to a soldier who was, by definition, from outside their own ranks.

The political legacy of the French Revolution: conflict

The leadership of the French Revolution changed with bewildering rapidity and violence between 1789 and 1795, but common to each ruling clique was the desire to force clear choices on those they ruled. This manifested itself in their insistence on the swearing of public oaths to each new con-

stitution by public officials, from the King downwards, which extended to
the clergy in 1791, and to a demand for open, public votes among deputies
on important issues: the execution of the king, the declaration of war, the
expulsion or execution of other deputies. The desired end was to achieve
'transparency' among citizens – openness, honestly, commitment[24] – but
the human result was to root the political history of the Revolution in a
series of conflicts, with lasting consequences. Once people were forced to
choose sides, it was not easy to renounce the allegiances – or accusations –
that went with them, at least not until after the fall of Robespierre in 1794.
These conflicts and divisions formed the immediate political background to
Napoleon's own regime, and he had to base all his political calculations on
them. This is even reflected in the questionnaires used by the regime when
vetting candidates for posts in the administration or the elected assemblies:
'What did he do before 1789?' 'What did he do, 1789–92?' 'What did he
do during the Terror, 1792–94?' 'What has he done, since 1795?' It was
something the regime had to care about.

In general terms, by 1799, the Revolution had bequeathed two kinds of
division to France: rivalries within the ranks of the revolutionaries, themselves, and the greater, more menacing division between revolution and
counter-revolution. The headings of the Napoleonic job-applications reflected, rather than defined, the chronological and the political character of
the internal splits in the Revolution. The first years of the Revolution,
1789–91, were more notable for major institutional reforms than political
violence. However, the debate over the new constitution, propagated in
1791, drove a fundamental wedge between the majority of legislators, who
wanted an electorate based on a set of property qualifications, and a
smaller group, determined to achieve universal manhood suffrage. The split
between liberals and radicals, which would bedevil the politics of the early
nineteenth century, was born. Its first, brutally clear manifestation, was at
the massacre of the Champs de Mars in July 1791. A few months before
the new constitution was to be proclaimed, Louis XVI attempted to flee
Paris, declaring his own, counter-revolutionary opposition to the new political order over which he was to preside. This was the occasion for the
radicals to reassert their own objections to the narrow franchise. The result
was their suppression, while organizing a mass petition against the constitution, not by the forces of the King, but by the moderate revolutionaries
of the majority in the National Assembly, which framed the constitution.

In the spring of 1792, France went to war with Prussia and the
Habsburg Monarchy. The subsequent military reversals led to panic at the
heart of the new government, created by the 1791 constitution, and by the
summer of 1792, the radicals – now generally called Jacobins, after the
name of their largest political club – used the war emergency to seize
power. On 10 August 1792, backed by the artisan classes of Paris, most of
whom had been disenfranchised by the 1791 constitution, the radicals
overthrew the constitution and the monarchy, declaring France a republic.

A new National Convention was summoned, elected by universal manhood suffrage, to frame a new constitution, also based on a democratic suffrage.

This was only the beginning of further in-fighting, however. Divisions flared over how best to run the war and over what to do with Louis XVI. These issues were exacerbated by the growing influence of the Parisian populace on the central government, and by a seeming hesitancy among some Jacobin deputies – the Girondin or Brissotin faction – about the merits of direct democracy for the new constitution. Two more radical factions, truer to the revolution of 10 August, won the support of Paris, one based in the Convention and the Jacobin Club – the Montagnards, centred on Robespierre – the other with its power base in the municipal administration of Paris, the Commune, led by Hébert. In the last days of May 1793, they united to purge the Convention of the Girondins, executing or imprisoning several deputies and driving many more into hiding.

The next phase of the Revolution, between 1792 and 1794, was called the Terror by contemporaries; it is not a fanciful or convenient label created by later historians. It produced a ruthless attempt to recentralize power in the national government, the Convention, and its chosen instrument to direct the war effort, the Committee of Public Safety, composed of 12 deputies. Montagnards and Hébertistes jostled for power on the Committee and in the other new bodies set up to ensure that 'the government remained revolutionary until the peace', in the words of the edict of the Convention. This rivalry, probably more to do with cynical power-mongering than ideology, ended with the victory of .the Montagnards, in the purge of the Hébertistes in March 1794. This was a sign that the Montagnards, and Robespierre in particular, had outbid them for the support of Paris. The last round of internecine fighting during the Terror was a purge of a faction of the Montagnards themselves, when Robespierre had Danton, his last obvious rival, arrested and killed in April 1794.

Concurrent to the struggles at the heart of the government, in Paris, supporters of the Girondins raised a series of revolts, based mainly on the large cities of southern France, which the Jacobins – Montagnard, Hébertist and Dantonist alike – all opposed as treasonous, and labelled 'Federalist', seeing in them an attempt to split the unity of the country and the Revolution. Some were more determined than others; whereas the risings in Bordeaux and Marseille collapsed easily, those in Lyon and Toulon were ferocious, eventually moving beyond the parameters of an inter-revolutionary civil war, and joining the wider struggle of the counter-revolution.

The Montagnards were deposed in July 1794 – the coup of 9 Thermidor, according to the revolutionary calendar – by an amorphous group in the Convention. This led to the gradual dismantling of the institutions of the Terror, and the abandonment of the democratic constitution drawn up in 1793, which was to be implemented at the end of the war. The new regime, the Directory, was obviously suspicious of the remnants of Robespierre's supporters; 'Terrorism' and 'Jacobinism' were to remain dread spectres for those who survived the turmoil of these years, well into the future. The Terror period became synonymous with 'factionalism', a form of politics to be avoided at all costs in the future. Yet, on the whole, its political ethos was one of reconciliation among revolutionaries, in recognition of the need to confront the greater – and ever-present – enemy of counter-revolution.

Counter-revolution was very different from the internal quarrels of the radical revolutionaries. It is a complex phenomenon. It embraced ideological opposition to the political principles of the Revolution itself – as exemplified by Louis XVI in 1791 – based on the belief that the whole reform project was a usurpation of legitimate royal power; large sectors of the nobility and clergy came to accept this view. The Civil Constitution of the Clergy of 1790, which nationalized Church property and subjected the Church to state control, alienated a narrow majority of the clergy, the nonjurors or *réfractaires*, who refused to take the oath to the constitution of 1791. Their ranks were swollen by other clergy, alienated by the growing anticlericalism of the revolutionaries, culminating in a series of 'de-Christianization' campaigns, in which Girondins and Hébertistes were often more prominent than Montagnards. Even after the purge of 9 Thermidor, the Directory remained suspicious of the Church, so close had its links become with counter-revolution. In times of military crisis, the overt anticlericalism of the Terror was quick to reassert itself, even among those who rejected Jacobinism in other respects.

The demands of war, especially the increasing recourse to mass conscription by all the revolutionary governments, turned vast parts of rural France into battlegrounds after 1792. It also expanded counter-revolution, a largely political or ideological set of opinions, into what has been termed 'anti-revolution', an opposition to what the Revolution was doing to the daily lives of ordinary people. The overlapping lines between counter- and anti-revolution are complex, for the popular resistance engendered by anti-revolution soon blended with many aspects of counter-revolution, particularly its religious aspects. The most spectacular revolts produced by the meeting of counter- with anti-revolution were in western France: the rising in the Vendée, in the spring of 1792, which achieved almost the status of full-scale war, and the more clandestine guerrilla war of the Chouan bands – named after sparrowhawks, whose calls the rebels used as signals – in the hilly region between Normandy and Brittany. However, they were only the tip of an iceberg. Rebellions on a smaller scale simmered throughout southern France – the Midi – after 1792, particularly in the Rhone valley, Provence and the Pyrenees. Most of western and southern France was never really at peace after 1792; local officials of the state and those who supported the Revolution always felt themselves embattled, and tended to be loyal to whoever was in power in Paris, as long as they supported the struggle against the 'brigands' of counter-revolution, as the rebels were termed in official parlance. They were seldom disappointed. Apart from a short-lived attempt to appease the Vendéans, shortly after Thermidor, successive regimes met the often barbaric resistance of the peasant rebels with official repression that was often as savage.

France was a seething mass of hatred and fear throughout the 1790s, but a revolution whose popular base seemed to be shrinking rather than expanding continued to survive, if not exactly to prosper. It had particular reserves of strength, which even those at its helm were only beginning to understand.

The institutional reforms: from citoyens *to* administrés

Behind the political turmoil of the 1790s, successive revolutionary regimes laid the foundations of a powerful, centralized state. Broadly, the moderate regimes of 1789–91 created a unified economic, legal and administrative order within France, while the Terrorist regime of 1792–94 clawed back most of the political initiative for the central government that first reforms had devolved to local level. After 1795, the Directory began to use the powers created through these reforms in systematic ways, but never with the insight into their possibilities later grasped by Napoleon.

The institutional reforms of 1789–91 swept away the overlapping, complicated administrative and judicial units of the *ancien régime*. The great privileged corporations – the *parlements*, provincial estates where they still existed, the Farmers-General – were all abolished, thus clearing the way for a uniform system of administration and justice for the whole of France. The revolutionaries filled this gap quickly and with remarkable clarity of mind: France was divided into 83 fairly uniform departments. The new units rode roughshod over the traditional provincial boundaries, and did not even pay too close an attention to natural topography, the decision to name them after natural features – thus rejecting any *ancien régime* affiliations – notwithstanding. Together with clarity and logic went an arbitrary and artificial approach to local government, yet the departments proved the most durable creation of the Revolution:[25] Napoleon added new departments, as the Empire expanded, until they numbered 120. Within France, they still form the basis for local government, as they do elsewhere in Europe.

The department became the central unit of all administration; there was nothing above it, except the central government and, in theory, it controlled its sub-divisions, the districts, cantons and communes. During the 1790s, the departments were run, in theory, by elected councils of local taxpayers. Under the Terror, they were often bypassed by the central government, usually when a deputy of the National Convention – a representative on mission – was sent to a particular area to take temporary control of its affairs. In theory, the Directory sought to end this practice and return authority to the councils, but the trend of re-centralization had been established, and was never wholly reversed after 1793. The judicial hierarchy of courts was also given a uniform structure, which generally corresponded to the administrative units and, under the Civil Constitution of the Clergy, the Church followed a similar pattern. Work was begun to give France a single set of legal codes, but this was completed only under Napoleon.

Centralization was meant to be softened by the elective principle, but the political unrest of the period after 1792 made elections difficult to hold, or occasions for political confrontation when they were held. It was often next to impossible to govern much of France, but when and where Paris could exert its authority, there were no constituted, legal bodies at local level outside its control. This made the task of counter-revolutionaries very difficult, and proved a decisive advantage to the revolutionaries at every stage. When a decision was taken in Paris, it was binding on the whole nation, something impossible under the old order. Successive governments ordered mass conscription – the *levées en masse* – over the whole country; no longer were certain provinces or classes exempt from their obligations. In principle, taxation followed the same uniform rules, but neither conscription nor taxation were applied regularly or according to systematic rules, by the governments of the 1790s. It was a question of potential, rather than achievement, in both cases.

There had been a shift in attitudes within the revolutionary governments, difficult to assess, but deeply important nonetheless. Those in authority began to regard those they governed less as fellow-citizens than as 'the ruled' – *les administrés*, 'the administered', as they chose to term them. This meant the tacit abandonment of the concept of equality and openness in government, and it happened fairly quickly. As early as 1790, this attitude was apparent in the debates on the first institutional reforms.[26] It was shared by deputies and local officials alike, and its common factor was contempt for the popular classes, especially the peasantry. In troubled areas, local officials soon came to see themselves as alienated and embattled; in more tranquil places, they spoke of their *administrés* with condescension.[27] This outlook, rather than the more egalitarian ideals of 1789, was probably prevalent in government by 1799.

Outside the institutions of government, the reforms of the 1790s left a more confused heritage, which the Directory was only beginning to remedy by 1799. Freedom of trade and profession was one of the few original principles of 1789 which was not reneged on or watered down during the revolutionary decade. Its thorough application broke down the corporatism of the *ancien régime*, in ways crucial for the emergence of the new state, but it also led to confusion in the workplace. Most affected were the skilled crafts – whose life was regulated by the guilds until their abolition in 1789

– and the liberal professions. Formal qualifications were no longer required to exercise any profession. The practical disadvantages of this were soon obvious to all, but this chaos was not easy to redress. The wider ramifications of the nationalization of Church property led to the collapse of university education in France; consequently, the law and medical schools closed their doors, along with all the other faculties. Those who received any professional training got it from private colleges, set up by barristers or surgeons trained before 1789.[28]

The only profession that rapidly re-acquired its traditional ethos was the army. It was also becoming the surest, fastest road to worldly success as the utopian dreams of 1789 dissolved into nightmare or farce. The Terrorist regime made great efforts to politicize the troops along 'correct' lines and the first levies of 1792 were volunteers, usually town-dwellers, who were probably already imbued with revolutionary ideals. However, in the course of the 1790s, the basic composition of the armies changed; they were now full of conscripts, usually peasants, and their officers were not long in reasserting more traditional patterns of discipline and hierarchy. After Thermidor, the government virtually abandoned feeding soldiers political propaganda: the biggest single influence on them were their officers, and although they too had benefited from the 'career open to talent' – and with it the rejection of noble privilege as a criterion for promotion – they had not abandoned traditional notions of status and authority conferred by rank, however that rank was earned. The Terrorist government had raised the esteem of the common soldier to that of a citizen doing a valued, heroic task of public service, but as egalitarian ideology receded after 1794, this new-found sense of esteem was gradually converted, among the troops, into a sense of the privilege due to a caste apart from other citizens.[29]

The Revolution gave Napoleon the foundations of a strong, uniform state, and the guiding principle that this was how a well-run, rational state should be organized. He accepted this part of his legacy with glee. It had proved crucial in the struggle for survival against the counter-revolution and, above all, against the far greater threat posed by the international war, which began in 1792.

The war with Europe, 1792–1799

The war which began in the spring of 1792, initially between France and the Habsburg Monarchy, supported by Prussia, would last until 1815, almost without interruption. Its immediate origins stemmed from a remarkable mixture of cynicism, reckless optimism and revolutionary zeal, heightened by inexperience. This peculiar mixture did not last long, but by the time more established patterns of military and diplomatic behaviour had reasserted themselves, France had been branded a subversive state by the other major powers: a threat to their very existence, not just a normal military threat to their material interests.

The aims of the revolutionaries in 1789 were, at heart, to renew and strengthen France, and to a certain extent they achieved this, if not as easily or in the manner they hoped at the outset. France's traditional rival in western Europe, the Habsburgs, saw only the weakness inflicted on the French state by the Revolution, which was exactly what they wanted: this was why they – and the British – stood aside from the first phase of the Revolution. A France racked by internal strife and a politically emasculated monarchy, unable to control its own army or foreign policy, was to be welcomed. For the Austrians, who ruled what is now Belgium, it meant peace and stability on an often troubled border; for the Prussians, it offered the chance to grab territory in the Rhineland without the threat of French interference.

In 1791 the new constitution in France brought the Brissotin faction to office, in uneasy partnership with more moderate revolutionaries, with Louis XVI – who had already signalled his hostility to the new regime at Varennes – at their head. By 1792, the Brissotins were convinced of the inherent weakness of any state that had not followed the French path of reform, a judgement that included Prussia, the Habsburg Monarchy and Britain. Should regenerated France decide to liberate the rest of a degenerate Europe, not only would she be guaranteed the support of those to be liberated but, perhaps more to the point, her traditional rivals would be unable to oppose her.

Even the idealistic revolutionaries had baser reasons to want war by 1791–92, however. They had become enamoured of the logic of the 'doctrine of natural frontiers', as applied to France, at least, which entailed advancing the border eastwards, ideally to the Rhine, but at least as far as the Schledt in Belgium. Neither Britain nor the Habsburgs could tolerate such ambitions, on purely strategic grounds: it meant the loss of Belgium by the Habsburgs, and French domination of the Channel. Both Louis and the Brissotins hoped that war would bring the political crisis to a head, Louis in the hope that a shuddering military defeat by the Habsburgs would undo the revolutionaries once and for all, while the Brissotins hoped it would unite the country behind them and flush out all the counter-revolutionaries as traitors.

They were all wrong. France proved stronger than anyone had foreseen, causing Prussia to abandon the war by 1793, and Britain to join it early in 1793. However, the Habsburgs also proved impossible to crush; they were a far cry from the dilapidated, ramshackle state the revolutionaries imagined. Thus, two long wars of attrition for the domination of western Europe and of the Atlantic entered their final phase: France and the Habsburgs contested for the mastery of western Europe; Britain and France re-entered their long-standing contest for overseas empire and naval supremacy. These older patterns were not clear during the Terror, 1792–94, nor did the ideological element ever leave the minds of the contestants.

However, after 1794, the alliance patterns established in the mid-eighteenth century re-emerged: Britain and the Habsburgs confronted France, who trailed Spain with her, in a mutual effort to save their empires from British ambition. Prussia considered an alliance with France, but settled for neutrality; the Hohenzollerns had clearly ceased to regard the French Republic as a major threat, at a very early stage of the Revolution.[30]

The war dragged on, but it looked increasingly familiar to eighteenth-century diplomatic eyes. The French soon abandoned any pretence of being liberators in the border areas they seized in the course of the fighting. The Low Countries, the Rhineland and northern Italy were plundered and ravaged by French troops who retained sufficient vestiges of Jacobin propaganda to despise Catholic religiosity, but not enough of the spirit of the Declaration of the Rights of Man to wish to extend their revolutionary virtue to the conquered.

The war continued, partly because the revolutionaries feared that an allied victory would result in the restoration of a Bourbon dynasty bent on bloody revenge, partly because older, deeper issues of geopolitics had been brought too close to the surface of international relations to be easily resolved. The military balance between France and the Habsburgs swung to and fro, but their reciprocal strengths and weaknesses held them in check. France had unleashed the massive human and material potential of her huge population, and had laid the foundations of a state capable of organization on a vast scale; the Habsburgs drew on deep reserves of manpower, too, directed into a highly professional army, and rallied the support of the small German states. In 1796–97, France seemed to have gained the upper hand, when Napoleon drove them from Italy, although the Habsburgs gave far less ground on the main front in Germany.

Suddenly, in 1799, the deadlock seemed to be broken definitively, and it was in the allies' favour. As the Habsburgs and their new Russian allies pushed forward in both Germany and Italy, a new phase of the conflict began, as did a new course of the Revolution within France. France now faced her deepest internal unrest since 1794 and the war now exercised a new form of influence on domestic politics. The army had been a growing presence in national life since 1792; now it was to dominate it.

A new man for new forces: the personal rise of Napoleon Bonaparte

The career of Napoleon Bonaparte, to 1799

Much has been made of the 'meteoric rise' of Napoleon, from the lower ranks of the officer corps to general, during the Revolution, and of his youthfulness when he received the command of the Army of Italy in 1796, at the age of 27. His rise to world power, from the ranks of a relatively poor, obscure family of minor Corsican nobles, has been marvelled at by admirers and detractors alike. However, until he entered politics at the very top, in 1799, Napoleon's career had conformed to those of his peers who shared his level of ability. Napoleon owed his rapid rise to the Revolution, but so did almost everyone who emerged as leaders in the 1790s; his youthfulness was far from remarkable, as were his relatively modest origins. Napoleon was part of the same phenomenon that catapulted Robespierre, Danton and Brissot to the leadership of France from provincial obscurity, while still in their thirties. His experience of the revolutionary years might be best described as not untypical in an exceptional era. Nor was he even alone in this in his own family. His younger brother, Lucien, carved out a successful political career, parallel to Napoleon's in the army. Lucien was elected deputy for Corsica to the national legislature, the Council of the 500, in 1798, when still below the legal age for the post. He achieved this while Napoleon was in Egypt, and without his help.

Napoleon was among many able army officers, trained in the provincial military academies of the *ancien régime,* who won rapid promotion through a combination of gaps left by the defection of royalist officers from the revolutionary armies, the expansion of the army after the outbreak of war in 1792, and good political connections, which in Napoleon's case came from his links with Robespierre's brother, Augustin, who aided his career until 1794, when his faction was overthrown. Napoleon then found another political patron, in Barras, who gave him command of the Paris garrison during an attempted royalist rebellion in the capital in 1795. Barras ensured Napoleon received great publicity for his role in this, which led – with political influence – to his appointment as commander of the Army of Italy. Lucien, too, was a protégé first of the Robespierres and then of Barras; patronage from politicians was far more important to both brothers than any help they could give each other.

Throughout his early career, Napoleon always had rivals, generals who were almost as young, dynamic and successful as himself: Hoche, Moreau and Bernadotte, all five years older than Napoleon, and Joubert, his exact contemporary, were the most prominent. Both Hoche and Moreau were generally considered better soldiers, Bernadotte as more politically astute. Napoleon's position as commander of the Army of Italy was important, but Italy was very much the secondary front during the revolutionary wars; the major command went to Moreau. Napoleon's military career before 1799 had been glamorous rather than distinguished: his conquest of Italy in 1796–97 had been revealed as fragile and over-ambitious. He had avoided direct involvement in the collapse of this front, in 1799, only by leading a catastrophic invasion of Egypt and Palestine, which ended in abject defeat and his selfish, almost cowardly decision to abandon his army to its fate and return to France.

While in Italy, however, Napoleon had shown a marked capacity for politics and diplomacy. His main rivals had all courted ambitions of creating 'sister republics' in the territories conquered by the French in the Rhineland and the Low Countries, but Napoleon, alone among them, actually managed to do so. In 1796, in northern Italy, he manoeuvred the defeated Austrians and the handful of pro-French collaborators into setting up a puppet state carved out of the captured Austrian province of Lombardy, the Cispadane Republic, with himself as President. It was later extended to include captured Papal territory, and renamed the Cisalpine Republic. Napoleon directed the writing of its constitution and the organization of its administration. The consitution of the Cisalpine Republic foreshadowed many of Napoleon's basic political preferences: a strong, one-man executive, able to dominate a legislature composed of several chambers, with different and very limited powers. Out of the way, in northern Italy, he first showed many of the political skills that would set him above his rivals, and ahead of them in the race for power. .

However, this power base was lost in 1799, with the reconquest of Italy by the Austrians. When Bonaparte returned to France from Egypt, in 1799, he was as in need of patronage and as far from the centre of power as at any time before 1796. In 1797, he was called upon to help the government suppress elections that had gone against it; he was both politically reliable, and had an army to carry out the purge. In 1799 he had lost his army; the most powerless of the generals, he was therefore thought to be the most compliant by the politicians.

It was in late 1799 that Napoleon's career deviated markedly from those of his rivals. This was not because he now entered politics, but because he did so at the top, through a set of circumstances he had not helped to shape. Divisions within the Directory led to plans for a coup within the government, aimed at strengthening the executive at the expense of the legislative assemblies. It was planned from within, and Napoleon was recruited to its ranks.

The Directory and the evolution of politics, 1795–1799

The Directorial regime was an intriguing blend of success and failure, of stability and instability. It was the creation of a heterogenous group of deputies in the National Convention, who had survived the Terror and backed the coup of 9 Thermidor, Year II (27 July 1794), hence their usual labels, the Thermidorians or ex-*conventionels*. Many were moderates whose convictions were never those of the Jacobins and who simply wanted to return to the principles of the constitution of 1791; others were those Girondins who were rehabilitated after Thermidor; still others had political backgrounds as radical as the Montagnards, but had fallen foul of them, such as Fouché, who eventually became Napoleon's Minister of Police. They had learned several lessons from the Terror, chiefly fear of direct democracy and also of a strong executive; they were as committed to the Republic as the Montagnards, and remained as frightened of military defeat as counter-revolution. They were determined to keep power in their own hands, and enacted the 'law of two-thirds', whereby they co-opted themselves from the National Convention into the new assemblies, created by the new constitution of 1795. This ensured their continued domination of the new regime, but the elections of 1797 and 1798 eroded their grip on power: those of 1797 saw the election of many constitutional royalists; those of 1798 saw the re-emergence of a large, coherent group of neo-Jacobin deputies. Most of the election results were annulled by the government on both occasions, with the help of the army. These two coups removed most of those new deputies who were perceived as beyond the pale, politically; the more obvious political opponents of the Thermidorians were easily defeated.

However, the elections produced another source of danger for the regime, all the more dangerous for not being obvious. Not all the new deputies were purged in 1797 or 1798; their numbers rose rapidly in each election until, by 1799, 52 per cent of those elected had never held national office before. These new men were not firmly committed to perpetuating the regime, as it had been established in 1795.[31] Most had made their mark in local office and had no clear political affiliations. It is probable that they were disillusioned with the idea of a powerful legislature, in the light of its failure to control extremism, and they shared the fear of more veteran politicians that a powerful legislature elected by a large electorate was a recipe for disaster: they, too, were usually survivors of the Terror, although at local level. Although their origins are still in need of clarification, the political outlook of the new deputies who avoided the great purges conformed to the efforts of many local administrators under the Directory, between 1795 and 1797, to govern by 'the rule of law', in place of factional strife.[32]

The new men showed a growing distrust of parliamentary politics *per se*, and turned their energies to practical, pragmatic reform projects. They were happier as technocrats, rather than parliamentarians. Nor did they harbour the fears of a strong executive which guided the politics of the founders of the Directory. Napoleon would build his own regime around these new men, and it proved easy for him to do so, not through dictatorial threats, but because they shared a common view of how government ought to work: factionalism would be replaced by technocracy; debate by analysis; intrigue by strong leadership. The 'new men' of the Directorial assemblies were developing a 'Bonapartist' approach to politics, at the heart of the government, simultaneous to – but independently of – the similar ideas Napoleon was implementing in the Cisalpine Republic. The new leader and the new state would be well met.

The Thermidorians could not, ultimately, prevent the evolution of the regime from within. Ruthless, suspicious and politically alert, they were adept at purging political rivals, but there was little they could do, in the face of a wider, more pervasive shift in attitudes to politics itself. There were signs that the extremists – Jacobins and royalists alike – were adapting to the electoral politics of the constitution of 1795, and may have been more at ease with the prospect of an alternating balance of forces than the founders of the regime themselves. This fragile experiment in electoral politics was shattered less by the violence of local cliques, than by the paranoia of the central government. Nevertheless, it is equally clear that the original ethos of the Directory was being overtaken by new political forces.[33] However, until 1799, the outlook that characterized the new majority in the chambers remained only a trend; the new deputies were still far from the real centre of power. It was only after 1798 that an influential group of established political leaders came to share their desire for a stronger executive, if not quite their contempt for parliamentary politics. When several of them were elected to the Directory, a powerful new alliance was created.

The coup of Brumaire, November 1799

Brumaire was the revolutionary month named after fog, and the coup that brought Napoleon to high office had a suitably murky background. This was thoroughly in keeping with the general pattern of political life under the Directory.

All the established politicians were uneasy at the political instability of the years after 1794, and in particular the unreliability of even so elitist an electorate as that created by the constitution of 1795. However, by 1797, some of them moved closer to the views of the new deputies, in calling for a revision of the constitution to provide for a stronger executive, hence their label, 'the revisionists', which was not technically possible until 1804. The most prominent exponent of 'revisionism' was Sieyès, and his election to the Directory by the chambers in May 1798 was a clear sign that the new majority in the legislature was looking for new policies from the executive. He was soon joined by another revisionist, Ducos. This tipped the balance on the five-man executive in favour of the revisionists, when two anti-revisionists, Merlin de Douai – a former member of the Committee of the Public Safety – and La Révellière, were forced to resign in June.

The resolve of the revisionists was hardened, and their minds concentrated, by the disastrous military defeat of the French armies in 1799. Now faced with the prospect of invasion, the new majority – and the

Thermidorians – were faced by demands for a return to the Terror. The chambers passed a series of emergency decrees that reminded many of the Montagnard regime: a new *levée en masse*, a forced loan on the rich, and the 'law of hostages', which allowed the government to take into custody ex-nobles, *chouans* and the families of deserters and émigrés, to protect local administrators from possible attack. The ascendancy of neo-Jacobin policies was short-lived: Sieyès and Ducos made Fouché Minister of Police, a man who, since Thermidor, had more to fear from Jacobins than from Jacobin policies, as he had been close to Hébert, Robespierre's rival for the leadership of the Left. Together, they closed the Jacobin club and began a campaign in the legislature to discredit pro-Jacobin ex-directors.

. Sieyès was the driving force for a change of government in the summer and autumn of 1799. He feared a Jacobin revival deeply, and saw the crisis as an opportunity to strengthen the constitution by creating a three-man executive with wider powers than the Directory. He drew up constitutional plans, and drew Cambacérès, an ex-director, into the plot: he became Minister of Justice, and played a key role in weakening the Jacobin opposition. The leading legal expert of the revolutionary decade, Cambacérès was probably the plotter whose attitudes were closest to those of the men of the new majority; he shared their pragmatism and technocratic approach to government, and placed a higher priority on concluding the codification of French law than on factional in-fighting. His constitutional ideas were certainly closer to Napoleon's than those of Sieyès. Cambacérès gave Napoleon crucial support immediately after the coup, to strengthen the power of the executive, and concentrate real power in the hands of one of the three 'consuls' – as the new directors were called – that consul being Napoleon. While first Joubert and then Napoleon were approached, to ensure that the coup had military backing and that its leadership was acceptable to the military, Sieyès also cultivated the leading bankers, Récamier and Perrégaux, and even gained the support of Moreau which, in turn, persuaded Bernadotte to remain neutral, if and when the blow came.

Napoleon was brought into politics by these well-established figures who thought him a 'safe' general, partly because he was not a royalist, partly because his military disasters had occurred far away, and partly because he did not seem very astute, judged on his record to date. Napoleon was a 'dark horse' in 1799; he had not even been the plotters' first choice among the generals. Hoche had been killed in 1797; Bernadotte was judged ablest for the role, but he was too close to the Jacobins; Moreau, in contrast, was tainted with royalism. The main goal of the plotters was to steer the government away from both these political extremes, and so their choice fell, initially, on Joubert. His death at the battle of Novi left the road clear for Napoleon.

The coup of 18–19 Brumaire, Year VIII (9–10 November 1799) was bloodless. The opposition of the Jacobin deputies in the chambers was vocal, but appeared stronger than it need have been only as a response to Napoleon's temporary loss of nerve when he attempted to confront the assemblies with the declaration of the new constitution; he was saved, first, by the presence of mind of his brother Lucien, who had been 'placed' by the plotters as President of the Council of 500 specifically for the coup, then by his troops. In an incident far more significant – and ominous – than the flurry of resistance from a few of the deputies, Napoleon showed an eloquence in front of the Directorial Guard that deserted him with the deputies: he told them the deputies were in the pay of the English, that there was a plot against the Republic. It was a denunciation straight from his own Jacobin roots, and it worked. The chambers were cleared, and the new regime was in place: it was headed by the three consuls, Napoleon, Sieyès and Ducos, but Sieyès was helpless to prevent Napoleon immediately declaring himself the President of the Consulate. Cambacérès and Lebrun, a financial expert imprisoned during the Terror, soon replaced Sieyès and Ducos, as second and third consuls, respectively. Brumaire was the victory of the new elements in Directorial politics – the army, as well as the new majority – not another step in the long line of coups meant to tighten the grip of the Thermidorians on power.

In the wake of Brumaire: a new dawn in the fog

Technocrats now usurped the politicians, and the majority of deputies in both chambers approved, as did almost all the embattled departmental officials, who were in the front line of the resurgence of counter-revolution and disorder that came in the wake of military defeat. Many of these local administrators were themselves neo-Jacobins, but, as Napoleon had already learned as President of the Cisalpine Republic, his regime had need of such men – at least at local level – if it was to survive.

Napoleon had a settled pattern of active support in mind, even as he seized power: it turned on a blend of the new men, who emerged from the shadows under the Directory, at the centre, and hardened – but increasingly apolitical – ex-Jacobins in the provinces. This pattern would be repeated in the new territories of the Empire as it expanded; these elements were to remain Napoleon's greatest sources of support, to the end. Later, attempts would be made to rally royalists and the ex-*conventionels* – the 'men of 1789' – to the regime, but initially, although Napoleon spoke of the revival of the principles of 1789–91, his true policies were those of the 'new wave' of Directorial deputies: politics was ended; elections gave way to appointment by an apolitical government.[34]

Perhaps the most remarkable part of Napoleon's career was the utterly unsuspected talents he suddenly displayed when handed office by a clique of experienced, astute politicians after the success of the coup of Brumaire: Napoleon understood that only office can be given, but that true power had to be taken. More than this, he showed, unexpectedly, that he knew how to take it. The first clear sign of Napoleon's singular genius emerged in his ability to discern where the strengths of the Revolution lay, and then to use them to overpower or neutralize its weaknesses.

Napoleon would draw forth the most effective aspects of reformed, revolutionary France, and he would draw both strength and confidence from the new forces unleashed by the Revolution. His first flash of genius was not on the field of battle, but in grasping political power, and doing so by recognizing the potential of the most powerful new forces at work in his state.

France was still a dangerous country to rule in 1799, closer to the verge of civil war than at any time since 1794. Napoleon had grave dangers in his rear, as he set about dealing with the crisis that had brought him to power: the unprecedented military defeats of 1799. In assuming the leadership of France, he was not only riding a tiger, he was riding it into battle. However, he had the means at his disposal to tame it, and turn its force outward against Europe. Throughout his inspired book, *L'Ancien Régime et la Révolution*, Tocqueville repeatedly urges the reader to push aside 'the debris' – the façade – of the anarchy wrought by the Revolution, for behind it lay the truth of its results, the essence of its achievement: the survival and resurgence of a state of terrifying power. Tocqueville hated Napoleon, in no small part because he did exactly what Tocqueville beseeched of his readers, and acted on it. A powerful tool passed into the hands of a man who knew its potential – and respected it – but who thirsted to use it. It was convenient that few at the time saw this.

Notes

1 In addition to Napoleon's own memoirs, written and dictated on St Helena, the crucial 'founder texts' of the myth are 'the four evangelists of St Helena', as Jean Tulard has named them: Las Cases, Montholon, Gougard, and Bertrand. For a modern anthology: *Napoléon à St-Hélène*, ed. J. Tulard, (Paris, 1981). Later, under the Second Empire, came the highly selective *Correspondance de Napoléon Ie*, 32 vols (Paris, 1858–70).

2 For a useful attack on the more recent literature of this kind: C.J. Esdaile, 'The Napoleonic period: some thoughts on recent historiography', *European History Quarterly*, 23 (1993) pp. 415–32. The classic, D. Chandler, *The Campaigns of Napoleon: the Mind and Method of History's Greatest Soldier*, (London, 1966), a monument in its own field, follows this path. A.J. Guérard, *Napoleon*, (Eng. trans., London, 1957), sets the modern pattern for many popular lives, in English and French, dwelling on the personal aspects and the romantic image.

3 Chateaubriand, *Napoléon*, ed. C. Melchior-Bonnet, (Paris, 1969) collects his disparate writings on Napoleon. Tolstoy's portrait of Napoleon is in *War and Peace*. G. Lefebvre, *Napoléon*, (Paris, 1st edn 1941, 2nd edn 1965).

4 For the span of classic judgements, see P. Geyl, *Napoleon. For and Against*, (Eng. trans., London, 1949). For a sneering, if inspired attack by an intellectual, E. Ludwig, *Napoleon*, (Berlin, 1926).

5 R. Holtman, *Napoleonic Propaganda*, (New York, 1950).

6 In contrast, J. Godechot entitles his chapter on the regime, in *Les Institutions de la France sous la Révolution et l'Empire*, (Paris, 1968), simply 'La dictature militaire'.

7 J. Tulard, *Napoléon, ou le mythe du sauveur*, (Paris, 1977).

8 J. Tulard, *Le Grand Empire*, (Paris, 1981).

9 See also, the brilliant F. Bluche, *Le Bonapartisme. Aux originès de la droite autoritaire (1800–1850)*, (Paris, 1980).

10 M. Lyons, *Napoleon and the Legacy of the French Revolution*, (London, 1994). G. Ellis, *The Napoleonic Empire*, (London, 1991).

11 L. Bergeron, *France under Napoleon*, (Eng. trans., Princeton, 1972).

12 Typical of this is V. Cronin, *Napoleon*, (London, 1971).

13 See especially, J.J. Sheehan, *German History, 1750–1866*, (Oxford, 1990). S.J. Woolf, *A History of Italy, 1700–1860*, (London, 1979). S. Schama, *Patriots and Liberators. Revolution in the Netherlands, 1780–1813*, (New York, 1977). G.H. Lovett, *Napoleon and the Birth of Modern Spain*, 2 vols (New York, 1965), and for the major examples in English.

14 For a full discussion, see pp. 269–70.

15 C.J. Esdaile, *The Wars of Napoleon*, (London, 1995) and D.G. Wright, *Napoleon and Europe*, (London, 1984) are important correctives to this.

16 Bluche, *Le Bonapartisme*, for the attack on 'factionalism' and the regime as 'above party'.

17 *The Autobiography of Goethe. Truth and Poetry from My Own Life*, 2 vols (Eng. trans., London, 1900) pp. 383–6.

18 F. Markham, *Napoleon*, (London, 1963).

19 See especially, W. Callahan, 'The origins of the conservative Church in Spain, 1789–1823', *European History Review*, 10 (1980) pp. 199–223.

20 Esdaile, *The Wars*. S.J. Woolf, *Napoleon's Integration of Europe*, (London, 1991).

21 A. Macintyre, *After Virtue. A Study in Moral Theory*, (London, 1981).

22 Among the major contributions: G. Ellis, *Napoleon's Continental Blockade. The Case of Alsace*, (Oxford, 1981), L. Bergeron, *Banquiers, négociants et manufacturiers parisiens du Directoire à l'Empire*, (Paris, 1978), and *Les 'masses de granit'. Cent mille notables du Premier Empire*, (Paris, 1979).

23 P.W. Schroderer, *The Transformation of European Politics, 1763–1848*, (Oxford, 1994).

24 M. Ozouf, *L'Homme régéneré*, (Paris, 1991).

25 I. Woloch, *The New Regime. Transformations of the French Civic Order, 1789–1820s*, (New York, 1994) p. 28.

26 N. Hampson, *Prelude to Terror*, (Oxford, 1988) pp. 87–8.

27 A. Patrick, 'The approach of French revolutionary officials to social problems', *Australian Journal of French Studies*, 18 (1981).

28 On the legal profession: M.J. Fitzsimmons, *The Parisian Order of Barristers and the French Revolution*, (Cambridge, MA, 1987). On the crafts and unskilled trades: M.D. Sibalis, 'Corporatism after corporations: restoring the guilds under Napoleon I and the Restoration', *French Historical Studies*, 15 (1988) pp. 718–30. For the wider perspective: Woloch, *The New Regime*.

29 J.A. Lynn, 'Towards an army of honour: the moral evolution of the French army, 1789–1815', *French Historical Studies*, 16 (1989) pp. 152–73. A. Forrest, *Soldiers of the French Revolution*, (Durham and London, 1990). S.F. Scott, *The Response of the Royal Army to the French Revolution*, (Oxford, 1978).

30 T.C.W. Blanning, *The Origins of the French Revolutionary Wars*, (Harlow, 1986) p. 122.

31 L. Hunt, D. Lansky and P. Hanson, 'The failure of the liberal republic in France,

1795–1799: the road to Brumaire', *Journal of Modern History*, 51 (1979) pp. 734–59, 752–3.

32 C. Lucas, 'The First French Directory and the rule of law', *French Historical Studies*, (1977) pp. 231–60.

33 C. Lucas, 'The rules of the game in local politics under the Directory', *French Historical Studies*, 16 (1989) pp. 345–71. I. Woloch, *The Jacobin Legacy. The Democratic Movement under the Directory*, (Princeton, CT, 1970). W.R. Fryer, *Republic or Restoration in France? 1794–1797*, (Manchester, 1965).

34 Hunt, Lansky and Hanson, 'The failure of the liberal republic', pp. 758–9.

|1|

Conquest, 1799–1807

Europe in 1799

The statesmen of western Europe were not overly concerned with the palace coup that made Napoleon Bonaparte head of the French state in November 1799. Nor were they entirely wrong in this. Past experience had shown them the inherent fragility of the regimes thrown up by the Revolution in France since 1789. These governments were always at their most vulnerable in times of military adversity and in 1799 the French Republic had just suffered a series of crushing defeats at the hands of the armies of the Second Coalition, which had driven the French out of Italy and Germany in the spring of 1799 and now threatened to carry the war into France itself for the first time since 1793. In these circumstances, a ruthless political purge, followed by yet another government under yet another new constitution – the fourth in eight years – was only to be expected. So often condemned for their inability to understand the nature of the Revolution inside France, the chancellories of Europe should be forgiven for drawing on recent experience in 1799 and thinking they had seen it all before.

A great deal has been made of the power and might of the state forged by the French revolutionaries, especially by posterity, yet in 1799, the truth is that most of this work was still to be done. The military fortunes of the French Republic were what most concerned the other powers of Europe and those fortunes had been decidedly mixed since hostilities had begun in 1792. Ultimately, every French advance had been repelled at some point or other and the reverses of 1798–99 were the most serious inflicted on France to date. The ruthless efforts of the Terror period, 1792–94, made France into a power to be feared and no state, large or small, was foolish enough to ignore the revival of French power and ambition. Nevertheless, the most important point about the nature of French power in 1799 was its limitations, not its extent. Throughout the 1790s France had emerged as a

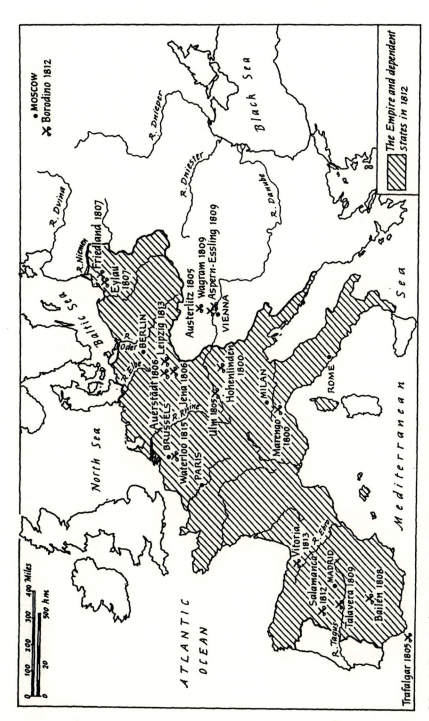

Map 1: Principal Napoleonic Battles, 1797–1815

strong *regional* power in western Europe, but she was far from capable of dominating the whole continent or even of being a determining influence beyond the ring of weak states to her immediate east and south.

No one questioned the subversive nature of the ideology of the Revolution, nor did anyone wish to see France become the dominant force anywhere in Europe, regardless of who might rule her. However, the leaders of Europe were not agreed on what priority to accord the French threat, because it was more of a threat to some than to others. In this way French weakness, rather than French strength, was what really sapped the determination of the first two coalitions assembled against France in the 1790s. This was very clear from the behaviour of the major European states in 1799.

Britain was the only major power to see the threat of France as unquestionably her first priority and the only one to remain in the war continuously. This tenacity is explained in part by the proximity of the two states but even more by their long-standing colonial and maritime rivalries outside Europe, many of which dated back to the seventeenth century. It had little to do with the growing power of France in continental Europe. In direct contrast, Prussia decided simply to 'write off' her minor territorial losses to France in the Rhineland and withdraw into neutrality. In 1799 this was still a sensible course of action; it was a position she retained until 1806 and an important illustration of how limited the scope of the French threat actually was. The issue most important to the Hohenzollerns was the fate of Poland, which France could not influence. Until 1798 Russia took even less of a practical interest in what to her was a very localized conflict at the other end of Europe. Even in 1798–99 Paul I was drawn into the Second Coalition only because France had tried to extend her aggression into the Mediterranean, but it was soon apparent that the French had overreached themselves there. Paul's withdrawal, early in 1800, was determined by the realization that the true interests of his country lay in defending the Baltic from British commercial domination, rather than in the fate of Germany and Italy.

The conduct of the Habsburg Monarchy is a clear example of the dilemma of how to deal with the resurgence of France, for there were deep divisions within the Court which sprang from two utterly opposed visions of where Habsburg interests lay. The more traditional view saw the Monarchy as a German power with vital interests to defend against French ambitions in the Empire. At the heart of this view was a deep attachment to the role of the Habsburg family as Holy Roman Emperors. This was the opinion that held sway at Court for most of the 1790s, when foreign affairs were directed by Count Thugut. Thus, the Monarchy remained a major force in the war against France. A different current of thought centred on the Emperor's brother, Archduke Charles. Less bound by traditional ties and convinced that the defence of the small German states was a waste of resources, this faction saw the future of the Monarchy as a territorially compact power, based in central Europe and the Balkans. Therefore Russia was the real enemy for them, not France.

The war with France exposed the chief weaknesses of the Habsburg state, but in a very particular way: the division of the Monarchy into the Austrian and Hungarian crowns was a traditional source of military, financial and administrative complications. The wars of the 1790s revealed less the inability of the Monarchy to defend itself – in fact it proved a formidable force – than the diverging priorities of the two crowns. As long as France remained a regional power only, the Hungarian Diet in Tressburg (now Bratislava) saw little merit in whole-hearted support of the war effort. This was reflected in the limited troops and taxes it contributed in the 1790s. For the Magyar nobles, the most pressing problem was the anarchy and disorder across the border with the Ottoman Empire which was much closer to them than the Rhineland or northern Italy. The view was very different from Vienna, however. To Thugut and his circle, French aggression was an established fact that had to be confronted; to the Magyars it was a distant noise.

All this points to the relatively restricted influence France had in Europe by 1799. The Habsburgs had been able to hold the French advance in check almost single-handed until 1797 and had more than restored the military balance by 1799 with only minimal help from Russia and the Ottomans. Moreover, when it is remembered that this had been done without the full co-operation of almost half the Habsburg Empire the extent of French power assumes its true proportions. Nothing was decided in the west by 1799; the French Republic and the Habsburgs still contested for domination in the region and no one was more aware of this than the policy-makers of the Directory. That was why a faction among them panicked and turned to Napoleon. The Directory deserves great credit for its consolidation of French power but it had not proved itself capable of sustained, secure expansion. By 1799 its own weaknesses stood exposed. Perhaps the best tribute that can be paid to those at the centre of the regime was the realism that made them turn to reform led by a stronger executive under Napoleon. Ultimately this is what would separate France from her rivals: the ability to adapt in the face of relative failure.

The end of the beginning, 1799–1801

The military position in 1799

The armies of the Second Coalition stood poised for victory in 1799 in all the major sectors of a front stretching from the Rhine, across the Alps, to the Mediterranean, the withdrawal of Russia from the war notwithstanding. However, France regrouped its forces in the winter of 1799–1800. At no other time during the wars of 1792–1814 were the advantages so clear of having a commander-in-chief as civilian head of state. Napoleon was able to co-ordinate his tactics, planning and resources very impressively and to a degree not possible under the Directory.

The inactivity and indecision of the Austrian leadership allowed the initiative to pass to the French in these months more than anything they could do to help themselves. The contrast between the approaches of the two states to the coming campaign marks the first of several major changes within France connected to the creation of the new regime. Whereas Napoleon could proceed with a coherent plan and subordinate political aims to military necessities, Habsburg policy was dictated by a mixture of both. Thugut, a diplomat, influenced purely military affairs to a degree already unthinkable for Talleyrand, his French counterpart, although such interference had not been unknown under the Directory. In a diplomatic effort to win over the south German states by making a show of protecting them, Thugut allowed the French to consolidate themselves in Switzerland where Kray now saw no possibility of an Austrian offensive. Even before the new campaign had started, the Austrians had been forced on the defensive and divided their forces in such a way as to lose their numerical advantage.

The greatest constraint on both sides, and not one often recognized as a levelling factor, was the cumulative exhaustion wrought by seven years of war, mainly with each other. Neither Napoleon nor Archduke Charles really wanted to fight in the spring of 1800. The French armies, often unpaid and underfed at the best of times in the 1790s, had suffered heavy desertions in the wake of the defeats of 1799, while the new more systematic conscription law introduced by the Directory in 1798 not only failed to replenish the depleted ranks of the armies, it also fostered serious disorder inside France, as well as in the Belgian departments. It is hardly surprising that Napoleon sought peace talks with Britain and the Habsburgs almost as soon as he took power. When his offers were rebuffed he was at least in a position to decide to fight on and, more importantly, on how to do so.

Archduke Charles had no such freedom; he was subject to the will of Francis II and had to compete with Thugut for influence at Court. He lost the argument in 1799–1800, and resigned. Charles saw that the army was as exhausted as Napoleon's and wanted time to rebuild it. Reform was needed as well as repair, but he argued neither could be done without a period of peace. In the event, when Thugut – who was confident that war and army reform could take place simultaneously – overruled Charles, both armies were forced to fight against the better judgement of their commanders. Napoleon was able to plan for a quick victory, sure in his own mind that France could not sustain a prolonged war.

The campaigns of 1800–1801

Napoleon entrusted Switzerland, the main sector, to his closest rival, Moreau, while he led the smaller Reserve Army over the Alps and attacked an Austrian army under Melas in southern Piedmont. The early stages of the fighting revealed the fragility of the French armies as well as the strategic brilliance of Napoleon and Moreau. Suddenly Thugut's elaborate, ambitious plans for a two-pronged Austrian offensive into France – across the Rhine into Lorraine and from northern Italy into Provence – evaporated. Kray withdrew to stronger positions on the Danube. It was a wise decision, if hardly what Thugut wanted. The quality of Kray's army had declined sharply since the winter; desertion was rife, the supply system had broken down and disputes broke out between Kray and his staff. In these circumstances it is not surprising that Moreau was able to advance as far as the Danube but he could not bring even this battered army to a decisive battle.

In Italy, Melas confronted Napoleon at Marengo, in southern Piedmont, on 14 June. At this stage, the most striking feature of Napoleon's campaign was a mixture of good leadership and stretched resources. The Austrians proved a match for Napoleon in the field. Marengo has been seen as the most fortuitous of Napoleon's victories,[1] and it need not have been decisive. It turned into a quick French victory because Melas, shaken by the fighting, asked for an armistice even though he could have withdrawn his troops to the Austrian fortresses in central Italy, the Quadrilateral, where there were another 80 000 fresh troops. As it was, the armistice ended the war in Italy. This was what Napoleon knew he needed most because even this short campaign had stretched his army; it had to rest and regroup.

By the terms of the armistice the Austrians left the French in virtual control of all Italy outside the Veneto. For the Habsburgs, this meant the loss of all the territory they had reconquered in 1799. Kray then concluded an armistice with Moreau and surrendered most of Bavaria to the French, and peace talks began at Luneville, in eastern France. When the Austrians insisted that they would not make peace without Britain, Napoleon renewed hostilities in November 1800. This time the French could concentrate on the one remaining front, the Danube, and Moreau won a major battle at Hohenlinden on 2 December 1800. It was the decisive blow that Napoleon had staked the campaign and his own survival on and Moreau gave it to him. Napoleon's masterplan had succeeded because in Moreau and his troops a new, more disciplined army had emerged. This was the first clear sign that the awesome power many contemporaries had detected in the revolutionary armies since 1792 was now almost a reality.

Habsburg resistance all but collapsed. Thugut resigned and the alliance with Britain was repudiated. On 9 February 1801 France and the Habsburgs concluded the Peace of Luneville. The war of the Second

Coalition was now over in continental Europe. Only Britain remained at war with France and her isolation was further increased by the successful diplomacy of Tsar Paul in the Baltic, where his League of Armed Neutrality closed northern Europe to British trade. The Danes and Prussians, with Russian backing, sealed the Baltic and the North Sea coast of Germany. Simultaneously, but independently, Napoleon initiated a joint Franco-Spanish invasion of Portugal, also aimed at stifling British commerce. By June 1801 the continent was sealed more effectively to the British than at any other point in the Napoleonic wars. The combined efforts of the Franco-Spanish alliance and the League of Armed Neutrality came much closer to defeating Britain than the Continental System which evolved from 1806 onwards. Whereas the later system was built on coercion and centred solely on France, the pincer movement of 1800–01 stemmed from a spontaneous identity of interest between France and Russia. It was potentially devastating but, as events turned out, unrepeatable. In part, this was because in 1801 British commerce still centred on European markets but by 1807 Britain was drawing most of her essential raw materials from the New World. The assassination of Tsar Paul in March 1801 did not immediately shatter the effectiveness of the League; in the first four months of 1801 not one British ship passed the Danish straits. The blockade – and the League – were broken by a ruthless naval action off Copenhagen on 2 April 1801 led by Nelson, which destroyed the Danish fleet. In the wake of this the new Tsar, Alexander I, moved to restore good relations with Britain.

Copenhagen was the British equivalent of Marengo and Hohenlinden but Britain, like France and the Habsburgs, had been driven to breaking-point by the latest round of fighting. She now needed to reorganize not only her armed forces but her commercial networks. This was the context in which the British finally made peace with the French Republic at Amiens in March 1802. The only period of complete peace in the whole period 1792–1814 now began. It resulted from the mutual exhaustion of the three major protagonists, Britain, France and the Habsburgs, and the net result was to give Napoleon a free hand in continental western Europe. This was the price the partners of the Second Coalition saw they had to pay to consolidate their own positions. Napoleon, however, had no illusions about French limitations. The future of Europe for the next decade would now turn on how each of the great powers used the time they had just bought themselves.

The watershed: the great powers at rest, 1801–1805

The collapse of the Second Coalition wrought many vital changes at the heart of the major states of Europe. In the course of 1801 Tsar Paul was assassinated and replaced by his son Alexander I. The government of the Habsburg Monarchy also saw sweeping changes, as Archduke Charles returned to the military high command with the brief to reform the army, while the conduct of foreign affairs passed to Cobenzl, an experienced diplomat, and to Colloredo, the Emperor's former tutor. In Britain, the long period of political stability under the ministry of William Pitt the Younger was shattered when he resigned in March 1801. This had been provoked by his confrontation with George III over the issue of Catholic Emancipation, itself a by-product of the hastily enacted abolition of the Irish parliament and its amalgamation with the British one as a panic response to a serious, French-backed rebellion in Ireland in 1798. It would be several years before a ministry of comparable authority emerged to lead the country. Pitt was replaced by Addington, a less decisive leader, if a better financier and administrator than Pitt. Pitt proved ruthless in opposition; together with his former rivals Fox, Grenville and the Whigs, he made the life of Addington's government untenable and forced him to resign by 1804.

With the other powers thus absorbed in their own affairs, Napoleon set about exploiting the terms of Luneville to the full. France was now confirmed in the possession of Belgium, Luxembourg and the west bank of the Rhine, areas she had seized early in the revolutionary wars. Napoleon was also tacitly allowed to annex most of Piedmont directly to France, the first step beyond the 'natural frontiers' proclaimed in 1792. The French advance was further confirmed by the recognition by Britain and the Habsburgs of several 'sister republics' created by the French in the course of the 1790s. Napoleon became their official guarantor.

Luneville reclaimed for France much of what had been won under the Directory, but not all of it, due to the cautious approach adopted by Napoleon at this early stage in his rule. The old idea of a western Europe composed of small, weak buffer states, so central to the concept of balance in eighteenth-century diplomacy, had not yet been abandoned. Set beside the resurrection of those sister republics closest to the borders of France, was the sacrifice of the further-flung ones in central and southern Italy, where the Pope and the various branches of the Bourbons were restored. Nebulous plans for a sister republic on the eastern bank of the Rhine were definitively abandoned. Instead, from 1801 until 1805, the French preferred to exercise an indirect influence on the rivalries of the German princes. This was a consolidation for France, but not an advance. In Switzerland, in 1803, Napoleon actually dissolved the centralized 'sister' Helvetic Republic he inherited from the Directory, replacing it with a cantonal federation over which his control as 'Mediator' was indirect, if decisive. A firm commitment of 16 000 Swiss troops per annum was preferable to direct political control.

Indirect control or, more correctly, determining influence was all Napoleon actually sought beyond France itself and the sister republics. He did not want to over-extend his territories because he saw very clearly that internal reform and consolidation had to be his first priority. He fought the 1800–01 campaign with the military and administrative machinery he inherited from the Directory and had seen how overstretched they were becoming. In seeking peace to reorder his state, Napoleon was conforming to the general pattern in these years. But France alone among the great powers in 1801 was able to enter into this process without major changes in its leadership; these had taken place already. Whereas for the other major states of Europe confused politics had to go with the process of reform, in France reform was part of a process of political consolidation. Ironically, France now had one of the most stable governments among the great powers, in stark contrast to her position at the start of the war of the Second Coalition in 1798. This difference was to prove crucial for the future. Just how much is revealed by an examination of the policies of the other great powers between 1801 and 1805.

In the immediate military and diplomatic context of 1801–05, the crucial point is that no other major state was able to reform itself to the degree achieved by Napoleon in France and its sister republics. Only the middle-sized German states matched the French bloc in the effectiveness of their internal reforms and they remained too small to influence the balance of power directly. Above all, no other state was able to revitalize its army to the extent Napoleon had by 1805. Those aspects of reform where Napoleon proved most successful were in local government and the army. They were not only those most essential for political survival in the early nineteenth century but exactly those areas where the other great powers enjoyed the least success.

Russia, Britain and the Habsburg Monarchy all suffered severe traumas in 1801. The strains of war had everywhere revived older fears and intensified many domestic difficulties for the governments of the three major members of the Second Coalition. Social anarchy haunted all of them and was intrinsically bound up with the war against France. The 'peace party' led by Archduke Charles in Vienna was firmly convinced that another war lost would lead to the disintegration of the Habsburg Monarchy. In Russia the fear of serf revolts united the upper classes more than any other issue, while Paul's foreign policy had disrupted lucrative trading links with Britain. The war years had seen the British government become obsessed by 'Jacobin' conspiracies among the urban working classes and political radicals, the overwhelming patriotism of the majority of the popular classes notwithstanding. The strain of war produced widespread mutinies in the navy in 1797, while the serious revolts in Ireland the following year awakened far older, deeper fears than the immediate political crisis centred on Pitt's resignation and George III's mental breakdown. The British ruling classes would continue to rally behind the war effort. Indeed, they would forge a new and vital role for themselves in national life as a result of the struggle. But in the first years of the new century they were on their guard just as much as their erstwhile allies on the continent.

These fears of social anarchy had a paradoxical effect on the rulers of all three states. In this anxious climate many saw the urgent need for reform not only of the armed forces but of society and government as a whole, especially of taxation and local government on which military reform depended. An efficient administration at provincial level came to be seen as the prerequisite for coming to grips with social anarchy and sustaining a good army through effective recruitment. However, the prevailing insecurity among the ruling elites also inhibited them from pushing their reforms far enough to be effective, where it did not thwart the process completely. Each state suffered a different kind of trauma but they all had the same result of retarding, warping or stifling reform when it had become essential. This was why Napoleonic France was able to gain a marked advantage over the other powers. At the moment France was able to forge ahead under the first stable government she had had since 1789, her rivals failed to keep pace. And they failed for reasons largely of their own making.

The manner in which Alexander I came to power in Russia left him little time or scope to do more than preserve his own position and gradually, if skilfully, free himself from the Court factions that surrounded him. Alexander eventually wrested control of the government for himself, and the tsarist autocracy emerged stronger than ever before by the end of the Napoleonic wars. However, in the period 1800–05 and beyond, his absorption in power struggles at the centre meant that vital military and local government reforms were neglected, which greatly reduced Russia's capacity to oppose Napoleon in the struggles ahead.

In Vienna, Francis soon disregarded most of Charles's administrative reforms when he saw that a streamlined system of ministerial government also meant one less under his direct control. To Francis, it was better that local government remain inefficient than that it become self-assertive and independent. Whenever this question was raised, he saw the example of the dreaded, over-mighty Hungarian Diet before him. Francis clung to this attitude despite the fact that the wars of the 1790s had virtually bankrupted his state, a problem to which the only permanent solution was a reform of the tax system which itself depended on a better bureaucracy. This attitude frustrated even his most faithful servants. As Cobenzl confided to Colloredo in 1802:

> I tremble when I think . . . about what I see and know. All is in flux . . . no area, no department is organized, nothing has order in it, general confusion, no co-operation, an utter lack of direction, no energy, total nonchalance . . . then contentment when business actually makes it from one day to the next. Oh God, where will it all end! . . . I lack the means to reform anything.[2]

Cobenzl and Charles saw that military reforms turned on the financial well-being of the state, and so did foreign policy. As Cobenzl put it, 'it is not sufficient that we have a strong army; it is equally necessary that we have the means to pay for it.'[3]

The financial shambles of the Monarchy was the main constraint on Charles's plans to reform the army after the battering it had taken in the last phases of the war. His problems were further compounded by the deep suspicion of the military Francis had inherited from his predecessors. Little of substance was achieved in such circumstances. By 1803 it was clear that Charles had no powers. His association with a desire for wider reforms made him distrusted at Court. Fear of Charles's reforming reputation also intensified the traditional independence of the Hungarian Diet. In 1802 it refused to make any further peacetime contributions of men or money to the army.

Yet Charles was far from a radical in military reform. He rejected ideas for a militia and distrusted mass conscription as it had been applied in France in the 1790s. In the light of the relatively good performance of well-trained, professional Austrian troops in these campaigns he was not unjustified in this view. Charles accomplished little because nothing could be done to improve pay or conditions. The military budget in 1804 was less than half its level in 1796, while the cost of essential military materials doubled in the same period. As a result, the parity with the French enjoyed by the Austrian troops in the 1790s was lost in these years. In 1804 Charles told Francis openly that Austria was in no condition to fight. He was right.

Indifference to the apparent success of the reforms of the Revolution in France set Britain apart from the states of the continent, who were torn between fears of its ideological subversiveness and a desire to imitate many of its practical reforms. Britain did not need to look elsewhere when it came to raising revenue. Her system of taxation was the best in Europe and was further strengthened by the introduction of income tax in 1798, further refined by Addington a few years later with the adoption of the principle of deduction at source. This was one of the most fundamental reforms adopted anywhere in Europe in this period and it was done with and through the consent of the ruling classes, surely the single most striking example of the continued, intensifying loyalty of the British elite to its own system and cause. Between them, Pitt and Addington set war finance on a firm footing. Unlike so many of their continental counterparts – most notably the Magyar barons – the British elite put its money where its mouth was. The introduction of these taxes supplemented one of the most efficient, rational systems for raising revenue in Europe, based for the most part on indirect taxation. London was rivalled as a financial centre only by the great cities of the United Provinces in the late eighteenth century and, as a consequence, the British government found it easy to raise loans for the war effort. Nevertheless, this money was never meant to be used to create an effective army, only to finance the campaigns of others. While British entrepreneurs shrewdly reoriented their markets away from an insecure, increasingly hostile Europe, their political masters did nothing of consequence to reform the small, ramshackle British army.

Prussia – although a second-rank power – was regarded as a model of military and administrative efficiency. The campaigns of 1806 would soon reveal that Prussia had been living on her reputation for some time, but until she entered the war against Napoleon in that year, her policy of neutrality concealed the fact. There was a great deal of complacency in the higher ranks of the Prussian state and its military high command, fostered by the elderly composition of the general staff. These circumstances were not propitious for major reform, although there was a growing concern after 1801 among the officer corps and the bureaucracy that modernization was needed in most sectors of the state. The army reformers received limited encouragement from the new king, Frederick-William III, who acceded the throne in 1797. He had a considerable, if deeply traditional interest in military affairs, and these years are remarkable for the ferment of ideas generated on army reform, which proved popular with younger officers, although they drew a cool reception from more conservative elements. Nevertheless, many younger, reform-minded officers went on to become the spearheads of the great period of army reform after 1806.

The leading proponent of reform, Scharnhorst, tried to urge radical change on Frederick-William III because he was genuinely alarmed at the prospect of fighting Napoleon in 1806, but his plans for the mass mobilization of a popular militia, the Landwehr, were rejected along with the concept of an army stripped of its aristocratic character. In their growing – and thoroughly justified – fear of Napoleon, the Prussian reformers asserted their belief that the only way to defeat him was to adopt without reserve the military methods of revolutionary France.

Even had Scharnhorst and his colleagues achieved the reforms they wanted, they would still have been one massive stride behind Napoleon. The Prussian reformers were transfixed by the French successes of the 1790s, and they overestimated the revival of French power. Napoleon and his advisors did not. Worried rather than elated by the nature of his victory over the Second Coalition, Napoleon had moved both his army and his state on to a further stage of development. By 1805 even the most determined, radical military reformers in Prussia and elsewhere were truly fighting the last war. An examination of Napoleon's use of these 'quiet years' between 1801 and 1805 will reveal why.

Napoleon turned to the task of reform and consolidation before the fighting had actually ended. It is important to remember that the crucial reforms he enacted in these years were applied to the French satellite states and the considerable territories annexed to France, as well as France itself, and many of these domestic reforms enabled Napoleon to strengthen his armed forces to a far greater extent than the other great powers.

In 1798 the Directory replaced the *ad hoc*, unsystematic conscription of the Revolution – the *levées en masse* – with a regular tri-annual system for raising conscripts. Napoleon refined it still further. It was obvious from the start that conscription could be enforced only by coercion. The national paramilitary police force created in 1791, the Gendarmerie, was also thoroughly reformed at this time and it proved vital to the process of conscription. So did the more centralized, streamlined restructuring of local government that took place in these years centred on civil servants appointed by the central government, the prefects. These changes proved vital for the rebuilding of the army. Through the diligence and dependability of the new prefects and the ruthlessness of the Gendarmerie, the heavy losses of the last campaigns were replaced by regular levies every year between 1800 and 1805. By 1805, when large-scale fighting resumed on land, it has been estimated that only about a quarter of the French army were veterans of the revolutionary armies; the rest were mainly conscripts raised since 1799.[4] Thus, in a very real sense, when war resumed in 1805 the allies faced a very new French army just as they were trying to come to terms with the old one.

It was what Napoleon did with these new troops that really mattered, however. Here, his dynamism sets him – and his war machine – apart from the other powers. Nelson's emphatic naval victory at Trafalgar on 21 October 1805 ended Napoleon's hopes of invading Britain. In preparation for that invasion, Napoleon had gathered his main forces along the Channel coast. This prolonged period of garrison duty could easily have led to the degeneration of the conscript army, but the period 1803–05 saw the largest standing army yet gathered by a single state in the revolutionary wars trained more thoroughly than was possible at any other time, before. or after, by a French officer corps that was younger, better schooled in war and more dynamic than any of its rivals. From the futile plan to invade Britain emerged the awesome Grande Armée, the force which would become the arbiter of Europe for the next ten years.

The Grande Armée could not have been assembled in the first place without the basic reform of the structure of the French high command which made Napoleon its sole supreme commander and ensured that there was only one army under one general staff, a step none of the other powers had been able to take. Henceforth, the French army developed a cohesive, highly centralized command structure unique among the armies of the period. In time this came to be seen as a drawback but until Napoleon's powers of leadership began to waver this system formed the basis of a stunning series of victories. Even before the war resumed with Britain, Napoleon began enhancing the officer corps by founding a military academy at Fontainebleau, later transferred to St Cyr. By 1805 it had produced over 400 highly trained young officers and continued to be a source of renewal throughout the wars.

The real rebuilding took place in the six big camps on the Channel coast, each camp the base of an army corps. The corps system was based on the concept of a fairly large unit, in theory between 20 000 and 30 000 men, composed of all branches of the army – infantry, cavalry and artillery – with adequate support services to make it self-contained. Its tactical use in war was its ability to fight large enemy forces unsupported, at least until reinforcements arrived. Moreau experimented with the corps system in 1799–1801 but it was only in 1803–05 that it became the standard unit of the French army. Henceforth all strategy was shaped around it. At the tactical level, Napoleon made fewer innovations; the crucial changes came through continuous drill. This produced better discipline under fire and a very high level of morale. The intensive training of the camps brought units together and also imbued the new conscripts with considerable physical toughness. In this way even seemingly futile exercises for the planned invasion of England proved useful: swimming practice produced high levels of fitness while training for amphibious landings instilled co-operation and cohesion at company level.[5] This discipline proved vital, as little emphasis was placed on marksmanship, partly through a lack of ammunition, partly because the '1777' musket was too inaccurate to merit it. This period afforded Napoleon the time to transform the French cavalry from something close to an embarrassment into the best in Europe. The artillery also underwent a thorough reorganization and its fire-power was increased. For the first time since the war began, the troops were properly armed and fed. Morale was lifted perceptibly by the issue of proper uniforms. Every soldier in every arm was kept busy all the time. At the heart of the Grande Armée was the Imperial Guard, an elite force which set the standard for the rest of the army. Membership was open to any soldier who proved himself worthy, and in the campaigns of 1805–07 it represented a level of training, expertise and, above all, commitment no other army possessed.

Discipline did not extend far beyond the battlefield or the parade ground, however. On campaign, indiscipline was rife. The troops marched quickly and desertions were practically non-existent in the early campaigns, but unofficial foraging was still accepted along with the plunder, violence and rapine that were always part of the army's behaviour. Frightening excesses always followed its victories. The Grande Armée was also noted for its 'Jacobin' zeal, especially its impiety; churches and shrines were its favourite prey. Significantly, Napoleon never allowed the Grande Armée to have chaplains.[6] The growing professionalism of the Grande Armée was tempered by many characteristics that made it as much the last great early modern army as the first modern one.

However, the Grande Armée had become the greatest army of its time by 1805, a new, more formidable army, very different from its predecessors of the 1790s, if still modelled on them. It has been suggested that this period saw the beginnings of a change in the ethos of military service from one of revolutionary patriotism to one based on professional honour.[7] This may be difficult to prove at a personal level but there is no doubt that the camps of 1803–05 forged a very different force from the dispirited, disorganized armies that finished the war in 1801. By 1805 the veterans had confidence in themselves, the conscripts had confidence in the future and they all had faith in their officers, their commander above all. And all this had been done without the knowledge of the other powers. Certainly, the governments of the great powers were aware that a large army was encamped on the Channel and that it was being trained, but they had no idea what it all meant, especially for them. At the outbreak of a new war in 1805 the military balance had tipped decisively in favour of Napoleon. This was in no small part because the other powers were preparing for the last war, if they were preparing at all. Had they sensed the true nature and power of the Grande Armée, it is doubtful the Russians or the Habsburgs would have joined Britain as readily as they did.

Europe in 1805: from diplomacy to *blitzkrieg*

The road to war

To the major states of Europe, the years 1801–05 were little more than an uneasy truce. The renewed fighting between Britain and France in 1803 only strengthened the climate of scepticism about preserving peace on the continent.

For the smaller states the period 1803–05 was crucial as their fates became bound up in the conflict between Britain and France. The naval character of the war drew in the small states of coastal Europe but their experiences were varied in these years. While Italian ports like Livorno, in Tuscany, suffered from the conflict, the great North Sea ports of Lübeck, Hamburg and Bremen boomed as they acquired trade driven out of the Low Countries by the war. Portugal, too, profited in this way. However, they all shared a desire to stay neutral in a quarrel between two powers they perceived as equally dangerous to them. French expansionism was already a known fact, but there was also a growing fear of British economic aggression, felt from Portugal to the Baltic.

Napoleon was able to tighten his grip on the Italian states in this period without any effective opposition, but he did so in the face of vehement – if impotent – protests from the governments of Tuscany, Naples and the Papal States. In the course of 1803–05 Napoleon flooded these states with troops against their wishes. Portugal and the Hanseatic ports were more successful in preserving their profitable neutrality but it was becoming increasingly difficult. The British had forced Napoleon to guarantee the integrity of Portugal as part of the Peace of Amiens but there was a growing suspicion that Britain would seize the Portuguese colonies in the same manner as she had those of France and Holland. By 1804 the influence of the French ambassador, General Lannes, had grown to the extent that he was able to oust the pro-British Rodrigo de Sousa Coutinho and help to power a pro-French faction centred around Antonio de Arajuo de Azevedo.[8] Nevertheless, even Arajuo refused to join France in the war of 1805. Faced with ever-increasing bullying from Paris on the one hand and cynical breaches of economic neutrality by the British on the other, he strove in vain to strengthen Portuguese defences against future threats from several sides. The Hansa ports had become vital centres of credit and commerce to both Britain and France. Thus their position as 'islands of neutrality in a Europe at war'[9] enabled them to remain neutral – and rich – when the war spread into Germany in 1805.

The period 1803–05 witnessed many important developments in the other small states of the Holy Roman Empire – the Reich – as well as the Hansa towns. The fate of these small states had been under discussion by France and Francis II, in his capacity as Holy Roman Emperor, on and off since 1797. Influenced by his defeat in the war of the Second Coalition, Francis refused to serve as the representative of the Reich any longer. This forced the Reichstag, the congress of the rulers of all the imperial states, to devise its own plan for the reorganization of the Holy Roman Empire. Their final decision, the Hauptschluss, was completed in April 1803. It was informed by a desire to strengthen the Reich in the face of great-power conflict. As such, it was the last attempt by these states to save themselves and to confront the realities of a new European order. In the short term, they failed: the Reich was swept away in 1806. But it did not die from lack of interest or support among its smaller members. Some statesmen were still bound by out-moded – and increasingly unreciprocated – ties of loyalty to the Habsburg dynasty, such as von Kruse the Chief Minister of Nassau. Others, mainly the Imperial Knights, saw that the very particular form of political organization of their tiny states could not exist outside a framework like the Reich.

Nevertheless, by withdrawing from the Congress of Rastatt, Francis II left the deciding influence to Napoleon: effectively, he admitted that France was now the dominant regional power in western and southern Germany, although he soon repented of this. In practice this meant that the states to gain most from the Hauptschluss were those large enough – and unsentimental enough – to negotiate directly with France. The tiny 'patchwork' states were reduced with great ruthlessness, and their lands divided among the middling states: Bavaria, Baden, Württemberg, Hesse-Kassel, Hesse-Darmstädt, Nassau, and Prussia all made gains. Within their ranks, however, the least sentimental about their allegiance to the Reich and the Habsburgs did best. The scruples of von Kruse cost Nassau considerably in comparison to the less inhibited diplomacy of Hesse-Darmstädt or Baden, for example.

A new political world was clearly emerging in western Germany in 1803 and Napoleon was its controlling influence. He fostered this redistribution of territory, thus beginning to convert these states into his allies and winning them away from the Habsburgs. Only he could ensure that they kept their new gains. In the short term the princes hoped to conserve the Reich through collaboration with Napoleon, but the real importance of the Hauptschluss went much further. It took the first major step in the creation of a new, lasting territorial basis for the German states which Napoleon would reinforce in 1806.

In the immediate context of 1803–05, the obvious influence Napoleon now wielded in Germany frightened both Russia and the Habsburgs. In May 1804, Napoleon transformed himself from First Consul of the French Republic into the hereditary Emperor of the French and brought the Pope to Paris for the coronation. In the light of his recent interventions in the Reich, Francis now feared Napoleon would try to make himself Holy Roman Emperor: he did not reject the idea until 1806. Habsburg policy towards Germany vacillated in this dangerous period. Francis was torn between a desire to withdraw from German affairs to concentrate on expansion in the Balkans and his traditional role as Holy Roman Emperor. The first trend is illustrated by his decision to take the title 'Emperor of Austria' in August 1804. This was not only a challenge to Napoleon, but a sign that Francis sought to shift the main role of the dynasty outside the Reich. However, from 1804 onwards, he began to intervene again in the affairs of the Reich in his traditional role. Francis now used his imperial status to protect the Imperial Knights of Swabia from the aggression of Max-Joseph of Bavaria, who was trying to stretch his authority over them beyond the terms of the Hauptschluss. All but driven from Italy and now fighting to control the new enlarged states of the Reich, the Habsburgs were increasingly prepared to listen to British proposals for a new coalition.

Russian diplomats were also alarmed by the extent of Napoleon's influence in the Reich, particularly because Alexander had assumed that the reordering of Germany was to be shared between Russia and France. Until 1804, Russia inclined towards a policy of co-operation with France aimed at containment, but the creation of the French Empire and Napoleon's gratuitous execution of a prominent French aristocrat, the Duc d'Enghien, pushed Alexander into the waiting arms of the British.

Pitt returned to office for the last time in 1804 and he thoroughly re-evaluated British war aims. The goals remained the same: of forcing France back behind her pre-war borders and the restoration of the Bourbons. However, most of the details Pitt put before the Tsar in 1804 were new, and many would find their way into the final settlement of the Napoleonic wars at the Congress of Vienna in 1815, above all the creation of a ring of strong states along the eastern border of France. When a new generation of British statesmen took over from Pitt after 1805, they would have to re-learn these lessons for themselves and it would be some time before British policy rediscovered the realism he imparted to it. Pitt's immediate priority was to rebuild the coalition and he made no specifications about the shape of any future peace settlement, 'for the limited object of preventing the future progress of French armies is of great importance in itself',[10] as he told the Russian ambassador. Russia was confident that she could withdraw behind the safety of her own, remote borders if the war went wrong, and had no tangible quarrel with the French Empire. In contrast, Austria felt threatened by the French domination of Italy, as much as by the reordering of

Germany, and took the field in desperation rather than hope. Only Prussia refused to fight.

The allies assumed that the Grande Armée would stay concentrated in northern Europe and that if the French opened a second front, it would be in northern Italy. They were wrong, for Napoleon decided to strike into the heart of the Habsburg Empire. More vital still, the partners in the new coalition had no idea of the awesome nature of the army Napoleon now unleashed against them.

The Ulm–Austerlitz campaign of 1805

The fighting that followed the formation of the Third Coalition transformed western and central Europe. The victories won by the Grande Armée in this campaign were shattering; they had none of the inconclusiveness of so many conflicts in the 1790s. Not only did Napoleon strike where least expected, he did so with unforeseen speed: the Austrians under Mack overestimated the time it would take him to reach the Rhine from the Channel camps by three whole weeks, just as they badly underestimated the time it would take the Russians to reach central Europe. As it was, the Grande Armée left its camps on 23 August 1805; by 30 September all its units had crossed the Rhine in good order with virtually no desertions – the surest evidence of its high morale – and by 11 October it had crossed the Danube.

Mack and Archduke Ferdinand had invaded Bavarian territory in September and moved slowly with their forces scattered over a wide area. When Napoleon attacked Mack at Ulm, on the upper Danube, he had 200 000 troops in seven corps under veteran commanders as well as 50 000 more good troops collected from his German allies, Bavaria, Württemberg and Baden. The French victory at Ulm has been denigrated on the grounds that Napoleon caught Mack only by chance, having overshot the Austrians because he did not know where they were – 'conducting a *Blitzkrieg* into thin air'[11] – and even exposing his own lines to a possible Austrian counter-attack. This is certainly possible, as armies of the time often became poorly co-ordinated over limited spaces, but it is often forgotten how poor the maps available to soldiers were in this period, particularly ones giving details of roads and villages on a small scale. It was usually only after campaigns that the French army could make good maps of its own with the information gathered during the fighting.[12] However, regardless of the close manoeuvres, the strategic and administrative superiority of the French war machine ensured Napoleon a clear advantage in both the quality and quantity of his army when he did catch Mack, who was forced to surrender his entire force of 33 000 men. On 15 November, Napoleon entered Vienna unopposed.

There was still a joint Austro-Russian army of 90 000 men concentrated north-east of Vienna, near Olmutz, however. The Russian army was under

Alexander's personal command and, convinced that he outnumbered Napoleon, he advanced against him. The armies met at Austerlitz on 2 December 1805. It proved the greatest victory of Napoleon's career. It was won by his own abilities, the excellence of his marshals – the corps commanders – and the men they commanded who were as highly motivated as they were well-drilled. There was now no doubt about French military superiority; the Grande Armée showed itself superior in every arm. Ulm had been a victory based on strategic planning; Austerlitz was a triumph of battlefield tactics, the fruit of the hard graft of the Channel camps.

A national cult soon sprang up around the battle of Austerlitz and its heroes. Its immediate impact was to convince Alexander to retreat behind his own borders. Left alone, a stunned, humiliated Francis surrendered. On 26 December 1805, Napoleon imposed the Treaty of Pressburg on the Austrian Empire from a position of undisputed superiority for the first time. The Napoleonic Empire was now emphatically the dominant power in western and central Europe, but its aims were still relatively limited and this was reflected in the peace settlement.

For Napoleon, the hallmark of the Treaty of Pressburg was consolidation; none of the worst fears of the Austrian Court were fulfilled. Napoleon used his position less to expand his Empire at Austrian expense – although this did happen in northern Italy – than to consolidate what he had already acquired. In Germany, this meant rewarding his new allies in ways that bound them to him definitively rather than the Habsburgs: the rulers of Bavaria and Württemberg were now styled kings, the Margrave of Baden was promoted to Grand Duke, and they all received substantial territory. This served to weaken the Holy Roman Empire and Habsburg influence in it, rather than the Austrian Empire itself. Napoleon, rather than the Holy Roman Emperor, was now officially recognized as the guarantor of the sovereignty of the three south German states, perhaps the gravest blow of all to the Reich. North of the Alps, Napoleon still preferred an indirect, if effective, form of hegemony. This was characterized by the creation of the Confederation of the Rhine in July 1806. The Confederation always remained a loose body, linking the German princes together under Napoleon as its protector. Napoleon's hopes to see it develop into a centralized, united state along French lines were never realized. The princes remained determined to preserve their independence and Napoleon did not challenge them, especially because the Confederation proved a reliable military ally. In only one instance did he deviate from this policy of indirect control, when he created the Grand Duchy of Berg early in 1806. It was assembled from lands in north-western Germany ceded by Prussia and Bavaria in exchange for territories elsewhere. This brought Napoleon control of both banks of the Rhine and also of the River Wesser, thus strengthening the blockade against Britain. The new state was ruled briefly by Murat, Napoleon's cavalry commander and brother-in-law, and then by Napoleon himself, as regent for his young nephew, the son of his brother Louis.

In Italy, Pressburg was used to confirm the series of annexations made by Napoleon in the months preceding the campaign. In June the Ligurian Republic became three French departments and the Duchies of Parma, Piacenza and Guastalla were formally occupied with a view to annexation. The Austrians also lost the lands of the old Republic of Venice. Now the Veneto itself and the Balkan territories of the old Republic – Istria and Dalmatia in modern-day Croatia and Slovenia – all passed to the Kingdom of Italy. Further south, the Neapolitan Bourbons were made to pay far more dearly for joining the Coalition than the Habsburgs, and chased into exile in Sicily. The mainland part of the Kingdom of Naples now became a French satellite state under Napoleon's older brother, Joseph. All Italy except Tuscany and the Papal States was now under direct French control.

At this point, the affairs of western Europe seemed settled to Napoleon's satisfaction. Although it was unlikely that this would have led to the end of the war with Britain, this need not have entailed further territorial expansion by Napoleon: war and domination are not always synonymous with territorial expansion. The next phase of Napoleonic expansion was not caused by British or Russian aggression, nor by French ambition, but by the unforeseen entry of Prussia into the Coalition in the summer of 1806. Although the resultant campaign was brief and conclusive, its diplomatic results changed dramatically the character and scope of French hegemony in Europe. By the end of the campaigns of 1806–07, France had been transformed from a regional into a continental superpower.

The zenith of French power, 1806–1807

The war with Prussia: Jena and Auerstädt, 1806

The entry of Prussia into the war came as a shock to all concerned. Britain and Russia had made strenuous efforts to bring her into the Coalition but the defeat of Austerlitz ended even these slender hopes. If Prussian neutrality were to be broken, it seemed most likely that it would be to join the French side: her annexation of Hanover was followed by the closure of Prussian ports to British commerce. Prussia was behaving like a French puppet state and that was just how Britain treated her, declaring war on Frederick-William III in June 1806. Hanover notwithstanding, the British government now allied with Prussia. Frederick-William had found the hidden costs of an alliance with Napoleon too high: the British had virtually impounded the Prussian merchant fleet. Above all, he now saw that future Prussian expansion in Germany depended on playing off France against Austria, but after Austerlitz this could only be possible by inflicting an equalizing defeat on France. In July, Prussia also reached agreement with Russia.

Militarily, Frederick-William could not have chosen a worse moment to fight. The Prussian army was now to pay the full price for its failure to reform itself during the long years of neutrality. Added to this was the growing strength of the Grande Armée. Napoleon imposed extortionate financial demands on Austria at Pressburg, which enabled the army to remain in winter quarters in Germany during 1805–06. There were more new, hastily trained conscripts in the French ranks by the summer of 1806 but they integrated well with the highly trained veterans of the 1805 campaign. Above all, they were superbly led by Napoleon and the marshals, all of whom were younger than their Prussian counterparts and more experienced in combat as well.

The gap between the two armies was soon driven home. Napoleon trapped the Prussians at Jena and Auerstädt, and crushed them. These battles destroyed the reputation of the Prussian army, a clinical deconstruction of a myth. The Prussian commanders had been inept and their tactics obsolete. In contrast, the French marshals displayed their ability to work together under Napoleon and independently as corps commanders, epitomized by Davout at Auerstädt, the supreme vindication of the corps system developed in the Channel camps.

The military humiliation of Prussia was followed by a peace which was marked by a justifiable vindictiveness on the part of Napoleon. Smarting from Frederick-William's duplicity, Napoleon proceeded to do to Prussia what the Habsburgs feared had been in store for them in 1805. The Treaty of Posen in December 1806 awarded Prussian territory to Saxony and raised its Elector to the status of King, thus creating a loyal ally in eastern Germany, and a viable counter-weight to Prussia. Further losses of territory and humiliations followed in the course of 1807, but even as the northern winter set in, the Russian forces were concentrating further east.

In the first days of November 1806, Napoleon ordered the army into Russian Poland and for the only time in the history of the revolutionary wars, the French found an indigenous, large-scale popular revolt on their side. On 28 November, the French occupied Warsaw but with his troops exhausted, fighting in difficult terrain and in appalling weather, Napoleon could not prevent an orderly Russian withdrawal. Unable to pursue his real enemy, Napoleon contented himself by stripping Prussia of her Polish lands and transferring their administration to a 'Committee of Government' composed of native Polish aristocrats. This was the first step towards the creation of a new Polish satellite state, the Grand Duchy of Warsaw. Far behind his front lines, Napoleon ordered French troops to occupy Hamburg and the rest of the North Sea coast that had been under Prussian control. A few days later he issued the Berlin Decrees, intensifying the blockade against Britain. In January 1807, the Russians launched a new offensive across northern Poland to surprise the scattered, over-extended French garrisons there, thus initiating the final round of the war of the Third Coalition, and of Napoleonic expansion.

The war with Russia: Eylau and Friedland, 1807

The Russians were now fighting closer to home while the Grande Armée was reaching the limits of its endurance. The cumulative losses of the campaigns of 1805 and 1806 had been heavy and because the fighting had continued unabated since the autumn of 1806 there was little time for training new recruits or organizing proper supplies. The Grande Armée now had a higher proportion of raw conscripts than at any time since 1801. In the 1806 campaign, one-third of the army had seen only six months' service but the well-trained troops of the Channel camps still formed the majority and the new troops learnt from them. By 1807, however, this proportion had been seriously reduced and it has been suggested that the quality of the Grande Armée had been seriously eroded. The best of the reinforcements to reach the front in late 1806 were not French, but the Poles and troops from the army of the Kingdom of Italy. Supplies were also a problem. Indeed, the new Russian offensive had been provoked, in part, by foraging expeditions so large that the Russians mistook them for an all-out attack. In many ways Alexander and his commander, Bennigsen, a German in Russian service, had picked a good moment to strike.

Napoleon responded to the Russian attack with inventiveness and calm, but was unable to plan his operations properly. Until now he had been obliged to plan his campaigns with poor maps and over bad roads; now he had to work entirely without either. When Napoleon led the Grande Armée into northern Poland he took it off the edge of the existing maps. The only information he had was from one topographer who moved ahead of the army with the scouts, collecting information which was then made into a map as the army went along. A full map of the region was completed only after the campaign was over.[13] The advance of the Grande Armée became an elaborate game of 'hide and seek'. Napoleon guessed rightly that the Russians would turn and fight at some point but he had no idea when or where. Bennigsen feigned a battle several times, only to slip away again. The big battle did not occur until 7 February 1807, at Eylau, when Napoleon simply blundered into Bennigsen. The battle was inconclusive but the losses were horrific; the experience convinced both sides to withdraw to winter quarters.

As Bennigsen drew strength, the Grande Armée reached its lowest ebb to date. The countryside was inhospitable, and by the spring, the marshals were fighting among themselves for supplies; desertion became a major problem for the first time. However, the following campaign soon showed that the powerful machine forged in the Channel camps was far from crippled. The bonds that united the Grande Armée had not been broken by adversity and Napoleon used his time wisely; great emphasis was placed on training the new conscripts that winter. Indeed, a new and deeper professionalism has been detected in the army that emerged from this campaign.

It had marched almost 3 000 miles in just over two years, annihilating two great armies and savaging a third. Reinforced from Italy and Germany as well as from France, and far from home, the focus of its loyalty was shifting from a patriotic, nationalist ethos to one based on personal loyalty, first to Napoleon and then to its own corps commanders. The army which emerged from the trials of 1807, was battle-hardened and resilient, if less thoroughly trained than in 1805. The useful administrative practice of calling up conscripts a year in advance had evolved by 1807 which allowed recruits to receive several months' extra training in the depots.

Bennigsen reopened the fighting in June 1807. Again, the armies had trouble finding each other, and when they did, at Friedland on 13 June, it was by chance. Friedland was a masterpiece of tactical improvisation by Napoleon. It is probable he could have inflicted more damage on the Russians had he pursued them, but the army had been pushed far enough. Napoleon had achieved his objective, to catch and maul the main Russian army.

On 23 June 1807, Alexander and Napoleon concluded an armistice at Tilsit. The last great continental power of the Third Coalition had been hounded across Europe behind its own borders and defeated. But Napoleon knew how severely this had stretched his resources. To be a dominant regional power was one thing; to aspire to the status of a European superpower was quite another, as any soldier of the Grande Armée knew all too well – in his own hard-boiled way – by the spring of 1807. Napoleon and Alexander, after his own rout at Austerlitz, had come to see this too, if somewhat later than their troops. Full peace talks began on 25 June 1807. When the two emperors met on a raft on the River Niemen, near Tilsit, Napoleon had the good sense to treat Alexander as an equal with whom he would construct a new European order. In Russia, Napoleon sensed a power beyond his range, but one his own Empire now counted as a near neighbour.

Europe in 1807: the new order of Tilsit

The two treaties of Tilsit embodied the ruthless reordering of the European mainland. In the first, signed between France and Russia on 7 July 1807, Alexander sanctioned almost all the territorial changes Napoleon and his predecessors had made up to this point in Italy, Germany and the Low Countries. He also conceded two more: the creation of the new Grand Duchy of Warsaw with Napoleon's new ally, the King of Saxony, as its ruler, and the wholly new state, the Kingdom of Westphalia, under Napoleon's youngest brother, Jerome.

By recognizing French hegemony in western Europe, Alexander bowed to reality for, as will be seen in the following chapter, Napoleon had consolidated his grip on these areas even as he advanced into new ones. It was an admission by the only state still capable of resistance that France was not only the master of western Europe, but that her power there was too well entrenched to be opposed. When he sanctioned the creation of Westphalia and the Grand Duchy of Warsaw, the Tsar also acknowledged the transformation of Napoleonic France from a regional into a pan-European superpower. This was the true turning-point for the French Empire: its power, resources and commitments were now of a much greater magnitude than in 1805. The second treaty of Tilsit effectively turned Prussia into a pawn of Napoleon. Its real importance lies in the fact that Alexander let it happen. Shaken by successive military defeats, he abandoned central, as well as western, Europe to Napoleon.

Napoleon moved quickly to enlist Alexander to the blockade. The destruction of his best fleet at Trafalgar convinced Napoleon that economic warfare was the only way to defeat the last great power still at war with him. This, in truth, made him reliant on Alexander to close his own ports to Britain and to help him police the Baltic. It also left Napoleon wholly dependent on Alexander from that point on: he represented the only friendly power in the Baltic region with a fleet. It was a dependence disliked by Talleyrand, the experienced French Foreign Minister. He saw the best hopes for French security in continuing to sow divisions among the other powers rather than in alliances with any of them. Tilsit led to his resignation.

With hindsight it is easy to see the wisdom of Talleyrand's assessment of the position in 1807. To contemporaries, however, it was obscured by the third consequence of Tilsit. Although Napoleon's control of the coasts of Europe was unsure, his military grip on central Europe was indisputable by 1807. The bulk of the Grande Armée was now in central Germany. Here, in comfortable quarters and amid plentiful countryside, the war machine showed every sign of renewing its formidable strength. While its veterans rested and drew breath, its new conscripts received the most thorough training of any since 1805. To friend and foe alike, their presence in Germany seemed permanent. Stadion and Archduke Charles were convinced that this presence on their borders made neutrality the only realistic option for Austria in the wars of 1806–07. In 1806 this led Stadion – normally a strong proponent of the German character of the Habsburg Monarchy – to persuade Francis II to dissolve the Holy Roman Empire because he feared Napoleon would get himself elected to the throne. A year later the Peace of Tilsit made Napoleon – and his army – a permanent, menacing neighbour. The predicament was summed up by Metternich, then the Austrian ambassador to France, writing to Stadion in 1808:

we no longer go through the intermediate steps which formerly were necessary to precede the opening of a campaign. Napoleon has no preparations to make; he has two hundred thousand men in front of us, on our two flanks and at our rear. He has not to pass the Rhine with new troops to fall on us. He can enter Galicia [on the border with the Grand Duchy of Warsaw] before we know at Vienna that he has made war upon us.[14]

By 1807, all British efforts to draw the Habsburgs into a new coalition were doomed to failure; British resistance was now confined to the fringes of Europe.

The rise of France from a regional to a continental power had been meteoric, established only in 1805 and confirmed in 1807. Its swiftness took Napoleon and his diplomats by surprise and this is reflected in the settlements they imposed on their enemies. Haste rather than a megalomaniac masterplan of domination is the defining characteristic of Napoleonic policy at its high point. Brothers were placed on thrones only after the treason of allies: Louis in Holland after the failure of the Batavian government to enforce the blockade, then Joseph in Naples and Jerome in Westphalia, following the defection of Naples, Prussia and Hesse-Kassel to the Third Coalition. Bonapartist dynasticism was, in every case, a last resort, not a burning ambition, but it extended Napoleonic hegemony.

Within the limits reached by 1807, that hegemony was more indomitable than the allied leaders dared imagine, extending far beyond the purely military and diplomatic, to the creation of a solid administrative hegemony that allowed Napoleon to harness to his service the human and material resources of the richest, most developed parts of the continent. Nevertheless, the limits France reached at Tilsit were the most she could cope with, as would be proved in the period 1808–14. When Napoleon attempted to extend his control beyond them he overreached the resources of his Empire as much as his own ambition.

Notes

1 O. Connelly, *Blundering to Glory: Napoleon's Military Campaigns*, (Wilmington, D.E., 1987) pp. 65–8.
2 Cited in K.A. Roider, 'The Habsburg foreign ministry and political reform, 1801–1805', *Central European History*, 22 (1989), pp. 160–82, 165–6.
3 Ibid., pp. 173–4.
4 Chandler, *Campaigns*, p. 333.
5 J. Morvan, *Le Soldat impérial*, 2 vols (Paris, 1904) i, p. 289 takes a more critical view of the value of these exercises.
6 Ibid. ii, pp. 507–8.
7 See especially J.A. Lynn, 'Toward an army of honour: the moral evolution of the French Army, 1789–1815', *French Historical Studies*, 16 (1989).
8 G. and J.S. de Silva Dias, *Os Primordios da Maçonaria em Portugal*, 4 vols (Lisbon, 1980) vol. I, tom. ii, pp. 423–30.
9 M. Bruguière, ' "Remarques sur les rapports", financiers entre la France et l'Allemangne du Nord à l'époque napoléonienne: Hambourg et "le parti de la paix" ' *Francia*, 1 (1973) pp. 467–81.

10 Cited in J. Sherwig, *Guineas and Gunpowder: British Foreign Aid in the Wars with France, 1793–1815*, (Cambridge, MA, 1969).

11 O. Connelly, *Blundering to Glory: Napoleon's Grande Armée*, (New York, 1988) pp. 113–14.

12 J.R. Elting, *Swords around a Throne: Napoleon's Grande Armée*, (New York, 1988) pp. 113–14.

13 Ibid., pp. 113.

14 Cited in E. Kraehe, *Metternich's German Policy*, 2 vols (Princeton, NJ, 1963 and 1988) i, p. 57.

|2|

Consolidation, 1799–1807

The Napoleonic Revolution in France

Ralliement, amalgame *and the Reconstruction of France, 1800–1807*

Much to the surprise of many who had brought him to power, Napoleon set about reshaping the civil and judicial inheritance of the Directory with as much energy and determination as he gave to the reform of the army; indeed, the need to strengthen the army quickened the pace of many other aspects of reform. The first years of the Consulate saw tremendous activity at the heart of the French state, if not always great innovation.

The process of reform is usually addressed solely in a French context, which inevitably judges Napoleon in the light of the revolutionary regimes of the 1790s. This is legitimate, in that the reforms of the 1790s represent Napoleon's inheritance and set the parameters he worked within. However, the contemporary context of the Napoleonic regime was not the Revolution, but the international climate post-1799. To neglect the comparative context of the times is to fail to grasp the true nature and importance of the Napoleonic regime. The activities of the Consulate and the early Empire are often attacked as derivative, or labelled as retrograde, when approached in the context of the French Revolution alone. When set beside its major rivals, however, Napoleonic France emerges as the most dynamic and inventive state in Europe by 1799, if not the most liberal or enlightened in comparison with some of the smaller German states.

Napoleon's was the first French government since 1791 to accede to power without recourse to a violent purge. Almost all the personnel of the Consular regime were drawn from the Directory, both at the centre and in local government. Indeed, through the policies of *ralliement* and *amalgame*, the regime actively sought to broaden its base of support beyond the untenably narrow confines it had reached under the Directory.[1] In fact, although many royalist émigrés and Jacobin activitists returned under the amnesties of 1800 and 1802, the men of the Directory remained the mainstay of the regime until a new generation of administrators emerged after about 1807. By 1804, Napoleon had tightened censorship to levels undreamt of in the 1790s, and expelled his most outspoken critics from the Tribunate, in a prelude to converting the Consulate into a hereditary Empire. Even the emasculation of the Tribunate – abolished in 1807 as a 'useless institution' – and the gradual retirement of critical deputies from the Corps Législatif after 1802, did not amount to the wholesale elimination of opposition that characterized the 1790s.

The authoritarian, often repressive nature of the Napoleonic regime is beyond question; it suffers by comparison with its revolutionary predecessors and by modern standards in its rejection of parliamentary supremacy for that of a powerful, centralized executive. Nevertheless, the transition from the elitist parliamentarianism of the Directory to the absolutism of the Consulate and the Empire was done with the consent of the bulk of the French political and propertied classes, and it was smoother than any previous change of regime. Evidence of this consent is not to be found in the meaningless plebiscites which marked each revision of the constitution of 1799, but in the willingness of the 'men of the Revolution' to work with the new system, and to help push it along the path to absolutism. The French Revolution had been an experiment in government, in which parliamentary politics was only one part. By 1799, most participants in the revolutionary experiment no longer regarded this as its essence. For contemporaries, this had become the protection of the Revolution from its enemies – internal and external – together with security of persons and property from arbitrary rule and efficient, modern administration, all subsumed under the concept of the rule of law. Napoleon offered them this, in exchange for surrendering real political power, but the true point is that the politicians and administrators of the Directory had come to this conclusion on their own. The nature of the Revolution had changed for them.

Napoleon kept his bargain with them, both through his practical reforms and in the way they were formulated. The First Consul and his collaborators stultified the legislative assemblies with remarkable speed – and few complaints – but in place of parliamentary debate, they instituted a system of consultation that made the regime responsive to the propertied and political classes to a far greater extent than any of the great powers, save Britain. This was expressed through the Council of State, at the apex of government, and in the *conseils de préfecture* and *conseils généraux*, in the departments; the latter acted as 'an administrative arbitration service, a local buffer between the propertied public and the state'.[2] Their other role was to submit proposals on local matters to the central government; their petitions were solicited by the regime and taken seriously.[3] Within the confines of the Council of State, Napoleon encouraged open discussion of practical affairs. These bodies placed no formal or effective check on Napoleonic absolutism, but they represent the sort of channels of communication sought in vain by reformers of the 'unofficial committee' and their rivals in the Senate in Russia and of Archduke Charles in the Habsburg Monarchy, in the same years.

It was in this atmosphere – that of a 'well-ordered police state', rather than a parliamentary government – that the great, practical reforms of the years 1800–05 took place. There is much truth in the assertion that the regime was a military dictatorship in spirit, and that it injected a military ethos into the state and society as a whole,[4] and few organizations are as tightly self-regulating as armies. The Napoleonic regime was an absolutism tempered by law; it played by its own rules but did not break them. Thus, the Code Napoleon became a guarantee of the conduct of the regime, as well as the summation of earlier attempts by the revolutionary regimes to give France a rational, uniform body of law. The constitution of 1799 studiously ignored the 'Rights of Man and the Citizen' proclaimed in the constitutions of the 1790s, but through the Code, it gave the citizen a clear, practicable set of legal entitlements which made a reality of its more specific, if limited pledge to respect the inviolability of property and individual liberty.

The Code met the needs of contemporary French society to a remarkable degree, bringing together a myriad of local statutes into a coherent code, based on a compromise between Roman and common law, and stands as one of the regime's greatest achievements, even if it represents the consolidation of earlier projects more than innovation. Enforced by a well-paid, professional judiciary, working through a structured, national hierarchy of courts, the Code provided French society with the relatively cheap, rapid system of justice sought under both the *ancien régime* and the Revolution. The Code was the major reason why the absolutism of the regime did not degenerate into despotism. As one scholar has observed, 'Civil liberty ... is the necessary counterweight of political authoritarianism ... [It was] as if citizens had exchanged their political rights for the guarantees of regulated and egalitarian [legal] statutes.'[5]

It is exactly because the Napoleonic regime rested on such tightly defined, legalistic foundations, that the arbitrary atrocities of the winter of 1804 stand out in its history; they were exceptions to the rule. In February 1804, a royalist plot to oust Bonaparte was discovered, directed by the Chouan leader, Cadoudal, and General Pichegru, both of whom had already been exiled from France. Cadoudal was executed and Pichegru found dead in his cell in irregular circumstances, but both were certainly guilty. The real lapse into brutal illegality surrounded the execution of the Duc d'Enghien, a well-connected but ineffectual émigré aristocrat living in Baden. There was little hard evidence to link him to the plot, but he was seized on 15 March and spirited to Paris, where he was executed by a hastily convened military court a week later. This caused a scandal at the time, and poisoned Napoleon's relations with Russia, in particular. Equally arbitrary, if not as vicious, was the arrest and exile to Guyana of Moreau, Napoleon's long-standing rival and an outspoken republican critic of the regime, who was accused of complicity with Cadoudal and Pichegru, their political differences notwithstanding.

The social conservatism of the Code, particularly in its assertion of patriarchal control of family life after the more liberal legislation of the 1790s, must not obscure its wider affirmation of standardized justice and legal equality. Indeed, its provision for divorce and insistence on civil marriage made these aspects of the Code anathema to many European societies, notably in the Italian peninsula, however retrograde this appears compared to the legislation of the Revolution. The very success of the Code would blind French policy-makers over its applicability to the rest of Europe. It also led some reformers outside the Napoleonic Empire, notably Michael Speransky in Russia, to copy its contents almost slavishly, in the reform of their own legal systems, often with disastrous results.

Napoleon took a direct interest in the Code, presiding in person over 57 of the 102 sessions of the Commission of Legislation charged with its formation.[6] He delegated far more authority over the financial reforms, however, but with impressive results in many respects. Stabilization of the currency gave tax revenues real value, and the creation of a hierarchy of trained tax administrators under the Ministry of Finance ensured that they reached the state's coffers. Professionalized auditing and regular, efficient tax collection enabled the government to work to annual budgets. This sets the Napoleonic regime far ahead of all its major rivals, save Britain, from whom he copied the model for the Bank of France, founded in 1800, which provided the government with a reliable source of credit, especially after it was brought under stricter government control in 1806. The tax system may have been burdensome, especially with the revival of many detested direct taxes such as those on salt and local tolls known as *octrois*, but as with the legal system, they were standardized, clear and broadly equitable, as well as efficient. It was underpinned by the successful compilation of accurate, systematic land registers, *cadastres*, for the whole country, which provided the statistical basis for calculating tax assessments. The *cadastres* set taxation on a fair, open foundation; they belong among the most useful and important achievements of the regime.[7] Until 1806–07, the revenue they provided was adequate for the needs of the regime – at least when supplemented by the contributions of its client states – but, significantly, the system proved itself increasingly unable to cope with the burden of imperial expansion after 1808.

The common goals of these reforms, together with those in higher education, were the strengthening of the state and a greater degree of national unity. They were yet another attempt to conclude the revolutionary process, which had been the goal of every regime since 1789, but the reforms of the 1790s had left Napoleon a valuable heritage of centralization that enabled him to think in terms of 'remodelling' French society, rather than 'regenerating' it from its foundations. The degree of this centralization also set France apart from most of its major rivals. The steady process of reform in Prussia produced results at least as modern and effective as the Code Napoleon and the economic reforms of the revolutionary years. Yet, the Prussian reforms did not annihilate the potential for traditional corporate resistance to the centre, as is revealed by the sudden revival of the noble provincial assemblies during the crisis of 1806–07.[8] Even in his darkest hours, Napoleon had no such fears. He had the Constituent Assembly to thank for these foundations.

The reforms of 1800–06 were an investment in the future: stability was not an empty term; it was embodied in the new *grandes écoles*, the refounded University, the *lycées*, and the new military academy at St Cyr. The legal profession was also reorganized by ending the total freedom to practise granted during the Revolution to anyone, regardless of their qualifications. The law of 22 Ventôse, Year XII (13 March 1804), established an official course of study for the bar in government law schools, delineated the legal hierarchy and envisaged a compulsory law degree for all those wishing to practise, by 1808.[9] These years of relative peace allowed the regime to think in the longer term, although much of this work would be dissipated in the years after 1807.

The speed with which a centralized state emerged was remarkable in the first years of the Consulate, but the convulsed circumstances of the early years altered its original forms. The essence of the Napoleonic system has long been seen as centred on the prefect not only as the linchpin of the system, but as its only important component, able to dominate all its various branches. However, the reality was more complex. The source of the supposed power of the Napoleonic prefect rests on three assumptions. First, that he alone of local officials could correspond directly with the central government, be it in Paris, Milan, Naples, Kassel or the Hague as the system spread. Second, that the department was the only unit of local government of any real significance. Finally, that the sections of the administration he controlled directly – the sub-prefects in the arrondissements and, below them, the *maires* in the communes – were the most important sector of local government. There were five main branches of local government in the Napoleonic administrative machine: the civil administration, headed by the prefect, which was under the Ministry of the Interior; the Gendarmerie, under the War Ministry; the civilian police – known as the administrative police – under the Ministry of General Police; the tax bureau, under the Ministry of Finance; and, finally, the tribunals under the Ministry of Justice. The prefect controlled only his own section directly; all the others had the right to correspond directly with their own ministers in the capital, and this is exactly what they did, and where they got their orders from. Only the civilian police, the police commissars, had a specific obligation to liaise with the prefect, but they could also appeal to their own superiors against him. What emerges from this system, in practice, is not a single chain of command descending from the capital via one man, the prefect, to all spheres of local administration.

The reality was quite the reverse, with five distinctive, and often competing, chains of command, running directly from the centre to their own local agents. More often than not, they merged into a tangled mesh of rivalries and mutual suspicions which converged on the department and then became a knot in the administrative chain, rather than a lock in a smooth, straight canal. The Napoleonic system was centralized in the manner of a spider's web.

Napoleon changed the ethos of the structures of 1789–91, less by creating the prefects than through the elimination of elected departmental councils and *juges de paix*, although the defusion of vicious factionalism this achieved was not unwelcome at local level. Yet, shorn of its elective elements, Napoleon resurrected the original administrative hierarchy of the Constituent Assembly in its entirety, a tribute to its essential efficacy. This was made possible by the conscious suppression of partisan politics. The departments became suspect under the Terror, through the moderate composition of so many of their councils, and were bypassed for their immediate sub-divisions, the districts. Unsurprisingly, the Directory abolished the districts, extending the role of the departments, above them, and the cantons, below, to fill the gap. Napoleon restored the functions of departments and districts – renamed arrondissements – to the proportions originally intended for them. The departments, under the prefects, became the hub of administration; the arrondissements were usually logical local crossroads – often well-established, larger market towns – as were the cantons, although the districts were regarded as generally possessing more men able to staff the administration than the smaller, cantonal seats.[10]

It has been assumed too readily that the Consulate 'jettisoned the cantons' in 1800.[11] The loss of elected administrative officials would, indeed, have represented an end to their usefulness, had such institutions been important to the regime, which they were not. Nor did the absence of a purely administrative figure – the equivalent of the prefects and subprefects above them, or the *maires* of the communes, below – matter as much as is often assumed. As will be seen, the Napoleonic state depended on competing strands of local government, that were largely independent of each other, if not of the centre. The cantons remained the seat of the *juges de paix*, the lowest rung of the judicial ladder, and became that of the new Gendarmerie. The authoritarian nature of the regime made the police and the judiciary at least as important in local government as the civil administration, if for different reasons and in different ways. As the outposts of the police and the courts, the cantons became the focal point of the conscription process and, wherever the regime lacked support, the cantons became its 'front line', as will be seen.

The communes were at the base of the administrative ladder, and successive revolutionary regimes had tried, largely in vain, to bring them under tighter central control. The Concordat of 1801 with the Papacy offered Napoleon a better hope than any regime since 1791 of enlisting the help of the clergy in local government. Their hostility and absence had hindered the work of practical administration in the communes, denying the state the services of literate clerks, to say nothing of their moral authority in the countryside. The existence of the Concordat was, at one level, an admission of their importance in this sphere. Where clerical support for the regime became a reality, the results were impressive, as in the Breton diocese of Vannes, where the *curés* represented almost the only link between the state and many rural communities, and where their influence was crucial for the operation of conscription.[12] Nevertheless, the Concordat was among the most fragile of Napoleon's successes, as was his grip on the countryside. French expansion into Italy, Germany and Spain stretched the relationship between the Papacy and the regime until it broke, and a new 'Concordat' replaced that of 1801 by 1810, devoid of Papal approval. Similarly, the strains of conscription, which fell on the countryside, at once tightened and strained the bonds between Napoleon and his *maires*. This is a reminder that the institutional reforms, which so strengthened Napoleon against his rivals, depended for their success on a ruthless pacification of the countryside in many parts of France, as well as in the newly acquired territories.

The social foundations of the state

The nature of Napoleon's seizure of power made him aware that his regime could not hope to survive without support beyond the political and administrative ranks of the Directory. He interpreted this need for support in wider terms than those of factional politics: broadening the basis of the regime meant more than just appeasing known royalists; it meant having a social policy which would appeal to those best placed to support – or destabilize – any government, throughout the country. Napoleon had a vision of the regime that reached beyond who participated in its running, to those who simply approved and co-operated with it willingly.

Throughout the life of the regime, the essence of this policy was to seek out the most stable and influential elements in the society of any given area – first in France and then beyond – and to win their approval, if not really to work through them. Almost invariably, Napoleon discerned these elements to be the landed, propertied classes. This was a rational choice, as the events of the 1790s had proved the resilience of the landowning classes of provincial France: the political upheavals had not dislodged them from their positions of social and economic prominence. Their influence was usually limited to a small area, as was normal in a predominantly agricultural economy based on local markets, and was often indirect – political power having passed to small groups of urban-based politicians who emerged in the 1790s. 'Notable' was an official term; it denoted a class of landowners who were both noble and non-noble, in terms of the *ancien régime*. It reached beyond factional politics, and, to a degree, indicated the wish of the regime to make them irrelevant; it expressed its policy of replacing ideological divisions with shared material interests: 'notable' was how Napoleon wanted them to see themselves. Any regime had to please these men, whether noble or non-noble, if it hoped to survive.

What impressed Napoleon was less the scale of their wealth, than its solidity, for he grasped that very little landed property had actually changed hands in the course of the Revolution. As the rapidly made fortunes of war speculators and entrepreneurs came and went at an alarming rate, these provincial landowners remained at the centre of local life, as if immoveable. This was what counted for the regime, and why these notables were dubbed 'the masses of granite'.[13] Landownership was essential, but the scale of wealth was not the essential criterion for notability. The official definition was expressed in the lists of the 600 *plus imposés*, drawn up to provide membership to the departmental electoral colleges, and based on the highest taxpayers, in a tax system based on property, not income. They did not exclude men of modest property, but they were almost exclusively propertied. The surest alternative route to notability was state service, but the regime always ensured there was room for 'new men' to enter this elite, even less-stable elements such as military contractors and the banking and commercial classes. However, the constant nexus was landownership.[14]

The regime always hoped to draw on the notables as a source of active support and, indeed, to convert them to the professional ethos of government service, but this was not its priority; passive acceptance was enough. Real political power was always denied them as a group, although official policy effectively defined them as such. Only as individuals, accepted into the ranks of state service, could they hope to influence the course of events. Most chose not to do so. The older aristocratic families were always conspicuous by their absence from public life in the provinces,[15] but their reluctance was shared by many non-nobles within the ranks of the notables. It was in their diffidence to the active policies of the regime, particularly over war and foreign policy, that social fusion became most evident, rather than through enthusiastic support for them. This emerged only gradually, however. In the first years of Napoleonic rule, it was clear to most of those who found themselves defined as 'notables', that the Code Napoleon, the restoration of order and the reordering of finance and taxation, were the pillars of a policy meant to please them. Most behaved accordingly. The professional civil servants and tamed revolutionary politicians were left to their work, unhindered, if unseconded by the immobile – but immortal – 'masses of granite'.

The Napoleonic Revolution and Europe

The emergence of a powerful, centralized state in France aroused great admiration in Europe during the 1790s. Even its most embittered adversaries were forced to pay tribute to an administrative machine which, most ironically, was able to tax, repress and conscript its citizens on a scale the traditional absolutist monarchies had only dreamed of. Napoleon emphasized those elements in the revolutionary state that best suited these more traditional ends, and improved on them between 1800 and 1806. This system was the way in which most of western Europe was to be governed between 1800 and 1814. The constitutions of all the satellite states were closely modelled on the one Napoleon gave France in 1800. Most were the work of French officials: Roederer drew up those of Italy and Naples; Cambacérès and Regnault de St Jean drew up Westphalia's; and the Grand Duchy of Berg's was drawn up by Maret – all high-ranking jurists under Napoleon. Only the Dutch kept a steady grip on their own constitutional affairs until their annexation to France in 1810; nevertheless, like the south German states, they readily adopted many aspects of the French system. Everywhere, the legislative assemblies were overawed by the executive powers. In Naples the legislature created by the constitution never even met, while in Westphalia it had very irregular sessions. Bureaucracies always counted for much more than elected legislatures.

Terms such as 'modern' or 'advanced' are always dangerous, especially in the context when reform and change form the essence of the history of a period, as in Europe between 1789 and 1814. Their use often poses more problems than it solves. However, most contemporaries – both supporters and adversaries – recognized something new, as well as dynamic, in the state that emerged in France after 1789, and they did not see the Napoleonic reforms as a return to the old order. Goethe spoke of Napoleon as the moving spirit of a new age; the state he fashioned from the legacy of the French Revolution was, reasonably enough, also regarded as the vanguard of change. For contemporaries, it was 'modern'. Yet, it was not the only model of modernity visible to Europeans, nor, in the eyes of many, was the Napoleonic Empire the most advanced, enlightened or efficient state then in existence. Many of the much-vaunted Napoleonic reforms had already been achieved in Prussia by the 1780s, particularly the codification of the law, the centralization of local government and the implementation of conscription. No state had a saner, more effective system of taxation than Britain. Few had more humane, advanced legal systems than Tuscany or the Hansa ports, nor richer cultural achievements than the small German states or the Dutch Republic.

However, the French path of reform made its achievements unique, in two ways. Most of the other states generally acknowledged to be 'advanced' were small or, like Britain, on the fringes of Europe. France was a giant, in every sense: no state of comparable size and resources reached her level of modernization. If France was not the most advanced, reformed, enlightened or 'modern' state in Europe, she was, under Napoleon, the most powerful to try to modernize. Further, France was the only state to achieve so wide a range of reforms, in most spheres of government, for the very essence of that state was to be all-embracing. The Napoleonic state always defined itself as 'modern', and in its terms, modernity meant a desire for uniformity of government and culture, and a desire to guide and control every aspect of public life. This version of the modern state sought to order the education of the elite, in its *lycées*, to inform its farmers what crops it was best to grow, to control the movements of its subjects. These controls extended beyond the popular classes, into the highest levels of the elite.

The state was there to govern and to lead everyone, without exception. To this end, in 1807, Napoleon himself ordered the most ambitious land survey ever undertaken in France, the Cadastre Parcellaire. This sought to register every piece of property in France, according to ownership and usage. France was divided into twelve districts, each with an inspector-general in charge of the survey, and by 1814 9000 French communes out of a total of 40 000 had been fully surveyed, and the work continued under the Restoration.[16] The practical aim of the survey was to set taxation on a more accurate footing following complaints from officials and property-owners, alike, over the less detailed *cadastre* drawn up in 1805. Its signif-icance is much wider, however. Napoleon had both the will and the means to undertake the survey; he had the untramelled power to make landown-ers open their properties to government agents, and a civil service ready to carry out the work. He told his Finance Minister, 'Half measures are always a waste of time and money. The only way forward is to survey all the land in all the communes of the empire.'[17] This was an assertion of power and efficiency, and it was not empty: it was a clear manifestation of his ability and intention to be master in his own house. The full impact of this becomes more apparent in the light of the failure of the Habsburgs and the Neapolitan Bourbons, among other rulers, whose similar ambitions were thwarted by aristocratic resistance in the eighteenth century.

This desire to control and direct the whole of society led the professional bureaucracy to begin at the beginning, as it were. From the outset, the state gathered statistics and facts on every conceivable aspect of life. The decree of 19 Germinal, Year IX (1804) ordered the prefects to begin this task at local level, with the double aim of quantifying the material aspects of society, and analysing them. The results were uneven, at best, and depended on the enthusiasm – or lack of it – of individual prefects and, even more, on the level of co-operation they received from the notables, who held most of the information they sought. This was a project conceived in peace; after 1806, the objectives of official enquiries narrowed, concerning themselves with particular problems or industries; by 1812, the Statistical Bureau, created as the repository of these findings, was disbanded.[18] What the prefects believed they found was a France riven by localism, divided into a multitude of geographic micro-climates and mutually incomprehensible dialects, a fragmented country. This reinforced their determination to impose cultural, administrative and political uniformity on French society. Indeed, their conclusion was often that France scarcely existed. Their prejudices, as well as their determination, to impose a uniform culture on a population they perceived as backward, hardened still further as the Empire expanded to include non-French peoples. The agents of the Napoleonic state saw themselves as the vanguard of modernity, and acted accordingly.

However imperfectly, many of their more practical goals were attained in France, to a degree sufficient enough to set the Napoleonic state apart from its rivals, and to make it a clear symbol of a new order. It was also the most successful model of reform, if far from the most popular. Among the other great powers, the British state regarded such ambitions as alien to its very essence. The realistic heirs of enlightened absolutism in the Habsburg Monarchy and even Prussia had decided that the acceptable limits of state power had already been reached; they refrained from further assaults on aristocracy, preferring unequal partnership – tipped in their favour – to true absolutism. The French revolutionaries and Napoleon, after them, did not recognize such limits.

For the peoples of the Low Countries, western Germany and Italy, the most lasting experience of the state created by the French Revolution would not be the liberal or democratic aspects of its earlier phases, but that of a powerful bureaucracy now harnessed to autocratic politics. They would gain a practical grasp of the administrative achievements of the Revolution in far greater proportion to any acquaintance with its political innovations. None of the sister republics of the 1790s lasted more than three years, indeed many counted their existences in months, but the Napoleonic state would dominate most of western, continental Europe for over a decade. 'The well-ordered police state' became a known fact, representative government remained a less familiar experience.

Internal conquest

The Napoleonic reforms produced a model of government which the French and non-French parts of its domains absorbed simultaneously, but the conditions in which it was applied differed enormously, inside and outside France. To the majority of Germans, Italians and Netherlanders, the French revolutionary conquests, prior to 1799, had amounted to little more than brutal, exploitative military occupations, while for the tiny minorities of pro-French 'patriots' scattered throughout western Europe, they had amounted to hopes raised and then dashed by a combination of French treachery, domestic reaction and then, in 1799, military defeat. Despite the many important continuities between the Directory and the Consulate, their attitudes to the administration of occupied Europe could not have been more different, a difference crucial to the fate of the peoples of western Europe.

The Napoleonic regime had a very clear set of policies for its internal administration: every area in the Napoleonic sphere of influence, whether annexed directly to France, erected into a satellite state, or already a part of metropolitan France, was to be governed by administrative and judicial institutions which were being created by the new Consular regime. The newly acquired territories and the original departments of the Republic underwent these reforms together. Indeed, pacification began in the imperial capital itself. The Consular regime was quick to repress Jacobin agitation in Paris, but combined this with measures to secure cheap food provisions for the city, linked to artificially low conscription quotas. Jacobins were contained; extreme royalists were simply expelled. In 1804, Napoleon told Fouché, 'My intention is that any Vendean rebel who has been amnestised, ought not to be allowed to stay in Paris.'[19] This set the tone for the rest of the French Empire. The Belgian, Italian and Rhenish territories, together with the sister republics and kingdoms established by 1802, form a coherent whole, the core of the Napoleonic sphere of influence, where the early reforms took root between 1800 and 1807.

Simultaneously, a policy of internal pacification was begun, not simply to restore order, but as the first step in winning support for the new regime among the occupied populations and establishing confidence in the regime in France itself. The driving force behind this policy of internal conquest was still securing the resources for the French war effort, albeit in a less ruthless manner. Its subjective, almost primal urge, was the regime's ingrained confidence in the superiority of French culture and its exportability. This mixture of clarity and confidence fuelled a remarkable period of dynamic administrative activity, behind the advancing armies. The goal of the regime was to spread across Europe the results achieved first in Paris, expressed in a police report of 1800: 'What gives the most satisfying idea of the kind of contentment inspired by the revolution of 18 Brumaire is that it is not of the sort that is born and then dies almost immediately... It is in the heart of the family where it expresses itself most freely.'[20]

Until 1808, French military success created a shield behind which coherent, sustained domestic policies developed. The war zone moved well away from the core of the Napoleonic state system, so that although Napoleon was at war for most of the period, the core of his Empire was not in the front line. The lives of the peoples of Italy, western Germany and the Low Countries, as well as France itself, were profoundly affected by the wars, but not in a direct sense, save for those who were conscripted. Therefore the internal histories of these areas turn on the ramifications of the wars, not the wars themselves. The state's constant need for soldiers and taxes brought them under an administrative machine more powerful, permanent and demanding than any they had experienced before.

This increasing distance from the war zones also greatly reduced the potential for overt, mass resistance to French rule in these parts of Europe. Popular revolts on the scale of those which took place in Italy, southwestern France or the Belgian departments in 1798–99 simply became impossible to repeat with success. This was not always immediately clear to those directly affected, however, as revealed by the ferocious revolt of 1806 of the peasantry of the Piacentino, the mountain valleys between Parma and Genoa, in north-western Italy. After the French occupied the area, these communities fiercely resisted initial attempts to tax and conscript them. Although the revolt was put down in only a few weeks, it offers several valuable insights into the general nature of French rule. It was crushed so quickly precisely because it was isolated, for unlike similar risings during the 1790s, there was no allied army fast approaching to bolster the rebels or to encourage other areas to join them. Consequently, although the French forces in the area were hard pressed, they succeeded because they could concentrate all their available strength against the rebels. The fighting took place in rugged mountains in the depths of winter, but even these ideal conditions for armed resistance could not sustain it for long against a handful of troops; rebellion was seen to fail disastrously and was not repeated. It was now starkly obvious that French rule had come to stay, in sharp contrast to the chronic instability of the 1790s, and this, in turn, altered the way in which the occupied had to view the occupiers. Yet it did not mean that the earlier hatreds were forgotten, rather that they had to be worked out in a new context, that of French domination.

By 1807, the Napoleonic regime had an inner core of territories, firmly under its control. The distinction between the satellite states and the imperial departments is of little practical importance when set in the context of contemporary perceptions. What mattered most, in the first instance, was the level of control the French could exercise over an area, and they were able to do this in the satellite kingdoms just as effectively as in the Rhenish or Piedmontese departments, or within France itself, if not better.

Bavaria remained under its native rulers, the Wittelbachs, throughout the period, but it was very much a part of the inner core of the Napoleonic state system, both because its rulers loyally supported Napoleon militarily and diplomatically, and also through their concerted attempts to reform their state along French lines. Bavaria adopted the French administrative system and a great deal of the Code Napoleon without any prompting from Napoleon. In practical terms, King Max-Joseph and his Chief Minister, Montgelas, were key collaborators in the policy of internal consolidation. The other major states of southern Germany, Württemberg and Baden, followed a path broadly similar to that of Bavaria.

Indeed, the French exercised a firmer control over the satellite states and the south German kingdoms than they did over some parts of France itself.

This control was no less valuable for being indirect; it was the degree of collaboration and the determination of those at the helm of the administration that really counted. The Confederation of the Rhine, Switzerland, Italy and Westphalia supplied conscripts and taxes – and had a higher level of law and order – than many parts of France. Whereas Napoleon crushed the revolt in the Piacentino, he made a formal peace with the Vendéan leaders.[21] The nine departments of the Vendée militaire were exempted from the first application of regular conscription in 1798 and then granted low quotas under the Napoleonic regime.[22] In contrast, the Swiss Confederation supplied its full contingent of 24 000 men until the last years of the war.[23] The states of the Confederation of the Rhine and the Kingdom of Italy proved better sources of recruits than the French department of Pyrénées Orientales[24] or the 12 departments which had high levels of desertion or non-appearance in 1799–1801.[25] Similarly, in 1801, the 32 French departments were placed under the jurisdiction of special criminal courts – half civilian, half military – and denied the jury system, because of the threat of disorder. These courts embraced nine annexed departments, but the remaining 23 were all within France, including the Vendée militaire.[26]

In the context of defining the reality of French power in Europe, the Kingdom of Holland was the exception that proves the rule. It was abolished in 1811 and its territories annexed directly to France because Louis was the only satellite ruler to hold out against the secure control of western Europe through general policies laid down in Paris by Napoleon. It is not his defiance which defines the general pattern, but the co-operation of his colleagues in Westphalia, Italy, Naples and the Swiss and Rhenish Confederations, which made French rule a practical reality in these areas, their formal diplomatic status notwithstanding.

However, below the level of the state, this hegemony had to be imposed by force. A relentless application of military-style policing was applied throughout Europe in the period 1799 to 1807, breaking the last vestiges of open resistance to French occupation, while creating the basic conditions for the reintroduction of a normal administrative system, following the chaos of the 1790s. Here, the great contradiction of the Napoleonic regime emerges. Its first goal was pacification, but this usually turned into internal conquest; the new order established peace through force, a glaring contradiction, if a perennial one, in the history of state-building in modern Europe.

The Napoleonic administrators were deeply aware of this incongruity, but they also saw their presence in occupied Europe to be as permanent as in France, which demanded a responsible attitude towards the people they now governed. They now had a clear policy to guide them, based on administrative and cultural assimilation of the occupied areas. In all of this, they differed from their predecessors of the revolutionary decade and, even though they were faced by the climate of hatred and suspicion created by the traumas of the Revolution, they could also hope that the military vic-

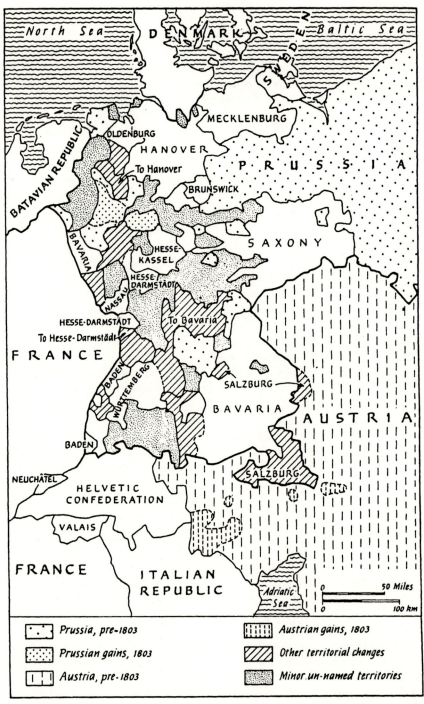

Map 2(i): The Napoleonic State System in Germany: Reorganization in 1803

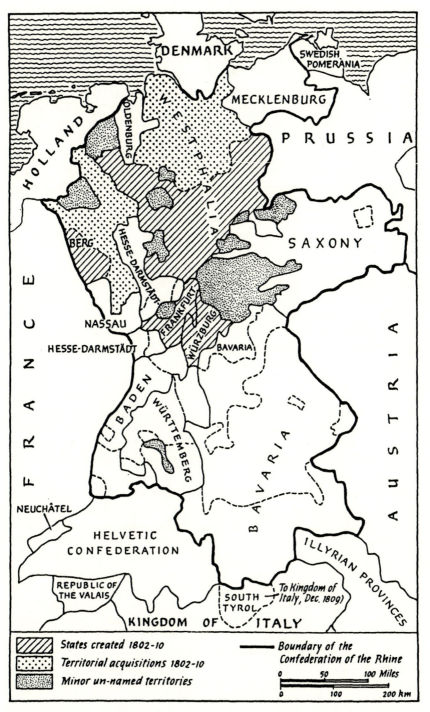

Map 2(ii): The Napoleonic State System in Germany: September 1809

tories of the years before 1808 would buy them the time they knew to be their best hope of success. Yet all this hinged on the successful continuation of the war which, in its turn, depended on a steady flow of men and money from the inner empire. The grounds for tension and conflict were clear from the outset, but complete failure was not inevitable, and there was a considerable degree of success. If there was a period when the establishment of French hegemony – political and cultural as well as diplomatic and military – looked most likely, it was in the first eight years after Brumaire, before the serious military reverses began. Indeed, as these years progressed, the permanence of French rule seemed increasingly assured. Contemporaries, whether supporters or enemies of the regime, dwelled on its obvious strengths, rather than its inherent frailties.

The Napoleonic state was still establishing its grip on power as it acquired new territories and a wider sphere of influence. Napoleon set out to centralize as much power as possible on himself and the higher levels of the administration he controlled, but it was the breakdown of civil order in many parts of France and the new territories that gave him the mandate to do so. Many of the key administrative practices and institutions of the Napoleonic regime were formed in response to the Consulate's first domestic task, the restoration of order. The Consulate undertook simultaneous campaigns against bandits and counter-revolutionaries in the new Belgian and Piedmontese departments and over most of the French Midi and the Vendée between 1800 and 1803. Pacification was achieved more quickly in some areas than others, and this had little relation to whether a convulsed area was newly annexed or part of France proper. Royalist brigandage was over in the Gard and most of the Cévennes in south-central France by 1802, following a vigorous campaign by General Gouvion.[27] The process took much longer further east, however. In both the 'French' department of the Var and the newly annexed departments of southwestern Piedmont, large-scale, neo-political banditry was not crushed until 1807, although steady progress was made throughout these years; the process of pacification was remarkably similar – and synchronized – on both sides of the southern Alps. The reports of Menou, the Administrator-General of the Piedmontese departments, and of Fauchet, prefect of the Var from 1801 to 1807, are marked by a constant, if cautious optimism in these matters.[28] In contrast to both, the departments of the eastern Pyrenees – the Pyrénées Orientales, the Ariège and the upland parts of the Haute-Garonne – were never fully pacified in these years, or afterwards.[29] They shared a border with Spain, which was never properly controlled by Napoleon, as well as the physical geography and violent political history which contributed to disorder right across the western Mediterranean in these decades, from Valencia to Tuscany. It is less the failure of the Consulate to tame the eastern Pyrenees that is remarkable, than its success elsewhere, however.

The crisis of the early years led the regime away from its administrative norms and it soon came to rely on two marginal administrative units – the Military Divisions, above the department, and the canton, below it – to achieve its three chief goals in its early years: the restoration of order, the enforcement of conscription, and replacing military occupation with a regular, civilian administration. These urgent problems required a level of co-operation among various branches of local government beyond the competence of the prefect. The more amorphous units of the canton and the military division were able to provide the scope for this exactly because they were the least well-defined links in the administrative chain. Neither of them was created by the Consulate. The canton became an important centre of local government for those branches of it which were both most independent of the prefect and most essential to the maintenance of public order, the Gendarmerie and the *juges de paix*, and, especially, for the enforcement of conscription, throughout the life of the regime. The Military Divisions were the real hubs of administrative activity as long as problems of law and order dominated the regime's agenda. This role is epitomized by the Vendée militaire and was repeated in most of the annexed departments in the first phases of their organization.

The restoration of order

The Consulate realized that the military occupations of the 1790s had had a catastrophic effect on public order throughout western Europe. The conduct of the French armies together with the Directory's policy of naked exploitation destroyed whatever fragile order that existed prior to the revolutionary wars. The Consulate sought to restore order, not solely by force, but through the creation of a stable, predominantly civilian administration. Force was a means to create order; regular, regulated administration was a means to maintain that order.

The Consulate faced a monumental task; banditry was rife over most of western Europe by 1800. Initially, the regime found it difficult to separate causes from cures, but it soon perceived the need to rid the new territories of the grosser aspects of military rule. In a bid to end this, there was a headlong rush to fill the courts and prefectures with members of the local elites. In France this meant a determined search for 'the men of 1789'; outside France, for the local notables of the *ancien régime* period. However, reliance on local men merely reintroduced factionalism into the heart of the very administration that was meant to restore order and confidence. This was the result when the regime got what it thought it wanted – participation by the indigenous elites – for in many cases they remained aloof. The most typical result was administrative paralysis and the continued degeneration of law and order.

The solution was threefold: the introduction of French personnel at almost every level of administration, further centralization and a more flexible administrative hierarchy. The Military Divisions were the first step in this process. They consisted of a group of departments and in the newly annexed areas of Germany and Italy the Military Divisions were virtually equivalent to the *ancien régime* states. In relatively peaceful areas, the departments, under their prefects, did indeed become the cornerstone of local government, but most of the new departments were not peaceful in these years.

The Military Divisions were placed under administrators-general, answerable only to Paris. They co-ordinated the work of other specialist commissioners and acted as heads of the security forces in their areas. In time, a core of administrators emerged who were specialists in the process of annexation, such as de Gerando, Roederer, Menou and Sàliceti. The rulers of the satellite states fulfilled a role comparable to that of the administrators-general in co-ordinating the restoration of order, employing police tactics identical to those used in the annexed departments and inside France itself.

The administrators-general, unlike the prefects, were able to operate over several departments, and so were better able to deal with bandits who often, themselves, ranged over wider areas than single departments. They were able to combine, co-ordinate and direct all the various forces available within the region – gendarmes, regular troops, national guards and even customs officers – in a crisis. This administrative structure smashed the revolt of 1806 in the Piacentino, as it had first done in the Vendée and the Belgian departments, under the Directory.

Less spectacularly, but probably of even more importance, this co-ordinated structure based on the military division was also the instrument by which the small but widespread brigand bands were eventually uprooted from the Belgian, Rhenish and north Italian departments. Other factors were important in this process – the co-operation of the local populations was crucial – but the flexible structure of the military division was the instrument by which it was achieved. Even in those areas where the post of Administrator-General was eventually phased out, responsibility for general security passed to the director-generals of police, whose jurisdictions remained those of the Military Divisions. In matters of security, the department never became the most important administrative unit, nor did the prefects have the pivotal role in the restoration of order.

The tactics employed in the pacification of western Europe followed a uniform course within each individual area as it was annexed. The pattern was one of the paramilitary presence of the gendarmerie in the countryside and a judicial policy based on notions of the collective guilt of communities and families, administered by military commissions rather than civilian courts. Gradually, depending on local circumstances, these coercive measures were meant to be replaced by the Napoleonic administrative system of prefects and civilian tribunals, not dependent on extraordinary powers or policies. This was the ultimate goal the French never lost sight of. They judged the success or failure of their policy on whether a given military division could eventually be governed normally or not, which ultimately depended on how well law and order was restored. In most of the areas which came under French control before 1808 – including both areas ruled directly from Paris and the satellite states – this was largely, if often imperfectly, achieved. Essentially, this was what distinguished the territories of the 'inner empire' from those of the 'new' or 'grand empire', which were acquired after 1808.

Within the 'inner empire', some areas were pacified and brought under normal administration more rapidly and more completely than others. The geographical pattern that emerges from this process offers important insights into the future development of the Napoleonic Empire, as it does for the evolution of the modern state in western Europe. Broadly, there were three categories of region, distinguished from each other by their respective responses to pacification by the French. The first comprised most of the Belgian departments, the Batavian Republic (the ex-Dutch Republic), the lowland areas of the Republic/Kingdom of Italy and the Piedmontese departments, the Rhineland departments and most of the Confederation of the Rhine. The widespread disorder which beset these areas during the 1790s was quickly overcome once the effects of war receded. None of these regions had been marked by large-scale banditry before the revolutionary wars, being lowland areas possessed of neither the topography nor the isolated, tightly knit communities where organized banditry thrived during the early modern period.

The second category comprised those regions where French administrative norms – and the law and order they depended on – were eventually imposed, but only after a prolonged period of concerted struggle, marked by frequent recourse to coercion and military force. The upland regions of the Piedmontese departments and the Republic/Kingdom of Italy, together with most of Liguria and the Duchies of Parma and Piacenza, fell into this category, along with many parts of western France and the Midi. French counter-insurgency policy reached maturity in these areas between 1800 and 1807, developing the tactics used later in central Italy, occupied Spain and parts of northern Europe. The mountain communities of the Pyrenees, Apennines and southern Alps had built a whole economy on highly organized, widespread banditry, usually based on smuggling. It is of great significance for the future development of these regions that the French destroyed the most obvious facets of banditry there in these years. Henceforth, this fact would distinguish these parts of the Mediterranean from other areas where a similar process either did not take place or failed. They were now brought closer to those in the first category, the results of the French occupation thus marking a genuine turning-point in their histories.

French tactics were based on the establishment of permanent, five-man gendarmerie brigades in the rural cantons. To try to guarantee impartial policing, these brigades were composed of three French and two local gendarmes, a policy the regime always did its best to continue in all the 'foreign' departments, throughout the period. Their presence was meant to bolster the will of the local national guards to oppose the bandits and, therefore, to stiffen the resolve of the propertied classes as well. There is strong evidence that a modicum of co-operation was, indeed, achieved between the local notables and the security forces, but the process took nearly eight years and it was punctuated by the frequent use of draconian measures against those the policy was meant to protect.

The Kingdom of Naples was the one area within the 'inner empire' that did not witness the successes achieved over most of the rest of western Europe in these years. Although its mainland territories became a satellite kingdom in 1805, ten years of continuous Napoleonic rule – and considerable efforts by the security forces – failed to eradicate large-scale banditry there. Most of the Kingdom of Naples was never really brought under normal forms of government; its gendarmerie was used for military-style campaigns against large, powerful brigand bands; for most of the period, much of it was under martial law, a set of circumstances which would be repeated in the decades following the unification of Italy in 1860. Geographically, the Napoleonic Kingdom of Naples was the furthest-flung component of the imperial state system at the point when Joseph deposed the Bourbons in 1805. It was separated from the fairly compact mass of the rest of the 'inner empire' by the as yet unabsorbed states of Tuscany and the Papacy; equally, it was exposed to attacks by the English fleet and the intrigues of the exiled Bourbon Court in Sicily. There were also more complex reasons for this failure, but the experience of Napoleonic rule helped to foster a growing gap between northern and southern Italy as regards the development of the state, at its most basic – and arguably most crucial – level.

The enforcement of conscription

No other single issue is as central to Napoleonic Europe as conscription. The French imposed it throughout the Empire and the satellite states and, although overt resistance to it followed a geographic pattern almost identical to that of banditry, unlike banditry it did not disappear. The policy of conscription continued from the start of French rule to the end, as did the many ramifications it had on the lives of the peoples of western Europe. Conscription became a unique, unifying experience for them, just as it provided the 'acid test' for the administrative machine of the Napoleonic state. No other process brought the state and society together as closely as conscription; no other policy pushed the state so far and so frequently beyond its own laws and ideals; no other aspect of French rule engendered as much administrative activity or popular loathing. The Napoleonic administrators knew only too well that the introduction of conscription could lead straight to revolt on a massive scale; their reminders of this stretched from the Vendéan revolt in 1793 – the first of its kind – to the Belgian peasant risings of 1798–99. In neither case was conscription the only cause, but it had been the trigger of both, and many others besides.

As the French advanced into northern Italy and western Germany, the newness of the Consular regime must be remembered in this context. Conscription inside France had been systematized only as late as 1798, with the Jourdan Law, which established categories of eligibility for conscription – 'classes' – based on age, men born in a certain year becoming liable for it in a certain year, with each commune being assigned a quota of men it had to fill. Thus France, the annexed territories and satellite states shared in its teething troubles and their resolution.

The enforcement of conscription seriously compromised the French model of administration, based as it was on the central position of the prefect as the head of a department where the *maires* of the communes were directly subordinate to him, and where the civil administration was supposed to be paramount. The first administrative problem was the inability and unwillingness of most rural *maires* to draw up lists of eligible conscripts and make them comply with the call-up. The reasons for this are fairly obvious and emerge with striking uniformity all over Europe. In most rural communes, in an empire whose population was overwhelmingly rural, the *maire* was usually only a peasant, at best barely literate and usually as opposed to conscription as those he administered. In any case, to side with the state in such a climate of opposition was to run a very serious risk; most *maires* found discretion the better part of valour where conscription was concerned.

At a higher level, it was evident that the civil authorities could not treat conscription as an administrative matter; it was part of the military enforcement of the state's authority and, as with the eradication of banditry, the degree of an area's assimilation to Napoleonic rule would be judged not just by the effectiveness of conscription in terms of men successfully enlisted and sent to the armies, but whether that process could be carried out by normal administrative means – through the prefects and *maires* – with the minimum amount of force. Again, as with the problem of banditry, some areas would reach these norms sooner and more smoothly than others, but by about 1811, most parts of the Empire had done so. For most of the period 1799–1807, however, this was still very much more a goal to be attained than a reality.

Conscription could be implemented only by the use of force, at best by threat, at worst by what amounted to officially sanctioned guerrilla warfare. This automatically relegated the civil authorities to a junior partnership with the other branches of local government. The administrative answer was to turn the canton into the pivot of the enforcement of conscription; it was where the actual rounding up of those eligible took place, and where those to be conscripted were chosen, by means of a public lottery. Just as the military division was useful because it covered several

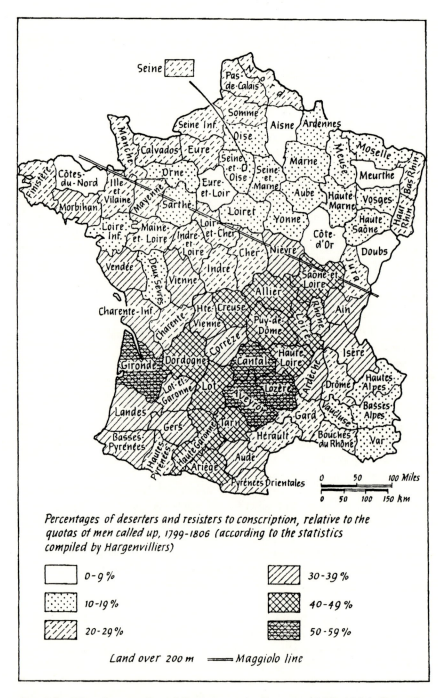

Map 3(i): The Geography of Resistance in France, 1800–1814: Desertion and Resistance to Conscription

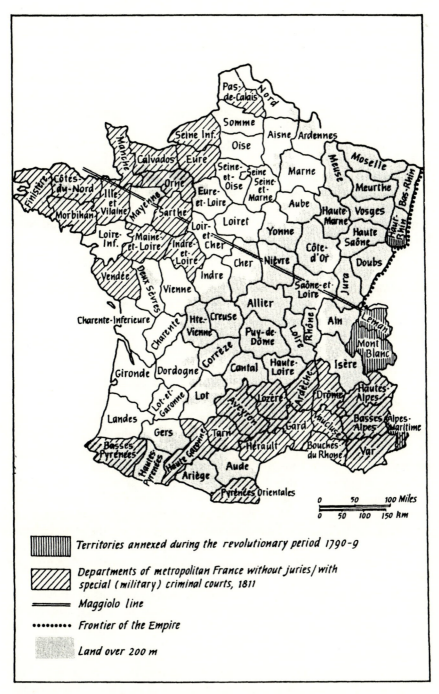

Map 3(ii): The Geography of Resistance in France, 1800–1814: Departments without Juries/with Special (Military) Criminal Courts (1811)

departments, so the canton covered several communes and corresponded with the jurisdictions of the justices of the peace and gendarmerie brigades. The prefects supervised the conscription operations and toured their departments, accompanied by a military escort, stopping in each cantonal seat to oversee the process in person. Given that this could take place as many as five times a year, the prefects came to know their departments much more intimately than might otherwise have been the case, as they were only obliged to do one annual tour, in normal circumstances – which never, in fact, prevailed.

This was how the Napoleonic state entered the lives of its subjects in a frequent and regular manner. Napoleonic administrators had a passion for collecting factual information of all kinds, and the bulk of it was usually acquired during the conscription tours. In this way, too, the different branches of local government were welded together. The prefect, *juge de paix* and the commander of the canton's gendarmerie brigade worked together on a regular basis to ensure that the communes supplied their quotas, usually by force; what turned threat into brutal reality was the concentration of a considerable armed force and high-ranking officials in each canton, in turn. To clear up those conscripts who had been missed on the regular tours, special 'mobile columns', composed of gendarmes and regular troops, were frequently authorized to sweep an area, as and when the prefect thought fit. In 1806, mobile columns were used in 20 departments of the Empire, divided almost equally between France and the annexed departments. They yielded good results, both in terms of arrests made and for a better, smoother process the following year.[30] Clearly, over most of the Empire itself and most of the satellite states – with the notable exception of the Batavian Republic which did not yet have it – the process had become fixed and a workable system was in place.

However successful, this process was a brutal business, which even the central government found distasteful. Following the ruthless manhunts of 1806, there were calls within the Council of State in Paris for 'measures that were gentler', but the local authorities protested that these tactics were the only ones that worked; the central government gave way.[31] As was often the case with the Napoleonic state, the insistence on a 'hard line' came from below, not above.

There was a battle line within the Empire, as well as on its military fronts and, unlike the 'real war', this was a battle the state ultimately won. It was a slow, grinding process, but one in which most local administrators – the *maires* excepted – showed remarkable energy and an almost unique ability to bury their rivalries. From the outset, the crucial importance of the success of conscription was clear to them. Marshal Murat, then military commander in the Italian Republic, gave very rare praise to the civilian administrators during the first application of conscription there, in 1803: 'Everything is conscription at the moment, they dream only of conscription. The executive, the council, the ministers have all become the Sons of

Mars...'[32] In the satellite states much of this enthusiasm was fuelled by the hope that the creation of a national army would mean the end of a direct French military presence. One of the first goals of all the administrators-general in the new departments, and of Melzi in the Italian Republic, had been to dislodge the French military administration and replace it by a civilian one, based on legality. This had been achieved in Italy and the Rhineland in the first months of Consular rule, but at local level, the demands of conscription soon compromised it. Nevertheless, the drive and determination of all concerned continued, virtually until the end of the Empire.

Between 1804 and 1806, the initial bureaucratic imperfections in the process were progressively corrected until a system emerged which functioned well enough to be persevered with. As their collective defiance in 1806 reveals, the local authorities had faith in it. The cost of success was high, so high as probably to be incalculable because of the rift conscription drove between the state and its people. However, the Napoleonic regime was getting what it needed most, at least within the territories of the inner empire. This had not been achieved by normal administrative means, nor by methods which even those in charge approved of. The enforcement of conscription perpetuated a military presence in civilian affairs, flouted legality and denatured the state at local level, but it worked.

This success appears even more striking when its geographic pattern is analysed. As with the suppression of banditry, the initial success or failure of conscription depended on topography more than anything else. Its imposition was a crude business which, appropriately enough, was tied to the most basic circumstances. Urban areas and the flat plains of most of northern Europe and the Po valley in northern Italy offered little refuge to the prospective deserter; mountains and forests did. Thus, even within regions or departments, great differences in recruitment could emerge. In Belgium, conscription met with little overt resistance in the settled, farming areas of the north, but the forests of the Ardennes to the south provided refuge for large numbers of deserters in the early years of the Consulate. A set of circumstances emerges. In the ex-Piedmontese department of Marengo, in northern Italy, the arrondissement of Casale, in the plain of the Po, provided conscripts without recourse to undue force, while the uplands of the neighbouring arrondissements of Alessandria and Asti were among the most problematic in the Empire. The same pattern was repeated across the border in the Kingdom of Italy, where the prefects' reports on the relative success of conscription varied exactly with the lie of the land, as well as in the French department of Pyrénées Orientales and many other French departments.[33] In this context, the lowland regions of the Kingdom of Italy, together with the whole of the Confederation of the Rhine and the Kingdom of Westphalia, were effectively more part of the Napoleonic system than the mountainous Auvergnat departments, in the same years.[34] The Kingdom of Westphalia, created out of diverse – but always flat – territories in north-central Germany in 1807, produced more conscripts per capita than any other region in the imperial system.[35]

The needs of conscription were also a spur to reform. Meeting the quotas set by the French was the high price of the territorial gains Napoleon bestowed on the rulers of the new Mittelstaaten – Bavaria, Baden, Württemberg, Nassau, and Hesse-Darmstädt – as well as for the new states of Westphalia and Berg. It was soon clear that only through policing and bureaucratic centralization, coupled with the eradication of collective or local privileges in matters of military service, could they meet Napoleon's demands and so assure independence. These states had no choice but to attack the remaining vestiges of privilege with all their might. Baden, for example, emerged by 1806 almost quadrupled in size, with over one hundred political entities which had been autonomous under the old Reich within its new borders. The need to raise men and taxes for the Napoleonic war effort made it urgent to wield them into a coherent, uniform whole: the concept of 'citizenship' simply had to be imposed on the mass of ex-fiefs of Imperial Knights, the former prince-bishoprics and the many 'home towns', semi-independent large villages whose sense of their 'liberties' was very much alive at the moment they were absorbed into Baden. The process of assimilation was ruthless and no attempt was made to compromise with local traditions. Legal and administrative uniformity was simply imposed without consultation by a determined civil service. The political culture of the Reich, based on lobbying and lengthy arbitration, was swept away. The hard-pressed princes of the Confederation were no more inclined to listen to the 'feudal relics' within their borders than was Napoleon. This was as true of states like Nassau, which had contained many such communities within its borders prior to the period of expansion 1803–06, as of Baden, with a strong tradition of centralization in the eighteenth century.[36] Württemberg was a state where the power of the prince had been hemmed in by an assertive diet, whose influence had grown considerably since 1770. In 1797, on the eve of a new war against France, the diet strongly contested the crown's demands for taxation and conscription.[37] After 1803, when Württemberg had changed sides, such institutional independence could no longer be tolerated.

The demands imposed by Napoleon on his German allies were ruthless – Nassau alone had over 2 per cent of its total population under arms between 1806 and 1813[38] – and the cost of failure to meet them was high. It soon became clear that if the small states – such as the Grand Duchy of Frankfurt, one of the few city states to survive in 1806 – failed to produce their quotas Napoleon would make them up from the Mittelstaaten. To avoid this, these states took their role in the Diet very seriously, exerting their own pressure on the smaller members of the Confederation. Thus, Napoleon was able to hold whole countries to ransom over conscription when it was combined with shrewd diplomacy.

The truly remarkable fact is that all blots on the landscape of the state were wiped clean as time went by. At the height of Napoleonic rule, the Lombard and Piedmontese highlands, the forests of the Ardennes and the mountains of the Auvergne, alike, all yielded their men. In southern Piedmont, the 'breakthrough' came with the final defeat of the great brigand bands between 1805 and 1808, while in parts of southern France, it seems to have taken rather longer. Nevertheless, by 1811 – the *annus mirabilis* for conscription[39] – the traditional pattern of resistance had been broken. That year saw an increase in the state's demands for men, but throughout those areas integrated into the imperial system early in the period, these demands were met with an ease which contrasts sharply with both the problems of the earlier years and the increasingly difficult circumstances of the last years of the Empire.

This is not to say that resentment or even resistance to conscription disappeared. Indeed there is some evidence that the latter increased in parts of Germany in the last years of French rule, but it could not halt the system. Organization, coupled with ruthless persistence and, above all, time, had overcome that most formidable enemy of the early modern state, geography. Napoleon, unlike Mohammed, had made the mountain come to him, but he had dragged it to him by force, and he sought more from it than blind obedience.

The normalization of public life

The Consulate had two important tasks facing it, which required far more subtlety than either the restoration of law and order, or the imposition of conscription. First, it had to heal the wounds of the 1790s, both inside and outside France, which were economic and social as well as political, especially in the non-French parts of the Empire. The second step was to create a sense of loyalty to the regime among its subjects. Taken together, these two goals embodied the reconstruction of most of western Europe following the ravages of war and revolution. To emphasize its commitment to this moderate course, the Consulate extended the amnesties of 1801 and 1802 to those who had fled French occupation in the newly annexed departments. An amnesty was also granted to deserters.

Contemporary administrators saw reconciliation and reconstruction as their real tasks; in comparison, the restoration of order was only a necessary prerequsite and the enforcement of conscription was only a transient irritant. For French administrators, the ultimate answer to both major aspects of reconstruction – healing the wounds of the 1790s and creating a stable base for its own rule – was the rebuilding of western Europe according to French practices, under the tutelage of French culture. It is here that the clarity of their vision emerges. Ultimately, this was interpreted as cultural imperialism by most of the non-French peoples of western Europe, but in the period prior to 1808, there were signs that considerable progress had been made towards these goals. Napoleonic plans for reconstruction encapsulated all facets of life: educational reform, the restructuring of religious life under the terms of the Concordat, and the rebuilding of economic infrastructures such as roads and bridges on a massive scale. All of this was to be laid down by the central government, but the first step had to be confronting the political legacy of the Revolution – the European civil war.

POLITICAL RECONSTRUCTION: HEALING THE OLD WOUNDS

There was much more to restoring order to a ravaged western Europe than efficient policing or the destruction of banditry. For the first time in almost a decade, as the war moved further away and the process of internal conquest triumphed, it was no longer feasible for people to resort to collective violence. The European civil war engendered by the Revolution was over – or, at least, ending – and public life could now re-emerge in a new context, where the French presence guaranteed a minimum of peace and protection.

The most striking feature of French policy, from the outset, was the determination of the regime to rule impartially and not to use its new-found, hard-won monopoly of power in the interests of any one political faction. These hopes were shared and predated by many non-French collaborators. In the words of a member of the new government of the Batavian (Dutch) Republic, early in 1799:

> Our policy is altogether new and . . . we will give ample proof that its object is none other than, with the strictest honesty, to deal a blow to all intriguers, to bring the constitution into full operation, to make it national and, once and for all, to destroy all factions on whichever side they may stand.[40]

The pursuit of these goals was riddled with complications, but the drive to create an administration free from factional strife was never abandoned.

In those areas annexed directly to France, an important aspect of the policy of reconciliation was the introduction of French officials into key judicial and administrative posts, partly to guide their non-French colleagues in the ways of the new system, but principally because it was hoped they would be as 'above faction' at local level as Napoleon himself was supposed to be at the centre. In the early years of their rule, the French saw this presence as essential in order to protect the patriots and counter-revolutionaries from each other. This was also the real reason why French administrators-general of the new Military Divisions preferred to assign ordinary criminal cases to the military commissions rather than the civilian courts, and why the jury system was never introduced into many of the new departments. This was well put by Jourde, the commissioner charged with organizing the tribunals in the ex-Piedmontese departments in 1801: 'It will be most necessary to employ Frenchmen in the criminal section [of the courts] ... given the personal hatreds which exist among the people of this lovely country.'[41]

Frenchmen served as magistrates, prefects, gendarmes in the annexed departments, thus creating a French presence even as low as cantonal level. In time, Rhenish, Belgian and Italian administrators also assumed posts in France. The 'highest flyer' among them was probably Botton de Castellamonte, a Piedmontese magistrate who became a president of the Cour de Casassion in Paris. Napoleon hoped to create a multinational civil service within the areas directly annexed to France, but initially he wanted simply a modicum of peace and efficiency, which only a French presence could guarantee. This was often more the case in theory than in practice in the first years of French rule, as two important factors hindered this aspect of the policy of reconciliation. First, the French themselves often proved to have powerful biases of their own. This was most marked within the ranks of the gendarmerie, two-thirds of which was composed of French soldiers in the annexed departments. Despite concerted efforts to recruit reliable soldiers into its ranks, gendarmes were often veterans of the early campaigns of the revolutionary wars. As such, they were usually ingrained with republican sympathies and a deep hostility to the people they now policed, who had been their enemies only a few years before. This was a problem particularly in the Belgian, Piedmontese and Rhineland departments, which had endured harsh occupations in the 1790s and been the theatres of large anti-French revolts as recently as 1798–99.

The imperial bureaucracy also needed such vast numbers to staff the lower levels of administration that it had to accept almost any literate man willing to serve. In practice, this meant allowing the patriots of the 1790s back into power, albeit at a lower level than they had occupied before Napoleon. In the Italian and Batavian Republics and the Kingdom of Naples, as well as in those areas ruled directly from Paris, patriot factions became entrenched in the cantons and the sub-prefectures, thus perpetuating the tensions of the revolutionary period. The radical complexion and partisan behaviour of the lower ranks of the magistracy and civil administration contrasts starkly with the moderate political backgrounds of their immediate superiors, the prefects and the magistrates of the appeal courts, the *cours d'appel*. Both within the Empire and in the Italian Republic and the Kingdom of Naples, the gap in outlook between the upper and lower echelons of the administrations remained striking.

In this climate, the more senior administrators developed a clear concept of the state as an adjudicator – a referee – between citizens hostile to each other, as much as to the state. Throughout the Empire, an uneasy alliance of French gendarmes and local patriots – both with fresh memories of the violence of counter-revolution – was watched with vigilance and concern by its less intransigent superiors. A close examination of the mass of denunciations and demands for arrests which flooded into the ministries of the Napoleonic police shows that these denunciations usually came from below, emanating either from private individuals or the local authorities. Most were found by the central authorities to be the results of malice, and were dropped following investigation. This experience of uncovering what they regarded as a society of vendetta and vipers' nests was formative for the Napoleonic administrators, convincing them further of the need for an authoritarian approach to the process of civilizing society – and that the society they ruled was a long way from civilized.

Frenchmen often dominated the higher echelons of the governments of the satellites. In the Kingdom of Naples, Saliceti and Roederer held important ministries, and in the Grand Duchy of Berg, Beugnot, once Voltaire's secretary, was the guiding influence. However, in the Batavian and Italian Republics, native statesmen were in almost complete control; by 1810, the same applied to the Kingdom of Naples, when Neapolitan citizenship became a prerequisite for public office. However, French and non-French officials faced similar problems and worked through compatible, increasingly identical administrative structures. Not surprisingly, the men who emerged to guide the inner empire shared a common outlook, if not always a common background. The early years of the Consulate saw a quest for men of moderate politics. Within France this usually meant those who had been active in the first years of the Revolution – before the Terror – and had re-emerged under the Directory. Among such men who went on to serve outside France were Roederer, Lesperut – who administered the Principality of Neuchâtel – and D'Auzers, the Director-General of Police in the north Italian departments. All were men of moderate views, who had 'gone to earth' under the Terror. The Napoleonic regime actively sought out the enlightened reformers of the 1780s outside France. The most prominent individual examples of this stamp of official approval are probably Melzi d'Eril, President of the Italian Republic 1800–06, and Schimmelpenninck, the 'Grand Pensionary' of the Batavian Republic, 1805–06. In Tuscany, where the French assumed control in 1808, it was official policy to bring 'the men of Archduke Peter-Leopold' into the administration.

The newly enlarged states of the Confederation of the Rhine were especially notable for the able, ruthless reformers at their helms. Baden produced an administration full of some of the most determined reformers of the period, led by von Reitzenstein. He divided the country into ten French-style departments, *kreise*, each with a civil servant as its prefect. This enabled von Reitzenstein to destroy the old, collegial style of local government so prevalent in the newly acquired parts of Baden. In Württemberg the prince himself led the drive for reform and administrative consolidation at the head of one of the most uncompromising, thoroughly professional bureaucracies in Europe. In Nassau, an equally capable administrator, von Bieberstein, had to work within the context of a much weaker state than the others, where the ex-Imperial Knights were potentially strong enough not only to thwart the process of centralization, but to dominate the government. They did not succeed in this and, although von Bieberstein often had to proceed more cautiously than his colleagues in the other Mittelstaaten and reform in a more piecemeal fashion, his work still proved far-reaching and enduring. Montgelas, First Minister of Max-Joseph of Bavaria, headed the drive for reform in the largest state of the Confederation. As a young man he had served under Joseph II of Austria, many of whose ideas he revived in the Napoleonic period, and stands as a living link between two major periods of reform in Germany.

All these statesmen epitomized what Napoleon sought of his chief collaborators in these years. All were of noble status, but had been associated with the reforming projects of pre-revolutionary regimes. It is interesting that most of the ministers of the German states were both younger and more uncompromising reformers than those in the satellite states. The first generation of Napoleonic leaders in these new states had been touched more deeply and directly by the French Revolution than their German counterparts. The foremost among them were older men of progressive views, rendered more conservative by the traumas of the 1790s. Determined to restore order and fearful of a return to the Terror, they were also firmly part of the propertied elites of their areas. Later, as the crisis intensified, Melzi and Schimmelpenninck would be replaced by younger, more dynamic men, in Melzi's case by the interesting combination of Eugène de Beauharnais and Antonio Aldini. The former was probably the most loyal member of the imperial family, while the latter had a republican past and had long played the radical opponent of Melzi in the early years. They complemented each other usefully in being more aggressive in implementing imperial policies and, above all, by being wholly reliant on the Napoleonic regime, if for very different reasons.

However, in the circumstances of the early years, Napoleon chose to try to rally the enlightened elements of the propertied classes to him, through men of their own kind, united as they were to Napoleon in a belief that the elites they belonged to could prosper only in a secularized, centralized and more efficient state. The advent of Napoleonic hegemony seemed to them to offer a chance to renew the assault on those aspects of the pre-revolutionary order they felt stood in the way of this vision – noble privilege, regional and municipal autonomy and the secular power of the Church – but without the democratic excesses of the 1790s.

THE 'CONCORDAT' – RELIGION AND CULTURE IN THE NEW STATE

The Napoleonic regime saw a settlement with the Church as an essential part of the internal pacification of France and the non-French territories it was in the process of absorbing. The Concordat of 1801 confirmed many important gains made by the revolutionary regimes, as regards state control over the property, activities and personnel of the Church. In many respects, the Concordat was as important for those aspects of

Church–state relations it said nothing about, as those it did. The French National Assembly had begun to nationalize all Church lands in 1790, and dissolved almost all the religious orders and corporations; it dealt with their properties as it saw fit, either selling them off or converting them to a variety of public uses. The Concordat left all this alone, which meant that not only did the orders of regular clergy remain suppressed in France, but that they – and their lands – could now be abolished wherever direct French rule was extended, and in any state which adopted the Code Napoleon.

The Concordat itself dealt with the secular clergy – now the only tolerated branch of the Church. The Directory's policy of the separation of Church and state was ended; Catholicism was recognized as the 'religion of the majority of Frenchmen', and public worship was again allowed. Churches were restored to the parish clergy and normal parish life was allowed to begin again. In return, the state received great latitude in the appointment of bishops and priests – they were salaried by the state and made to swear an oath of loyalty to it – their routine affairs to be administered by a newly created Ministry of Religion. In addition, a new reorganization of dioceses was sanctioned, along the lines Napoleon wanted; in theory, dioceses were to correspond exactly with departments which, in fact, entailed a considerable reduction in their number.

In a French context, the Concordat was an important improvement on the condition of the Church, but to those areas only now coming under French control, it looked very different. These regions had not experienced the religious policies of the Revolution, the momentary depredations of the French armies and the short-lived reforms of the sister republics notwithstanding. Now, a true revolution in religious life was to be unleashed over northern Italy and western Germany, where the *ancien régime* Church had remained intact, however battered by the winds of revolution and war. To statesmen like Melzi d'Eril in Milan and Montgelas in Munich, it presented a chance to renew the course of enlightened reform, and they pounced on it. The Catholic Church was a diverse body which had disseminated its influence and presence into every aspect of European life; the Napoleonic reformers now intended to impose a compact uniformity on it. The violent fitfulness of the Revolution was to be replaced by vigorous, systematic social engineering.

The policy-makers of the inner empire saw the Concordat as an opportunity to advance the power of their states. Their unanimous, enthusiastic support for it is an interesting indication of what they had in common. Its terms were welcomed because they brought the Church more comprehensively under state control than previous reforming monarchs had been able to achieve. Indeed, initially Melzi objected fiercely to the Concordat because he thought it too lenient to the Church. He was outspoken in his insistent belief that much tighter state controls over the Church were needed in the Italian Republic than in France, because the Church played a far more prominent role in Italian society. His strong views on this subject did not prevail over those of Napoleon, but were important enough to drive Melzi to the brink of resignation.

In concrete terms, the way was open to seizing the vast, often valuable properties of the Church, for those who followed the lead offered by the French example. The fate of these properties was no side issue; many of the lands embraced by the inner empire were among the most intensely pious in Europe, replete with the accumulated wealth of the Church. Both wealth and power beckoned.

The Concordat, particularly the dissolution of the regular orders, was implemented with more ruthlessness and vigour in the south German states, especially Bavaria, than in those areas directly under France. This was one area where the degree of control exercised from Paris mattered a great deal. The terms of the Concordat were introduced gradually, if determinedly, in the Rhenish and Piedmontese departments, while in the Italian Republic, Napoleon's intervention was able to restrain Melzi, but in the states of southern Germany, no such checks could be applied. Here, it was not just a case of seizing abbeys, priories and landed estates, but whole states which had been ruled by their prince-bishops until the reorganization of 1803. Bamberg, Freising, Augsburg and Passau were all ecclesiastical states which passed to Bavaria in 1803, together comprising 880 000 inhabitants. It was a coincidence of history that where the pickings were richest, the moderating influence of French policy was weakest, but it was exactly this set of circumstances that turned these states – led by Montgelas in Bavaria – to ruthless secularization on a grand scale. In Nassau, von Bieberstein proceeded carefully over the dissolution of the regular orders between 1803 and 1806, abolishing the monasteries one by one, but the process became more ruthless after the abolition of the Holy Roman Empire and the end of all legal restraints on the process.

The assault on the Church was pursued with an enthusiasm which was fuelled by more than just rapacious, financial greed. For Melzi and Montgelas this was the chance to finish unfinished business, to fulfil Josephist hopes of subordinating the Church to the state and to break its cultural grip on society. They relished the struggle. In 1802, Montgelas castigated the Bavarian monasteries he was about abolish because they 'encouraged the perpetuation of superstition and of most baneful errors; they have built up obstacles against the spread of enlightened principles, and they have sown suspicion against every institution working for true moral education.'[42] It was an outlook Melzi shared whole-heartedly; he extended his sense of disgust to the secular clergy, telling Napoleon in 1802 that the Italian clergy 'were of a caste of mind scarcely conforming to the views of the government and secretly supported all that was opposed to it'.[43] Similar sentiments can be found among many French officials within the Empire proper, but only rarely were they expressed in so outspoken a fashion, or acted upon quite so aggressively at the top of the administration; these at-

titudes were widespread at local level, but Paris held them more or less in
check. Clearly, in the cases of Montgelas and Melzi, the earlier influences
of Joseph II's reforms dominated their actions. Melzi acknowledged this
openly when he advocated the wholesale reintroduction of these policies in
his project for a separate Italian Concordat, in July 1802.

Over the length and breadth of the states within Napoleon's orbit, the
treasures of the great abbeys and monasteries were meticulously seized by
state commissioners, along with those of churches closed as part of the
rationalization process laid down by the Concordat. To the men driving
this work on, it was much more than the acquisition of material wealth.
Each object of beauty, every book or manuscript seized from the clutches
of the Church, was something recovered for the benefit of society,
through the agency of the state. Many priceless treasures were lost or
destroyed in the process – the full extent of the cultural loss has never
really been calculated by historians, perhaps because many do not wish
to know – but what mattered to contemporary reformers was that the
Church no longer had them; its intellectual grip on society had been dealt
a severe, well-calculated blow. Thus stripped of its temporal wealth, it
could now be 'reset on its proper way', as Melzi put it. That path had
been carefully laid down for what was left of the Church – that is, its
secular arm, the priests and bishops – by the governments of the
Napoleonic states; these plans, too, had their roots in what is broadly
termed Jansenism. The French Civil Constitution of the Clergy of 1791
had resurrected it; Napoleonic hegemony was to let it have its day. When
the Napoleonic state turned its attention to reforming the secular clergy,
the intended result was to change people's lives through the direct intervention of the state. These reforms touched a raw nerve in European
society; from an administrative point of view, only the process of conscription was calculated to bring the citizen so close to the state.

Whereas previously religious life had been the preserve of many institutions – the lay confraternities and the various orders of mendicant friars,
for instance – now it was to centre on the parish and the diocese alone, the
ecclesiastical equivalent of the commune and the department. The reforms
of the Concordat allowed for just this, the abolition of almost all Church
bodies except these two. The new monopoly of the parish was expressed
in concrete, material terms when it became the recipient of many goods –
from organs to chapels, from revenues to candlesticks – which had been
confiscated from the regular clergy. However, it was not only the structure
of the Church that was to be simplified; religious practices were also to be
reformed, and the role of the priest in society redefined. This is where the
Napoleonic state drew on a set of ideas which predated both itself and the
Revolution. The reform or abolition of clerical institutions was intended to
tighten state control over the Church, but the drastic reform of religious
practices was meant to change and reshape the way people lived. With the
Concordat came the abolition of scores of saints' days and, consequently,

the loss of the local festivals and holidays which sculpted the pattern of a person's year. Even those few high days which survived – Christmas, Easter, Corpus Christi, the Assumption – now had to be celebrated differently. An end was to be put to most public processions – just as an end had been put to most of the lay confraternities who marched in them – and with all this, it was hoped the drunkenness, brawling and general public disorder they engendered would end too.

Through all of this, the Napoleonic officials hoped to achieve two goals which had been striven for by enlightened reformers for decades. On a practical level, they hoped to encourage a more orderly society, not simply by banning the obvious circumstances which gave rise to disorder, but by breaking the identification of the Church with those circumstances. On a different plane, they sought to make religion itself more spiritual and austere. The parish priest became a civil servant in practice, as well as theory – he was already on the state payroll, following the abolition of the tithe. Thus, he was to combat superstition, ignorance and disorder; in human terms, this meant loyalty to an official culture of reason and enlightened progress, not just to a functional state.

Nowhere are the deeper ambitions of the Napoleonic state made clearer than in this aspect of its policy. As a means of advancing the power and influence of the state, the governments of Napoleonic Europe had struck on a route into the heart of the society they ruled, when they turned their backs on the policy of separation practised by the French Directory, and that of co-existence which most previous rulers had been constrained to accept. As with the imposition of conscription and the French administrative system, the opposition would be fierce, but the stakes were very high, nothing short of the character of European civilization itself.

The momentous implications of this aspect of the Napoleonic reforms can easily be lost in the mundane evidence needed to support them, because its administrative execution was done through seizures of Church properties, with the lists of goods and financial accounts it generated, and in the maze of involved negotiations between Napoleon and Pius VII over the appointments of bishops, the redrawing of dioceses and the minutiae of Church–state relations. Just as with conscription, the dry figures disguise an undertaking of epic proportions; the numbers crunched their way into the history of the period, echoing the tramping of the boots of the soldiers who closed the abbeys and the nunneries and the hill chapels. The Church was everywhere in western Europe, but everywhere it was sought out – just as with the conscripts – from the smallest, most decrepit mountain chapel to the fattest abbey, and from the poorest nun to the proudest prince-bishop. On this level, bureaucracy won an impressive victory, which its meticulous records both prove and disguise. Beneath it all, however, lay the regime's belief in the superiority of a culture rooted in the secular, rational world of the Enlightenment, over the popular culture of the people of western Europe.

Even in its appeals to social stability and conservatism, the Napoleonic regime still had to confront those aspects of the old order that had stood in the path of state power. The power of the Church was one such obstacle; that of noble privilege – often termed 'feudalism' – was another.

THE ABOLITION OF NOBLE PRIVILEGE AND THE INTRODUCTION OF THE CODE NAPOLEON, 1799–1807

The years 1806–08 were the last time when new acquisitions could be absorbed in relative peace, and when proper attention could be given to domestic reform. As one historian has noted in the case of Bavaria, the most decisive year for the formation of the modern state there was 1808, in the brief gap between two wars, when the Franco-Russian alliance seemed to have created a lasting peace.[44] The same was true of all the new territories in these years.

The regime faced a delicate problem over anything that touched the nobility. On the one hand, it sought to rally the landed element of the propertied classes to itself – and all nobles were landowners, almost by definition – while on the other, to tolerate the noble privileges of the *ancien régime* was incompatible with the concept of a powerful, centralized state. This latter aspect of the problem is better understood when it is remembered that noble privilege extended well beyond exemption from taxation. 'Feudalism' also included a noble's right to hold his own courts and enforce his own justice on his fief; it extended to his rights over many aspects of the economy through monopolies of mills or wine presses, for example, all of which were far more important than the often repeated 'totems' of feudal oppression: tax exemption, hunting rights, or monopoly of high office. 'Feudalism' as the late eighteenth century understood it, was a complex mesh of judicial and financial privileges, made still more complicated by the fact that many feudal privileges had passed into the hands of non-nobles in the course of the century.[45]

When the French revolutionaries had tried to abolish all feudal privilege in 1789, they assimilated many of its financial aspects into the realm of private property: feudal dues were commuted into rents; fiefs into private estates which were not confiscated from their owners, even if they were, henceforth, to be taxed. These lessons had been well absorbed by the Napoleonic regime when, in its turn, it had to confront such institutions beyond the borders of France, and Napoleon often turned to the same men who had pioneered the abolition of feudalism in the first years of the Revolution. Simeon, the Chief Minister of Jerome's Kingdom of Westphalia, and Beugnot, in the Grand Duchy of Berg, were representative of this. They shared a set of legal principles that turned on the fine distinctions between feudal services and property rights. Once these distinctions had been made, however, French jurists tried to pursue the abolition of the former with the same single-mindedness they had shown in France; conversely, their approach to those aspects of privilege connected with property were treated with great caution. Broadly, their policy aimed at the uncompromising destruction of the rights of nobles to exercise judicial authority or demand personal services – serfdom in its purest form – that is, to destroy privilege before the law. However, it did not always embrace measures which would violate private property or overturn the social order in the short term, although their avowed goal was always to create a wider distribution of property among the peasantry and bourgeoisie. The attack on legal privilege was to be short and sharp; that on property was much more gradualist.

In many areas – the Batavian Republic, Piedmont and Lombardy, for example – feudal privilege was not very extensive, and the French reforms met with little difficulty. It was otherwise in the Kingdom of Naples and the German states, however. In the Kingdom of Naples, a feudal baronage had been powerful enough to thwart concerted attempts to create an efficient state in the course of the eighteenth century, while in the German states, the political character of the Holy Roman Empire had perpetuated the existence of the micro-states of the Knights of the Empire – true 'fief-states' – as well as considerable noble privilege within states such as Bavaria, Baden and Württemberg. The northern and central states from which Westphalia and Berg had been created also embraced nobilities possessed of extensive privileges.

Noble privilege in these areas could not be sanctioned within the Napoleonic order, in part simply because of its sheer extent within these states, and the new regimes made tremendous efforts to destroy seigneurialism in its most obvious forms. Seen in a wider context, the abolition of the secular privileges of the Church had been the first salvo in a war whose next victims would be the nobles. In Germany, the princes now set about the Imperial Knights and the Free Cities of the south and centre with the same rapacious glee with which they had gobbled up the lands of the prince-bishops, soon after the Austrian defeats of 1805, with the only state with an interest in protecting them now reduced to impotence. Max-Joseph and Montgelas seized the Free Cities of Nuremberg and Augsburg, the latter already weakened by the destruction of its neighbouring prince-bishop, without great ceremony. They used a calculated policy of coercion and concession to end the independence of the Imperial Knights within their states, which reduced them to the status of other nobles. Those who resisted were dealt with harshly, as was also the case in Baden and Württemburg, whose king told his commissioners that 'Whoever among you attracts the most complaints is the most gratifying to me.'[46] As for those knights who came under direct French rule, Napoleon coldly rebuffed a delegation sent to plead their case in 1806.

In some of the smaller Mittelstaaten it was less easy, however. In Nassau the nobles had the potential not only to perpetuate their economic domination of the countryside, but to usurp the lower rungs of the judiciary and administration: the new state stood in danger of going backwards and slipping into a truly feudal structure. Von Bieberstein was acutely aware of this, writing in 1806 that if seigneurialism was not curbed, 'a state within a state would exist', and so the ex-Knights 'need to become what their new status mandates, namely rich property owners within the state, equipped with a few privileges ... but without infringeing on the unity of the state'.[47] Von Bieberstein proceeded with caution, usually making concessions over taxation to deprive the Knights of their judicial privileges. It was a successful policy, as not only did the state come to control the entire judiciary by 1813, but gradually seigneurialism in Nassau was reduced from a threat to the existence of the state itself to a series of private lease arrangements between landowners and tenants. One of its most far-reaching results was the emergence of a sizeable class of relatively secure and independent peasant smallholders. This process began with the wise decision to sell off monastic lands in small affordable lots and accelerated after 1812, following the abolition of almost 1000 forms of feudal due. This was done in such a way as to let the peasants keep their land as well as free themselves of their obligations. The peasantry of Nassau became free tax-paying landholders and the nobility lost its grip on them to the state. The work of von Bieberstein in this sphere was probably the most successful in Germany. It was a victory for persistence, moderation and pragmatism, and in the wider context of Napoleonic Europe, it was a rare one.

The assault on feudalism in the Kingdom of Naples was among the most thrusting of any Napoleonic regime, mainly because Joseph Bonaparte, and then Murat, inherited a vibrant anti-feudal tradition in the higher levels of the *ancien régime* administration. This tradition, with its roots in the eighteenth-century Enlightenment, was epitomized by Zurlo and Ricciardi, two native Neapolitans who were Ministers for the Interior and Justice, respectively, for most of the period 1806–14. They showed a remarkable zeal in their attack on the powerful barons of the Kingdom which, although not crowned with the comprehensive victory they sought, still dealt the barons a series of blows from which they never recovered. Murat, himself, had no doubt where his internal priorities lay, writing to Zurlo in 1810, 'Without doubt, the greatest benefit of my reign will be the total abolition of feudalism.'[48] In Zurlo and Ricciardi, he had servants who were determined to make this a reality. Their commitment to the destruction of feudalism is all the more striking because they often opposed the introduction of other aspects of the Code Napoleon; it becomes even clearer when the extent of the barons' power is revealed. Judicial privilege was concentrated in the hands of barely 90 nobles – 15 per cent of the aristocracy as a whole – which they exercised over about two million people, roughly one-quarter of the population of the kingdom. Their economic power, although less easy to assess with precision, dominated directly the lives of about five million people, 70 per cent of the rural population. Seen against this background, the gradualist approach adopted by the reformers to the redistribution of property becomes more explicable, while the daring of their legal reforms appears as a truly radical assault on the old order. The dynamic phase of reform was concentrated between 1806 and 1810, beginning with the decree of 2 August 1806, by which the barons and the traditional municipal councils – the *università* – lost all their judicial powers to centrally appointed magistrates. This policy often ran aground in practice because the barons were still able to overawe local government, and because there were not enough new magistrates to fill the void created by the abolition of the baronial courts. Nevertheless, the barons themselves were all too aware that they could only control their power bases by indirect means. A special commission for complaints against them operated between 1806 and 1810. The true importance of this legal aspect of the Napoleonic reforms was that they swept away many obstacles to future reforms, as the changes in the laws of inheritance opened vast tracts of property to the free market. Above all, the barons could no longer hide behind their own courts; their continued – if indirect – grip on local affairs was not mirrored in the higher courts to which they were now subject.

The land reforms attempted by Zurlo in these years were, potentially, among the most far-reaching of the Napoleonic era. Obviously, it was unrealistic to think in terms of despoiling the barons of their vast estates as such, but the reforming ministers were able to undermine its feudal character by asserting the concept of private property against it, which they did through the judgements of the special commission. Zurlo tried to go further, through an attempt to sell off in small units parts of land surrendered by the barons when they could not produce legal titles to them, a project dear to him, as he made clear:

> Its general aim has been to raise the neediest class of citizens to the status of property owners ... If particular, transitory matters oppose these beneficial aims, we must set about ending them, but they must not in any circumstances be allowed to deflect the most important objective of the law.[49]

The barons lost appreciable amounts of land as a result of this policy, but not to the peasants, who could not afford to work them under the added burden of state taxation. Most of these plots reverted to the common lands administered by the municipalities; a blow to baronial power, but not one for the diffusion of private property to the peasantry. In general, it was the rural bourgeoisie who dominated the municipalities, and they emerged the winners in this process. The overall result had been a limited victory, centred on negative achievements rather than positive ones – destructive of baronial power, rather than creative – but set in its contemporary context, the work of Zurlo and Ricciardi was impressive and fundamental.

In the Grand Duchy of Berg and the Kingdom of Westphalia, the French did not inherit an administrative tradition that was either unified or sympathetic, but a collection of former states and parts of states with legal traditions deeply imbued by seigneurial privilege. Nevertheless, the initial determination of Simeon and Beugnot to impose the Code on these areas, and the consequent abolition of privilege, was as great as that of Zurlo and Ricciardi. The same could be said of Berthier's attitude to the Duchy of Neuchâtel, which Napoleon had given him in 1806. Neuchâtel is an example notable for its sheer irony, in that Berthier, having been awarded the duchy as something close to a personal fief, launched a ruthless assault on feudal and local privileges there. Although often thwarted in these efforts because of his permanent absence on campaign – and tempered in his drive by his commissioner, Lesperut – Berthier's aggressive, reforming attitude stands at odds with his position as the duchy's personal overlord. The influence of enlightened absolutism was stronger than the trappings of Napoleonic nobility.

Napoleon ruled the Grand Duchy of Berg as regent for his young nephew; therefore, it was virtually under direct French control, through Maret, who headed a bureau for Berg's affairs in Paris. Initially, Paris insisted on the outright abolition of seigneurialism. Beugnot saw this had to be tempered where property rights were concerned, given the dominant position of the barons over most of the country, but he shared Napoleon's insistence on the abolition of serfdom as such – that is, all personal services and private jurisdictions. As in Naples, these reforms were driven through; as Beugnot put it, if the new settlement 'hurt the pride of the privileged classes, it did not hurt their interests'.[50] Most services were abolished only if the peasants could buy themselves out of them – which they could not do – making Beugnot's reforms among the most timid of the period; there were no far-reaching enquiries into titles as in Naples. To contemporary reformers 'on the ground', however, they were meant to be the first stage in a gradualist process which would create a peasantry of secure leaseholders. As in Naples, the legal restrictions imposed on life and property were swept away with alacrity and ruthlessness in 1806–07 by a French-dominated executive. However, the drive against the existence of the great estates themselves was slowed to a virtual halt under the influence of native administrators, deeply conscious of the revolutionary potential of the sweeping decrees on abolition which Napoleon continued to issue, such as that from Valladolid of 11 January 1809, insisting on the suppression of all fiefs in the Grand Duchy. Similar demands were still being issued into 1811. Beugnot, on the other hand, soon learned that it was easier to create an administration from scratch – and even to impose conscription – than to introduce changes that would jolt the entire structure of society.

Even in the face of these circumstances, Beugnot maintained his basic commitment to fundamental reform in the long term. This was the case in 1809, when he refused military protection to the nobles of Arenberg from a peasant revolt because they were flouting those reforms which had been enacted. Napoleon backed Beugnot fully in his handling of the revolt, and nearly always sided against the nobles when local disputes of this nature reached him. Distance from the central government was a problem for the reformers and local government was still in the hands of the nobles, causing Beugnot to remark that, 'far from central power, the petty barons take their revenge for the audacity of their tenants'. In these circumstances, Beugnot's words to Roederer, in 1809, reflect a mixture of realism touched with defiance, and idealism thwarted by reality:

> Conscription or taxes paid in kind are the price of political inde-
> pendence; the price of individual freedom and the liberation of
> the land market is payed for in taxes in cash; thus, when a citizen has
> submitted to conscription and payed his taxes, he is even with society,
> but society, in its turn, must guarantee him the advantages he has
> payed the price of.[51]

Conscription and taxation continued on their way in Berg, but so did bitter disputes between peasants and landowners over the implications of the French reforms. Beugnot's hopes that they would be resolved in the courts – and thus, usually, in favour of the peasants – were thwarted by his lack of control over local administration. Paris concluded the problem was administrative, that power was too far away. Napoleon determined that this would not be the case in the next – and last – new state created in Germany in these years, Jerome's Kingdom of Westphalia.

Westphalia was envisaged as a 'model state' by all those involved in its creation, from Napoleon downwards. As such, it is easy to see it as a new initiative in imperial policy, as a bright new dawn. In reality, it was the final stage in a cumulative process, begun in 1799 and meant to end at Tilsit. Thus, the kingdom was created in an atmosphere of tremendous confidence, to be an example to the rest of Germany of the superiority of the French system and, in particular, to encourage the other German states to adopt that system in full. With such great hopes resting on its fledgling shoulders, the abolition of feudalism and the introduction of the Code Napoleon carried a greater urgency in Westphalia than elsewhere. They were the key to the creation of a new social order in Germany which, in turn, would secure that part of Europe firmly within the inner empire.

This urgency is clearly evident when the uncompromising approach to the feudal question of Jerome's Chief Minister, Simeon, is contrasted to the gradualist moderation of Beugnot in Berg – himself also now a part of Jerome's team – where the prevailing conditions were broadly similar. The aristocracy retained its privileges and power at local level very much intact in Hesse-Kassel, despite the presence of an efficient state bureaucracy. In these conditions, the reforms could not be gradualist; the basic administrative structure could not be set up without an immediate confrontation between the old order in its most unreconstructed form, and the new one, at its most uncompromising.

Speed was of the essence; a constitution written by French jurists was promulgated within a few months. The hope was for a clean break with the past, the means was a short, sharp shock. Freedom of commerce and enterprise was introduced at a stroke; the guilds, the nobles' personal tolls, along with those of the towns, were all abolished, as were all personal services and dues. The revolutionary intentions of Jerome and Simeon were not lost on the native administrators, who recoiled from the possibility of a sudden abolition of feudalism in the countryside. Like their colleagues in Berg, they sought a gradual evolution away from seigneurialism, towards private property, in ways which would not jeopardize patterns of inheritance within the landed nobility, which the introduction of the Code would entail. They sought peasant emancipation, but in stages. Simeon, in contrast, steadfastly refused to admit that the Napoleonic state was not a universally applicable model, or that the vast differences between French and Westphalian society really mattered. The winter of 1807–08 was a period of frenetic reform, as Simeon systematically prepared for a definitive legal assault on the nobles' estates, but the confrontation would not take place. The feudal dues were abolished only on condition of compensation, which amounted to leaving them alone.

These reforms would be the last of their kind that Napoleonic Europe would witness in a spirit of optimism. Henceforth, those areas which came under French rule were administered with few long-term goals in mind. Until 1807, the French challenged feudal privilege wherever they found it. In Naples, they breathed fresh life into an ancient struggle; in the south German states, they set the key example for native reformers; in much of northern Germany, they posed the question for the first time. A consistently hard line was taken against seigneurialism by those at the centre of power – Joseph, Murat and Zurlo, in Naples; Berthier in Neuchâtel; Jerome and Simeon in Westphalia; and, above all, Napoleon himself – a hard line which stands in contrast to the gradualism of their subordinates. Where moderates like Beugnot or Lesperut differed from Simeon and Zurlo was not over the desire to eradicate feudalism, but how to do so. In those vast areas where it formed the basis of the whole social order, the gradualists prevailed. Time seemed to be on their side in the victorious years between 1805 and 1808, but it was not, and in this fact lies much of the explanation for the failure of the Napoleonic regime to change the structure of society in much of rural Europe. Gradualism was a doomed policy in the convulsed world of the Napoleonic era, but this is clearer to posterity than it was to contemporaries.

If Westphalia marks the last, half finished, stage in the consolidation of the inner empire, the creation of the Grand Duchy of Warsaw marks a new transitional phase in the emergence of an outer empire. It was not an unsuccessful creation, in terms of recruits and tax revenue – the Grand Duchy raised almost 200 000 men in its six year existence, from a population of 2 600 000 – but this was due less to any assimilation of the Grand Duchy into the Napoleonic system, than to forces of nationalism best understood in the context of collaboration. The Grand Duchy appeared more a part of the French state system than it actually was, if judged by the standards of the inner empire as a whole. The limits of assimilation are particularly evident over the question of feudalism and the introduction of the Code Napoleon.

Napoleon is usually accused of being as ignorant of Polish realities, as is seen in his – by now standard – insistence on the full-scale adoption of the Code Napoleon into the Grand Duchy, a code whose terms only made a real impact on the small, urban sector of society. Nevertheless, ignorance is not the same as insensitivity. Napoleon knew he was dealing with the remnants of a proud, well-defined polity, and he behaved accordingly. Both the Emperor and, after 1809, Frederick-Augustus, who was the Grand Duchy's absentee ruler as well as King of Saxony, left internal affairs to an executive council of Polish nobles. Sensitivity to Polish conditions meant supporting the nobles and led to a distinct rejection of the new constitution's bold affirmation that 'serfdom is abolished'. In fact, the regime deliberately interpreted the legal ambiguities surrounding the emancipation of the serfs in ways that actually strengthened the nobles' position over their tenants. This stemmed from a discrepancy in the terms of emancipation, by which peasants were granted freedom of movement without any security of tenure – which was actually weakened under the new system. The nobles saw their real powers increased, and were able to make contracts with their tenants with a very free hand. Although few peasants were dispossessed because their labour was too valuable, neither did their legal position change in any fundamental way. The formal contracts which the new law code insisted on between landlord and tenant were often described as 'conforming to local usage'.[52]

No other satellite state gave its military or political support to the French cause as readily as the Grand Duchy of Warsaw. Although there were Jacobin and reactionary elements within the Polish aristocracy opposed to French hegemony, the great mass of the gentry rallied to Napoleon at every crucial moment. Yet, the price for this was a refusal to implement many central aims of Napoleonic policy, the abolition of *de facto* serfdom chief among them. The deeper lesson seemed to be that a greater sensitivity to local traditions entailed the renunciation of liberal, reforming ambitions. In the context of the Grand Duchy of Warsaw, the bitterness of this lesson was reinforced by the fact that this state created a viable, centralized bureaucracy on the French model, while all but ignoring its social and legal reforms. The Grand Duchy was a living monument to the contradictions in the Napoleonic state system.

Towards the crisis of the Empire: French imperialism and the origins of the Continental System, 1806–1807

In 1806–07 Napoleon still needed to consolidate his regime within France itself and to defeat Britain, now his only remaining adversary. To achieve these two ends, he initiated two policies which would disrupt much of the inner empire in the years to come, if with different degrees of intensity. Napoleon created a new nobility in 1806 to consolidate the new imperial dynasty, and to bolster its financial position he began a policy of extensive land grants – the *dotations* – most of which were in the non-French territories of the Empire. In an effort to defeat Britain by economic, rather than military means, he initiated a series of policies known as the Continental System heralded by the Berlin Decrees of 1806.

The dotations

Napoleon was deeply aware of how shallow the foundations of his regime were, and of the need to create a solid basis of support for it. Three maxims guided him in this process: Napoleon always showed a marked preference for men who had risen through service to him which, in practice, tended to mean soldiers. He also had a deep distrust of fortunes which were not based on landed wealth. Finally, his unswerving belief in authoritarian rule precluded any attempt to found a new elite through parliamentary institutions. Put another way, Napoleon somehow had to create a new elite without giving it political power – so he had to give it social and economic security instead – and he *had* to give it to them, because he wanted men loyal to himself alone. Moreover, he wanted it done in the traditional way, through landed wealth; he had to invest new men with old money. To cap it all, he saw that this would have to be done outside France – indeed, outside most of the territories acquired before 1805 – because the principles of feudalism had been too thoroughly uprooted in them. In these circumstances, the creation of *dotations* in the Italian, German and Polish territories, from 1806 onwards, was tailor-made for the creation of a new European elite. This, at least, was how it looked from Paris.

The *dotations* were lands – usually former royal domains of deposed sovereigns or Church lands – which the Emperor seized for himself and then earmarked their revenues for distribution to whoever he chose. Once assigned, these revenues were to remain within the family of the recipient, descending by primogeniture through the male line. The rents from the lands could be alienated only with the permission of the Emperor, and the recipient had to swear an oath of loyalty to the dynasty. Their size, in terms of income, was to be proportionate to the dignity of the holders. The social

and economic connotations of the *dotations* were overwhelmingly aristocratic. Two important caveats kept this institution firmly within the political framework of the Napoleonic state. These land grants did not involve
the residence of their holders *in situ* – indeed, they were actively encouraged to transfer the revenues to France – and as a consequence the lands
were managed by French commissioners. More importantly, the *dotations*
did not carry any political or judicial rights; neither equality before the law
nor the state's monopoly of power were compromised in any way.

The same could not be said of the economies of the satellite states
affected by this policy. The first land grants were in the Venetian
provinces annexed to the Kingdom of Italy and the former Duchies of
Parma, Piacenza and Guastalla; the revenues of the smallest duchy,
Guastalla, were turned over to Napoleon's sister, Pauline, *en bloc*. Six
more followed in the Kingdom of Naples, to which first Joseph and then
Murat strongly objected, but to no avail.

This was as nothing compared with what was to follow in Berg, Westphalia and, above all, in the Grand Duchy of Warsaw. The Venetian and
Neapolitan creations had been hindrances to Eugène and Murat, but the
dotations in the Grand Duchy of Warsaw amounted to a loss of 20 per cent
of the fledgling state's revenues, a loss which had to be absorbed in a period
of severe economic dislocation in the wake of war and Napoleon's fresh
demands for the Duchy to form an army of its own. The magnitude of these
grants is well illustrated by the mere fact that Davout's was Lowicz, the old
benefice of the Primate of all Poland – a principality kept virtually intact –
while Lannes's was Siewierz, the former benefice of the bishops of Cracow,
which included some of the most important paper mills and glassworks in
a country where industry was as important to economic development as it
was scarce. In Berg, Beugnot complained continually that the Emperor was
not setting a proper example in the abolition of feudalism. In Westphalia,
the ever-swelling numbers of *dotations* were a crucial check on the much-
vaunted transformation of rural society through land reform, quite separately from the significant revenues it denied the 'model state'.

The deeper resentment provoked by these land grants can be imagined
by examining the behaviour and attitudes of the French commissioners,
who were accountable only to the Emperor: Vincent, a commissioner in
Warsaw, claimed the *dotations* were part of France itself. However inge-
nious a solution to the regime's policy of retrenchment within France, it
proved a serious miscalculation in the territories where it was applied.

The Berlin Decrees

The policy initiated by the Berlin Decrees of November 1806 had momentous consequences for the future of the Napoleonic state system. The emergence of the Continental System was a policy forced on the French by the

unique threat still posed by Britain. However, as with the *dotations*, it was a policy born of unprecedented success as much as of frustration in the face of long-standing problems, internal insecurity in the case of the *dotations* and external threat in that of the Continental System.

The naval calamity of Trafalgar in October 1805 ended any hopes Napoleon had of beating the British at their own game, and the Berlin Decrees of November were an acknowledgement of this. They declared Britain in a state of blockade by France, her allies and satellites, officially ending all trading contacts between them and Britain. The British had begun their own, formal blockade against the Empire the previous May, but following the Berlin Decrees, both sides sought next to extend their grip on neutral shipping. The British did this through Orders in Council in January and November 1807, which obliged neutral ships to get British permission to trade with enemy ports; Napoleon countered with the Milan Decrees of November and December 1807, which extended his ban on the importation of British goods to neutral ships. Although Napoleon introduced further measures in 1810, the Berlin and Milan decrees henceforth formed the essence of blockade policy.

There was a clear distinction within the Continental System between the blockade proper and the wider restructuring of the economies of the Napoleonic state system.[53] After 1807, both aspects of the policy initiated in 1806 changed the character of the Empire in equal – if different – measure. Both policies were as Francocentric in nature as the *dotations*, but their most important consequences were reserved for the rest of western and central Europe. When set in the wider context of European economic history, the complex experience of Napoleonic economic policies becomes by far the most important element of the Continental System.[54] Its aim to create 'an uncommon market', 'a one-way common market', produced varied and complex results from region to region, and from state to state. The blockade was but one component of a much larger economic design for Europe. Seen in this way, the importance of the blockade assumes its proper proportions, as part of a greater whole. The exclusion of Britain from the economic life of continental Europe was to be a starting-point, the foundation upon which the rest of the Continental System had to rest.

The decision to blockade the continent against Britain altered the new order created at Tilsit, and its ramifications were political and military, rather than economic. The success of the blockade depended on a control of the coasts beyond the scope of the settlement of 1806–07. The need to enforce it compelled the Empire to expand into new areas – Spain and central Italy – and to seek to control some regions already within its orbit in new ways, principally the Kingdom of Holland and the North Sea coast of Germany. Thus, a new 'outer empire' began to form, against which the degree of consolidation, pacification and assimilation of the older, 'inner empire' can be measured.

So far, this process has been viewed largely from the side of the French conquerors and their collaborators, in an effort to understand the nature of government activity and the kind of empire those in power were trying to create. This is only one side of the story, as has already become clear when examining many aspects of Napoleonic policy in action, particularly the enforcement of conscription. It is essential to know what the people of the Empire thought of the new Napoleonic order.

Notes

1 F. Bluche, *Le Bonapartisme*, on the theory. E.A. Whitcomb, 'Napoleon's prefects', *American Historical Review,* 69 (1974); and J-P. Bertaud, 'Napoleon's officers', *Past and Present,* 111 (1986) pp. 90–107, for the practice.

2 I. Woloch, *The New Regime. Transformations of the French Civic Order, 1789–1820s,* (New York and London, 1994) p. 55.

3 Ibid., pp. 56–7.

4 Bertaud, 'Napoleon's officers', p. 107.

5 J-I. Halperin, *L'Impossible Code Civil,* (Paris, 1992) pp. 264–5.

6 R.B. Holtman, *The Napoleonic Revolution,* (Philadelphia, PA, 1967) p. 88.

7 P.M. Jones, *Politics and Rural Society. The Southern Massif Central, c. 1750–1880,* (Cambridge, 1985) p. 154, sets this alongside the great reforms of the 1790s.

8 R.M. Berdahl, *The Politics of the Prussian Nobility: the Development of a Conservative Ideology, 1770–1848,* (Princeton, NJ, 1988).

9 Fitzsimmons, *Parisian Order of Barristers,* pp. 147–53.

10 Woloch, *New Regime,* pp. 118–19.

11 Ibid., p. 127.

12 C. Langlois, *Le Diocese de Vannes au xixe siècle,* (Paris, 1974), 'Complots, propagandes et répression policière en Bretagne sous l'Empire, 1806–1807', *Annales de Bretagne,* 78 (1957). On conscription, A. Forrest, *Conscripts and Deserters,* (Oxford, 1988) pp. 220–3.

13 L. Bergeron and G. Chaussinand-Nogaret, *Les Masses de Granit. Cent mille notables du Premier Empire,* (Paris, 1979).

14 G. Ellis, 'Rhine and Loire: Napoleon's elites and social order', in *Beyond the Terror,* (Cambridge, 1983) eds. G. Lewis and C.M. Lucas, pp. 232–67, 246.

15 Ellis, 'Napoleonic elites', p. 266.

16 R.J.P. Kain and E. Baignet, *The Cadastral Map in the Service of the State. A History of Property Mapping,* (Chicago and London, 1984) pp. 228–31.

17 Cited in Kain and Baignet, *Cadastral Map,* p. 228.

18 M-N. Bourguet, *Déchiffrer la France. La statistique départmentale à l'époque napoleonienne,* (Paris, 1989) pp. 301–6.

19 E. d'Hauterive, *La Police Secrète du Premier Empire,* 4 vols (Paris, 1908–64) i, p. 59.

20 Cited in A. Aulard, *Paris sous le Consulat,* 4 vols (Paris, 1903–14) i, p. 2.

21 J-C. Martin, *La Vendée et la France,* (Paris, 1987) p. 335.

22 Woloch, *New Regime,* p. 390. Tulard, *Napoleon,* p. 225.

23 Schroeder, *Transformation,* p. 233.

24 On the Kingdom of Italy: A. Grab, 'Army, state and society: conscription and desertion in Napoleonic Italy (1803–1814)', *Journal of Modern History,* 67 (1995) pp. 25–54, 50. On the Pyrénées Orientales: M. Brunet, *Le Roussillon. Une société contre l'Etat, 1780–1820,* (Toulouse, 1986) pp. 307–21.

25 See the map and figures in Forrest, *Conscripts and Deserters,* p. 88.

26 Holtman, *Napoleonic Revolution,* p. 87. *Almanach National,* 1802.

27 G. Lewis, *The Second Vendée. The Continuity of Counter–revolution in the Department of the Gard, 1789–1815,* (Oxford, 1978) pp. 114, 117.

28 On the Var: M. Agulhon, *La Vie Sociale en Provence Intérieure au lendemain de*

la Révolution, (Paris, 1970) pp. 369–404. On Piedmont, M. Broers, 'Policing Piedmont, 1797–1821', *Criminal Justice History*, 16 (1994) pp. 1–47.

29 Brunet, *Le Roussillon*. P. Sahlins, *Forest Rites. The War of the Demoiselles in Nineteenth Century France*, (Cambridge, MA, 1994) pp. 20–1. A. Forrest, *Deserteurs et Insoumis sous la Révolution et l'Empire*, (Paris, 1988) pp. 214, 226, 239–41.

30 I. Woloch, 'Napoleonic conscription, state power and society', *Past and Present*, 111 (1986) pp. 101–29.

31 Woloch, 'Napoleonic conscription', pp. 120–1.

32 L. Antonielli, *I Prefetti dell'Italia Napoleonica*, (Milan, 1983), p. 456.

33 On Piedmont: M.G. Broers, 'The restoration of order in Napoleonic Piedmont, 1796–1814', (Unpubl. D.Phil. thesis, Oxford, 1986). On the Kingdom of Italy: Antonielli, *Prefetti*. On the Pyrénées Orientales: Brunet, *Le Roussillon*, pp. 297–321. On France as a whole: Forrest, *Déserteurs et Insoumis*, especially Chapter 9.

34 Woloch, *New Regime*, pp. 218–19.

35 Sheehan, *German History*, p. 261.

36 L.E. Lee, 'Baden between revolutions: state-building and citizenship, 1800–1848', *Central European History*, 24 (1991) pp. 248–67.

37 D. Moran, *Toward the Century of Words: Johann Cotta and the Politics of the Public Realm in Germany, 1795–1832*, (Berkeley, CA, 1990) p. 73.

38 C. Anderson, 'State-building in early nineteenth century Nassau', *Central European History*, 24 (1991) pp. 222–47.

39 Woloch, 'Napoleonic conscription', p. 122.

40 Cited in S. Schama, *Patriots and Liberators, Revolution in the Netherlands, 1780–1803*, (New York, 1977) p. 356.

41 Archives Nationales de Paris, BB(5) (Organisation Judiciaire, Cour de Turin) 304, Jourde to the Minister of Justice, 29 messidor, Year IX/18 July 1801.

42 Cited in Sheehan, *German History*, p. 356. Also cited in K. Epstein, *The Genesis of German Conservatism*, (Princeton, NJ, 1966) p. 607.

43 Cited in C. Zaghi, *Potere, Chiesa e Società, studi e ricerche sull'Italia giacobina e napoleonica*, (Naples, 1984) p. 527.

44 M. Dunan, *Napoléon et l'Allemagne, le systeme continental et les debuts du Royaume de Baviere, 1806–1810*, (Paris, 1942) p. 100.

45 See for example, the definition of its economic connotations by F. Furet, 'Feudal system', in *A Critical Dictionary of the French Revolution*, (Eng. trans., Cambridge, MA, and London, 1989) eds. F. Furet and M. Ozouf, p. 687.

46 Cited in J.J. Gagliardo, *Reich and Nation*, (Bloomington, and London, 1980) p. 230.

47 Cited in Anderson, 'State-building in early nineteenth century Nassau', p. 235.

48 Cited in A. Valente, *Gioacchino Murat e l'Italia meridionale*, (Turin, 1965) p. 278.

49 Cited in P. Villani, *Mezzogiorno tra riforme e rivoluzione*, (Rome and Bari, 1973), p. 209.

50 Cited in C. Schmidt, *Le Grand Duché de Berg (1806–1813)*, (Paris, 1905) p. 184.

51 Schmidt, *Berg*, pp. 195–6.

52 The major works by these historians dealing with the Continental System are: Ellis, *Napoleon's Continental Blockade*; Bergeron, *France under Napoleon*. Francois Crouzet has written copiously on this topic; his major contribution in English is: 'Wars, blockade and economic change in Europe, 1792–1813', *Journal of Economic History*, 24 (1964). His seminal work is *L'Economie Britannique et le Blocus Continental*, (Paris, 1987 edn).

53 Ellis, *Napoleonic Empire*, p. 96.

54 Bergeron, *France under Napoleon*, p. 173.

|3|

Collaboration and resistance: the Napoleonic state and the people of western Europe, 1799–1808

The nationalist historians of the last century were among the most successful myth-makers of all time, so much so that three generations later, even the most historically aware modern European can slip all too easily into their carefully crafted belief that the natural political order of the continent is that of nation-states, and that this has always been the case, regardless of whether they actually existed as organized polities or not. In this view of European history, the dynastic states of the *ancien régime* appear as artificial, intrinsically flawed creations, propped up only by the cynical diplomacy of eighteenth-century statecraft.

Napoleon was under no such illusions; neither was he deluded into thinking the peoples of Europe would automatically thank him for overthrowing their rulers, in contrast to the diplomatic 'Never-neverland' inhabited by the first French revolutionaries. Napoleon saw that although the small states of Italy and Germany may have become unviable in the new international climate, they were not often unpopular with the majority of their subjects. Nor were they the artificial creations of recent diplomacy. The Wittelsbach dynasty in Bavaria and the House of Savoy in Piedmont-Savoy were among the oldest in Europe; together with the House of Orange in the Dutch Republic, they enjoyed a sense of loyalty from their peoples – at least among the popular classes – as genuine and intense as that commanded by any later nation-state. This was equally true of the many, unfairly despised 'postage stamp states' of the Holy Roman Empire. The Archbishop-Elector of Mainz, for example, was highly regarded by the mass of the people, and was welcomed back ecstatically during his brief restoration in 1793. Indeed, the Holy Roman Empire itself still commanded a great deal of affection among many of its subjects. Hindsight occludes the hopes raised among many contemporaries that the changes imposed by Napoleon in 1803 could actually provide a more rational basis for prolonging the life of the Empire and making it better able to survive effectively in the new international climate. To many at the time, the hope – if not always the expectation – was that 1803 was a new beginning for the old order, not the beginning of the end, as it actually proved to be in 1806.

Territorial integrity was more common among the Italian states than the German ones. Ruling dynasties had come and gone in the Kingdom of Naples and in Tuscany, but they had survived for centuries as political units by the time of the Napoleonic wars, as had the Duchy of Milan, which became the core of the Italian Republic. The Papal States and the two maritime republics of Genoa and Venice were probably the oldest surviving states in Europe by the end of the eighteenth century; the essential forms of their political orders had remained in place for a millennium.

Napoleon may have toppled all of this, but he had a healthy respect for it, as was evident in his initial reluctance to depose dynasties like the House of Savoy. The most obvious evidence of this respect is the aping of its outward trappings – the panoply of the Imperial Court, the titles and, more significantly, the decision to establish a hereditary dynasty of his own. However, outside France this was not the most important aspect of his quest for stability. Inside France, Napoleon found a heritage of revolutionary instability conveniently set between his regime and a thousand-year history of monarchy. His clarity of mind in the non-French territories was to face the fact that circumstances there were different. He himself had swept away the legitimate order of things and he knew he could not draw on the concept of legitimacy as a basis for his rule. Accordingly, legitimate government was to be replaced by efficient, rational, enlightened government.

Westphalia was arguably the most artificial of the Napoleonic states, but it was also meant to be the most advanced, successful and enlightened. This was no coincidence; Westphalia was there to prove, conclusively, that efficient, modern government was better than legitimate government. Napoleonic rule was to be an alternative to the old order, not a straight replacement for it, which amounted to an admission of its limitations, as well as an assertion of confidence in the 'civilizing mission'. There was no point in aspiring to anything but support built on utilitarian, pragmatic successes. As Napoleon told Jerome on ascending his throne in 1807, 'this way of governing will be a more powerful barrier between you and Prussia than fortresses or French protection'. Napoleon spoke from a knowledge tempered by eight years of state-building, from experience acquired in the creation of the inner empire. Old loyalties died hard, be they to great powers or to the pettiest of the Imperial Knights; this lesson – at long last – had been learned.

However, even the chosen remedy held within it the seeds of discord. Napoleon's definition of 'good government' reveals a different lesson still unheeded: the assumption that the peoples of western Europe wanted a more effective, modern state to govern them. This assumed not only that they would welcome specifically French reforms, but that they wanted reforms at all. 'Moral conquest' was still conquest.

The French reforms met with collaboration and resistance, both of which took many forms. Most groups and individuals moved uneasily between these extremes. Perhaps an essential, defining characteristic of the lands which became the 'inner empire' (those acquired up to 1807) was that the balance slowly – and usually grudgingly – tipped away from resistance, towards collaboration. The consolidation of Napoleonic rule was a turbulent process, and the initial response it met with among the vast majority of people was resistance.

Resistance

Only a few months before the coup of Brumaire in 1799, the new regime had a foretaste of how deeply the people of western Europe had come to hate the French, the conduct of their armies, their revolutionary ideas and, perhaps the most chilling thing for the future empire-builders, those native 'Jacobins' – more correctly called republicans or patriots – who had collaborated with the French. In 1798, the Belgian departments and almost the whole of Italy had been the theatres of large, widespread counter-revolutionary risings, sparked by allied military successes. They were the culmination of several years of upheaval, caused in part by the transitory ravages of war – usually in the shape of the French armies – but also by a more complex reaction to the political, economic and religious reforms of the short-lived 'sister republics', which were imbued with the example of revolutionary France. The relative importance of the transitory and the more deep-rooted reasons behind the revolts is complex, but the Napoleonic officials who returned to rule these populations had to hope their major cause had been the former, not the latter. However, close examination of Napoleonic rule in its initial phase reveals a picture of an unremitting detestation for the French and their revolution, in roughly equal measure.

Revolt

By definition, the lands first brought under Napoleonic control bordered on France. On one level, this appears little more than a simplistic platitude, but borders are complex areas; the ravages of war and invasion surge around them – and break over them – like waves against shorelines. Few borders in history have been as relentlessly, savagely contested as those around France in the seventeenth and eighteenth centuries. This ugly process had left a particular mark on its otherwise varied peoples; they had developed a traditional hatred of the French which had little, if anything, to do with the French Revolution. To the border communities of the Low Countries, the Rhineland, Piedmont and Catalonia, the campaigns of the 1790s were the latest round in what they saw as a primordial conflict with their large, looming and pitiless neighbour. Consequently, the revolutionary wars reawakened a whole host of atavistic hatreds, fears and, above all, loyalties to their own rulers.

The French armies had no need to behave like a Mongol horde in these regions, because they were already perceived as such, their subsequent atrocities serving only to reaffirm their folk image. Seen through the eyes of those 'on the receiving end', there was nothing new in any of this. France – the greatest state in western Europe – had always posed the same threat. In the Rhenish Palatinate, the devastation caused by the troops of Louis XIV had become part of the collective memory of its people. An Irish traveller noted its persistence – and vivacity – as late as the 1790s:

> The particulars of that dismal scene have been transmitted from father to son, and are still spoken of with horror by the peasantry of this country, among whom the French nation is held in detestation to this day.[1]

The Piedmontese and Spanish governments channelled the residual hatreds of their border populations into irregular guerrilla forces – the Piedmontese *barbetti* and the Catalan *michelotis* – and larger provincial militias, all of which offered very effective opposition to the French long after formal hostilities had ceased. Their activities were as spontaneous as they were ferocious, making the Piedmontese Alps, especially, an area the French feared well after their annexation of the area.

Perhaps the greatest 'slap in the face' of all for the French was the massive revolt of the peasantry of the Belgian departments of 1798–99. The region's ingrained hatred of its habitual invader notwithstanding, these former Habsburg provinces had been under French rule intermittently since 1792, and continuously since 1795, circumstances which indicate that the experience of French administration – as opposed to French conquest – had not engendered assimilation, to put it mildly. Embodied in the Belgian uprising were the hallmarks of new resentments, as well as atavistic fears, in that it embraced revolts against the religious policies of the Directory, against the loss of municipal and provincial autonomy through the introduction of French administration and the enforcement of mass conscription, which triggered the initial outbreaks of violence in late 1798. A dread spectre raised its head out of the Belgian forests to haunt the minds of Napoleonic administrators in the years to come: even if the old hatreds could be eradicated and the old political allegiances abandoned through years of 'the wise and liberal administration' Napoleon urged on Jerome, it was more than possible that this same administration – by its very nature – would give rise to new, equally virulent resentments. The events of the immediate past yielded no comfort for the French reformers. Several parts of the inner empire – the then Austrian Netherlands, the Dutch Republic and Lombardy, as well as Tuscany which still lay outside the French Empire – had reacted against attempts at enlightened reforms in the course of the 1780s. The course of reform in Bavaria, Baden and Württemberg remained halting and uncertain in the face of ecclesiastical, noble and peasant opposition right up to 1805, when Napoleonic hegemony over the region was definitively confirmed. Added to this list must be the futile attempts of the Neapolitan Bourbons to humble the feudal baronage throughout the eighteenth century. The cumulative impression is of the tide of reform being rolled back defiantly in many of those places where the Napoleonic regime would soon be trying to revive it.

There were also parts of the 'inner empire' without any history of enlightened reform in the eighteenth century. These areas were often the ones that raised the greatest hopes in the minds of Napoleonic reformers; Berg and Westphalia were seen as virgin territory, perfect conditions for the kind of fresh start enlightened thinkers dreamed of. In the fiefdoms of the Imperial Knights and many of the small states of Italy and central Germany, the presence of government in local life had been less oppressive than non-existent. This was anathema to the Napoleonic administrators, and they ascribed the social and economic ills of these societies to the absence of strong government. Typical of this are the comments of a French official on the lawlessness and violence he found in the mountain communities of the Apennines, between Genoa and Parma, the capitals of two of the weakest, most unreformed states in Italy:

this country, without justice, without an administration, without policing, offered impunity to one and all; ordinary crimes multiplied endlessly.

The morality and customs of the inhabitants still lead them into vile vendettas, [which are] the general reason for all [the other] offenses.

The young peasant of this region is brought up to carry a knife at every important moment in his life. This knife becomes a decoration, a sign of valour [and] from this custom, naturally, comes the use of this vicious weapon, and attacks at every gathering, at the slightest provocation, are the lamentable result; [they] were never pursued under the old government or, at least, they remained unpunished; no example [was set].[2]

The Imperial Knights were given an equally bad press, for broadly similar reasons. Some of them were corrupt, idle and grasping, but, in common with the rest of the galaxy of weak states swallowed up by the early Napoleonic advances, they were incapable of making any consistent impact on the daily lives of the subjects. The French failed to grasp that the essential popularity of these states lay precisely in their weakness. Too small to play any part in international affairs, few of them had conscription or high levels of taxation. Imperial Knights offered their own swords and services to the larger German powers, but not those of their subjects, a role which would be reversed under Napoleonic rule. The 'mercenary state' of Hesse-Kassel was an exception to this general rule. Internally, most of these states were usually content with a minimum level of control, leaving local communities, particularly isolated rural areas, to their own devices. This left a mass of local customs and usages untouched, to a degree intolerable – and almost unimaginable until seen at first hand – by those tutored in the tradition of French absolutism, whether in its Bourbon or revolutionary guise.

Thus, it is hardly surprising that the French model of the state – containing as it did a wholly alien concept of civil society – met fierce initial resistance in equal measure from areas with no tradition of reform and those which had actively rejected it. The revolt in the former Duchy of Piacenza in 1805–06, referred to in the last chapter, shows this when approached from the rebels' perspective, rather than the state's. The people of the mountain valleys were among the least governed in western Europe before the French occupied the Duchies permanently in 1805 – 'in the midst of torrents and mountains . . . without communications to Parma and Piacenza . . . [and] still a long way from Civilization', as their French Administrator-General described them in 1806[3] – and what little there was had broken down during the war. The dukes collected only a few indirect taxes, but even this had ceased by 1803. Suddenly, in 1805, came French demands for taxes – and in new forms – together with orders to 'mobilize' the supposed members of the ramshackle local militia for service in Lombardy. The valley communities rose in revolt almost immediately against these unprecedented and therefore, to them, illegitimate demands. The calls to arms they issued, on entering the plain of the Po Valley, reveal their motives to have been to preserve their freedom not from French rule as such, but from any new form of state interference. These remote valleys had never been 'administered', nor did they intend to be. As has been seen, the revolt was crushed by the French – 'a government whose power they did not appreciate', as a French officer tellingly remarked[4] – but to those left to pick up the pieces, it was the initial, violent reaction that mattered most. They would have to live with the consequences – and the causes.

The mountain valleys put up stiff resistance not only because they had the Apennines to shield them, but because their communities were still tightly knit and imbued with just enough sense of collectivity to organize resistance, their profusion of private blood feuds notwithstanding. This same spirit emerged in the struggle against conscription, whether in the larger opposition still posed by more isolated communities, or at the level of the family, as shown by the enormous financial sacrifices peasants would make to buy replacements for sons or nephews. By recalling the collective character of their resistance, the attitudes of those subjected to conscription can best be glimpsed.

However successful conscription was on one level, it backfired on another, not simply because it was resisted, but because that resistance kept residual collective loyalties alive, in defiance of both the liberal individualism the Napoleonic regime had inherited from the Revolution, and the new national and imperial allegiances it was trying to establish. The continuous imposition of conscription, particularly in the closely knit rural communities where most of the people of Napoleonic Europe still lived, engendered more than a specific hatred of a particular policy or regime; it kept alive older patterns of allegiance and sharpened people's awareness of them, in direct opposition to the centralized, modern state.

Organized brigandage has many affinities with resistance to conscription; indeed, brigandage was often the direct result of attempts to avoid it. The other link between them is their mutual dependence on the collective goodwill of local communities to defy authority. This was just as true whether banditry was apolitical or had counter-revolutionary undertones, as it usually did in Calabria or Spain. Thus, when the new governments launched their determined campaigns against brigandage, they were, in part, another aspect of the struggle between the state and local collectivism. The French were genuinely successful only when they had patiently severed the links between the bandits and their communities. It was a protracted operation which usually ended with the bands being forced into doing the unthinkable, turning on people within their own areas. Significantly, examples of this kind of success came mainly from the Rhineland, Piedmontese and Belgian departments, and from the Italian Republic, the true core of the Empire beyond France, where there was enough time for these tactics to work. Even here, it must be remembered that although the most deeply entrenched bands were beaten, looser groups of deserters and *réfractaires* remained throughout the inner empire. Pacification seldom brought the regime the kind of support its other policies strove for. Moreover, there were more forms of resistance other than armed rebellion.

Passive resistance: the defence of cultural freedom

THE EMOTIONAL AND INTELLECTUAL CLIMATE, 1799–1807

It is ironic that the more violent and overt the resistance they faced, the easier the French found it to deal with, at least until 1808. It was a ruthless, straightforward job for which the experience of their own internal counter-revolution had prepared them well; they often referred to revolts in this period as 'little Vendées'. The subtle forms of resistance proved more elusive for them; less menacing in their manifestations than the peasant revolts, but often no less dramatic, they were taken seriously by all involved, and with good reason. The French had a deliberate policy of cultural imperialism and those who opposed it soon developed strategies to preserve their indigenous cultures from modernization, standardization, or both. They had one vital attitude in common, their commitment to diversity notwithstanding: for all of them, Napoleon was the heir of the Revolution, before all else.

The major outlines of the French policy of cultural imperialism emerged most clearly in the introduction of the Concordat and the Code Napoleon, but once the structures of the Napoleonic administrative system were in place, it imbued a wide range of the state's activities from education to municipal improvement, with an ethos of the crusade of Gallic reason against Gothic or Jesuit obscurantism. It provoked a wide variety of adverse responses, but a pattern emerges when related, first, to different social classes within society, and then, to the political experience of individual states under the *ancien régime*.

Armed revolt was dominated by the popular classes, but it depended on the collective support of whole communities. Revolts were often led by members of local elites – priests, small landowners, lawyers and local officials – but many forms of passive resistance were marked more often by class and cultural differences. Popular resistance turned on the defence of popular culture which, however difficult to generalize about in detail, usually centred around Catholic religious practice. The French reformers had no doubts about what they were trying to eradicate. Thus, popular resentment usually stemmed from the introduction of the Concordat and pitted itself against French attempts to standardize cultural life and modernize society or, put in their terms, to enlighten it.

Elite resistance was more diversified, in the sense that it divides more clearly into what might be termed reactionary and liberal wings and, increasingly, it also came to include radical, pro-French patriots of the revolutionary period who had been alienated by Napoleon. The key to the reactionary and progressive responses lies in the character of the *ancien régime* states. Reactionary opponents of Napoleonic rule were drawn from those sections of the ruling classes who opposed all modernizing reforms. In common with the elements of the popular classes who resisted the new model of the state, the feudal barons of northern Germany and the Kingdom of Naples, or the Imperial Knights and the elites of the Free Cities of the Holy Roman Empire supported the status quo precisely because it was based on a weak, archaic state. Their whole existence depended exactly on a political culture rooted in corporatism which the Napoleonic state meant to annihilate. The 'weak state' found many learned defenders in the great universities of the Holy Roman Empire in its last days. Prominent among them was Christian Weisse, a professor at Leipzig, who challenged directly the concept that a state should be judged on its ability to resist other states. For Weisse, its *raison d'être* was the preservation of civic freedom, something best achieved in the small, weak states of the Holy Roman Empire. His argument gained a wide appeal in the years of Napoleonic hegemony.

In contrast to this, there were other political elites who felt their states to be more advanced, more enlightened than anything the French had to offer them. What makes them identifiable as a distinct group is the conscious air of cultural superiority they exhibited in the face of Napoleonic rule, their confidence in their higher level of enlightenment. However, even within this group, there are striking differences – and seeming contradictions – which arise from the rich diversity of the political world of the *ancien régime*, especially when it was confronted with the 'universal model' of the state being exported by Napoleon. It embraced most of the political classes of the Dutch Republic, elements of the Piedmontese aristocracy and many intellectuals throughout the Holy Roman Empire, particularly in the small Protestant states and the more liberal prince-bishoprics, such as Mainz. Beyond the confines of the Napoleonic state system, this attitude was also reflected in the outlook of William Pitt the Younger, the British Prime Minister, who had a record of moderate reform despite his opposition to revolutionary France. It also characterized the mainstream of the Prussian bureaucracy, until the crushing military defeats of 1806. These strands of enlightened opposition to the tenor of French reform formed 'the conservative enlightenment', rooted as they were in pre-revolutionary reforming traditions. If so complex a category can have a thinker who is representative of it, it is probably Edmund Burke, a Whig who had supported the American revolutionaries against England, but after 1789 was driven to conservatism by the violence of the Revolution.

If the peoples on the frontiers of France had their special, atavistic view of the likely consequences of French rule, the rest of western Europe had been subjected to a strident campaign of anti-revolutionary propaganda before 1799 and had often experienced direct French occupation as well. At this point, the pro-French patriots divided from the reformers of the conservative enlightenment; the patriots were those still loyal not just to the French, but to the ideology of the Revolution. The French Revolution received 'saturation coverage' throughout the states Napoleon would later bring under his sway; that coverage ranged from the ecstatic to the terror-crazed, but there is little doubt that the 'bad press' gained a considerably wider audience among contemporaries than the 'good one'. The main reason for this was the course of the Revolution itself. As the early hopes of 1789 gave way first to the war and then the Terror, even many journals of liberal sympathies turned from outright – if usually cautious – support, to apprehension and then horror. This was the process that forged the 'conservative enlightenment', and prepared it to be a source of opposition to the Napoleonic regime in the years ahead.

The responses of Goethe to events in France are probably representative of the majority of the German intelligentsia. As an administrator in the service of the Duke of Weimar, Goethe saw the value of enlightened reform to the extent that he felt little sympathy for the fate of the French monarchy, but saw little to hope for in the popular violence that surrounded these events. In his *Venetian Epigrams* written in 1790, Goethe expressed a fear

of the Revolution, together with a belief in reform from above, to prevent
the spread of anarchy:

'Those men are mad' you will say, when we hear the
impassioned hysterics
Declaiming in the streets and squares of France.
They are madmen to me, as well; but
the free fool can talk sense,
While the learned, if oppressed, can
remain but silent.

Goethe never underestimated the power of the Revolution, especially after
he had witnessed the French victory at Valmy in 1792, but by the advent
of Napoleonic rule, its failings had come to obsess him. On both a personal
and a cultural level, he shuddered at the fate of Italy, a deep source of his
own creativity, during the French invasion of 1796. Goethe is probably exceptional in his ability to imbue a deeply personal response to public events
with a sense of historical destiny, but he was probably typical enough of
his milieu in the words he wrote to his friend, the poet Schiller, also in 1796:
'The French tempest is reaching the Thuringian forest. In future, we will
venerate the hills, which usually send us cold winds, as a goddess if they
break the storm.'[5] This was the cast of the greatest mind of the age, when
that wind blew his little court and country away by 1806 – and Napoleon
straight to his own doorstep.

A similar attitude emerges in the journals which flourished in many
Italian cities in the 1780s and 1790s. Most Italian journals were progressive in their views, catering for an enlightened, urban readership. Consequently, they were largely favourable to the Revolution until 1791; what
destroyed this was the flight of the King to Varennes. If reform could no
longer come from above, it was obvious that its desirable limits had been
exceeded; the outbreak of war and the execution of Louis XVI only served
to confirm this for them. Well before the French invasion of 1796 and its
privations, 'the Revolution had become a single block [for the Italian press],
to be condemned as a gigantic monstrosity'.[6]

If the educated classes were able to generate their own visions of hell,
the Church mobilized itself to provide one for the masses throughout the
length and breadth of Catholic Europe. The Church was an international
organization – the only one in Europe at the time – and when the French
revolutionaries crossed swords with it, the repercussions of their actions
spread far beyond France, and well in advance of their armies. From 1792
onwards, the pastoral letters of the Calabrian bishops, in the heel of Italy,
dwelt on both the need to oppose the atheistic ideas of the Revolution and
on loyalty to the King; anti-reformist clergy in Tuscany were equally active
and influential among the masses in these years, painting a similar picture
of blaspheming hordes, long before a French soldier ever set foot there.
Everywhere, preachers portrayed the French invasion as the Apocalypse.

The likening of the war with France to the crusades against the Moors touched atavistic passions as far away from the fighting as Andalusia. It worked, as testified by a traveller in Eifel, a remote part of Germany. As late as 1798,

> the population of this desolate corner, hidden away behind barren rocks, has hardly ever seen French soldiers during the entire course of the war. But they have been depicted as bandits and atheists, who plunder churches and drag pictures of Christ on the Cross through the mud, tied to their horses' tails.[7]

This psychological preparation outlasted the vicious conduct of the French armies, as it did the phase of mass resistance to them; it was bolstered, sustained and confirmed by the peacetime policy of the introduction of the Concordat, an occurrence which astounded the regime.

THE PASSIVE RESISTANCE OF THE MASSES: THE DEFENCE OF BAROQUE PIETY

The Napoleonic regime sought to dispel the fears inherited from the 1790s about the anticlerical nature of the Revolution, and Napoleonic officials, particularly French ones, might be forgiven their optimism over the introduction of the Concordat as a potential source of reconciliation and reconstruction, as it had shown useful results within France and in the Belgian and Rhineland departments, up to a point. In those areas subject to France before 1802, the terms of the Concordat permitted a restoration of sorts. However, to see this as a sign of its likely success elsewhere was to forget a crucial difference between the past histories of France and the rest of Europe, as regards the experience of the Revolution. The religious life of those areas invaded by the French had endured destruction, desecration and despoilment, but not a sustained official policy of de-Christianization of public life, as had happened in France with varying degrees of intensity between 1790 and 1799. In these circumstances, the enforcement of the Concordat in Italy and Germany beyond the Rhineland did not imply a qualified deliverance from the worst excesses of the Revolution, but the exact opposite, a dreaded, all too predictable confirmation of the fears stirred up in the 1790s. Put bluntly, it backfired on the French.

There was a second source of false optimism abroad in the French bureaucracy, drawn from too official a reading of past history. The early revolutionaries had a selective view of the immediate past of western Europe, believing that peasant disturbances and the plots of a few radicals could be transformed into a mass revolution. Napoleonic bureaucrats were no less selective; it was just that they chose a different period to bolster their hope, that of enlightened reform, which had been equally disastrous. The French felt that the general reforms of the Concordat were in step with the recent work of Catholic reformers in the 1780s, such as the supporters of the Synod of Pistoia, who had sought to create a more spiritual, less worldly Church. In reality, these reformers had seen their plans brutally smashed against the rocks of violent popular resistance and their defeat assured the perpetuation of these aspects of popular religious and social life into the early nineteenth century. The terms of the French Concordat categorically condemned them all to extinction. The Concordat, then, appears a very inauspicious instrument for collaboration when put into its full historical perspective; its terms were utterly at odds with the society it now faced.

The role played by the Church in French society before the Revolution had been important, but vocations for the regular orders and the activities of lay organizations had been declining during the eighteenth century, which may point to the gradual emergence of a more secular society, although there were crucial exceptions in vast parts of the west and the Midi. In the Rhineland and Italy, even such tentative signs of change were absent, which meant that the terms of the Concordat ran against the cultural tide, not just too far ahead of it. Consequently, its introduction produced serious social disruption as well as cultural affront. If the centrality of the Church in the life of these regions needs to be stressed, it can be seen simply by the omnipresence of passive resistance to the French reforms in societies and settings otherwise so diverse. Resistance occurred in the great cities of Italy and the Rhineland, as well as in the remotest mountain hamlet. The Napoleonic state sought to be everywhere, but the Church – in one form or other – had got there first, and so the clash between them touched the lives of almost everyone in western Europe, but especially those of ordinary people. The regime made strenuous, if usually clumsy efforts to win the support of the bishops and parish priests – the only parts of the clergy it intended to retain – but failed to take into account the adverse effects of the rest of its policies on the laity.

There is a crucial difference in all of this between the Napoleonic state and its eighteenth-century predecessors. The Habsburgs, most of the south German rulers and the Neapolitan Bourbons had all indulged in bouts of secularization, while the policies developed by Joseph and Peter-Leopold were as radical and ruthless as the Concordat, but unlike the Napoleonic state, they had not been powerful enough to enforce them for long. Even in those areas where previous generations of rulers had enjoyed some success, this had always been because they were limited in scope. Many of Joseph II's reforms survived him, but they did not match those of the French. The new order saw things in more general terms; whereas the House of Savoy or the Wittelsbachs had contented themselves with seizing the odd abbey or shutting the occasional monastery, revolutionary and Napoleonic regimes destroyed almost all of them in the manner of Henry VIII.

Under the Concordat, the parish and the secular clergy were the only important elements of religious life. This was utterly at odds not only with the practices and structures the reformers found, but with the practical needs of southern Germany, the Rhineland and central and southern Italy, all areas which would feel the full force of the Concordat. There is strong evidence that popular religiosity had intensified in these regions in the course of the eighteenth century, even if it had not been made more orthodox. Not only had participation in religious life increased in forms usually abhorrent to enlightened, elite opinion, this renewed enthusiasm had been achieved by methods banned under the French reforms. Missions by regular orders to rural areas, especially, were central to this. A new order specifically devoted to this work, the Redemptorists, was created in the Kingdom of Naples in 1732 and got Papal approval in 1749. The dramatic sermons of its friars made an enormous impact in isolated rural areas and great cities alike. By 1784, the order was active in Germany and Poland as well. When the French struck at the very existence of the missions, it was not at all akin to closing a useless, almost empty monastery, but a powerful force at the grass-roots of ordinary life. Similarly, they had little understanding of the important role played by many regular clergy in supplementing the work of parish priests. In effect, the introduction of the Concordat into Italy and Germany disrupted ordinary religious life, even those aspects it sought to strengthen.

The regime had to live with popular reactions to the spectacular raids of its commissioners on the temporal possessions of the Church, just as when it tried to stamp out disorderly or superstitious practices, it ran straight into the same powerful resistance that had defeated eighteenth-century reformers. Shock and consternation followed the sudden, almost wholesale abolition of convents. The twin reactions of social disruption and cultural affront were both evident in popular reaction, as was tenacious, if peaceful, popular resistance. Even leaders of the Counter-Reformation as generally popular and successful as St Charles Borromeo, the great sixteenth-century Archbishop of Milan, had fought shy of reforming convents, for fear of provoking public opinion. Not so the authors – or executors – of the Napoleonic Concordat. The regime's efficiency when it came to closing convents and expelling their occupants was not matched by its ability to arrange pensions or alternative accommodation for their occupants. The result was a series of spectacles of suffering and distress, heightened because it concerned women, which probably did more to confirm the popular image of Napoleon as a bully and an ogre than all the high-brow fulminating of Madame de Staël or Chateaubriand in their writings. Some of the initial traumas were compounded by administrative bungling, especially as regards the payment of pensions, and were eventually resolved, but the first impressions were probably the lasting ones for public opinion – they were what people actually saw. When the regular orders were abolished, the monks and nuns were expected to return to their families, that is, to wherever they

had originally come from. Often this caused the nuns, in particular, considerable distress, which became public knowledge. An example from
northern Italy, drawn to Napoleon's attention by the Cardinal Archbishop
of Genoa, illustrates the many factors involved. When the Concordat was
introduced into the Piedmontese departments, many nuns were deported,
virtually penniless, to their families in Genoa, their place of origin. When
their relatives refused to take them back, or were found to be dead or
too aged themselves, many turned to begging in the streets. They were
still doing so, with considerable success, when the Concordat caught up
with them, as it were, when the French annexed Liguria in 1806.[8]

Nuns were also capable of subtle defiance. So adept were they at quietly
reassembling their communities in the Kingdom of Italy, that it was forbidden for them to live in groups of more than four, but these clandestine
convents were still finding shelter and support in Bologna as late as 1810.
As the prefect told his superiors in Milan:

> their reclusion was voluntary, their practice of retreat came from a
> sense of conversion... For these reasons they have received the not
> indifferent generosity of the townspeople, and have been given a
> house where twenty of them live.[9]

The example of the nuns poignantly pitted the strong against the weak,
with disastrous consequences for the image of the new regime. This was
not helped by the way the terms of the Concordat were enforced by local
officials marked by the radical politics of the 1790s, as in the Rhineland
departments, where prohibition of pilgrimages and many other external
symbols of religion was zealously enforced on sullen populations. The same
happened in Naples, with similar results. The abolition of the regular orders
'does not please the Neapolitans', as a French official put it, with marvel-
lous understatement.[10] This, of course, was when the regime could enforce
the Concordat. Defiance was easier, and more blatant, when it came to the
ban on the celebration of many religious holidays, as the exasperated
Minister of Religion (Cultes) told Napoleon in 1808, as part of a general
survey of the state of the Church:

> The priests read out the list of abolished holidays from the pulpit,
> they summon the people by the sound of the bells [and] they celebrate
> the rites with the same pomp... I have written to the bishops... that
> it is a mockery to announce the abolition of a holiday and then cele-
> brate it, right away, as if it had not been abolished.[11]

This kind of thing persisted at every level, and with such mass support that
even the most zealous local officials were too intimidated to intervene. In
1811, in the Ligurian town of Novi, an infuriated sub-prefect stood by
powerlessly as the populace celebrated the banned feast of their patron saint
for two whole days. All he could do was write an indignant letter to the
Archpriest, 'who answered me calmly'.[12]

This was the point where even a powerful state had to pull back, but there were many instances where it did not, with bloody consequences. In Pisa, in 1808, when the French stood by the outlawing of those passages in the traditional Easter lesson blaming the Jews for the death of Christ, there was trouble in the town throughout Holy Week which required the use of troops.[13] French officials dreaded Easter all over the Empire, as a time when feelings ran high and an essentially hostile Church reasserted its hold over the people. At few other moments did the gap between rulers and ruled appear so great. In open defiance, banned feasts and processions went ahead, usually with as much rowdiness as in the past and now, at times, with an added political colouring. Where armed resistance had failed, street parties prevailed. The corkscrew and the Cross often proved mightier than the alliance of the quill pen of the Enlightenment and the sword of the Grande Armée.

At times, ministers themselves had to back down, especially in the satellite states. In Naples, the otherwise aggressively anticlerical Minister of Justice, Ricciardi, simply did not circulate those articles of the Code Napoleon which allowed the civil marriage of priests, for example. All over the peninsula, the French laws on divorce were studiously ignored by landed families anxious about the disruption they might cause to carefully constructed marriage strategies. In this case, religious scruples went hand in hand with material interest.

The prospect of Jewish emancipation, promised by the Code, caused resentment everywhere. Napoleon himself was obliged to impose some restrictions on their civil rights in 1808, on grounds of public order: there was a dark side to the defence of popular piety, alongside the defiant desire to process, pray and revel as a community, in the open air. The Grand Duchy of Warsaw in 1808 suspended Jewish political emancipation for ten years, stating that Jews were not yet properly assimilated into society; this ban did not extend to those who converted to Catholicism. In Germany, the Jews gained full emancipation only in direct proportion to the degree of French control. It was most complete in the Rhenish departments under direct French rule, Berg and Westphalia. Many progressive measures were taken in Baden, but they did not grant full political equality. Bavaria did nothing at all until 1813. There is more than a little irony in the fact that the most active, successful and assimilated Jewish community in Germany between 1799 and 1806 was in Berlin, the capital of Prussia, a state with an older, more conservative tradition of reform.

When the Napoleonic regime was at its most enlightened, it met its fiercest internal, popular resistance, a truth soon to be reinforced by the peasant risings of 1808 in Spain and the popular reactions to the seizure of the Pope in 1809. Yet, if worse was still to come, it was already clear by 1807 that the reforms of the Concordat ran counter to the deepest values of the common popular culture of Catholic Europe, to the point that most Napoleonic officials did not recognize these practices as such, but as barbarous superstition, for this was how they described it. In 1798, a French official in the Rhineland spoke of processions, pilgrimages, statues, crosses and all 'external signs of religion' as 'standards of fanaticism', insisting on their prohibition.[14] Thirteen years later, by 1811, Napoleon called a national council of the Church, which enshrined this attitude in official ideology. Number 49 of its policy document, entitled 'Views on the organization of Catholic Worship' declared it the duty of the Church 'to lend a hand in the eradication of superstitious practices, these shameful leftovers of mediaeval barbarism'.[15] The Napoleonic Concordat brought to the surface all the tensions between elite and popular culture which had been building up throughout the eighteenth century. It placed the state, with all its new-found power, emphatically on the side of the elite culture engendered by the enlightenment, while increasingly it pushed the Church into the arms of popular culture. Above all, the impact of the reforms of the Concordat did nothing to resolve the conflict, only to sharpen it.

Withdrawal: intellectual resistance – from the conservative enlightenment to Romanticism

A large segment of the propertied classes had opposed enlightened reform during the *ancien régime*, on both material and ideological grounds, and they renewed their intransigence under Napoleonic rule, a sound reason for seeing Napoleon as 'the last of the enlightened despots'. These men had been able to pose a considerable threat to the French before their military control was assured, because these reactionary elements could find common ground with popular sources of resistance and provide leadership for them. This happened in Italy and the Belgian departments in 1798–99 and would happen again, in Spain and southern Italy, after 1808. However, at the height of Napoleonic rule, roughly from 1802 to 1807, most gave up active resistance and retired to their estates, a sign in itself of consolidation. At the apogee of Napoleonic domination, between 1806 and 1808, a few collaborated with the regime in a half-hearted way, but most of those who could not afford exile remained as aloof as humanly possible from the new order.

Their numbers included most of the feudal barons of Naples and the petty German states, or Polish noblemen who disliked their loss of control over their peasants and looked enviously across the new border at unreformed Russia. The great nobles of Bavaria and Württemberg fought a particularly spirited – and fairly successful – rearguard action against reform throughout the period. The reforms of the Concordat offended the piety of many within the propertied classes; this was particularly marked among women. If they did not exhibit the exuberant defiance of artisans and peasants, noble houses of this stamp gave refuge and patronage to ex-monks and friars as tutors and private chaplains. Their conspicuous presence at masses held on suppressed saints' days or conducted by anti-government clergy was a constant source of irritation to the authorities. Dynastic loyalties also played a crucial role in determining their attitudes, a scruple they had in common with many less reactionary opponents of Napoleonic rule. The career of the Piedmontese noble Thaon di Revel is a case in point. Thaon spent almost the whole 14 years of French rule on his estates, steadfastly refusing office under the new regime. Although his loyalty to the exiled House of Savoy was unswerving, his disdain for the French was based on ideological grounds, as well as purely dynastic attachments, borne out by his reactionary conduct as Chief Minister during the brief restoration of 1799 and after the collapse of French rule in 1814, when he again played a large part in a deeply reactionary government.

Reactionary nobles became stock hate figures for the liberal Romantic writers of the early nineteenth century, epitomized by the gloom-laden, tight-fisted Marchese di Dongo in Stendhal's novel, *The Charterhouse of Parma*, who 'professed a vigorous hatred for the enlightenment: these are the ideas, he said, which lost Italy'. Their conspicuous absence from government was an embarrassment for the French, but one which they had come to expect after the experience of emigration in France before 1790. When pushed too far, the French could resort to considerable coercion against such opposition, as when several noble officers of the Hessian army were imprisoned, in 1807, until they agreed to take service with the French. In the main, however, great efforts were made to placate even the most reactionary among them, but they were not the most serious source of opposition within the nobility or the educated classes as a whole.

The real problem for the new governments was less that the inveterate opponents of enlightened reform did not change their spots, but that many who did see themselves as enlightened and progressive also refused to join them, either from a belief that their societies had no need of French-style reform, or a sense of dynastic loyalty, or a mixture of both. This was the resistance of the conservative enlightenment, whose reservations about the new French order were already acute before Napoleonic rule.

They formulated a complex but emphatic rejection of the Napoleonic vision of the state and society. Many enlightened reformers, particularly in the Netherlands and Germany, did not necessarily believe that the rational reform of society needed to be carried out by a large, powerful, centralized state or, at least, not one developed to the degree of the Napoleonic state; they were satisfied with the progress being made within the existing structures. Humbolt propounded a plea for states based on less government, rather than more, in a corpus of work devoted to devising a political order in harmony with the ideals of the '*Bildung*'.The small prince-bishoprics of the Rhineland or semi-autonomous Dutch towns were ideal vehicles for progress. When these polities were swept away, they took no interest in the new political order. A second area of difference, often tightly bound up with the first, arose where an influential, sophisticated tradition of reform predated French domination, and found many aspects of the Napoleonic model incompatible with it, as in the Kingdom of Naples and in Piedmont, and, to a degree, in the Netherlands, all states where dynastic loyalties were particularly fierce throughout society.

Finally, there is a phenomenon which stands at a crossroads in European cultural life, between the conservative enlightenment and Romanticism. Its very association with Romanticism makes this intellectual current extremely varied, but it carried with it some of the finest minds of the era: Goethe, the Schlegels and Herder, in Germany; Alfieri in Italy. The direction they were carried in was a course they had already set out on: the supremacy of personal, moral preoccupations over public life, a set of priorities which the unambitious status quo of the old, petty states had allowed them to pursue, but that the new order would not. While the first two currents of thought – the reactionaries and the men of the conservative enlightenment – tended to look back to pre-revolutionary political models, the third looked away less in apathetic incomprehension, but in disgusted conscious rejection. Turning one's back on politics was a very political gesture, indeed, as those who did so were well aware.

Just as the *ancien régime* had been good to the reactionary sectors of the elite because they embodied its politics and controlled its economy, so had many enlightened thinkers, both materially through patronage or state employment, and intellectually – spiritually, as many of them put it – because they had been left alone, if not under one state, then in another. Such circumstances, now vanished, made all these groups little inclined to rally to the new order. Ultimately, their reformist ideas were rooted in particular dynastic loyalties, cultural traditions or spiritual hopes that overrode any similarities between older concepts of state-building, such as German Cameralism or Piedmontese absolutism, and the Napoleonic model.

The most extreme sign of this reluctance to collaborate was emigration, a phenomenon that preoccupied the Consulat enough to include stiff terms in its amnesty of 1802, which threatened to confiscate the estates of those who refused to return; Jerome did this again, in Westphalia, in 1807. Emigration had included enlightened reformers from the very start of the Revolution; the last reforming ministers of the French monarchy in the 1780s, Calonne, Necker and Brienne, were notable among them. The trend abated under the Consulat, but it did not end, as personified by Napoleon's most vociferous opponent, Madame de Staël, who, as Necker's daughter, stood in a family tradition of enlightened reform, as well as an intellectual one. Emigration also expanded its ranks to embrace several enlightened reformers from the foreign states now under French rule. Prominent among them was the Polish nobleman, Czartoryski, the tsarist Foreign Minister between 1803 and 1806, who was deeply committed to the cause of reform of the

Russian Empire's institutions, and to autonomy for Poland within a reformed Russia. Alexander I dismissed him from office amid great acrimony in 1806, ruthlessly abandoning Czartoryski's hopes for a Polish state, as the price of a Prussian alliance. His disgrace coincided with the first intimations that Napoleon might himself create a Polish state, but Czartoryski drafted a paper for his former master, entitled 'On the necessity of restoring Poland to forestall Bonaparte'. Nor did he rally after the Grand Duchy of Warsaw became a reality, despite his long-standing belief in the need for political and administrative changes very like those taking place in the new satellite kingdom. Although betrayed by St Petersburg, this disciple of Montesquieu steadfastly refused to collaborate, seeing in Napoleon only a tyrant.

Earlier in the period, Napoleon had encountered similar reticence among a group of reformers he had a particular admiration for, the military-technocrats of the Piedmontese aristocracy. The late 1770s and 1780s had seen the emergence of a generation of young nobles within the officer corps, many trained in Prussia and with a great admiration for Frederick the Great. Their general attitude to reform of the state had much in common with Napoleonic ideas, but the loss of independence and a powerful tradition of dynastic loyalty kept most of them deeply estranged from Napoleon. Their opponents within the Savoyard state in its last years were reformers of a different kind, more enlightened than absolutist in outlook, but with an equally proud tradition of service to the House of Savoy, particularly in the higher ranks of the judiciary and the civil administration. There were those among them who would slowly develop an association with the Napoleonic regime, notably Prospero Balbo, but there were just as many who rebuffed concerted attempts by Napoleon to reconcile them. Clemente di Priocca was an enlightened reformer 'who got away'. Priocca was the last Savoyard Foreign Minister before the fall of the monarchy in 1797. Appointed in desperate circumstances, he strove to win the King over to an alliance with France as a means of saving independence and the cause of reform but, not unlike the experience of Czartoryski, he saw his policies betrayed by his own sovereign. Nevertheless, he followed the Court into exile in Tuscany, where he lived until his death in 1813, in considerable poverty, his estates having been confiscated under the terms of the amnesty. The French even made a second attempt to recruit him when they annexed Tuscany in 1809, but to no avail.

Another Piedmontese who felt himself more enlightened than the French was Galeani Napione, a thoroughgoing liberal reformer in the last years of the *ancien régime*, whose 'salon' became a centre of liberal thought and subtly restrained cultural resistance to French 'homogenization' throughout the years of Napoleonic rule. Napione consciously abandoned active politics, shifting to deliberate cultural resistance through the study of Piedmontese history and Italian literature. His circle of young noblemen never discussed politics directly, but it was never far from the surface. In common with pious peasants and their priests, these aristocratic intellectuals gathered around Napione ostentatiously refused to celebrate official marriages, birthdays or French victories. Even at the height of the Empire, this kind of opposition mattered to the French, not because it posed a threat – indeed, the regime was remarkably lenient to these men – but because of its source. These were exactly the men who the French felt had every reason to be with them. They found considerably more of the same when they entered Spain in 1808. Liberal ideas devoid of absolutist politics linked, somewhat paradoxically, to powerful dynastic loyalties, were a potent combination for stubborn resistance. A French official, speaking in a Piedmontese context, dubbed this attitude 'an invisible apathy'.[16]

Even when Italian intellectuals chose the path of cultural resistance it was always as a second best, a substitute for direct political action, imposed by circumstances. However, the leading minds of German cultural tradition sought something quite different from anything, political or otherwise, the French Revolution had to offer them. This is not to deny their engagement with politics, which was very real, but it had a character all its own. Politics, as the French and Italians understood it, was something the German intellectuals had thrust upon them; their rejection of it was a powerful gesture of resistance.

Intellectuals such as Goethe and Schiller believed that a reform of society depended not on political or administrative reform – nor on institutional change of any kind – but on moral reform, achieved by cultural means, centred on the individual. These concepts had very deep roots in the Protestant culture of northern Germany and, although many German intellectuals were distracted from it in their early enthusiasm for the Revolution, it was quick to reassert itself as the dominant current when disillusion set in. Most of them had rallied to the defence of the Holy Roman Empire in its death throes between 1803 and 1806. Goethe, usually so atypical in his subtle approach to life, was fairly representative of the intelligentsia in this respect, at this time, in his belief that the old, ramshackle constitution had its merits, specifically because its weakness permitted the intellectual – and the individual intent on moral reform – enough freedom and peace to lead his own life, within the context of a well-ordered state. Similarly, most doubted that the Code Napoleon, and the whole social system it embodied, could take root in so alien a culture. It was not by chance that, between 1802 and 1806, many German intellectuals joined Goethe in Saxe-Weimar and the other tiny duchies clustered around the western borders of Prussia. They were taking refuge in the only states which still bore some resemblance to those aspects of the old order they depended on. Here, as Goethe put it, they clung to their last hope, that these little states would be forgotten about, and their last firm belief, that Prussia was still too strong for France. They were wrong on both counts.

The crushing French victories of Jena and Auerstadt had repercussions far beyond the purely military, throughout Europe. In many cases the shattering of the myth of Prussian invincibility began a shift from passive resistance to reluctant collaboration, as will be discussed below. However, the most common reaction within the German intelligentsia was to reassert the necessity of a withdrawal from public life, into the unsullied, edifying realms of high culture. As Goethe put it, Germany's emphatic political decline, sealed by the defeat of Prussia, had to be compensated by a cultural grandeur; its very weakness made Weimar the ideal cultural capital. Ultimately, in 1806, the defence of German culture, and the preservation of the specifically spiritual German approach to reform – *Bildung* as it came to be known – was more important than politics. *Bildung* was not a substitute for political action, it was an alternative vision of life. Goethe's three meetings with Napoleon in late 1808, at Erfurt and Weimar, encapsulated this reaction. He emerged from them with a profound respect for Napoleon, and with a lasting fascination for the forces that produced him – which must be touched on again, in another context – but also with a deepened awareness that the only way to confront the gap between them was further withdrawal. Goethe's implicit reply to Napoleon's parting assertion that 'politics is our destiny', was 'no'; it is emblematic of the collective response of the new generation of intellectuals, German and non-German, who would lead the Romantic movement. This rejection was all the more striking because Napoleon had a high regard for German literature. He requested the meeting with Goethe because he admired his work and he was aware that, in Germany, the French faced an elite culture at least the equal in sophistication to their own. For this reason, he sought to persuade Goethe to write for the Imperial Court in Paris. Napoleon sensed the importance of academics and intellectuals in German public life and, therefore, he tried to recruit the most influential of them all to lend him active support.

Few of his French servants in Germany shared Napoleon's enthusiasm for German high culture, but those who had to contend with it often developed a grudging respect for its complexity. In contrast to the use of literature and music as a means of withdrawal, the jurisprudence of the great universities became a powerful weapon at the disposal of the feudal baronage in its rearguard actions against the introduction of the Code Napoleon. Beugnot snarled that 'They write about the law more than they understand it', but he saw that the German legists were both respected and clever enough to stultify and emasculate the Code under the sheer weight of their erudition.[17] The great legal schools of northern Germany were the mainstays of an unreformed order, but one which – unlike either Bourbon or Revolutionary France – looked after its intelligentsia. 'The clerisy', as it was known, was nurtured and employed within the universities, bureaucracies and the established Protestant churches of the states of the old order. Thus, the intellectual establishment of northern, Protestant Germany tended to side with the old order against the new.

The intellectual life of the German and Italian states had been turbulent before the French Revolution, and they had their share of renegades.

However, it is important to remember that the greatest minds who had rebelled against the *ancien régime* – Alfieri in Piedmont or Schiller in Württemburg – did so in response to authoritarian, assertive regimes. Schiller and Alfieri soon took refuge in the weakest, most tolerant states they could find in the vicinity, and proceeded to turn their backs on conventional politics. Among such rebels, the ground was not propitious for the Napoleonic state to win adherents, and there is a certain irony in this. Later in the nineteenth century, many artists and writers – mainly, but not entirely French – would remake Napoleon as a symbol of Romanticism, but the leading contemporary exponents of the movement, however fragmented and contradictory in other ways, drew identity and inspiration from a determined rejection of the values of official, exultantly neo-classical French culture, that is, of the cultural models Napoleon fostered and tried to foist on them.

The resistance of the radicals

The radicals of the 1790s occupy a peculiar place in the pattern of resistance to Napoleonic rule. They were a weak, usually isolated minority almost everywhere, something their own militants admitted, themselves; yet there is no doubt that the moderate conservatives in power after 1800 – Melzi and Schimmelpenninck, for example – feared them to the point of paranoia and persecution. Attempts to resolve this paradox have not been helped by generations of left-wing historians who have been determined to place them at the centre of resistance to the new, authoritarian order after 1799[18] – when their true importance as a force for radical reform actually came through collaboration with the regime, at local level.

Contemporary fear of the 'Jacobins' – to use the scareword of the day rather than the more accurate 'patriot', 'radical' or 'republican' – was rooted in fears that they would be able to exploit the extensive agrarian unrest prevalent in western Europe in the 1790s. It was a fear utterly without foundation; nowhere outside France did the peasantry rise against the old order, only for it. It was widespread and deeply felt, although faded after the reimposition of French control after 1800, even if it never really subsided. The real source of fear, for men like Melzi or the restored Dutch politicians, in the first years of Napoleonic rule, was that these 'Jacobin' elements had been prominent in the governments of the short-lived 'sister republics' of the 1790s. The radical cliques had a practical experience of politics and administration as well as conspiratorial tendencies which, it was feared, would be used to unseat the new regimes. This threat was much more real than any prospect of popular revolts led by the radicals, who had been the chief targets of the mass counter-revolutionary risings of the late 1790s.

Added to their conspiratorial acumen, the radicals had another worrying characteristic: their wide, diffuse territorial distribution, which proved a real source of strength throughout the years of Napoleonic rule, first as opponents and then as collaborators. Although few in number, the radicals in the Rhineland, the Batavian Republic and north-central Italy were scattered throughout provincial towns and cities, not concentrated in a handful of centres where they could be dealt with easily. In the first, fraught years of Napoleonic rule, this made the prospect of wide – if thin – conspiratorial networks appear feasible. Later, as conspiracy gave way to collaboration, it meant that a small clutch of loyal, if often over-zealous men, could be found to administrate the departments, arrondissements and, especially, the cantons.

The response of the radicals to Napoleonic rule was shaped by three major experiences, common to all of them, whether Italian, German, Dutch or Belgian: their growing disillusionment with the French in the 1790s; the ruthless purges carried out against them in the first years of Napoleonic rule; and their experience of being the chief targets of counter-revolutionary fury. Viewed in the long term, for most of them, the last experience far outweighed the other two, binding them to Napoleon, however reluctantly. In the early years, however, this was by no means clear to them, or to their political opponents.

Before the French had decided to alienate the Left, the Left had become alienated from them, on its own terms and for its own reasons. Even at the height of their power and prestige during the sister republics of the 1790s, most radicals shared the anger and indignation of their fellow countrymen in the face of French rapaciousness and military exploitation. In 1799, the Piedmontese radical, Carlo Botta, wrote to a friend denouncing 'the new French conquest of Italy'; while in Koblenz, in 1798, Jacob Hann was equally indignant, openly denouncing 'the French leeches' for their ill-treatment of the Rhinelanders. It is striking evidence of their intrinsic weakness and isolation that even shared feelings of such an urgent kind could do nothing to bridge the gap between the radicals and the society they sought to govern. In their hatred of French exploitation, they were only following a flow of popular feelings, not leading it. Only true counter-revolutionaries or, later, those prepared to countenance the Napoleonic restoration of order, had more effective answers to the havoc created by French military occupation. Diplomatic betrayal embittered those Rhinelanders and Piedmontese who desired their own republics, while those in Venice were simply sold to the Austrians at Campo-Formio, an act of cynical, old-style diplomacy that frightened all of them.

French treachery and greed made a particular impact on the radicals; it disillusioned them as only idealistic intellectuals are capable of being disillusioned. The misconduct of the French at every level – as brutal military occupiers and calculating diplomats – had done more than enrage the radicals, it had surprised them. The Revolution was meant to produce new men with a new morality, but it had not, and this shattering discovery produced, in its turn, a series of repercussions within their ranks. The most idealistic among them had turned their backs on the French well before 1799, and they took one of two very different roads, usually conditioned by their native cultures. The radicals in the Rhineland were among the most deeply idealistic in Europe. They were imbued with the same intellectual morality of the *Bildung* as the more conservative elements of the intelligentsia and, through the universities most of them were connected with, they had come under the recent, invigorating influence of Kantian philosophy. The Rhenish Jacobins were as convinced of their cultural parity with France as the conservatives, and so were in for a double shock, for not only did the French cynically abuse their country in a material sense, they also spurned German intellectual culture. Their dream of an exchange of ideas, based on the penetration of France by Kantian notions of moral self-education, were brusquely swept aside. Faced with these early manifestations of cultural imperialism, the more committed among them turned away from politics and retreated into private study, as exemplified by Josef Goerres, in the manner of more conservative intellectuals. There were a few Italian radicals, such as Carlo Botta, who also followed this path, but most were conditioned by their culture to political, rather than cultural resistance. At the risk of oversimplification, it is still true that disillusioned Germans turned to lyric poetry, while Italians produced history of a highly politicized kind.

When they remained active, the Italian radicals turned to political conspiracy through shadowy secret societies such as the 'Black League' in Piedmont or the more widespread but equally nebulous Società dei Raggi ('the Rays of Light'), whose members had been influenced by the French radical, Babeuf, and his colleague, Buonnaroti, unreconstructed Jacobins who had used these tactics against the Directory within France. Although few Italian radicals shared the social and economic ideas of the French conspirators – in itself a good reason to be wary of labelling them 'Jacobins' – they were quick to embrace their conspiratorial approach to politics in the wake of Napoleon's rejection of the idea of Italian unity. In most cases, the main point to make about their conspiracies is their ineffectual nature. Nevertheless, there were important exceptions to this which were both the product and the justification for persecutions by conservative Napoleonic collaborators.

These persecutions followed hard on the heels of the creation of more conservative regimes in the Italian and Batavian Republics, and the reoccupations of Piedmont and the Rhineland; their high point was between about 1800 and 1805. In the Batavian Republic, a French-backed coup brought a small group of unitarist democrats to power in 1797. Although these radicals were swept aside in the course of 1799, to be replaced by more moderate politicians less hostile to traditional provincial autonomy, the radicals still commanded vocal, well-organized newspapers and clubs in most of the large Dutch cities. There were fears of another coup well into

1802, which seemed feasible enough to contemporaries because the radicals seemed to have two totally unrelated, ultimately incompatible sources of support. Their desire for a thoroughly centralized state could be expected to gain them French support, as it had in 1797 when the naval defeat of Camperdown had momentarily galvanized the French into an attempt to gain more efficient support from the Dutch. By 1802, Napoleon's preference for the support of secure local elites far outran any desire for uniformity within states outside the Empire proper. The second source of radical support came from urban artisans, particularly those whose livelihoods had been damaged by the war. They could put sizeable crowds on the streets through their active network of clubs. The closure of these clubs was one of the first steps taken against them by the conservative Batavian Directory in 1802–03. Indeed, the Dutch radicals were among the few leftists with any real claim to popular support outside France. Yet even the Dutch radicals still had too limited a basis of support to keep them in power without French help in 1798, or to get them back into it in 1802. It is striking in a comparative context, but must not be exaggerated. Nor were they persecuted; the restrained world of Dutch politics stayed their hand when in power, and that of their moderate opponents, when out of it. Although much less prominent in government than before 1799, they were not hounded to any great extent, nor did they lose all influence in public affairs. As so often in this very advanced society, its political culture never quite plunged itself into vicious extremes.

The same could not be said of the course of events in Melzi's Italian Republic, which saw the most successful radical conspiracy of these years, that of Bologna in 1802. Even this *cause célèbre* was not without enough qualifications to its success to make it an exception to prove the rule. Melzi was intent on a thorough purge of men connected with the sister republics of the 1790s and the period 1800–02. Furthermore, he was determined to curb their political activities outside government and to expel the numerous radicals from other parts of Italy who had gathered in Bologna, as refugees, in the period 1800–02. The strong radical presence in Bologna was not, in itself, enough to cause the revolt, however. The radicals of Bologna returned to the fore of politics in 1802 over the issue of local separatism, which is ironic when it is remembered that most of the radicals were pan-Italian nationalists, committed to some form or other of unification. Bologna and its surrounding province had been part of the Papal States, until given to the second Cisalpine Republic in 1800. The city had enjoyed considerable autonomy and privileges under the weak government of the popes, which Melzi's proto-French government in Milan was determined to remove. This led to resentment among the whole elite of Bologna, their many political differences notwithstanding. The ill-feelings among the traditionalists, still loyal to the Pope, also less obviously extended to moderate republicans, led by Aldini, who were happy to encourage the radicals in their opposition to the new prefect sent by Melzi to Bologna, the conservative, formerly pro-Austrian nobleman, Carlotti. In particular, the Bolognese elite was united in its fight to preserve its powerful national guard from Melzi's attempts to disband it. The guard was full of radical democrats and had become their real source of influence in local affairs.

Then came the bad harvest of the spring of 1802, which led to high prices and food shortages in the town, culminating in a surge of popular discontent that the radicals seemed to be tapping. Tension mounted throughout the summer of 1802, and with the prefect unable to control the city, order had to be restored by the French garrison. Local solidarity held firm during the trials of the ringleaders, the local magistrates refusing to convict them. It was all a huge embarrassment for Melzi, especially because he was forced to replace Carlotti with Somenazi, a man with a radical past who had served the Cisalpine Republic in the 1790s – just the kind of man Melzi was desperate to avoid appointing. Somenazi restored order and won the confidence of the radicals, bringing many of them back into local government.

In many ways, the events in Bologna illustrate how potent radical opposition could still be in the first years of Napoleonic rule. Melzi now had to temper his policy of purging the republicans and could no longer refuse to employ them. Equally, the revolt of Bologna showed that it was not impossible for the Left to take the lead in a popular insurrection, albeit in very particular circumstances. However, there were two things which worked greatly to Melzi's advantage when he finally chose to compromise with them, and they are of more importance for the future than those circumstances which had led to the revolt. On the one hand, as the violence increased the moderates led by Aldini began to distance themselves from the radicals in the national guard, leaving them increasingly isolated. In the last analysis, mainstream republicans would support them only so far. Perhaps more significantly, the subsequent success of Somenazi's policy of reconciliation showed how eager most radicals were to collaborate with the new regime. The real lesson of Bologna for Melzi was that only a minuscule hard core of radicals could not be brought safely into the official fold. The road of refusal was for the – often unemployable – few. Whether in Italy, Germany or the Low Countries, most radicals rejoined the system; indeed, most would never have turned to resistance in the first place, had they not been driven from it. By 1804, in the Belgian departments, the Jacobins still under police surveillance could only grumble and were no longer seen as a threat, as they watched their closest relatives take office under the French.

The main reason for the loyalty of the radicals, even in the face of official persecution, was fear of counter-revolution. The violence of the brief restorations of the 1790s did more to shape their political outlook than anything else. Henceforth, even the wildest-eyed idealist knew that the radicals were 'a tiny little group, spurned by the great majority of their fellow citizens', as it was put by one of the most committed of their number, the Rhenish Jacobin Georg Forster.[19] This was one lesson of popular counter-revolution. The other was that the ousted governments of the *ancien régime*, briefly restored in the Rhineland in 1793 and throughout Italy in 1799, had been particularly vicious and unforgiving towards collaborators. Once the plunge had been taken, there was no going back for these men. At first, it produced a reluctant acceptance of the new regime, but the embers of radical dissent were not dead. As radical opposition faded within the inner empire, it would reach its pinnacle in Spain by 1810, while in the Kingdom of Naples, perhaps as early 1807 but certainly by 1809, radical secret societies began to flourish, the most famous of which was the Carbonari. In the next phase of Napoleonic rule, after 1807, radical resistance, now dwindling in the inner empire, would be reborn on its margins.

Seen another way, there was the gradual, qualified triumph of collaboration over resistance within the inner empire between 1800 and 1807.

Collaboration: the human reality of consolidation

The Napoleonic regime knew it had few real friends beyond the borders of France in 1799, and it did not really want the support of many of those it did have. This was knowledge born of experience; the men at the helm of the Napoleonic state system had lived through the ravages of the 1790s alongside the ravaged populations of the lands they now ruled. They saw the 1790s for what they were – an unmitigated disaster that all concerned had now to put behind them. Put another way, the regime was desperate for its twin policies of *ralliement* and *amalgame* to work. The official aspect of this policy has already been examined; its reception by those it was aimed at must now be considered.

The hatred and suspicion inspired in most of the occupied populations by the prospect of another bout of French rule created a symbiotic relationship between resistance and collaboration which was to be altered profoundly – but only momentarily – by the stunning military victories of 1805–07. Until this point, the onus was on the Napoleonic occupiers to prove not only the merits, but the durability of their rule; after the defeats of Austria, Russia and Prussia, it was up to the occupied to come to terms with the realities of the new order. Thus, for most of the period 1799–1806, the line between resistance and collaboration was thin and blurred.

The 'new forces'

For all its aristocratic, elitist proclivities, the Napoleonic state was the direct heir of the Revolution. There was no escaping the fact, and nowhere is it clearer than in the nature of the support it got in the annexed territories and the satellite states. That support came, however grudgingly, from the Left, the majority of the republicans of the 1790s; from religious minorities freed by the Concordat; from suppressed national groups, the Poles above all; and from those more moderate enlightened reformers of the late eighteenth century who had fallen foul of the reactions of the 1790s, usually those who had bought *biens nationaux*, served in the governments of the sister republics as an exercise in damage limitation, or had belonged to the generally suspect, often outlawed Freemasons. All of them had been welded to the Napoleonic cause by the vengeful, highly arbitrary persecutions of counter-revolution. Fear was the initial spur, a negative force which the regime sought to turn to positive use.

The French had to turn to the republicans of the 1790s to staff their administration, especially at local level. During the initial organization of the Italian Republic, Melzi employed them with great reluctance and only as a last resort, but when they finally were given posts in the administration, former republicans such as Aldini, Brunetti or Somenazi, proved themselves among the ablest servants of the new state. Indeed, Melzi's hope to create an administration totally free of ex-republicans quickly came to nothing. Partly, this was due to the reluctance of more conservative men to serve the Italian Republic, but it was also because many of those who did accept lacked the competence and direct experience of the French administrative system which only ex-republicans possessed. Above all, Napoleon disliked Melzi's policy of deliberate exclusion on grounds of past political allegiance; he saw it as running counter to the twin concepts of *ralliement* and *amalgame*, with their goal of reconciliation.

Predictably, there was a more pragmatic side to Napoleon's opposition to Melzi's narrow concept of what was politically acceptable. In 1806, following Melzi's resignation, Napoleon told Aldini, 'Treat the patriots well... The patriot party is the one which has always been the most energetic for France and for the throne.'[20] He was right. As shown in the case of Bologna in 1802, Melzi had to turn to the republican prefect, Somenazi, not only because of his political affiliations, but also for his administrative experience. Their ideological position made them sympathetic to the technical innovations of the new state. Even if they often resented its authoritarian politics – or lack of them – the goal of enlightened progress remained a common cause with Napoleon. Quite deliberately, in 1806, Napoleon insisted on the use of experienced prefects from the Kingdom of Italy, most of whom had patriot backgrounds, to organize the newly acquired Venetian departments. In this, he took Aldini's advice over Eugène's, and was thoroughly vindicated by their competent response to the administrative chaos they found. This particular example is also striking proof that an inner empire had emerged between 1799 and 1806, possessed of a loyal, professional class of administrators, now themselves experienced enough to cope with the challenge of new areas and who were not French. Here, consolidation and collaboration merge into one.

Throughout the Empire, men of similar backgrounds provided the backbone of the administration, especially where those in central government were less reluctant to turn to them than Melzi. Simeon used his masonic connections to recruit loyal, enlightened administrative personnel, first in Berg and then in Westphalia. Hesse-Kassel, a part of Westphalia since 1806, had seen a flowering of freemasonry in the late eighteenth century which attracted many reformers to its ranks, but the lodges were banned in 1793, at the height of the reaction against the Revolution. Jerome and Simeon reopened the lodges in 1806 and they enjoyed a particularly close association with the regime.

These examples reveal that even in states without a concerted tradition of enlightened reform prior to French rule, there had at least been interest in it among a fraction of the elite, and it was that fraction the Napoleonic rulers could most readily count upon, in the face of stubborn opposition to their reforms. The legal protestations of the peasantry around Dortmund against attempts by the feudal barons to negate the French assault on feudal dues was organized by a radical lawyer, Arnold Mallinkrodt. A writer and journalist, as well as a lawyer, Mallinkrodt had been in and out of trouble under the *ancien régime*, but he proved a valuable ally to Beugnot's reforming intentions at local level. Men of a similar stamp, who had often been victims of Bourbon persecution in 1799, staffed Zurlo's special anti-feudal tribunals in Naples. As a general rule, where or when the old order was strongest, the French drew on those radicals they felt they could trust and, in these circumstances, their support was usually enthusiastic. They perceived the progressive aspects of the new regime and threw their energies into its service. The police and tribunals of the lower levels of the administration were full of such men; it was through their efforts that conscription and the Concordat were enforced. They hounded both bandits and 'fanatical' clergy with alacrity, tasks which would have been beyond the regime without them. At what might be termed the 'cutting edge' of government – in the small towns and rural backwaters which comprised most of the Empire – men with republican and masonic pasts proved invaluable. The wide, if thin, dissemination of the patriots now proved a vital asset to them, and to the regime.

Another source of enthusiastic support was the business communities of the Rhineland. Their adherence to the French is indicative of the change in priorities which took place under the Consulat; it signals the end of the policy of naked exploitation and its replacement by one of positive reconstruction in an area that had been particularly despoiled and embittered in the 1790s. The businessmen of the major cities of the Rhineland drew important advantages from French rule through integration into a larger economic unit. Of at least equal importance was the prominent place they were accorded in the Napoleonic administration. The *maires* of Aachen, Crefeld and Cologne were all drawn from the business community, as were the occupants of many other administrative posts, in sharp contrast to their marginal position under the *ancien régime*. The whole process of consultation, through departmental councils and chambers of commerce introduced by the French, marked a real break with the past and gave these groups the opportunity to participate in political life in a more active, direct way than had been possible hitherto.

The agricultural entrepreneurs of the Po Valley, in north-western Italy, also proved a loyal, solid nucleus of support for the regime. Their motives for collaboration were not unlike those of the Rhenish business communities, in that their marginalized position under the *ancien régime* was significantly reversed under the French. In Habsburg Lombardy and even more in Piedmont, under the House of Savoy, mercantilist commercial policies and restrictions on the production and exportation of rice, by far their most profitable crop, were swept away under Napoleonic rule. Rice cultivation had appalling human consequences; the irrigation canals it depended on produced malarial swamps which ruined the health of the local population, to the horror of humanitarian prefects and even Napoleonic recruiting officers. As Jourdan, the Administrator-General of Piedmont, remarked in 1802, 'when travelling through these fertile plains, one is struck by the contrast presented by the richness of the soil and the pallid faces of those who till it'.[21] Nevertheless, the same rural entrepreneurs castigated by administrators for their callousness were acknowledged to be among the most loyal supporters of the regime in the whole of the Empire. Had there ever been an award for the 'most Napoleonic town in Europe', it would probably have gone to Vercelli, seat of the department of the Sesia – former Piedmontese territory – and the heart of the rice area of the Po. Its bourgeois national guard fought with distinction against the peasant rebels of the Val d'Aosta in 1800 and again in 1801; conscription always ran smoothly; brigandage was almost unknown among its emaciated inhabitants. To cap it all, before the Revolution, Vercelli had been the site of one of the most intensely Jansenist seminaries in Europe, several of whose alumni served the new regime in lay, as well as clerical posts; even the clergy could be counted on. Almost every stereotyped source of support for the Napoleonic regime was concentrated in Vercelli: a core of patriots, persecuted during the Revolution; a Jansenist clergy; a thrusting, capitalist rural bourgeoisie. There is considerable irony in the fact that the French themselves would have loved to see an end to the source of their wealth – and hence to their loyalty – the cultivation of rice, 'this injurious abuse' as the prefect called it in 1809, pleading 'It is of the utmost urgency that an end be put to so deplorable a state of affairs.'[22] His superiors agreed, but never more than in principle; the regime knew its heartland when it saw it.

The case of the Poles is inextricably bound up with diplomatic convulsions. Polish enthusiasm for the French cause stemmed from a truly nationalist patriotism, almost unique in Europe at the time. However imperfect or incomplete – in terms of real independence and territory – the

Grand Duchy of Warsaw provided most Poles with a far more satisfactory arrangement than the ignominy of the third partition of 1795, which had wiped Poland off the map. Here, nationalism in probably its purest form fuelled very successful collaboration on a wide scale. Despite attempts to curb their feudal privileges and centralize the state – to say nothing of the huge *dotations* within its borders – the mass of the Polish nobility threw itself behind Napoleon.

Nationalism has often been cited as a major factor in support for Napoleonic rule, particularly in the cases of Italy and Germany, but this has more to do with the wishful thinking of the nationalist historians of the nineteenth century and their successors than historical reality.[23] Many factors were involved in collaboration, but nationalist aspirations – as they are now understood – were seldom among them, the modern concept of nationalism being only barely perceptible at this time. The Grand Duchy of Warsaw is an exception to this, not an example of the general rule. The particular circumstances of Polish history in the eighteenth century had forged a consciously nationalist outlook within the ranks of the Polish nobility, a nobility that also happened to be unusually large by contemporary European standards. The Grand Duchy of Warsaw does, indeed, provide a clear example of how potent a force nationalism could be for collaboration, but it is a unique case.

The introduction of religious toleration offered by the Concordat, or under the auspices of related reforms in the satellite states, produced another source of support that was always, by definition, marginal. In a relative sense, Dutch Catholics, Protestant subjects of the German prince-bishops and Jews everywhere gained something from the reforms, even if it was seldom full emancipation, as has been seen. The religious groups who achieved most were probably those of the small, unreformed German states, who did not share the religion of their sovereign. The creation of the new states of Berg and Westphalia, or direct annexation to France, advanced the civil status of whichever denomination had not hitherto been the official religion, whether Catholic, Lutheran or Calvinist. A good example of the successful influence of emancipation on collaboration is the Mennonite community of Crefeld, a former Prussian city in the Rhineland. Their religious beliefs kept the Mennonites out of politics under the old regime, but they came forward to serve the French. This change is epitomized by the rich business family, the von der Leyens, whose influence in Crefeld shifted from the oblique to one of such public prominence that they played host to Napoleon in 1811.

This pattern is also present in the Batavian Republic, where a denominational patchwork of Catholics, Jews and non-Calvinist Protestants such as the Anabaptists, saw many of the restrictions on them lifted after the fall of the House of Orange and the disestablishment of the Dutch Reformed Church. The position of the Catholics, in particular, was still precarious under the Republic; there were plenty of Dutch politicians who wanted re-establishment and few Catholics, dissenters or Jews were found in local government before the creation of the Kingdom of Holland – and the advent of tighter central control – in 1806. Orangist outbursts against toleration kept most of these groups loyal to the new order, although the Sephardic Jews of Rotterdam resented losing their links with their co-religionists in London as a result of the war.

The Jewish communities of Europe present a very particular case, both in terms of the reality of their emancipation and their level of collaboration. The prospect of full Jewish emancipation raised by the Concordat was deeply – often violently – unpopular almost everywhere. Even within France itself, Napoleon was constrained to delay the full emancipation of the large Jewish communities of Alsace and Lorraine. The same delay was imposed in the Grand Duchy of Warsaw, which contained 80 per cent of the world's Jews at this time, a community of almost 800 000. Nevertheless, their status in urban communities was enhanced, particularly in the case of property rights. In general, there was just enough perceptible progress to worry the most Orthodox Jewish communities, who feared the prospect of assimilation. Most of these reservations emerged during the 'Grand Sanhedrin' of leading rabbis and scholars, called by Napoleon in 1807, to resolve the problems arising from emancipation. What is most striking about the attitude of this council is that it fought for less assimilation, not more, in its adamant opposition to mixed marriages, something Napoleon greatly favoured but had to concede. There was more enthusiasm for civic integration, enshrined by the use of the term 'fellow citizens' (*concitoyens*) for equal dealings with non-Jewish subjects of the Empire. Although many Orthodox communities were apprehensive about French rule and emancipation, the general trend was one of loyalty and cautious support.

In the wider context of resistance and collaboration, and a new regime in search of a solid base of support, these minorities probably gained more from the relationship than their new masters. Whether it was a case of suppressed Polish nationalists, persecuted radicals or religious minorities, the verdict given in a Dutch context has a relevance for the whole of Napoleonic Europe: 'Those who would be the real beneficiaries of a new order ... were together nothing like so strong a force as to overcome the resistance, passive or active, of the old elite.'[24] The forces most favourable to the French cause were all too often the weakest and most marginal in European society. In this sense, the Empire remained the true heir of 1789.

The cases of the Polish gentry and the Rhenish business communities reveal the importance of analysing collaboration in a comparative context. The businessmen of the Rhineland found the French system more representative – and so more responsive to their needs – than the *ancien régime* had been. Yet this was not the feeling in the great Dutch cities, whose economies and societies were broadly similar to those of the Rhineland. As shall be seen, the Continental System affected their respective economies differently in the years after 1807, but before that date, the past political histories of these two urban, trading regions counted greatly. Whereas the Rhinelanders – or some of them, at least – gained a greater share in politics than previously, the Dutch cities felt the relative loss of local autonomy under the Batavian Republic. Louis Bonaparte, as King of Holland after 1806, was acutely aware of this, as were all Dutch opponents of unitarism, but even the mildest centralizing reforms were always a source of alienation at every social level. The Dutch experience was generally one of a society which felt itself, with some reason, to be more advanced than the French, a condition they attributed to municipal independence and the civic pride it engendered. Their highly developed social services – orphanages and homes for the aged, in particular – are impressive evidence for this view of themselves.

A comparison between Piedmontese and Polish attitudes to independence reveals that the degree of collaboration the French achieved could never be divorced from how their presence altered the previous political order. Given the varied nature of the political patchwork of the old order, their interaction could never be uniformly predicted. For the Poles, the creation of the Grand Duchy of Warsaw represented a restoration of lost independence. In contrast, the annexation to France of the mainland territories of the House of Savoy was a severe shock for most of the Piedmontese elite. Many republicans shared this sense of loss, having vested their hopes in the conversion of their state into a sister republic; indeed, many of the most embittered anti-French conspirators of the Black League may have been Piedmontese, rather than Italian, in their loyalties.

The collaboration of the patriots was not always enthusiastic and was driven as much by fear of counter-revolution than anything else. As time passed and the French presence seemed increasingly unshakeable, even some of the most intransigent radicals drifted back into state service, probably through a mixture of admiration and resignation. When they did so, it was a clear sign that the revolutionary era was over. The majority of patriots who stood by the French had no illusions about the dependent nature of the relationship, whatever its source. In the words of the patriot *maire* of the Piedmontese town of Alessandria, in 1809: 'My political existence depends on the life of the government, its enemies are my enemies.'[25] Clear-sighted self-interest had replaced dewy-eyed idealism, where it had ever existed in the first place. Their dependence on Napoleon's hegemony was obvious, and ultimately it was determined by their marginal position in society. They provided a solid enough base for the regime, but hardly a broad one.

The establishment: conservative collaboration

The elite sections of European society were those the Napoleonic regime actively wanted on its side. By its own standards the degree of support the regime received from the ruling classes of the *ancien régime* was the bench-mark of success. This policy was pushed to its furthest limits by Melzi, in the Italian Republic between 1802 and 1805, while Schimmelpenninck and his colleagues pursued a similarly fawning policy towards the Dutch patri-cians in the same years. It was a difficult process, but the policy of *ral-liement* was pursued throughout the Empire with consistency and determination. The results were qualified, marked by subtleties and nuances absent from the starker choices which faced those more directly dependent on French hegemony. The very fact that the French were dealing with solid, well-established interests – political and cultural, as well as economic – made their task all the harder.

Melzi d'Eril's support for the regime marked him out from his peers as the exception that proves the rule. At the fall of the *ancien régime*, Melzi had been a disappointed, if moderate reformer; at the end of the revolu-tionary years, 1796–99, he was terrified of popular disorder and so dis-gusted by the radicalism of the Cisalpine Republic of 1796–99 that he retired to his family's estates in Spain. He turned to Napoleon because he felt the French had shed their own radicalism and could guarantee order, as well as a moderate policy of reform. Melzi was not over-successful in persuading many men like himself of the wisdom of his decision. In most cases, the reason was less a clash of ideologies than of confidence that French rule would, indeed, last. The reactionary persecutions of 1799 had frightened as much by their example as by their results – they had terrified the landed nobles who witnessed them, as well as the patriots who were their victims. The immediate heritage of this for Melzi was that the landed classes of northern and central Italy did not want to compromise themselves by serving the Italian Republic in its early years; they refused to accept the posts as prefects that Melzi was so anxious to offer them. It was this con-tinuing sense of insecurity that did most to thwart Melzi's dream of 'a dic-tatorship of the notables'. As he told Napoleon in March 1802, 'external conditions are still considered unreassuring here'.[26]

How crucial the military and diplomatic climate was to collaboration – in northern Italy and elsewhere – emerges when Melzi's problems prior to the great victories of 1805–07 are contrasted to the ease with which his successors, Eugène de Beauharnais and Aldini, had in recruiting the Venetian nobility to state service following the annexation of Venice to the Kingdom of Italy in 1806. Many of the oldest Venetian families served in the provisional administration which presided over annexation, and they often expressed a wish to continue in their posts. The problem here was twofold: first, they were reluctant to serve outside their own areas; and second, those few who could be persuaded to do so often proved tempera-mentally incapable of adapting to the disciplined, professional attitudes required of Napoleonic administrators. The landed nobles of the old Venetian Republic did not want and, indeed, could not afford to live away from their estates, a problem Melzi had also found in Lombardy. Despite

Eugène's wish to make concessions to them, Napoleon remained adamant over maintaining the rule of prefects serving only outside their own departments. In the event, only three Venetian nobles accepted prefectures and all of them had left them for seats in the Imperial Senate by 1809. While in their posts, although willing to work hard, they showed too much independence, a spontaneous sense of superiority and an ingrained authoritarianism, all of which denoted a psychological refusal to become modern, professional bureaucrats. Their experience is an important example of the problem of trying to adapt a traditional aristocracy to the needs of a modern state, and the Venetian aristocracy were among the most aristocratic of them all.

The experience of the Venetian nobility shows that a willingness to collaborate was not always matched by an ability to adapt. A more complex set of factors influenced the collaboration of the elites of Piedmont and many of the German states, who had strong traditions of state service within administrative systems closer to Napoleon's than those of the ramshackle Republic of Venice. Among the Hessian and Piedmontese nobility, a subtle but real distinction emerges between the collaboration of the bureaucrats and magistrates, on the one hand, and the older, landed nobles with their tradition of military service, on the other. The same negative forces of dynastic loyalties, aversion to the revolutionary heritage of the new regime and scepticism about its survival were at work among those who refused to collaborate; therefore, the key to understanding why some nobles chose participation rather than rejection lies mainly in seeing how the French overcame these reservations. The complexities arise because these reservations were, usually, overcome only in part.

When the great judicial and administrative families of the German and Italian states took service under the French, their reasoning mirrored that of Melzi: the new regime was to be supported because it had restored order and offered the chance to resume the path of enlightened reform. However, this usually reflected an admiration for the Napoleonic way of doing things rather than genuine support for French rule, and it was often coupled with the same persistent cultural resistance to the 'Frenchification' of their cultural life that characterized the 'resisters' in their ranks. In the north German and Piedmontese cases, the private intellectual circles devoted to the preservation of indigenous culture provided points of regular contact between those who 'rallied' and those who did not. In Turin, for example, Prospero Balbo accepted a series of progressively more important posts under the French, becoming the head of the University of Turin in 1805. Balbo and Napoleon had a deep mutual respect for each other, and the Emperor always supported Balbo in his initiatives concerning the University. This collaboration was achieved with both hesitation and reluctance on Balbo's part and it never entailed Balbo breaking his links with those 'cultural rebels' grouped around his old friend, Napione. His decision to collaborate was a calculated exercise in damage limitation, based on a lucid realism, but even this did not deter him from treading a potentially dangerous line. Balbo was under police surveillance until 1808, and often used his position to protect intellectuals known for their royalist sympathies, who the French would otherwise have dealt with more severely. These tendencies are even more apparent in the career of his son, Cesare, who became the first constitutional Prime Minister of Piedmont-Savoy in 1848. The French administrative system had no greater admirer than the younger Balbo, who served it at a very high level, as an auditor of the Council of State; a generation later, in 1848, he was responsible for its wholesale introduction into his own country. All this notwithstanding, he was a leading light of the Concordi, a literary circle of young nobles devoted to resisting French cultural hegemony, while his private correspondence reveals his disgust at the role he had to play in the annexations of Tuscany, and then Rome, to the Empire.

Among the service nobilities, realism always had to be balanced against the strong ties of dynastic loyalty engendered by close ties to the crown; the timing and circumstances surrounding the collapse of the old order and the introduction of French rule often helped tip the scales one way or the other. The reticence of the Piedmontese ruling class infuriated the French in the first years of their rule, and it is noteworthy that it was only after Austerlitz that families such as the Balbos began to come forward in real earnest. Circumstances were different in the German states which were to form the Grand Duchy of Berg and the Kingdom of Westphalia. Here, French rule followed on a series of earth-shattering victories and seemed more imposing from the outset than it did in the earlier conquests, in northern Italy. Hence, most of the higher Hessian nobility, the Ritterschaft, took service with the French with an often shameless rapidity. They did so either out of financial necessity or a desire to continue their careers. Those who found collaboration easiest in Hesse-Kassel were usually from families with a long tradition of administrative service, often with university educations. Six out of seven senior civil servants drawn from the Ritterschaft joined the Westphalian administration, as did most of their subordinates, nobles and bourgeois, alike.[27] The new regime offered them faster promotion and higher salaries. Its permanence seemed confirmed when Jerome crushed an abortive revolt in 1808 with considerable ease.

There was a strong ideological attraction to the Napoleonic state for ruling classes with an experience of enlightened absolutism, when deeper dynastic loyalties were overcome or set aside. States such as Piedmont, Hesse-Kassel and the south German kingdoms contained many men of this cast of mind. Theirs was a rather different outlook from that of the more radical reformers, in that they would countenance reform only within the context of the existing political and social order. Thus, they came into Napoleonic service by a very different route, as a result of watching the old order collapse and being forced to turn to the French as a last resort. Many, especially in northern Italy and the Low Countries, did so in the course of the 1790s, and reactionary courts in exile usually failed to recognize the subtle distinction between these men and the more ideologically committed collaborators of the Left. This, in turn, bound them closer to the French, but there were other reasons which drew them to the regime. Provincial administrators, noble and non-noble alike, had borne the brunt of the anarchy of the 1790s; their lives and properties had been those most jeopardized by the demise of the states they had served so faithfully. These conditions produced a political outlook based on fear and disillusionment, which the French capitalized on through the restoration of order and the stronger support its administrative system offered to those who served it, in the course of their duties. Not the least important aspect of this support was the presence of an organized rural police force, the Gendarmerie. Its efforts did much to assure the support of the smaller nobles and rural bourgeoisie, whose lives and properties it protected, with however bad a grace.

Beyond this, the Napoleonic state system – based on much larger political units, closely integrated with each other in military and administrative terms – offered more potential for advancement than the smaller states of Italy or the Holy Roman Empire. These benefits were not confined to service in the army or the bureaucracy. The *lycées*, created throughout the Empire and imitated in the satellite states, may have been shunned by patricians such as Balbo – who, while Rector of the University of Turin, saw to it that his sons were educated at home – but the provincial notables went to great lengths to secure places in them for their sons. Again, the key to understanding collaboration is the relative context the French inherited. If Napoleonic rule meant a loss of power, privilege and status to feudal barons in southern Italy and northern Germany, or to those who had previously guided the destinies of significant, if limited states such as Piedmont-Savoy or the Dutch Republic, it had more to offer their subordinates. This particular element of the French system, dependent as it was on larger states, is a much more significant indication of the ways in which support for the concept of the nation-state would grow, later in the century, than the more ideological – and colourful – interpretations of Napoleonic influence favoured by nationalist historians. Bigger states meant more jobs in the bureaucracy and the army than in smaller ones; this gave reality to the concept of the career open to talent and an outlet for thousands of frustrated ambitions. The new imperial nobility was based wholly on the concept of service. The career open to talent is a concept of the Revolution which the Napoleonic regime can be accused of betraying all too easily, but the reality is far more complex.

The greatest incentive for the military nobility was undoubtably the prospect of service in the largest, most dynamic military machine as yet seen in Europe. In light of this, what is most striking is their initial reluctance, followed by distinguished service in the French war effort. Some did so out of financial necessity, but a younger generation in Piedmont and the

German states was genuinely impressed by Napoleon. In general, the regime found its most willing volunteers among junior officers of the swollen, underpaid ranks of the Hessian and Savoyard armies. There had been considerable attempts to institute noble preferment for military promotion in many *ancien régime* states, but it had been resisted in most of them. Thus, paradoxically, the arrival of the French often accentuated existing patterns among the meritocratic officer corps of the more militaristic *ancien régime* states. In 1806, non-nobles made up 43 per cent of the Hessian officer corps, in a state which had consciously shunned noble preferment; by the end of the Napoleonic wars, it had reached 63 per cent, many of whom had spectacular careers in the Russian and Spanish campaigns of the last years.[28]

Nevertheless, the loyalty of most nobles did not run very deep and, in Germany and Naples, it was always compromised by the continuous – if relatively moderate – assault on feudal privilege. It is worth recalling Beugnot's rueful comment that 'it hurts the pride of the privileged classes, it did not hurt their interests'. Noble pride is not to be underestimated, nor the mere fact that their interests were being tampered with in the first place. In Westphalia and Italy the French pinned their hopes on the attraction of larger, potentially more profitable courts, together with service in a truly powerful imperial superstate, believing that this would outweigh losses closer to home, such as the abolition of seigneurial jurisdictions. The results were, at best, qualified. In the Kingdom of Naples, the assault on privilege was more aggressive than in Germany, and thus more obviously alienating in its effects. Many barons were active – if careful – supporters of brigands. They were helped and encouraged in this by the proximity of the Bourbon Court in exile in Sicily and even more by the British navy. Rarely within the inner empire was the absence of collaboration quite so marked or its reverse quite so blatantly obvious.

More typical of the response of those affected by the loss of privilege was that of the nobles of the Grand Duchy of Berg, who collaborated to the extent of accepting key posts in the magistracy, but then used them to obstruct the reform process. Similarly, in Westphalia, although many nobles flocked both to Jerome's court and to the colours of his new army, they continued to complain about his reforms. It is of great significance to the dubious success of the policy of collaboration that the legislature of the model Kingdom of Westphalia met but once, and that of the Kingdom of Naples, never. In both cases, Jerome and Murat saw all too quickly that these bodies would become powerful platforms for the nobility to arrest the process of reform.

Noble *ralliement* was limited and fragile, a fragility which would be starkly exposed in the years of crisis ahead, in contrast to the relatively solid, genuine support it acquired from the ranks of enlightened bureaucracies. This is clear from the experience of the German Mittelstaaten. Their expansion in 1803–06 created problems of assimilation not dissimilar to those facing the rest of the inner empire, if on a smaller scale. If the business communities of Free Cities like Augsburg welcomed absorption into the larger economic unit of Bavaria, the Imperial Knights did not. They soon made common cause with the indigenous nobility against the reforms of Max-Joseph and Montgelas. In what amounted to a passive revolt, the Bavarian nobles were able to prevent the full introduction of the Code Napoleon. In Nassau, as has been seen, von Bieberstein feared it could endanger the state itself, while in Baden resistance to centralization spread far beyond the nobility to embrace the privileged but broad-based urban elites of the 'home towns': councillors, guild masters and many artisans.

This recalcitrance stands in sharp contrast to the loyalty received by Montgelas, von Bieberstein, von Reitzenstein, and Frederick of Württemberg from the professional bureaucracies they created. It was a loyalty forged in their acrimonious struggles with privilege which sharpened their absolutist convictions, which were strengthened rather than deflated by the resistance they met with. Territorial expansion and Napoleon's military demands were only the catalysts for reform in these states, not their deeper causes. When Frederick dissolved the ancient constitution of Württemberg in 1805 – freed from traditional constraints by Napoleonic protection – he turned to a bureaucracy which was as frustrated by the power of the estates as he was himself. Bureaucratic loyalty was already well established in the Mittelstaaten, and support for centralized absolutism cut across class lines, just as opposition to it did. Within the ranks of the administration, a shared political mentality emerged after 1803, centred on the desire to build a new kind of state, inspired by the model of Napoleonic France. In all these states, elements of the traditional elites and hitherto excluded elements of the bourgeoisie worked together to this end. The Mittelstaaten were the Empire in microcosm.

The inescapable truth is that Napoleonic rule imposed unpopular demands on the mass of its subjects, while assailing the power and privilege of the most influential among them. The benefits of collaboration usually came from within the system; they did not include the well wishes of those being ruled, for obvious reasons. There were important exceptions to this, to be sure. The restoration of order, particularly the destruction of banditry, won the regime considerable support where it took place, as did the reconstruction of economic life after the wars of the 1790s. Northern Italy is a good example of the former; the left bank of the Rhine, of the latter.

The most popular form of engagement within the inner empire was also the least political: the purchase of *biens nationaux*, a pattern well established in France early in the Revolution. In the non-French territories, the lands were usually drawn from former Church properties and, more rarely, the estates of émigrés confiscated by the state for failure to return under the amnesty. The Concordat legitimized the sales of the Church lands, although most of the courts in exile remained more Catholic than the Pope over this issue. Whatever their scruples in other respects, the chance to acquire some of the most valuable property in Europe was too much to resist, for those with the capital to do so. When Napoleonic hegemony began to look secure, sales rose, most markedly in Piedmont, the Kingdom of Italy and the Kingdom of Naples. In Naples, Zurlo intended to use the sales to create a new class of peasant smallholders, but he failed. Instead, the pattern already evident in France and northern Italy reasserted itself, whereby those with liquid capital, both nobles and the wealthier rural bourgeoisie together with some high-ranking bureaucrats, extended their grip on the rural economy. This is one area where *amalgame* of a sort occurred, with families of all political persuasions taking part in the sales. However, their real importance is economic and social, not political – at least in terms of collaboration. Buying *biens nationaux* may have been a sign that the new order was now regarded as permanent, but by no means did it equal direct collaboration of a political nature. Although for some families, such as the Cavours and Barolos in Piedmont, it did, in fact, mark the first step towards a change of allegiance, it is equally the case that the Neapolitan barons were also among the greatest purchasers of these properties.

In the end, support for the regime, especially for those at local level, meant identification with the enforcement of conscription, heavy taxation and the Concordat. Where seigneurialism was strong, it meant incurring the wrath of nobles, whose social and economic powers were still largely intact. Even at the height of French hegemony, collaboration had its price. In the face of this, it would be reasonable to assume that a strong *esprit de corps* would develop within the administration, but this was seldom the case. *Ralliement* (support for the regime) was intended to be the twin of *amalgame* (the fusing of the different elements who rallied) but the reality proved very different.

Internal rivalries: the Empire of the professionals

The Napoleonic state fostered rivalry by its very nature. Its power structure was ideal for nurturing competing interests, but it did not create them. Instead, the regime acquired these rivalries naturally, a palpable heritage of the divisions of the 1790s and of the highly competitive – if more restrained – world of *ancien régime* public life. Rivalries were latent, too, in the chequered nature of support the regime enjoyed. The achievements of the Empire must not be confused with its intentions, particularly as regards *amalgame*. The imperial nobility, the army and, indeed, the whole bureaucracy, were meant to merge the *ancien régime* elites with those new elites produced by the Revolution. Although something like this may have happened in France – and even this is being increasingly brought into question[29] – there is little evidence for it elsewhere.

Ralliement seldom produced *amalgame* in part, at least, because the structure of the state militated against the success of fusion. The structure of local government and other institutions enabled rival factions to seize – and then monopolize – its different branches. When this happened, it usually followed a traditional, predictable pattern, which was all the harder to break for being so. The patriots of the 1790s were quick to seize opportunities for office, which usually came at arrondissement or departmental level and in the lower tiers of the judiciary. In contrast, men with more conservative pasts, frequently the radicals' opponents, either received higher office – usually in the higher courts because of their longer experience – or, if they were more reticent, with less conspicuous posts in municipal government. The result was the perpetuation of old rivalries by new means. In the Rhenish city of Cologne, it led to attempts by the patriot business community – newly powerful on the General Council of the department of the Rhur – to oust the *maire* Wittgenstein, who had an *ancien régime* background. The lower echelons of the Piedmontese departments were consolidated swiftly into patriot strongholds soon after annexation and witnessed a string of allegedly biased decisions against known royalists and furious attempts to keep 'outsiders' – which meant ex-royalists – out of local office.

The renewal of the struggle against feudalism in the Kingdom of Naples resurrected the almost timeless feud between the former royal magistrates – led by Zurlo and Ricciardi – and the barons, even those who rallied and served with some commitment. Pignatelli di Cerchiara, the head of one of the Kingdom's most distinguished noble families, served Murat as a councillor of state, Minister for the Navy and then Secretary of State. His ultimate loyalty to the regime was never in doubt; he had been exiled by the Bourbons and his goddaughter married Manhès, the French general in charge of the campaigns against the bandits. Nevertheless, Pignatelli opposed most of Zurlo's reforms and remained a consistently conservative influence on the Council. The long-running feud between Melzi and Aldini in the Italian Republic is another example of this.

Similar quarrels broke out in other public institutions, such as the bitter struggle within the University of Turin, between Bonvicino, a patriot of the 1790s, head of the Medical Faculty which was dominated by patriots, and the crypto-royalist Law Faculty, supported by Balbo, the conservative Rector. The University became the unlikely focus for a series of power struggles which involved the French prefect, Loyel, on the side of the medics, and the more moderate General Menou, who supported the lawyers. In 1806, Balbo tried to appoint a known royalist as a sub-librarian, an unfortunate decision eagerly pounced on by the pro-patriot police. The affair escalated to a ridiculous degree, and was only resolved when Napoleon intervened personally on Balbo's behalf.

The pettiness of this incident is indicative of the seething suspicions and animosities which were still alive, even within the ranks of those with a common allegiance to the regime, epitomized by the fact that Balbo, a man known to have the direct confidence of the Emperor, was still being watched by the police in 1808. The general conclusion made in the context of southern France, that 'Napoleon, like all dictators, had merely placed many of France's problems "on ice" ',[30] applies to the whole Empire. There is a mass of evidence at every turn to support this judgement throughout the whole of Napoleonic Europe, and it is all the more poignant when that evidence comes from within the administration itself.

Nevertheless, other forces were also at work on the ruling classes of the inner empire and, however qualified, they should not be discounted for the future development of the political culture of western Europe. The lands of the inner empire had their problems kept 'on ice' for some time, and in that time most of them came to respect the Napoleonic system, if not its French purveyors or each other. This was an achievement with important consequences for the future. During Napoleonic rule, as under the *ancien régime*, rivalries and animosities were contested within civilized bounds and by largely peaceful means. To collaborate was to accept these rules, however grudgingly. The Napoleonic period cannot be understood without the traumatic experiences of the Revolution or the older problems of the *ancien régime*, but the extended experience of civil peace in most of the inner empire for most of the period deserves consideration.

There was a common strand among those who collaborated with the Napoleonic regime or, more accurately, among those who found something of value in it, even if their adherence fell short of genuine loyalty. It was based on a belief in the philosophy of the Enlightenment in its most general and least refined form, particularly as applied to the role of the state in society. When von Bieberstein struck at seigneurial dues in Nassau, he did so not only to strengthen the state he happened – as a foreigner – to serve, but because he regarded such practices as 'no longer compatible with the degree of civilization among the peoples'.[31] Their goal became 'to modify the traditional for the good of the whole'.[32] To this end they strove – against the odds – to persuade the 'citizens' created by their reforms to identify with that whole, the state, rather than with their older identities·of caste, province, occupation, or town. The Napoleonic Empire became the last – if not always the most popular – hope of most contemporary reformers, but it reserved its most profound influence for those who served it directly. The borders of Napoleonic Europe were created by military aggression; its internal history was driven forward as an act of bureaucratic will imposed on a recalcitrant population. To men of this stamp, a constitutional, advanced state meant a well-regulated public order, not a representative one. Reform in this context meant riding roughshod over traditional forms of representation as well as feudal strictures. This was as true of independent imitators as of the Empire itself. In Baden, von Reitzenstein disbanded the ancient local assemblies of the 'home towns', such as that of Breisgau,[33] in the same spirit as Napoleon abolished the Tribunate and local elections. None of those involved doubted it was for the best.

The Napoleonic regime has received many epithets – the 'bourgeois empire', 'the gangster state', 'the dictatorship of the notables' – most of which are not without foundation, but there is room enough for another: 'the empire of the professionals'. To christen it thus is also to admit that the regime did not achieve much success in laying its foundations where it most wanted to, among the landed classes, who had interests dearer to them than state service, at least on the thoroughly professional terms insisted on by the Napoleonic regime. By and large, they could not rise above narrow provincial horizons, but there were others who could, and they became more than the backbone of the army and the administration, but the heart and soul of the new order being forged in these years. Most were of bourgeois origins, but not all, especially within the army. Increasingly they were younger men to whom careers were more important than inherited, landed wealth. They were epitomized by Napoleon's adopted son, Eugène de Beauharnais, Viceroy of the Kingdom of Italy, whose ideal was a bureaucracy composed of men whose personal interests were bound to those of the state, rather than of men whose private interests were reflected by the state. Above all, they adhered to Napoleon's assertion 'that there cannot be true liberty, for either the Nation or its citizens, where good administration is not to be found'. Contrary to the myth cultivated later which based the success of the regime on the personal charisma of Napoleon, 'the true believer' worshipped the system, not the man. That was the contemporary reality, and the heart of true collaboration.

The false dawn of Tilsit

The victories 1806–07 marked the apogee of both collaboration and consolidation. It was no coincidence that the elites of the new German and Venetian territories swarmed to the regime in these years. However much disdain or disappointment they harboured, it did not express itself in their public behaviour. Within those areas already under French control, deeply royalist families such as the Barolos and Cavours, who had held themselves aloof since the late 1790s, now began to come forward, accepting posts and extending social acceptance to the French. Attitudes in the Belgian departments – which had been under French rule even longer and where the local elites had remained in resolute isolation – showed similar signs of change. In 1807, the French prefect of Liège observed that the clergy, landowners and merchants seemed 'confident and of goodwill' towards the regime. Suddenly, the Belgian upper classes accepted the prefects' invitations to official social functions. Madame de la Tour du Pin, an indefatigable ambassador for the regime to high society, claimed she had successfully reconciled the Belgian aristocracy to the imperial government.[34]

To a regime intent on staying and ruling, these things mattered; there was nothing trivial about them to those in power. When the imperial nobility was created in 1808, there were powerful indications that it would amalgamate the elites not only of France, but of the whole Empire. In the event, it was to be a false dawn. The aura of invincibility passed as suddenly as it had arisen. The phrase 'a turning point that failed to turn' is an over-employed one in modern European history, usually linked to the revolutions of 1848–49, but it has a striking relevance to the circumstances in Europe between the battle of Jena and the invasion of Spain.

Notes

1 J. Moore, *A view of society and manners in France, Switzerland and Germany*, (Dublin, 1779). Cited in T.C.W. Blanning, *The French Revolution in Germany*, (Oxford, 1983) p. 249.

2 Archives Nationales de Paris (ANP), F(1)E (Pays Annexés) 87/8, Prefect, dept. Taro, to the Minister of the Interior, 10 December 1808.

3 ANP F(1)E, (Pays Annexés) 87/8, Administrator-General, Parma, to the Minister of the Interior, 23 July 1806.

4 ANP F(1)E (Pays Annexés) 86, Lt. Lacroix to Lebrun, Administrator-General, Liguria, undated (*c.*1806).

5 Cited in G.P. Gooch, *Germany and the French Revolution*, (London, 1965 edn) p. 198.

6 M. Cuaz, *Le Nuove di Francia: l'immagine della rivoluzione francese nella stampa periodica italiana*, (Turin, 1990) p. 13.

7 Cited in Blanning, *Germany*, p. 88.

8 ANP AF(IV), 945, Minister of Religion (Cultes) to Napoleon, 18 June 1806.

9 Archivio di Stato di Bologna, (ASB) Sezzione Preffetura del Reno, Titolo xxiv, Articolo 19 (Soppressione dei Conventi) Prefect, dipt, del Reno to Min della Polizia, Milan, 6 July 1810.

10 Cited in G. De Rosa, 'La vita religiosa nel Mezzogiorno durante la dominazione francese', *Pratiques Réligieuses, dans l'Europe révolutionnaire*, eds. P. Larou and R. Darteville (Paris, 1988) pp. 103–11.

11 ANP AF(IV) (Cultes, 1807–1809) 1046, Dossier II (1808) Minister of Religion (Cultes) to Napoleon, April 1808.

12 Archivio di Stato di Genova (ASG), Preffetura Francese, Pacco 78, Fasciolo 106 (Culto), Sub-prefect of Novi to Prefect, dept. Gênes, 6 August 1811.

13 Archivio di Stato di Firenze (ASF) Buon Governo, 461, (1808), Archbishop of Pisa to President of the Buon Governo, 1 April 1808.

14 De Rosa, *Pratiques Réligieuses*, p. 63.

15 ANP AF(IV), 1303, 'Vues de l'Organisation du Culte Catholique', 3 June 1811.

16 ANP F(1)E (Pays Annexés), 74 (Piémont) 'Rapport de la Boulinière et Cappelle sur le Piemont', 1806.

17 Cited in Schmidt, *Berg*, pp. 221–2.

18 On Germany: T.C.W. Blanning, 'German Jacobins and the French Revolution', *Historical Journal*, 23 (1980) pp. 985–1002, forcefully redresses the unbalanced views of W. Grab, *Ein volk muss seine Freiheit selbst eroben: Zur Geschichte der deurschen Jakobiner*, 2 vols (Berlin, 1975, 1981). On Italy, M. Broers, 'Revolution as vendetta: Napoleonic Piedmont, 1800–1814', *Historical Journal*, 33 (1990), for views close to those of Blanning.

19 Cited in Blanning, 'German Jacobins', p. 993.

20 Cited in Antonielli, *Prefetti*, p. 254.

21 ANP F(1)E (Pays Annexés), 78 (Piémont), 'Memoire sur le Piémont', an XI (1802).
22 ANP BB(18) (Justice Criminelle et Correctionelle) 841 (dept. Sesia), Prefect, dept. Sesia, to the Minister of the Interior, 8 March 1809.
23 Among the better, standard works, Holtman, *Napoleonic Revolution*, pp. 179–93, incorporates many of these misconceptions. H. Kohn, 'Napoleon and the age of nationalism', *Journal of Modern History*, 22 (1950), encapsulates them. For a clear expression of more recent, realistic views, at a general level, Wright, *Napoleon and Europe*, pp. 71–3.
24 Schama, *Patriots*, p. 473.
25 Cited in Broers, 'Revolution as vendetta', ii, p. 802.
26 Cited in Antonielli, *Prefetti*, p. 68.
27 G. Pedlow, *The Survival of the Hessian Nobility, 1770–1870*, (Princeton, NJ, 1988).
28 Ibid.
29 For the most recent discussion of this, see Ellis, *Napoleonic Empire*, pp. 72–81, for his critique of the view of Jean Tulard, the major exponent of the concept of '*amalgame*'. Ellis cites in his favour the important article, Whitcomb, 'Napoleon's prefects'.
30 G. Lewis, 'Political brigandage and popular disaffection in the southeast of France, 1795–1804', in *Beyond the Terror*, pp. 195–231, 231.
31 Cited in Anderson, 'State-building in early nineteenth century Nassau', p. 239.
32 An apt phrase coined by L.S. Flockerzie, 'State-building and nation building in the "Third Germany": Saxony after the Congress of Vienna', *Central European History*, 24 (1991) pp. 268–92, 290.
33 Lee, 'Baden between revolutions', p. 252.
34 Cited in P. Verhaegen, *La Belgique sous la domination française, 1792–1814*, 5 vols (Brussels, 1923–1929).

|4|

Crisis, 1808–1811

The Continental Blockade and the reordering of Europe, 1807–1809

Expansion in Germany and Italy: coastal security

Napoleon's first priority in 1807 was to make Britain sue for peace by means of the economic Continental Blockade. Henceforth, its enforcement dominated the development of the Empire. Napoleon had to control the entire coastline of Europe, from the Baltic to the Mediterranean. This was a momentous and ultimately impossible ambition, but it remained central to French policy from 1807 onwards. Napoleon himself had few illusions about the privations in store. As early as December 1807, he told his brother Louis, the King of Holland, 'The blockade will ruin many commercial towns: Lyon, Amsterdam, Rotterdam . . .'. He could have extended the list to every port where his writ ran.

The long French tradition of economic protectionism received a new lease of life when the outbreak of the revolutionary wars in 1792 allowed successive governments to enact trade and tariff legislation aimed at strangling British commerce in the name of the war effort. Napoleon was building on this legislation even before the Berlin Decrees of 1806, just as he drew heavily on a mercantilist tradition of economic thought that stretched back to Colbert and Louis XIV. However, from the Peace of Tilsit onwards, the economic blockade of Britain became the pivot of all French policy, domestic and foreign, military and economic. It stemmed from a widely shared belief that the victories of 1806–07 seemed to make the blockade feasible.

Initially, the blockade was meant to work through co-operation, not coercion. Napoleon stood by the policy of maintaining as limited and indirect a French presence as was possible, in the states bordering the inner empire, confined to the military occupation of key installations crucial to the blockade. There was a great deal of bullying, directed at the small states of northern Germany, Tuscany, the Papacy, Spain and Portugal – and eventually of Louis in Holland, as well – to make them enforce the blockade, but there was no serious territorial expansion until December 1807, when Tuscany was occupied and March 1808, when Napoleon deposed the Spanish Bourbons in favour of his brother Joseph. The annexations of the Papal States and the north German coast did not take place until after the outbreak of war with Austria in 1809. The outer empire was created with as much hesitancy as the inner one had been.

Almost simultaneously with the issuing of the Berlin Decrees in mid-November 1806, French and Dutch troops occupied the three Hansa ports of Hamburg, Lübeck and Bremen, on the North Sea coast of Germany, together with some of the smaller ports and coastal fortresses. Beyond this, the senates of the Hansa towns continued to rule much as before. The occupation was accepted with resignation rather than enthusiasm, but the general view of the three senates was that a strong military presence would at least keep the area out of any further fighting. The enforcement of the blockade was merely irksome, at this stage; fiercer resentment was triggered by the conscription of 3000 sailors from the Hansa ports by the French in February 1808. Once again, the demands of the modern, Napoleonic state had intruded into the world of small, *ancien régime* countries – by now the last bastions of what had been the Holy Roman Empire – which had scarcely possessed armed forces, never mind conscription. This incident marks the point when resentment turned into hostility, but until the introduction of conscription occupation produced unexpected benefits which probably offset its burdens. Indeed, in the period between their occupation late in 1806 and annexation to France in 1810, this indirect – ultimately farcical – form of French control helped engender something of an economic 'boom' in the Hansa ports. Although Napoleon forbade the Hansa towns to trade directly with Britain after 1806, they were allowed to go on trading with neutral shipping, a concession he did not grant to his own ports. This loophole was exploited to the full, and was made all the easier by a succession of easily corruptible French military commanders – Mortier, Brune and, finally, Bernadotte, judged by the locals the most susceptible of the three – and by the permanent presence of Bourienne, the French ambassador to the Hansa ports from 1805 to 1810 when, significantly, he was recalled to Paris on charges of corruption. The rich cultural life of these city-states continued to flourish under their liberal, tolerant merchant elites.

By 1807, the last major vestiges of the old order on the Italian mainland were the Papal States and the former Grand Duchy of Tuscany, made into the Kingdom of Etruria in 1801 under a Spanish Bourbon. Both of these states witnessed periods of concerted reform in the late eighteenth century, under Pius VI in Rome and Peter-Leopold in Tuscany, but from the late 1790s they became bastions of reaction, their Francophile reformers effectively marginalized and intermittently persecuted by the new, wary regimes of Pius VII, Pope since 1800, and the Spanish Infanta, Maria-Luisa, who ruled Etruria after the death of her husband, Luigi I, in 1803, and who built on the reactionary policies of her Habsburg predecessor, Ferdinand III. The only major policy they preserved from the era of reform was neutrality and it led Napoleon to overthrow them. Initially, as in the Hansa ports, Napoleon preferred a policy of limited military occupation to direct rule. The main port of the Tuscan coast was Livorno, which Peter-Leopold had gone to great lengths to turn into one of the most important commercial ports in Italy by the 1780s. As with the Hansa towns, its neutral status had brought Livorno heightened prosperity, because it was open to legitimate, neutral shipping, and to the English as well, in violation of official agreements with France. Then, in the summer of 1807, a French garrison 'cleansed' Livorno of its English merchandise. In scenes soon to be repeated in the Hansa and Dutch ports, dumbfounded crowds saw confiscated goods piled high on the main square and ceremoniously set alight. Soon, it was very clear that the French would stay until they had broken blockade running.

French troops had been in Etruria since 1802, but a purely military presence was no longer felt to be enough in Paris by 1807. Napoleon regarded Etruria as a client state and interpreted its neutrality as pro-Austrian during the war of 1805 and as pro-British thereafter. Maria-Luisa was seen increasingly as an unreliable ally, not only because of her tolerant attitude to widespread blockade running, but because the French perceived her regime as ideologically unsound – reactionary – and, therefore, pro-Austrian. She dismissed most of Peter-Leopold's ministers, some of whom had been recalled in 1802 to restore the state's disastrous finances, replacing them with men who had fought the French in 1799. This had actually been done to remove men with Habsburg loyalties from the government, and so reinforce Etrurian neutrality. However, Clarke, the French ambassador in Florence, interpreted this in its domestic context, as a counter-revolutionary gesture. He saw the reactionary ecclesiastical policies of the Queen as a sign of unreliability; in 1805, his secretary told Talleyrand that 'all the jobs and all the positions at Court are being entrusted to men who stood in the ranks of the anti-French faction [in 1799]'.[1] On 5 December, Napoleon deposed Maria-Luisa.

The change of regime was not met with overt resistance – it had been only a Napoleonic imposition in the first place – but Maria-Luisa had allowed the anti-French faction to reassert itself, less in terms of power than of popularity. In the last months of her rule, under a constant hail of French threats, Maria-Luisa continued to patronize the arts and support the resurgence of popular piety through public processions as an overt form of passive resistance to the imminent arrival of the new order.

Tuscany was transformed into a Grand Duchy under Napoleon's sister Elise, but in practice it consisted of three departments ruled from Paris. In

May 1808, Menou was sent to Florence as head of the transitional administration, the Giunta, to oversee the integration of Tuscany into the Empire. It was another challenge for the same 'team' that had dealt with the Vendée, the Rhineland and Piedmont.

Events in the Papal States followed a similar pattern. Since 1801, Pius VII had watched the introduction of the Concordat into Napoleon's Italian possessions with increasing unease, just as Napoleon had become ever more concerned by the Pope's inability to close his ports – Ancona, Civita Vecchia and Rimini – against the British and by his refusal to convert his neutrality into an alliance. Cardinal Fesch, the French ambassador to Rome, was as suspicious of Pius VII's real sympathies as Clarke was of those of the Bourbons in Florence. Napoleon needed the ports' closure; the Papal States were too weak to comply. Following an Anglo-Russian attempt to attack the Bay of Naples in November 1805, Napoleon sent troops into the Papal States in force. The horrors of occupation followed, as Fesch admitted, in December 1805:

> we put pressure on the Papal States: we raise taxes by force, we make them feed our troops. The generals respect nothing [in order to] enrich themselves. The poor Pope is in a violent mood ... [The French generals] first impose arbitrary taxes and then commit acts of aggression ... What reprisals [there will be] if events allow the Allies into Ancona![2]

Pius VII met the French with much more determined, outspoken resistance than the Bourbons in Florence, albeit of an equally non-violent character. 'The French are detestable to them, and what would they not do to them, if they had the power?', as Fesch observed[3] – and Napoleon came to agree. In 1806, he sent troops into the ports without Papal consent; in March, the Pope refused his demand to expel the allied ambassadors. The separate quarrel over the introduction of the Concordat into Italy – particularly its provisions for civil marriage which horrified Pius VII – merged with that of the blockade in Napoleon's mind by July 1807, when he told Eugène:

> perhaps the time is not far off when I will recognize the Pope only as the Bishop of Rome, equal in rank to any of the other bishops of my realms. I am not afraid ... to conduct my business without the Pope ...[4]

The threats of deposition and annexation were thinly veiled; perhaps more significant is the fact that Napoleon had no qualms about deposing the Pope, who was more than just temporal ruler. A few months later the French demanded the Pope's co-operation in the war against Britain and that he close his ports and allow the French to occupy them. They also insisted on their right to extend the terms of the Concordat throughout Italy. Pius VII refused, and on 2 February 1808 the French occupied Rome.

In 1809, the Papal States became two French departments, Tiber (later Rome) and Trasimène.

The Pope had a powerful grip over his people, and he displayed a level of defiance which led Napoleon to remove him forcibly from the Vatican, first to Savona, near Genoa, and then to Fontainebleau, but not before Pius had ordered his treasury to stop supplying the occupying forces and his people not to serve the new government. He was widely obeyed. By early 1808, so many cardinals – who were the heads of the Papal bureaucracy as well as prelates – had been arrested that the administrative structure all but collapsed. 'A chaotic situation, pregnant with fear, characterized the first moments of institutional transition.'[5] So began one of the most intense and widespread instances of organized passive resistance to their rule the French had yet encountered. In its own way, the peaceful refusal to co-operate with the French in the Papal States rivalled the more violent resistance they were about to meet in Spain.

Roman and Spanish resistance sprang from almost identical roots which had little to do with the initial motives behind Napoleon's intervention. Expedient annexations to enforce the blockade soon showed signs of reverting to a French revolutionary crusade against the old foe of counter-revolution. The French ambassadors stressed the dangers of domestic counter-revolution in the states of central Italy, as much if not more than the military issues at stake. A pattern was already being set which emerged more clearly after annexation: geopolitics would, again, merge with an ideological mission. In Rome, the French had struck at the apex of the Church and at the most legitimate ruler in Catholic Europe; the ramshackle nature of this state in no way detracted from this, as those sent to rule the new territories were soon to learn. The standard of resistance had been raised by Pius VII as he was unceremoniously dragged away into exile, and it was answered, peacefully but determinedly. The annexation of central Italy was going to be messy and unpleasant, if feasible.

It was to be in Spain that Fesch's rhetorical question – 'what would they not do to them, if they had the power?' – would be answered. The decision to enter Spain also meant that all the newly annexed territories would come into the Empire at a time when its resources were stretched further than ever before. Tilsit had only seemed to be a turning point; Spain was the real sea-change.

Spain and Portugal, 1808–1809: tactical intervention, resistance and collaboration

Franco-Spanish relations had improved under Napoleon from formal conflict under the Directory to nominal ally, and by 1808 there were over

100 000 French troops in Spain. Their behaviour did not fail to produce tensions with local communities, but the reasons for their presence were generally interpreted as friendly by most Spaniards. French troop levels had been increased throughout 1806–08, mainly for a projected Franco-Spanish invasion of Portugal, and there is little evidence that Napoleon harboured plans to depose the Bourbons during these years; his distrust of them, although voiced at times, was never as intense as his growing quarrel with Pius VII, for example, nor was Spain as central to his security as central Italy or the North Sea coast. As so often before when he had extended the Empire, Napoleon moved out of exasperation rather than as a result of a premeditated plan.

However loyal, the Spanish Bourbons had proved incompetent military allies, and in the new world of the Continental Blockade, Napoleon could not afford Spanish inefficiency. His impatience grew because the blockade had turned Lisbon into one of the greatest centres of smuggling in Europe by 1807. Napoleon's initial goal even as late as 1808 was not to conquer Spain, but to control Portuguese trade. Ultimately, it was the internal turmoil of the Spanish royal family that led Napoleon to depose them,[6] and the initial reaction to this was not without encouraging signs for Napoleon's new course of action in Spain.

Spaniards were deeply aware of the need for a far-reaching reform of their country, but all such initiatives had foundered on powerful vested interests and engendered a bitter legacy of factionalism at Court. Charles III, who died in 1788, had been one of the most ambitious reformers of the late eighteenth century, and many of his progressive ministers were still active in 1808, such as the legal reformer Jovellanos, who spent the years 1801–07 in exile, the anticlerical Urquijo, and the ageing Floridablanca, Charles III's Chief Minister. By the eve of Napoleon's intervention, however they had become embroiled in the very web of power struggles their enlightened reforms were meant to curb. There was a sad inevitability about this, as they were faced by a rival faction – itself not intrinsically hostile to all reform – gathered around the new King, Charles IV. The high politics of the years between 1788 and 1808 were dominated by men who, although seldom reactionaries, were more committed to preserving themselves in office than exercising power, more concerned with defending themselves against their rivals than strengthening the state.

When the King and the heir to the throne, Ferdinand, became directly involved in the faction fighting, as deadly rivals, an urgent crisis developed that Napoleon could not ignore. Charles IV had relied on Manuel Godoy as his Chief Minister since 1798. Godoy was far from a reactionary; indeed, his army reforms had earned him the enmity of many of the traditionalist nobles, but his manoeuvring for office had implicated him in the disgrace of Jovellanos in 1798 and of Urquijo two years later, and so turned the progressive faction against him as well. Unjustifiably, Godoy became a thoroughly hated political figure in Spanish public opinion between 1801 and

1808, mainly because he had kept so many rivals out of office for so long. These circumstances made it all the easier for the diverse strands of opposition to gather around Ferdinand and to project him as an alternative ruler to Charles IV.

By October 1807, the rivalry between father and son led them both to appeal separately to Napoleon for protection against each other, but Napoleon did nothing. However, when, on 18 March 1808, Charles and Ferdinand openly turned on each other at the royal palace of Aranjuez, the political crisis in Spain moved from the endemic to the urgent. Organized and led by Ferdinand's supporters, a mob attacked Godoy's home and turned him over to Ferdinand, who imprisoned him. Panicked by the revolt, Charles IV abdicated in favour of his son, but then reneged on it and appealed to Napoleon for help. Aranjuez was the first step along a very long, momentous road; the country would not be united under a single government until 1814.

Napoleon now decided to depose both claimants in favour of one of his brothers. Spain was offered first to Louis, who refused – a worrying indication for Napoleon of how attached he had become to the Dutch – and then to Joseph, who accepted with some reservations. The craven manner in which Charles and Ferdinand signed away their throne to Joseph at Bayonne seemed to justify this course of action. Nevertheless, Ferdinand had come to the throne on a tide of popular euphoria which engulfed the whole of Spain as the news spread of Godoy's fall.

The news of the abdications produced three distinct responses in Spain. In the first days of May, the popular classes of Madrid – and then of most provincial centres – rose in a series of ferocious, specifically anti-French revolts, utterly spontaneous and almost hysterical in their determination. In contrast, the central government in Madrid froze and then retreated into a sterile legalism which amounted to collaborating with the French on the grounds that Charles had ordered them to obey Murat, the commander of the French forces in Spain, who he had appointed 'Lieutenant of the Kingdom'. Finally, the provincial notables and the local authorities were caught between these two responses: one came from below that was powerful, frightening, but essentially anarchic; the other from above, which was well-informed, with strong claims to legitimacy and spoke with the voice of reason against the tide of popular disorder, but it was as impotent as the other was frenetic.

Essentially, the central government and the French, on one side, and the popular, pro-Bourbon movements on the other, were bidding for the support of the only effective political authority left in Spain: the provincial administrations. As had so often been the case when the revolutionary storm had broken over other countries, the state had fallen back, momentarily, into its constituent parts. In Spain, this meant the traditional regions of the kingdom. Decades of determined efforts at centralization by the monarchy were disintegrating in a matter of weeks.

The crucial characteristic of the anti-French revolts of the spring of 1808 was their provincialism, in every sense of the word. Although the risings were widespread, they seldom reached beyond their own provincial borders; from the outset, then, Spanish resistance was organized on a provincial basis, which long remained its essence. All the strengths, weaknesses and paradoxes of counter-revolution come into sharp relief in Spain. The rebels rose for their King – Ferdinand VII, 'the hoped for one' – but also in response to a fear of the supposed atheism of revolutionary France and, not surprisingly, the clergy played a very prominent role in the first stages of the rising, as they would continue to do in most of the fighting to come. The appeal to religion touched a very particular, powerful nerve among the Spanish masses, urban and rural alike, and in this is to be found one of the deepest paradoxes in the relationship between national identity and the *ancien régime* world of provincial and local loyalties. The revolts of 1808 drew on, and probably strengthened, a deeply rooted sense of Spanish national feeling, inextricably linked to Catholicism and a shared sense of history that centred on the forging of a Catholic nation in the medieval wars against the Moors, the *Reconquista*. Yet this shared sense of identity and purpose was not equated with political or administrative unity, even when dynastic loyalty was as fiercely felt as it obviously was in Spain.

In the prevailing chaos, the provinces were forced to go their own ways, but they also found it very difficult to work together. A new national government, the *Junta Central*, was formed in September 1808, but its existence was beset by problems with the emergent provincial governments, the *juntas supremas*, as they chose, significantly, to call themselves.[7] These juntas had emerged at provincial level simply because the popular, localized movements of the first days saw the province as the natural political unit and instinctively allowed their own insurrectionary municipal committees to cede power to them to organize resistance through what has been called 'an instinctive federalism' that reasserted itself at the collapse of power at the centre.[8] The transfer of authority from provincial to national level was much harder to achieve. This lack of co-ordination had always been the greatest weakness within most resistance to French rule, and they had exploited it to the full in crushing revolts all over the inner empire.

The most powerful, co-ordinated force in Spain was the 118 000 troops of the French army; much depended on whether – and how many – Spaniards would see them as a force for order and stability, or as an instrument of foreign oppression. At this stage, the outcome was not as clearcut as the fury of the popular revolts of May and June 1808, or future events, might make it appear. The case of Spain must not be taken in isolation. The French had faced these terrors before – in Belgium, Italy and the Rhineland, as well as the Vendée – and, eventually, prevailed. There were signs in Spain that the patterns of earlier interventions were being repeated.

Shortly after the abdication of the Bourbons, Napoleon called an assembly of the leading figures of Spanish public life in Bayonne. Several refused, Jovellanos notable among them, but a significant number of royal ministers did attend, most of whom had reputations as determined reformers – 'the men of Charles III' – led by Urquijo. Napoleon responded by drafting a constitution for Spain which was far more conciliatory to the notables than those he had recently bestowed on Westphalia and the Grand Duchy of Warsaw, at least on paper. The constitution of Bayonne said nothing about the nationalization of Church lands, the abolition of the regular orders or the suppression of seigneurial rights; it also maintained Catholicism as the only tolerated religion of Spain; above all, conscription was not introduced. Only this final concession would survive Napoleon and Joseph's personal experience of Spanish resistance, but in 1808, at Bayonne, it seemed well worth conciliating the Spanish elite, lay and clerical. Indeed, in a comparative context, they were the most favoured in Napoleonic Europe, to the temporary disappointment of many liberals in their ranks.

Perhaps even more encouraging for the French had been the response of the central authorities in Madrid to the events of early May. The rising in Madrid, los Dos Mayo, acquired a potent symbolism in Spain almost immediately. The courage of the urban popular classes, organized and led by traditionalist nobles and clergy, gave the signal for the provincial risings that followed. However, los Dos Mayo was not a unified movement; the spectre of disorder frightened many within the propertied classes and almost everyone at the apex of government. There were good grounds for the French to believe that Murat's ruthless suppression of the revolt might be welcomed as the restoration of order, probably their most effective means of winning support hitherto. In his memoirs, the writer Mesonero Romanos recalled his parents' growing dread as the crowds sallied forth along their street on 2 May 1808. As his father paced the floor nervously, his mother said the rosary.[9] The future liberal politician Alcalà Galiano remembered that, as a youth, his parents had forbidden him to join the rebels on los Dos Mayo: 'it was for the lower classes ... sensible people did not involve themselves'.[10]

Their fears were shared by the men Ferdinand had left in charge when he went to Bayonne. The highest levels of the administrations – the Council of Castille and the Junta de Gobierno – desired internal order and to avoid war with France. This was coloured by a deep sense of resignation following the abdications; their last orders from Ferdinand had been to call a Cortes, but Charles had told them to make Murat President of the Junta de Gobierno which, in turn, would give him control of the Council of Castille, a body that was 'after the king, the cornerstone of the Spanish monarchy ... which represented the first rung of delegated royal authority'.[11] When these two bodies recognized Joseph as King, it gave the Bonapartes as strong a legal claim to the throne as they could hope for; more importantly, it was a sign, far weightier than the support given at the assembly of Bayonne, that Napoleon had the support of the leaders of the Spanish state.

They were led by Cabarrus, O'Farril and Azanza, enlightened reformers who had been victims of Godoy and, therefore, partisans of Ferdinand, who had appointed them to the Junta de Gobierno. By accepting Joseph, it is probable that they hoped simply to end the crisis, get themselves out of the way and avoid all further responsibility for what might follow. They saw this as their last act and set about mechanically issuing Murat's orders, most of which concerned repressing the provincial revolts in an effort to recall the regional juntas to order. In effect, they deliberately vacated power in the hope that the French would restore order and that an instinctive feeling of resignation, even apathy, would prevail in Spain. This was a much less enthusiastic form of collaboration than had been seen among the liberals at Bayonne. Its main aim was to avoid civil war by the only means to hand, Murat's troops. These hopes failed, as did their plans to leave office; Azanza, O'Farril and Cabarrus all went on to become Joseph's leading ministers, along with Urquijo. Almost by accident – certainly not by their own design – Joseph had reassembled around him the partisans of enlightened reform, much as he had already done in Naples, another early cause for optimism.

Far from all *ancien régime* reformers in Spain joined the French; in Spain, as in Italy and Germany, Napoleonic intervention split the conservative enlightenment. In 1808, however the die had not yet been cast. Jovellanos, who would emerge as a rebel leader, wrote privately to his friend, Mazarredo – already one of Joseph's ministers – that he thought well of the new King and was impressed by his achievements in Naples. His ultimate choice of allegiance notwithstanding, Jovellanos was as frightened by the spectre of popular revolt as his friends among the collaborators. His thoughts closely resembled theirs – and those of Joseph – when in the spring of 1808 he wrote:

> Civil war...the worst of all ills, is already inevitable... Vengeance and rage are in every heart, without a single exception, and shamefully, these feelings produce so great a fervour that it seems difficult to reduce them to order.[12]

Like the collaborators – the *afrancesados* or *josefinos* – Jovellanos felt a deep sense of regret and resignation at the course of events but, unlike them, his sense of resignation extended to the inevitability of conflict – and therefore to the need to take sides. Nevertheless, his reluctance to do so was obvious, as was his distaste at the prospect of a civil war based on popular risings and rooted in disorder. This tension was present at the heart of almost every provincial junta in 1808. Even at the very eye of the storm, the fragility of resistance could be sensed.

The provincial elites seldom responded with the fervour of the popular classes in the spring and summer of 1808. In the years ahead, the local notables and civil servants thrust into power at the head of the provincial juntas, would guard their powers jealously against a succession of central governments. However their initial reaction was usually tainted with fear, particularly where, as in Oviedo, the capital of Asturias, the populace was able to disarm the French garrison and, in turn, arm themselves; or when, as at Cartagena, in the province of Murcia, the Spanish garrison mutinied and joined the rebels. In many cases, provincial officials and military commanders who opposed resisting the French were driven from office. One who survived almost in spite of himself was the Captain-General of Valencia. On 23 May 1808, he was faced by crowds led by a Franciscan friar and an army captain demanding the formation of a provincial junta and a local army to fight the French. He complied with these demands, but also wrote to Madrid, begging the Council of Castille to send troops to quell the revolt. When Madrid did not react, the rebels prevailed, a junta was formed and Valencia went on to become one of the fiercest centres of resistance.[13]

These provincial revolts and the juntas they spawned have been interpreted as the core of a 'revolutionary process' within the Spanish counter-revolution.[14] In 1808, the evidence would seem to run firmly against such claims. The popular revolts were truly counter-revolutionary in character; they were not driven by class hatreds or economic motives, such as food shortages. Equally, the masses and the notables of the smaller towns were willing to follow the existing administration if it would fight the French. It is also striking how reluctant most provincial elites were to act without Madrid. As the example of Valencia makes all too clear, central government was paralysed, leaving its provincial administrators to face the popular tide alone. In most cases, they decided to lead this tide, rather than defy it.

The truly 'revolutionary process' began when, to maintain their control and a semblance of public order, the Spanish provincial elites assumed powers that, if territorially narrow, were fuller than anything they had ever known. Few of them were without experience of public life, if usually only at provincial level. Now they were on their own, and were quick to consolidate themselves. By supporting the war, they had secured an unprecedented level of popular support, averted the horrors of further popular tumult and reaffirmed their right to govern. Effectively, this was the turning-point; inertia coupled with sheer logistics had lost the new government the support of the provincial elites. Even with over 100 000 troops in the country, Murat had found Spain too large to control. The French garrisons in the key fortresses were too isolated and small to withstand the risings, while Murat's central force of about 40 000 in Madrid could not hope to strike out in several directions at once.

Dispersion and lack of co-operation among the juntas was quickly perceived as a vital problem by the Spanish themselves, especially because their initial plans turned on an offensive war to drive out the French; such attempts soon proved disastrous. The local armies raised by the provincial juntas were lamentably weak and the French crushed them repeatedly when they clashed directly. This was true even when they included regular Spanish troops, who proved no match for even second-rate French forces. Thus, Spain was made to pay the price for decades of failed or ineffective reforms. As early as 1808, however, it was clear that Spain's greatest weapon was her sheer size. The French could not be everywhere; they could not defeat all the juntas at once. Defensively, the scattered nature of the risings proved their salvation. Spain was by far the largest single piece of territory the French had ever tried to absorb at one time and, ultimately, it proved beyond them.

At only one point in the early stages of the war was the pattern of Spanish defeat in the field broken, at Bailen, in the south-east, on 22 July 1808. Its immediate impact was to stiffen the resistance of the provincial juntas and prompt them to create the *Junta Central*. It also panicked Joseph into abandoning Madrid and withdrawing north of the River Ebro. The news of Bailen finally convinced the British to strengthen the small military expedition they had sent to the peninsula in June. Without doubt, this was the most significant long-term result of this unheralded Spanish victory, but its significance was obscured for some time to come by the arrival in Spain of Napoleon himself at the head of almost 170 000 of his best troops.

Napoleon has usually been upbraided by historians for being ill-informed about Spain and Spanish affairs. At a practical level, this is probably un-justified; French troops had been there long enough to supply topographi-cal information and other basic, practical knowledge about the country, nor was the information supplied by his ambassadors quite as useless as has often been inferred.[15] At a more subjective level, his contempt for its 'monk-ridden', superstitious peasantry and degenerate ruling classes was not only shared by most of his compatriots, but often by the British, especially where the Spanish nobility was concerned. Nor did the French reserve this kind of contempt for the Spanish, as has been seen. Napoleon underrated the kind of resistance he found in Spain because he had met it before and overcome it. There was little new about Spanish resistance, except its scale, but even this crucial difference was temporarily obscured by his successes in the 1808–09 campaign. They would re-emerge when, literally, the dust settled.

Napoleon's personal intervention quickly proved Bailen to have been a success not to be repeated, but the sheer size of the peninsula remained the heart of the military problem facing the French.

The importance of diffuse resistance on a wide scale was underlined by the course of events in Portugal, prior to Napoleon's arrival. The years 1801–07 had been profitable for Portuguese merchants, but fraught for their rulers in their attempts to remain neutral. As late as January 1807, Araujo, the Portuguese Chief Minister still felt confident enough to tell the British ambassador that 'I have enough faith in Bonaparte to believe that he will continue to humour us',[16] but even as he spoke, the first of a flood of French ultimatums was on its way to Lisbon. Napoleon demanded the closure of Portuguese ports to the British, the confiscation of all British merchandise and the arrest of all British subjects in Portugal. After protracted negotiations, the ports were closed on 20 October 1807, but when this was followed by a French demand to garrison the coastal fortresses, the Portuguese ministers suddenly showed a remarkable unity and resolve to oppose Napoleon.

Unity at the apex of the state characterized Portuguese leaders throughout the conflict, giving a clear sense of direction to the resistance that was sorely lacking in Spain. Previously, the Portuguese cabinet had been divided into a small 'pro-French' faction centred on Araujo and a larger 'pro-British' one led by Rodrigo de Souza Couthino. Suddenly they agreed that French troops would not be allowed to occupy Portugal, even if this led to war, and, if the French invaded, John VI, the Prince Regent, should withdraw to the Portuguese colony of Brazil. Junot invaded Portugal in late November 1807. On 27 November 1807, the Court sailed for Brazil. Angry crowds gathered on the docks of Lisbon to revile John VI for deserting them; foreshadowing the actions of the Bourbons, he created a Regency Council and ordered it to co-operate with the French. However, more indicative of what was to come were the deserted towns and villages Junot found on his march to Lisbon. This passive resistance denied the French vital supplies, but it was also a clear sign that, should circumstances change, Portugal would resist. There were barely 30 000 French troops in Portugal, and reinforcements were far away.

From December 1807 until June 1808, Junot ruled Portugal without serious opposition. He took his administrative role seriously, hoping to become the head of a new satellite state. To this end, he dissolved the Regency Council in February 1808 and declared John VI deposed; the national militia was disbanded and he sent many units of the regular army to France for incorporation into the imperial forces. In these months, Junot also displayed those progressive elements of imperial rule so recently trumpeted in Westphalia. A constitution was drawn up, embodying religious toleration, equality before the law and freedom of the individual. Junot also proclaimed the more practical benefits to come: 'roads shall be opened, canals shall be dug to facilitate communications, to improve industry and agriculture . . . public education should be fostered and [widely] diffused'.[17] The popular classes of Lisbon remained hostile, their hatred of the French boiling over into violence during serious riots in December 1807, described by Lisbon's Intendant-General of Police as 'the impulse of a united people'.[18] Even those administrators who chose the path of collaboration in these months did so in a clear, open effort to maintain national independence. This was the paramount issue for them and is reflected in the projects for the future of the state they presented to Napoleon; they did not want Junot as their ruler but a member of the imperial family, specifically because this was seen as security against any attempts to annex Portugal to Spain, or to dismember it, both very real threats.[19] This project was most associated with Verdier and was countered by the proposals of Noronha who appealed to Napoleon to restore the Regency Council and summon a Cortes to settle the succession. Despite their important differences, both factions sought to preserve 'the independence of the kingdom subordinate to the protective authority of the Great Napoleon', as the leading journal, *Gazeta de Lisboa*, put it on 28 May 1808.[20] However, also apparent in the proposals of Verdier and Noronha is a political outlook which divorced patriotic nationalism from loyalty to the monarchy and the traditional social order it stood for in the minds of most Portuguese. This strong dynastic loyalty was sharpened by the brutality of the French occupation and, particularly among the nobles and clergy, by the fears for their privileges aroused by Junot's intended reforms, particularly his plans to introduce the French Civil Code.

These reforms far outweighed Junot's stated intention of acting as a bulwark against 'Jacobin anarchy', and the adverse effects of the blockade also alienated the bourgeoisie. Nevertheless, the threat of social anarchy and the rise of *juntismo* in the provinces frightened many within the traditional governing classes. Some believed a national war of resistance would end in a loss of their power to these unfathomed forces. Thus, even in Portugal, there were signs that the favoured Napoleonic tactic of the restoration of order might rally support for Junot, beyond the ranks of the enlightened reformers around Verdier. The Intendant of the Police of Lisbon served Junot without hesitation – and was retained by the Regency – for exactly these reasons. However Junot's rule was cut short.

The rising in Spain in May 1808 precipitated similar revolts in Portugal in June. They were strengthened further by the arrival of a British expeditionary force in early August, under Wellesley, the future Duke of Wellington. The British presence was crucial for sustaining Portuguese resistance, but beside it must be set the capacity for unity and co-operation, as well as courage, displayed by the Portuguese political classes. Collective, popular resistance was quickly channelled into the national cause and a properly co-ordinated war effort. The contrast with Spain was a subtle one, but it proved vital in creating a solid and extensive territorial base against the French south of the Pyrenees:

> In Spain, the principal resistance was simultaneous, but [it took place] in regions very distant [from each other]; ours took a more co-ordinated form, with its origins in a widespread discontent, provoked by a variety of reasons.[21]

The first major revolt was in Porto on 6 June 1808. Porto had overtaken Lisbon as the country's busiest port by 1807, and its merchants had much to lose from the imposition of the blockade, while its popular classes shared in the general resentment of French military occupation and the deposition of Prince John. The French were driven out by the united populace of the city and a junta was set up under the Bishop of Porto. The French retreat following the rising in Porto provoked a mass of small local revolts throughout northern Portugal, each under its own leadership at this stage. The coastal town of Viana became another important centre of resistance, its rising on 18 June being carefully planned by the municipality and led by an army lieutenant, Barretto, under an elected junta led by the military governor. The Algarve, in the far south, also followed Porto's lead in a series of isolated revolts, on a pattern which led one observer to remark:

> Such was the mania for juntas in Alem Tejo that right down to the smallest hamlets of 15 or 20 households... [there were] juntas composed of the parish priest and several tenant farmers... acting as in the name of the seigneurs.[22]

All of this seems very similar to Spain, but the crucial differences were the disciplined, almost deferential respect for authority shown in these risings – the initiative usually came from recognized local leaders – and, above all, the readiness of the local juntas to recognize the supreme authority of Porto. The junta in Viana, for example, wrote to Porto offering its allegiance almost immediately, as did the two major southern juntas at Beja and Evora, who learned quickly how futile it was to try to resist the French alone. All of them proclaimed their loyalty to the Prince Regent and began raising local troops to replace the disbanded royal army. This success rested on the undisputed respect for the authority of the Supreme Junta in Porto which, in turn, was based on the personal authority of its Bishop-President, Castro, and the sure knowledge that the true purpose of the revolt was the restoration of the monarchy and the Catholic religion. Significantly, an earlier attempt to raise a revolt in Porto, led by liberal army officers on 7 June, had failed; it was only later on 16 June, when Bishop Castro took the lead during the festivities of Corpus Christi, that popular support was assured. Similarly, he moved quickly to abolish any other sources of authority to the Supreme Junta within Porto; on 5 July he dissolved the Military Junta – the council of liberal officers who had helped plan the revolt – on a trumped up charge of treason. In this way, not only was the authority of the Supreme Junta assured, so was the traditionalist character of the revolt.[23] With its goals and ideological character firmly established, the Supreme Junta of Porto gathered the forces of northern Portugal around it, assured itself of the allegiance of the rest of the country and was able to present itself to the British as a viable, national government they had to respect. When Wellesley landed at Mondego Bay, on the central coast, in August 1808, the Junta Suprema in Porto had 2000 troops to give him, while the north and the Algarve had virtually liberated themselves.

Wellesley made straight for Lisbon and routed Junot's main force at

Vimiero on 21 August 1808. Junot thought a popular rising in Lisbon so likely that he did not dare retire behind its defences to fight on. The following day, Wellesley's less dynamic superiors, Dalrymple and Burrard, offered Junot generous terms for surrender, the Convention of Sintra, which he gladly accepted. The British commanders were ordered back to London to explain why they had repatriated Junot's army of 26 000 to France with all their weapons. It did little to please the Portuguese either.

The Convention of Sintra was not the disaster for the British that it at first appeared to be. The French had lost Portugal and would never regain it; the British began to entrench themselves there with Portuguese support, exemplified by the decision of the Prince Regent to appoint an English general, Beresford, as commander of the Portuguese army. By September 1808, the Regency Council had been re-established in Lisbon and, with admirable political acumen, it co-opted into its ranks the Bishop of Porto and representatives of all the major provincial juntas. Bailen had been a false start, but Vimiero was not. If Portugal was not the first part of the Iberian peninsula to raise the standard of revolt, it was the one to do so most effectively.

When Napoleon returned to Spain early in November 1808, the Empire was in the throes of its first crisis since Tilsit. The French now controlled only the northern provinces of Navarra and Aragon – and those rather imperfectly – together with the north-eastern coast around Barcelona. Napoleon was now faced with a *Reconquista* of his own. In the meantime, the Spanish juntas had been trying to follow the example of the Portuguese in an effort better to co-ordinate their resistance after Bailen, but with considerably less success.

Whatever they can be accused of in the way of incompetence or short-sightedness, the *juntas supremas* were not idle during the respite they were given after Bailen. At provincial level, they consolidated their leadership and forged their alliance with the Church, without question the greatest driving force in the war against the French. The Church was a massive presence in Spanish life, both numerically and in terms of influence; its 16 000 parish priests and 60 000 monks, friars and lay brothers were overwhelmingly anti-French. The first calls to arms had come from the pulpits and, as in Italy and the Belgian departments in 1799, they had proved the most effective. The clergy – particularly its lower ranks – shared the political outlook of the masses, urban and rural alike. Together with their flocks, prelates like the staunchly royalist Bishop of Orense fought for the dynasty and against what they perceived as a France still in the grip of the Jacobins. When the upper clergy – 'having discovered the irresistible force of popular feelings'[24] – first put themselves at the head of this force and then joined the *juntas supremas*, as they did in Galicia, Leon, Valencia, and Santander, they put popular force at the service of the juntas, as well as bringing it to heel more effectively than the secular authorities could. Despite the conciliatory gestures – or omissions, to be more precise – in the constitution of

Bayonne, the more traditionalist Spanish nobles also had no sympathy for the French, particularly those who possessed seigneurial rights. It was at this stage that men of this stamp came forward in the provincial juntas, such as Solano, the Captain-General of Andalusia, or the Marquis of Santa Cruz de Marcenado, in Asturias.

As has been seen, the liberal reformers were those most divided by Napoleon's promise to 'substitute order for disorder, law for whim, justice for oppression [and] to pluck Spain from the abyss'.[25] In the months after Bailen most *ilustrados* set aside their admiration for revolutionary France. Radicals like the poet Quintana were now in the process of convincing themselves that Napoleonic France was no longer liberal, but merely an aggressive military despotism which could be resisted with a clear conscience and that the collapse of central authority offered a far better chance for real reform than collaboration with Joseph. Such optimism was only possible in the aftermath of Bailen, for it seemed to offer Spanish liberals an opportunity to resist and to reform, a combination of options not open to many like-minded men in Italy and Germany when they had to confront the French before 1808. Together with the reactionaries, the liberals finally overcame their fear of using popular force against the French.

If the aftermath of Bailen rallied many waverers, it also produced the first clear signs that the anti-*afrancesado* fury, hitherto associated exclusively with the popular movement, had now infected the juntas as well. Liberal and conservative patriots found much-needed common ground in their mutual desire to persecute *afrancesados*. Decrees began to pour out from the *juntas supremas* sequestering the property of known collaborators. A poignant, if relatively innocuous example of this occurred at the usually dusty meeting of the Spanish Historical Academy. On 19 August 1808, the distinguished medieval historian, Capmany, made a speech of remarkable verbal violence, demanding the expulsion of those members of the Academy who had collaborated:

> What can we say about those scholars who, at some tyrannized secret meeting, fought among themselves for the glory and the prestige of who was going to be the foremost, or the vilest, admirer of our enemies ... [given] the extreme peril the country is in, there is no point in either pity or pardon for [those] who have shown courage only in helping to lose it with the weapons that ought to be used in its defence.[26]

The motion was defeated, but later when Capmany emerged as a national resistance leader he was able to translate his words into a concerted policy of persecution.

Many of those who had collaborated reluctantly, in the chaos of the spring of 1808, now felt themselves bound to the French, for better or for worse. Another phenomenon all too familiar to western Europe since 1789 was being repeated in Spain. Breaking the cycle of vendetta within the propertied classes was an important way in which the French gained acceptance for their rule. Joseph's regime in Spain would employ it with unswerving commitment, but now circumstances were different. Vengeance against the collaborators, as well as the French, was an important source of unity for the disparate coalitions of bishops, liberal intellectuals, provincial nobles, and royal bureaucrats. In this way, Jovellanos' dire predictions came true and, ironically, when he was elected to the *Junta Central*, the last years of his life would be spent supervising the process.

In their attempts to create the *Junta Central*, and in their attitude to it thereafter, the Spanish leadership showed all the weaknesses their Portuguese counterparts did not. Its legitimacy was contested by the Council of Castille, several of whose members had remained at the helm in Madrid, after Joseph's withdrawal, and now wanted to reassert the authority of the Council over the provincial juntas. Only when it realized that its timidity had forfeited the confidence and respect of the *juntas supremas*, did the Council accept the *Junta Central*, abandoning its own project to co-opt delegates from the *juntas supremas* into itself. Embittered, the Council of Castille renounced its claims to any supreme power; nevertheless, its remaining members continued to work for the creation of a Regency Council, to replace the *Junta Central*. They retained some influence because the eventual leadership of the *Junta Central*, Jovellanos and Floridablanca, shared the Council's qualms about the legality of what they were doing, seeing clearly that a link with the *ancien régime* had been broken. In the immediate context of the resistance, at least 'it put an end to the vacillations of the Supreme and Royal Council of Castille'.[27] However, it did not put an end to the suspicions and rivalries among the *juntas supremas*.

Those who created the *Junta Central* had no agreed idea of what they wanted it to be. Throughout the summer of 1808, calls for co-operation and projects to achieve it flew between the provincial capitals, while the British, desperate to have a central authority to deal with, willingly ferried provincial deputies from one meeting place to another courtesy of the Royal Navy. At heart, most of the juntas felt that the only way to create a legitimate national government was to summon the Cortes, but anxious to capitalize on the success of Bailen, they opted for the *Junta Central* as an expedient. The Junta's deputies finally met in September 1808, first in Madrid, then in Aranjuez. It was composed of deputies drawn from the *juntas supremas*, often with differing orders about what powers they could delegate to the new body, and all of them with provincial interests to defend against the others. While the juntas of Valencia, Murcia and Extremadura gave their deputies authority to delegate what powers they saw fit to the *Junta Central*, that of Aragon pledged its deputies to very restricted lines of action. The deputies from Asturias, although in principle among the most compliant, soon reasserted their province's long tradition of persistent 'lobbying' and hard bargaining with central government. This insecure, unwieldy body – an executive with 34 members with no powers to raise taxation by its own authority – was now given the task of preparing Spain to withstand the wrath of the Grande Armée. Not surprisingly, it failed abysmally.

The preparations by the two governments for the coming struggle in northern Spain could not have been more different. No more emphatic contrast could be found between the capacity of a large, modern, centralized state to wage war, and the inefficiency of a government dominated by provincial interests, half rooted in the *ancien régime*, half in a federalist revolt. With consummate skill, the Napoleonic administrative machine, civil and military, moved 170 000 soldiers from central Germany to northern Spain in the space of a few weeks. Although once in Spain and on campaign, the French troops were often abandoned to their fate, when they entered Spain, the Grande Armée was clothed, armed and supplied.[28] Napoleon himself was very displeased with the administration of this march, but this is a harsh judgement, inaccurate in itself and certainly unfair by contemporary standards. The troops went to war with what they needed and, although worn out by their long march, they remained well-disciplined and, above all, loyal; there were few desertions. The standards of administration did not match those of the 1805 campaign, but the task was more demanding in terms of both organization and material resources.[29] Historians have tended to dwell on the shortcomings of the logistical support of the Grande Armée in 1808 – and also in the following campaign of 1809 in central Europe[30] – but this is to see the matter in purely French terms, and to judge only by the standards of the Napoleonic state. What really matters is the wider comparative perspective. Armies matter in relation to their opponents.

In almost a parody of Napoleonic standards of organization even short of its best, the *Junta Central* struggled vainly to co-ordinate the separate armies raised by the provincial juntas and, unable to supply these troops itself, it was reduced to issuing a decree to the *juntas supremas* on 13 November 1808, ordering them not to provide funds for the war, but to open public subscriptions for the troops. The bulk of the Spanish army had stayed loyal to the resistance, despite the defeats of the first months. The 17 000 troops serving with the French in Hamburg, who mutinied *en masse* at the news of Dos Mayo, were spirited away to Galicia by the Royal Navy. The courage of all its ranks was never in dispute, but its efficiency had deteriorated in the course of the summer of 1808, if anything. The victory of Bailen had been won against second-rate troops; now it would be different.

The logistical problems faced by the *Junta Central* were probably beyond any government; it was highly unlikely that decades of neglect and mismanagement could have been put aright in the space of a few months. Their choice of tactics could have been avoided, however. Its troops were ragged, inadequately armed and badly officered before operations even began; the

Spanish leadership opted to advance north, and played into Napoleon's hands. He smashed the Spanish at the Somosierra pass on 30 November 1808. On 4 December Madrid surrendered, and Joseph was restored. The *Junta Central* fled south to Seville.

Napoleon now planned to drive west and south-west in a twin-pronged attack on Seville and Lisbon. There was little to stop him, but the events that followed serve as a reminder of how large a task the conquest of Spain was, geographically. The military commander who best understood this was the British general, Sir John Moore. Moore's force of 15 000 had marched from the safety of Lisbon to aid the Spanish offensive, but did not arrive in time. Hoping to draw Napoleon to him, he attacked the vital route centre of Valladolid; 'the British army, serving as the bullfighter's red cloak, would deliberately lure the Gallic bull away from its prey'.[31] Suspending all other operations, Napoleon and then Soult, in the final stages, raced Moore to La Coruna, a port in the very far north-west, where Moore's troops were rescued by a British naval squadron on 16 January 1809.

At the time, both Napoleon and the British regarded the campaign as a French success, if an incomplete one, but Moore's heroic diversion had spared Lisbon and Seville, giving Beresford and the *Junta Central*, respectively, time to regroup. Similarly, although Spain north of the Ebro and the roads from the French border to Madrid were now secure by military standards, the country was far from pacified by the standards of the inner empire. In the north, the cities of Gerona and Zaragoza resumed their determined resistance; along the Mediterranean coast, Valencia and Tarragona also fought on, supplied by the British from Gibraltar. The Spanish were proving adept at siege warfare, in contrast to their failures in open combat, while guerrilla activity was also emerging as a major problem.

Military security alone would not satisfy Napoleon. He now intended Spain to feel the full force of Napoleonic reform and cultural imperialism. Their experience of Spanish resistance had convinced the French even more of the need for a social and cultural revolution in Spain, as well as purely institutional reforms. Napoleon's famous outburst that 'countries full of monks are easy to subdue, I have experience of it', was soon repented of. On the last day of 1808, Fouché said the Spanish monks were the most dangerous enemies the French now faced. To judge by the terms of the new constitution he drew up for Joseph after the recapture of Madrid, Napoleon agreed. Gone were the concessions made to the Church and the seigneurs at Bayonne, and with them the policies of *ralliement* and *amalgame*, at least as far as the nobles and clergy were concerned. The monks and friars leading the resistance in Zaragoza and other less renowned strongholds of Spanish patriotism had convinced Napoleon to introduce a series of measures modelled on the French and Italian Concordats, a policy perceptively termed 'revolutionary Jansenism'.[32] On 18 August 1809, the total abolition of all religious orders was decreed throughout Spain. Napoleon personally abolished the Inquisition and a whole range of seigneurial rights.

Joseph's regime made efforts to reconcile liberals in the resistance to his cause, but his ecclesiastical and anti-seigneurial policies became progressively harsher.

In a wider imperial context, the new Spanish constitution is the first major sign of a more radical course in Napoleon's internal policies. It is probably no coincidence that it was at Valladolid, late in 1808, when he issued his most determined anti-seigneurial legislation for the Grand Duchy of Berg, or that the arrest not only of Pius VII, but of thousands of clergy in the Roman and Tuscan departments – priests and monks, as well as cardinals – followed hard on the heels of his Spanish experience. Faced by counter-revolution at its most determined, violent and unreconstructed, the regime was returning to at least some of its Jacobin roots. There might be no more talk of the Rights of Man or liberty and equality, but the clergy and nobility were once again to be feared and fought.

This change of direction was born – or reborn, perhaps – in the struggle to master the outer empire. Nevertheless, the single most important element in the French strategy of absorption was still the restoration of order and the normalization of life in the new areas under their control. Napoleon had shown the effectiveness of his military machine when he could bring it to bear on one point. The next stage of his Spanish policy was internal pacification, much as it had been elsewhere, but another set of events forced Joseph to face this task alone with severely reduced resources at his disposal. Early in 1809, Napoleon rushed back to Paris to meet the threat of a new war with Austria; the Portuguese and Spanish juntas were not the only ones to take heart from the victory of Bailen. The new, expanded Empire would now have to face war on two fronts, in great part because it tried to absorb too large a country, Spain, too quickly. Napoleon's 'Spanish ulcer' was caused by indigestion, the result of biting off more than he could chew.

The crisis in central Europe: war and revolt, 1808–1809

The war with Austria

Until Napoleon deposed the Spanish Bourbons, Vienna refused to countenance war with Napoleon, largely because the Austrian army was still too weak to fight. However the news of Bayonne convinced them of Stadion's firmly held view that Napoleon was bent on the destruction of the Habsburgs. Charles now agreed, telling Francis of Napoleon, 'Your Majesty can no longer mistake his plans. There is no further question of what he wants; he wants everything!'[33] This fear was rooted in the fact that the Spanish Bourbons had been loyal allies of Napoleon, not his enemies: Napoleon could be motivated only by a mixture of revolutionary radicalism and dynastic ambitions for his family. Missing from their analyses was the central issue of the blockade, a striking example of how outdated *ancien régime* diplomacy had become in Napoleonic Europe. Convinced that the days of his House were numbered, in April 1808 Francis prepared for a purely defensive war against France.

The plan shifted to an aggressive war when it became clear that the best troops of the Grande Armée were now in Spain; there were barely 80 000 combat-ready French troops in central and southern Germany, bereft of the directing intelligence of Napoleon. However, even the most astute Austrian analysts had failed to grasp the organizational powers of the Napoleonic state. On his return to Paris in the first days of 1809, Napoleon set in motion the machinery of conscription. Seventeen new regiments were raised from the conscripts of the levy of 1810 and, by the spring of 1809, Napoleon had about 174 000 French troops in Germany. Although most of them were raw recruits, they were stiffened by the arrival from Spain of the cavalry reserve and the Imperial Guard. For the second time in less than a year, the Napoleonic administrative system successfully transferred a large army across western Europe in a short space of time. This was helped by the fact that the troops involved were the Imperial Guard, who always enjoyed better support than the rest of the army; they travelled by horse cart, rather than marched. Nevertheless, the speed of their march was impressive by contemporary standards: the last Guard units left Spain on 24 March, reaching Paris on 30 April, and Strasbourg, the starting-point for the campaign, on 11 May.[34] Historians have often faulted not only the quality of the troops involved, but the level of preparedness of the Napoleonic army,[35] but a similar operation would have been unthinkable for any other European state. The Habsburgs were not yet on this level.

The patriotic fervour of the Spanish resistance raised hopes in Stadion's mind that an Austrian advance would trigger popular revolts throughout Germany. To foster them, Gentz, Madame de Staël and Friedrich Schlegel poured out a series of appeals to German values and patriotism, in the hope of turning the war into a popular struggle, but they fell on stony ground in the states of the Confederation of the Rhine, the German lands of the inner empire. There was little in it even directed at the popular masses; an appeal based on the abolition of conscription and the restoration of local usages and corporate privileges might have raised a degree of popular resistance, as it did in 1813, but such tactics were neglected in 1809. However, there was enough to frighten the princes of the Confederation. Habsburg declarations alluding to a return to the borders of 1805 and the restoration of the Imperial Knights and the prince-bishops drew the princes closer to France, ensuring Napoleon almost 100 000 more troops, as internal quarrels were set aside.

Austrian war aims became entangled with the restoration of the petty princes. This directed their offensive against Napoleon's main forces, in an attempt to march to the southern states and the Rhineland, the heartland of collaboration. As Montgelas put it:

> Count Stadion should see the enormous error he made in allowing the plan of preparations to be changed. He would have found plenty of supporters in northern Germany, whereas in Bavaria, he did not meet one. Instead of [attacking] the weakest part of the Confederation; he began by attacking the strongest.[36]

When war finally came, in April 1809, the fighting was relatively brief, although Austrian resistance was more determined than the French had expected. The main French army under Napoleon took Vienna on 13 May 1809. However, a week later Charles defeated Napoleon at the battles of Aspern and Esling, to the east of Vienna, but his desire to preserve the core of his forces prevented Charles from exploiting this success. The successful offensive to the north by the army of the Grand Duchy of Warsaw tied down the other Austrian army. Napoleon then launched a carefully prepared attack on Charles' forces at Wagram, north-east of Vienna, on 5 July 1809. The casualties on both sides were high and both commanders were now anxious for peace; an armistice was signed at Znaim on 12 July 1809.

Francis abandoned the 'war party', realizing that neither Russia nor Prussia would join him. In late July, Charles was dismissed, to be replaced by Prince Schwarzenberg, while Stadion stood aside to let Metternich conduct negotiations with the French, which resulted in the Peace of Schonbrunn (Vienna), concluded on 14 October 1809. Its terms reveal Napoleon's priority still to be the strengthening of the blockade. Austria lost the whole of her Adriatic coast: most of the provinces of Friuli, Carinola and Carinthia, together with the city of Trieste and those parts of Dalmatia and Croatia south of the River Save, were amalgamated with the rest of Dalmatia and the city of Ragusa, former Venetian territory which had been administered by the Kingdom of Italy since 1806, to form the Illyrian provinces of the French Empire, ruled from Paris. Their immediate purpose was to seal the northern Adriatic to the British, who had successfully occupied most of the Ionian islands, further south, in 1807. A very heavy indemnity was imposed on Austria and the army was to be limited to 150 000 men; above all, Austria was to join the blockade.

Hindsight has often portrayed the war of 1809 as the first clear sign that Napoleonic hegemony was in decline, but little of this was apparent to contemporaries. They saw yet another French victory, this time in the face of adversity and against improved opposition. The man who had to pick up the pieces, the new Austrian Chancellor, Metternich, who had stressed French shortcomings early in 1809, could write by August:

> Whatever the stipulations of the peace may be, the result will be the same, namely that we can seek our security only in adapting to the triumphant French system.[37]

It was a view shared by a large section of the British reading public. In 1809 even the most implacable enemies of Napoleon admitted not just his continuing military supremacy, but the genius of the system behind it. In the words of the *Edinburgh Review*, 'The diadem of Bonaparte had dimmed the lustre of all the ancient crowns of Europe; and her nobles have been outshone and out generalled, and out-negotiated, by men raised by their own exertion from the common level of the people.'[38]

In a wider, longer perspective, it is clear that Napoleonic France achieved its great-power status only through great strain. The country was economically backward in many respects; its political stability was far from assured even at the height of the Empire; it was becoming demographically stagnant.[39] But France continued to triumph. Organization was the key, and the campaigns of 1808 and 1809 were an accolade to a whole system of government. Not only had the French Empire, itself, surmounted the military crisis of 1808–09, so had the inner empire as a whole. Dutch and Belgian national guards had helped repel a British landing at Walcheren in September 1809; the troops of the Confederation states and the Kingdom of Italy had all distinguished themselves; while the Polish response had astounded the whole of Europe. The Grand Duchy of Warsaw had proved more than able to defend itself; in the course of the war, over 60 000 men had been put into the field in the space of a few months and had proved more than a match for both the Austrians and the Russians;[40] this did not include the 52 000 already serving in Spain, a success that frightened Alexander. There were clear signs that the inner empire was emerging as a solid, wider base for Napoleon. However, there was a price to pay, and it produced a wave of revolts within the inner empire, which would test its solidity even more severely than the war itself.

The revolts of 1809 in Germany and Italy

GERMANY AND THE TYROL

The revolts of 1809 in Germany and Italy make an interesting contrast. The Tyrol apart, the German revolts were aristocratic conspiracies with little popular backing and were crushed easily. Those in Italy were anarchic and dissipated themselves, but they also proved much harder to suppress. For very different reasons, all these revolts foundered on the rock of the inner empire.

The rigours of Austrian occupation in 1808–09 turned most Bavarians against them, thus ensuring the advancing French a rare warm welcome. In the words of a French officer:

> Bavaria seems to have remembered the accumulated damage done by the Austrian troops in so short a space of time: thus, we were everywhere received as liberators and brothers. Everywhere, the people ran

to greet our passing, blessing our presence [and] execrating the Austrians.[41]

According to Archduke Charles, 'Everywhere the Austrians appeared in Bavaria they were seen as enemies and found no supporters.'[42] Where they did not appear, the revolts in their favour were swept away.

There were three risings in Westphalia in April 1809, one led by Schill, a major in the Prussian army whose small paramilitary band careered across a fairly wide swathe of territory, raiding the treasuries of several towns along the way, but finding little popular backing as they did so. His men were crushed by Jerome's troops, as were those led by Dorenberg, a colonel in the Westphalian Royal Guard, who rose in Kassel in a carefully planned attempt to oust Jerome. When another Prussian officer, von Katt, tried to seize the fortress city of Magdeburg with a small force, he was repulsed with ease. The loyalty and efficiency of Jerome's new Westphalian army was crucial. Nevertheless, their collapse was less a sign of the popularity of Napoleonic rule than a general distrust or indifference to Austrian ambitions. Even German nobles who were angered by attempts to abolish feudalism, as well as peasants oppressed by conscription, still regarded the Napoleonic presence as unshakeable in 1809, if far from desirable. When the deposed Duke of Brunswick advanced into Saxony and Westphalia with 10 000 troops, he found little active support.

Some areas did show enthusiasm for the advancing Austrians. Promises to restore the traditional order had a powerful appeal in the former Imperial Free Cities, the suppressed prince-bishoprics and the abolished fiefs of the Imperial Knights, particularly in all those 'mediatized' lands now under Bavarian rule and so closest to the fighting. Although the commercial middle classes of cities such as Augsberg and Passau supported the new order the urban masses displayed considerable counter-revolutionary zeal. There were violent anti-Bavarian outbursts in these cities accompanied by calls for the restoration of an old order which had dispensed charity and patronage, rather than enforced conscription. In Augsburg the University was pro-Habsburg. Passau saw a municipal revolt akin to those of 1808 in Spain and its gates were opened to the Austrians. They were the only events of this kind, however, and these urban revolts were easily contained. They could not act as rallying points for their rural hinterlands.

The Tyrol was different. A rebellion broke out in 1809 to rival any of the resistance found in Spain or Portugal. Indeed, the Tyrolean rising was a classic, definitive example of counter-revolution. The Tyrol, spanning the German and Italian Alps, had been attached to the Habsburg crown since the fourteenth century but, traditionally, the association had been loose, even by the standards of the Habsburgs. It was characterized by respect for local liberties and customs on the part of the monarchy, and fierce dynastic loyalty on the part of the Tyroleans. In 1806, the Tyrol was given to Bavaria, a decision which soon led to calamity. Once again,

Bavaria appears as the Napoleonic Empire in microcosm: Max-Joseph soon found an outer empire of his own, in the new territories he gained in 1806. If the former Imperial Free Cities can be equated with Napoleon's Hansa ports and the ex-prince-bishoprics with his Papal States, the Tyrol was Max-Joseph's personal Spain. And that was how he decided to treat it.

Max-Joseph and Montgelas showed more conformity and aggression in their internal policies than those of either Louis in Holland or Joseph in Naples and Spain. The Tyrol, unused to being governed at all, was now to feel the full weight of Napoleonic imperialism, even if the perpetrators were Bavarians. Typically, the Tyrol disappeared; its estates were abolished and its territory divided into three departments. With its provincial privileges gone, taxation rose by almost 20 per cent. Then Austrian paper currency was withdrawn from circulation and made redeemable only in Bavarian silver coins, a measure which cost Tyroleans dearly. As an important route between Italy and Germany, the Tyrol's transport trade suffered appallingly from Bavarian adherence to the blockade. It is a familiar litany, and equally familiar is that these problems were as nothing beside the introduction of conscription and the anticlerical policies of Montgelas. 'To *Bavarianize* the country meant to *decatholicize* it', declared a Jesuit father,[43] and most of Tyrolean countryside agreed in the wake of reforms modelled on the Napoleonic Concordat. When the three bishops of the region protested at the ruthlessness of the reforms, two of them were exiled, while several hundred priests were gaoled in the course of 1807. Traditional loyalties to the Habsburgs intensified.

The Tyrol had an ability to fight back not possessed by Passau and Augsburg. 'The country can be compared to a natural fortress whose belligerent population constitutes an equally natural garrison', was the judgement of a French general who served there in 1809.[44] The Tyrolean Alps are among the most forbidding topography in Europe and their people, unlike many of their rebellious counterparts in Spain, had a long tradition of guerrilla warfare to draw upon. Montgelas was well aware of this and saw that resentment of his reforms was much more dangerous in the Tyrol than elsewhere. Constantly stressing the lack of troops in the area as war with Austria approached, Montgelas told the French ambassador in March 1809:

> You must believe that this business is of the very highest importance ... Small, partial disturbances have broken out, the young men flee in droves across the mountains to take service in Austria and to escape conscription.[45]

He was right, and the links with Austria were far more organized than this indicates. In Archduke John, the Tyroleans had a powerful spokesman in Vienna. Through Baron Hoymar, a Tyrolean noble, Vienna established contact with well-organized local resistance leaders. Most prominent among them were the innkeeper Andreas Hofer and the Capuchine friar Joachim Haspinger, both to become legendary.

The rebels had a limited amount of support from regular Austrian troops in the first months of the revolt, but the most important victories were largely their own work. Napoleon hoped the Bavarians could cope with the Tyrol on their own, but such was the rebels' success that by July, with the Wagram campaign over, it was obvious that the revolt could be put down only by the Grande Armée: without Austrian help, the Tyroleans retook the regional capital, Innsbruck. The military history of the Tyrolean revolt displays all the classic strengths and weaknesses of counter-revolutionary guerrilla warfare: an almost indomitable ability to resist at local level, but a total inability to carry the fight beyond regional confines. Although the revolt was crushed within eight months of its outbreak, its relative success had done severe damage to Napoleon's faith in his Bavarian ally; he entrusted the last stages of the campaign to Eugène's Italian troops, rather than the discredited Bavarians. Napoleon was also sufficiently impressed by the Tyroleans to offer them terms: 'I would not find it inconvenient to grant them privileges and a form [of government] to satisfy their views', he told Murat in August 1809.[46] In the end, the southern Tyrol was transferred to Italian rule. The north remained under Bavaria, but only with great reluctance on Napoleon's part: 'I think the German Tyrol will always be badly governed, that it will never be subdued, and will cause us serious trouble.'[47] When Max-Joseph protested at these remarks, Napoleon had his answer ready: 'The Tyrol would have revolted against the House of Austria, if it had behaved like the Bavarians.'[48] This was certainly right, but in the light of the resistance his own, identical policies had produced in Spain – and were producing in Italy even as he spoke – Napoleon's judgement was also unfair.

THE ITALIAN REVOLTS OF 1809

There were three main centres of revolt in the Italian peninsula in 1809: the far south of the Kingdom of Naples, particularly Calabria; that part of the Kingdom of Italy south of the River Po known as the Emilia-Romagna; and the Veneto, that part of the Kingdom of Italy that had once been the hinterland of the old Republic of Venice, particularly the Alpine valleys bordering on Lombardy.[49]

The Venetian revolts were a spill-over from the fighting in the Tyrol. Although fragmented and unorganized above village level, they outlasted the Tyrolean rising. Order was not restored in this area until November 1809 and isolated acts of arson and attacks on government officials continued into 1810 around Verona, Vicenza and Belluno, all important cities. After the revolt, nine military tribunals were set up; their severity resulted in hundreds of executions. Several of the areas involved, in the lowlands of the Po valley around Rovigo, and the Alpine valleys of the Vallentina and Valcamonica, had revolted in 1805–06 following their annexation by the Kingdom of Italy;

in 1809 they were quick to do so again. As in the Tyrol, the Alpine valleys deeply resented the economic dislocation caused by the blockade to their transit trade, as well as the loss of local autonomy which followed annexation. The most general cause of the revolts in all the areas involved seems to have been the increased demands of conscription for the war of 1809.

Underlying all of this was a detestation of the revolutionary-Napoleonic state. South of the Alps it was run by Italians in Milan, north of them by Germans in Munich; in both areas it produced a desire – however vaguely perceived at times – to return to a less demanding, more archaic political order. Such hopes emerge in the proclamation of the peasant rebels who took the town of Schio at the height of the rising, early in July 1809. In the words of its historian:

> When the musket fire ceased, they hoisted the flag of St. Mark [the flag of the old Republic of Venice]; they proclaimed the return of the old laws and [thus] they would establish a form of government after their own fashion, publishing decrees on the circulation of money, on the abolition of tolls and conscription, and, above all, on the restoration of Religion and Fairness.[50]

Everywhere, the French and their local collaborators were harassed, robbed and often killed. There are many instances of support for the Austrians as allies in a common cause, but the Alpine communities and several urban centres in the Po delta such as Este and Rovigo fought for the express goal of restoring the Republic of Venice.

As the revolts spread, a general breakdown of law and order followed in the countryside. By late July 1809, a decidedly criminal element came to the fore as the French drove back the larger peasant bands, such as the 8000 men from the valleys who besieged Vicenza for almost two weeks.[51] The peasants were reinforced by large numbers of deserters and men from the cities of the Po valley fleeing conscription; when they dispersed into smaller bands many turned to brigandage. This, in turn, drove many communities to support the restoration of order by the French. Several large towns stayed loyal to the French, at least in so far as a deep-seated fear of peasant animosity towards urban centres stiffened their willingness to defend themselves. Vicenza, Treviso and Feltre all defied the rebels; their national guards fought beside the French. Clearly, older animosities between town and countryside in north-eastern Italy influenced the course of these revolts to a very great extent; those urban centres which rebelled, such as Rovigo, did not neighbour the Alpine valleys and had little direct contact with them, while those at the foot of the valleys – their traditional administrative centres – were hostile to the rebels. The co-operation between town and country so prominent in the revolt of northern Portugal was missing in the Veneto, and was even less apparent in the revolts in central Italy.

The wave of disorder that swept Emilia-Romagna had also been building up for several years, but only reached its height after the war of 1809. It seemed utterly devoid of any explicit political content and was provoked by the growing burdens of conscription and taxation. As a result the revolts were without clear direction and never achieved a leadership beyond local level. If they possessed any constant organizing element it was probably the numerous deserters who joined the ranks of the peasant communities; of the 1000 rebels finally brought to trial by the military commission in Bologna, more than half were deserters, and when the initial risings degenerated into banditry, the organized bands that finally emerged were all led by deserters.[52] The risings began as tax revolts in the first week of July 1809, among the mountain communities near Bologna. The rebels soon swept into the plains; on 7 July they laid siege to the regional capital, Bologna. The prefect told a colleague:

> The horde of brigands, composed mainly of deserters, after having spread fear in many of the larger villages in the countryside – where they seized arms and extorted money – yesterday morning dared to show themselves under the walls of this city . . .[53]

The local authorities held firm. Led by the prefect, the national guard of Bologna – long suspected of 'Jacobinism' by the government in Milan – repelled the rebels without the help of regular troops. This did not deter the rebels; as late as October 1809, the prefect of Bologna reported that they had attacked many villages in considerable force, 'committing countless robberies they vented most of their fury on civil servants and especially, on the mayors'.[54] One such was the terrorized mayor of the hamlet of Crespellano, who wrote to the prefect that same month of 'these monsters, speaking in different languages, terrible in appearance, but more terrible still in their deeds', who ransacked his village hall and raped his wife.[55] Banditry did not shrink back to what the authorities considered its normal proportions until May 1810, when the armed columns of gendarmes finally ceased their operations. Only after ten months did these troubles finally lose the characteristics of a rebellion against the government.

These disturbances ended with a whimper rather than a bang, due partly to the firmness and determination of the local authorities, partly to the isolation and incoherence of the rebels. Try as they could, the authorities found no links with British or Austrian agents or with the Tyrolean rebels. The course of these revolts are an emphatic sign of the strength of the state, but even more of the capacity of the inner empire for internal combustion under the demands of war.

The serious revolts that rocked the Kingdom of Naples took place in more convulsed circumstances than any of the other risings of 1809 on either side of the Alps. The failure of all the others points to the resilience and power of the Napoleonic state in western Europe, but the revolts in southern Italy were never properly quelled. The southern revolts grew from a traditional pattern of banditry, but southern banditry never returned to its 'normal' levels, nor did it really lose its counter-revolutionary character. The events of 1809 have been represented as a tragedy for the south, especially in Calabria where the fighting was fiercest, because they shattered the fragile law and order fostered by Joseph and then Murat. This view, that the risings of 1809 revived banditry when it was on the verge of dying out, is probably far too optimistic, given the deep roots it had in these areas which were plagued by poverty and economic backwardness.[56] Nevertheless, considerable progress had been made between 1805 and 1809 in curbing the general disorder in southern Italy, but from 1809 onwards the trend went in the opposite direction. The Kingdom of Naples had never been absorbed properly into the inner empire; now it would almost be lost to it.

The turning-point for southern Italy came in 1809 with the introduction of conscription for the first time to meet the demands of the war in Germany. During the war of 1809, the British and the Bourbons in Sicily took the offensive, the British in a series of raids along the Calabrian coast, the Bourbons by sending material aid and encouragement to the bandits, which gave the bandits a new degree of independence from their usual patrons, the barons, several of whom had shown signs of preferring the prospect of law and order offered by the new regime. Despite signs that the local population – and certainly most local officials – were prepared to support the campaigns led by General Manhès to restore order, the most important bands retained their grip on vast tracts of the countryside and the fragile support of the *signori* was subtly withdrawn from the government as the prospect of a successful counter-revolution seemed more likely than the restoration of order by Murat.

As a result, a bitter but fragmented guerrilla war developed in Calabria, while resistance to conscription fostered disorder almost everywhere. All this was made easier by the rugged, remote nature of the countryside. As in Spain, the conflict soon produced atrocities on both sides; castration and even crucifixion were sometimes added to the usual catalogue of rapes, murders and mutilations. The British and the Bourbons have been condemned as callous and irresponsible by posterity for practising what amounted to a policy of destabilization in the Kingdom of Naples,[57] but their actions fell on fertile soil, where social tensions of all kinds had long been present and had often taken violent forms of expression.

By 1811, Murat's effective control was confined to the larger towns and was increasingly dependent on French troops. Even liberal opposition to the French had begun to emerge, in the form of revolutionary secret societies, the most famous of whom were the Carbonari, although they posed nothing like as great a threat as the bandits. There was a thin line separating the course of events here from those in Spain. Indeed, French counter-insurgency offensives made better progress in Navarre, Catalonia and Asturias between 1809 and 1812 than they did in southern Italy. There was strong pressure on the Bourbons and the British commanders in Sicily to commit British troops to a permanent presence on the Italian mainland, but it was decided to concentrate military resources on Spain and Portugal; the British

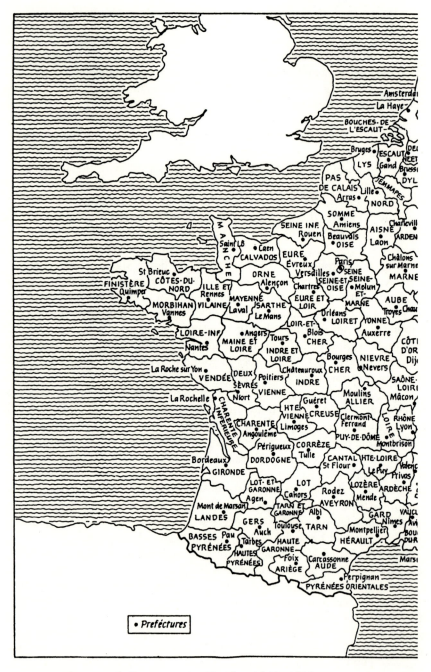

Map 4: The French Empire at its Height, 1811–1812

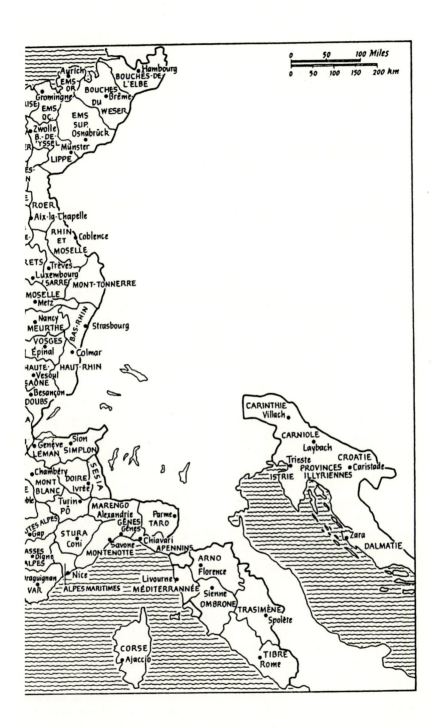

were stretched as fully as Napoleon. Murat was spared his throne for the time being, but his people were subjected to the horrors of war without the prospect of a clear victory by either side. Spain has sometimes been described as the Vietnam of the Napoleonic wars.[58] If so, then Calabria was their Cambodia.

The aftermath of 1809: the final reordering of the Empire

The wars of 1808–09 had not changed the fact of French military superiority. The real crisis of confidence was stirred by the internal revolts. There was a genuine crisis of confidence in the ranks of the administrators who had to deal with them in Italy and Germany. Simeon's early optimism for the future of Westphalia was shattered by the revolts, despite their ephemeral character. He interpreted them as a sign of fragility, remarking in 1811 that 'The Spanish example is referred to, and should war break out, all the country between the Rhine and the Oder will see a real insurrection.'[59] Fragility was also a term employed frequently by the prefects of the Kingdom of Italy, who saw resistance to the new state at every level of society, from the popular violence of the revolts themselves to the passive refusal of the nobles and clergy to calm them. From this point great stress was put on increasing the powers and efficiency of the prefects, juxtaposed to their own expressed feelings of weakness. These revolts brought to the surface a sense of uncertainty long present in the Kingdom of Italy and this fear, in turn, points to why the state began to place so much emphasis on social control, 'in the long term, the only practicable way of consolidating the insecure position of ... the Napoleonic government at local level'.[60]

Seen in this perspective, these anarchic, shapeless revolts attain a heightened significance. They were more than primitive responses to the burdens of conscription and taxation – although they were certainly this too – but a frustrated rejection of the modern state itself. Napoleonic bureaucrats saw this clearly and perceived the dangerous gap between the state and those it governed.

At the highest levels, Napoleon now doubted the competence of Max-Joseph in Bavaria, who had failed in the Tyrol; of his brother Joseph, who had handed most of Spain to the rebels; of Louis, in Holland, who had done little for the war effort and even less to enforce the blockade; of Murat, who had failed to enforce conscription in Naples; even Jerome – unjustly – was berated for his handling of the revolts in Westphalia. A further reorganization was undertaken, centred once again along the coasts, to tighten the blockade. The new Illyrian provinces and then the Hansa ports were annexed directly to France. In Spain, Napoleon removed the provinces north of the River Ebro from Joseph's direct control in February 1810, placing this area – which included the great port of Barcelona – under French military rule; the outright annexation of Catalonia to France would follow in 1812. However, the greatest display of fear and distrust was reserved for Louis in Holland. Finally, the demands of the blockade combined with the trauma of 1809 drove Napoleon to depose his own brother and annex a satellite state.

By 1809, the failure of Louis to suppress Dutch smuggling, most of it done directly with Britain, had decided Napoleon on a tougher policy towards Holland. The British landing at Walcheren had allowed the French to move a considerable number of troops into the southern Netherlands, which Napoleon now wanted to use to occupy the Dutch coast and its major ports. When Louis opposed this, Napoleon replied that 'you would have us believe that the Dutch had great energy ... Yes, they have energy all right – for smuggling.'[61] The French demanded the Dutch provinces of Zeeland and Brabant, the confiscation of all colonial goods found in Holland, and that the administration of the Dutch customs' service be turned over to French officials. There were other terms designed deliberately to humiliate Louis, but Napoleon's main aim was to strike 'the deadliest blow I can inflict on England', and he told Louis bluntly 'You will find in me a brother if I find in you a Frenchman.'[62] He did not, and it was only after excessive bullying, even by Napoleon's standards, that Louis allowed French troops into what was left of his kingdom. Their presence provoked many confrontations between the Dutch and the French troops, particularly attacks on customs' posts. Louis's reaction was to try to resist – even an alliance with England was considered – but his ministers refused to support him and on 2 July 1810 he abdicated. The whole of Holland became French departments: Amsterdam, Rotterdam and the Hague became 'French' cities.

The inner empire had arisen from the bewilderment of success; the outer empire was born in the uncertainty present at the very heart of the imperial family. There was nothing 'grand' about the 'Grand Empire' except the illusion it creates on the map, and no one knew it better than Napoleon.

Notes

1 F. Pesendorfer, *Fernando III e la Toscana in età napoleonica*, (Italian trans., Florence, 1986) p. 131.
2 A. Latrielle, *Napoleon et le St. Siège (1801–1808)*, (Paris, 1935) p. 447.
3 Ibid., p. 448.
4 Ibid., p. 567.
5 C. Nardi, *Napoleone e Roma: la politica della Consultà Romana*, (Rome, 1989) p. 53.
6 It should be stated that some historians have interpreted the French interventions in both Etruria/Tuscany and Spain as part of premeditated policy to eradicate the Bourbon dynasty by Napoleon. The lack of concrete evidence for this

view is further contradicted by the actual course of events. If such a concerted plan of action existed, it took a very long time to emerge. For a recent assertion of the 'plot theory', especially in a Spanish context, see: D. Hilt, *The Troubled Trinity, Godoy and the Spanish Monarchs*, (Tuscaloosa, AL, 1987). The opposite view is concisely put by J.R. Aymes, *La Guerra de la Independencia en España, 1808–14*, (Madrid, 1980), also published in French as *La Guerre d'Indépendence Espagnole, (1808–1814)*, (Paris, 1973).

7 The Spanish word *junta* literally means 'committee'; it was used in this period, as it still is in Spain, Portugal and Latin America, to describe a ruling body, usually thrust into power by convulsed circumstances.

8 Aymes, *La Guerre d'Indépendence*, p. 72.

9 G.H. Lovett, *Napoleon and the Birth of Modern Spain*, 2 vols (1965), New York i, p. 143.

10 Cited in Aymes, *La Guerre d'Indépendence*, p. 20.

11 A. Martinez del Velasco, *La Formación de la Junta Central*, (Pamplona, 1972) pp. 41–2.

12 Cited in H. Jüretschke, *Los Afrancesados en la Guerra de la Independencia*, (Madrid, 1962) p. 72.

13 M. Ardit, 'La crisi politica de l'antic regim (1793–1813)', pp. 195–215, in M. Ardit (ed.) *Historia del Pais Valencia, IV, Fins a la crisi de l'Antic Regim*, (Barcelona, 1990) pp. 205–8.

14 The term is that of Miguel Artola-Gallego, probably the leading historian of the Spanish War of Independence. This concept is central to three of his major studies: *Los Origenes de la España Contemporanea*, 2 vols (Madrid, 1959), *Antiguo Regime y Revolucion Liberal*, (Madrid, 1978) and *La España de Fernando VII*, vol. XXXIII of *Historia de la España*, ed. R. Menendez Pidal, (Madrid, 1978).

15 The traditional view is effectively undermined by X. Castro Perez, 'Réaction et idéologie en Galicie pendant la guerre d'Indépendence', *Les Résistances à la Révolution*, eds. F. Lebrun and R. Dupuy, (Paris, 1987) pp. 295–301.

16 Cited in D. Francis, *Portugal, 1715–1808*, (London, 1985) p. 268.

17 Cited in H.V. Livermore, *A New History of Portugal*, (Cambridge, 1966) p. 251.

18 Cited in A. Do Carmo Reis, *As Revoltas do Porto contra Junot*, (Lisbon, 1991) p. 77.

19 Reis, *As Revoltas do Porto*, pp. 65–70.

20 Ibid., p. 67.

21 L.A. de Oliveria Ramos, *Da Ilustracao ao Liberalismo*, (Porto, 1979) pp. 92–3.

22 Ibid., p. 100.

23 Reis, *As Revoltas do Porto*, pp. 101–19.

24 Aymes, *La Guerre d'Independence*, p. 24.

25 *Moniteur Universel*, 14 July 1808. Cited in Aymes, *La Guerre d'Indépendence*, p. 11.

26 Cited in Jüretschke, *Los Afrancesados*, pp. 88–9. The entire text is cited pp. 84–9.

27 Martinez del Velasco, *La Formación*, p. 167.

28 Morvan, *Le Soldat*, i, p. 485.

29 Ibid., i, pp. 151–9.

30 Morvan, *Le Soldat*, i, pp. 322–3. Elting, *Swords*, pp. 61–3. The major accounts of the Spanish campaign by Chandler, *Campaigns*, and Connelly, *Blundering*, do not mention the logistical organization.

31 Chandler, *Campaigns*, p. 646.

32 E. de la Lama Cereceda, *J.A. Llorente, un ideal Burguesia*, (Pamplona, 1991).

33 Cited in J.A. Vann, 'Habsburg policy and the Austrian War of 1809', *Central*

European History, 7 (1974) pp. 291–310, 305.

34 H. Lahouque, *The Anatomy of Glory: Napoleon and his Guard*, (English trans., London, 1962) pp. 150–1.

35 Chandler, *Campaigns*, pp. 732–5. Connelly, *Blundering*, p. 134. Elting, *Swords*, pp. 62–3. Morvan, *Le Soldat*, i, pp. 159, 325–31.

36 Dunan, *Napoléon*, p. 243.

37 Cited in Kraehe, *Metternich*, i, p. 104.

38 Cited in J. Cannon, *Aristocratic Century: The Peerage in Eighteenth Century England*, (Cambridge, 1984) p. 166, and in L. Colley, *Britons. Forging the Nation, 1707–1837*, (Bath, 1992) p. 150.

39 T.C.W. Blanning, 'The French Revolution and the modernization of Germany', *Central European History*, 22 (1989) pp. 109–29.

40 R. Biecki, 'L'effort militaire polonaise, 1806–1815', *Révue de l'Institut Napoléon*, 132 (1976) pp. 147–64, 157.

41 Dunan, *Napoléon*, p. 245.

42 Ibid., p. 244.

43 Ibid., p. 235.

44 Cited in F.G. Eyck, *Loyal Rebels, Andreas Hofer and the Tyrolean Revolt of 1809*, (London, 1986) p. 1.

45 Dunan, *Napoléon*, p. 236.

46 Ibid., p. 267.

47 Ibid., p. 270.

48 Ibid., p. 270.

49 In English see Grab, 'Army, state and society', and 'State power, brigandage and rural resistance in Napoleonic Italy', *European History Quarterly*, 25 (1995) pp. 39–70.

50 C. Bullo, 'Dei movimenti insurrezionali del Veneto sotto il dominio napoleonico, e specialmente del brigantaggio politico del 1809', *Nuovo Archivio Veneto*, 17 (1899) pp. 66–101, 84.

51 Ibid., pp. 81–2.

52 L. Valenete, *La Corte Speciale per i delitti di Stato del dipartimento del Reno (1809–1811)*, (Unpbl. Tesi di Laurea, Bologna, 1973) pp. 29, 36 note 2.

53 Antonielli, *Prefetti*, p. 506, note 62.

54 Archivio de Stato, Bologna, Titolo xx (Polizia), Busta 807 (1809), Prefect, dept. Reno, to Minister of the Interior, Milan, 18 October 1809.

55 Ibid., Sindaco of Crespellano to Prefect, dept. Reno, 10 October 1809.

56 See especially Valenete, *Murat*, pp. 137–48.

57 Valenete, *Murat*, and U. Caldora, *Calabria Napoleonica*, (Naples, 1960) are representative of this view.

58 D. Alexander, *Rod of Iron: French Counterinsurgency Policy in Aragon During the Peninsular War*, (Wilmington, DE, 1985) p. ix.

59 Tulard, 'Simeon', p. 567.

60 Antonielli, *Prefetti*, p. 507.

61 Schama, *Patriots*, p. 599.

62 Ibid., p. 603.

|5|

Coercion: the Europe of the Grand Empire, 1810–1814

Renewal and ambition

The final years of Napoleon's rule have often been portrayed as a period of stagnation and increasing conservatism, as a time when the Empire began to slip back into the patterns of the *ancien régime*, but nothing could be further from the truth.

The outward tone for the standard view of the late Empire as hardening into conservatism is set by Napoleon's marriage to Marie-Louise, daughter of Francis II of Austria, in April 1810. It caused consternation in France, was seen as a betrayal of the Revolution, and not just among avowed republicans. Yet the Austrian marriage was not what it seemed. It came at the height of Napoleon's quarrel with the Pope, when Napoleon was an excommunicate. This allowed Pius VII to refuse to recognize the marriage and then the legitimacy of the son it produced. Pius urged the clergy not to celebrate the marriage or the birth of the little prince, to whom Napoleon gave the deliberately provocative title, King of Rome. Even if the marriage was meant to lead the regime along more traditionalist paths, its practical consequences were to embitter the quarrel with Rome still further, thus reviving anticlericalism and much of the radical tradition that went with it. To the very end, the hereditary Empire was fighting the battles of the Revolution.

In turn, this threw the regime back on many of its radical, almost Jacobin roots at the very moment when it had sought to free itself from the past. Within the Kingdom of Italy, for example, the prefectoral corps became more heavily dominated by the Jacobins of the 1796–99 period as time progressed: the Jacobin element was less than 20 per cent of the corps when Melzi left power in 1806, but under Eugène they numbered 45.8 per cent by 1810 and almost 60 per cent by 1813, a clear majority.[1] These changes took place in the inner empire; they were even more marked in the

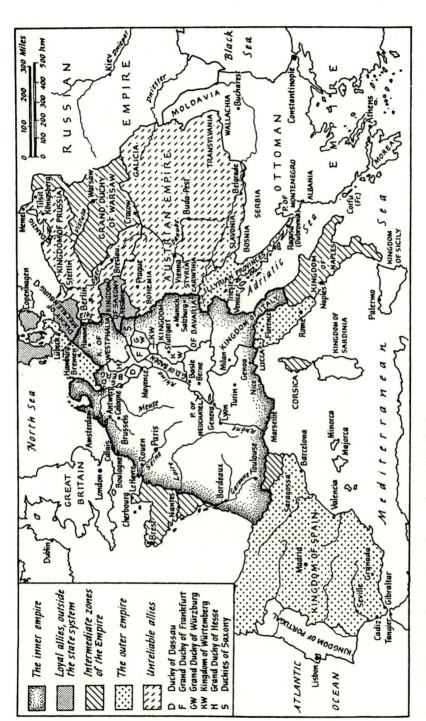

Map 5: The Napoleonic State System by 1811–1812

Legend:

- The inner empire
- Loyal allies, outside the state system
- Intermediate zones of the Empire
- The outer empire
- Unreliable allies

D   Duchy of Dassau
F   Grand Duchy of Frankfurt
GW Grand Duchy of Würzburg
KW Kingdom of Würtemberg
H   Grand Duchy of Hesse
S   Duchies of Saxony

new territories. At the centre of power, this return to revolutionary militancy is clear in the replacement of Fouché by Savary, at the powerful Ministry of Police-Générale, in 1810. Savary masterminded the brutal destruction of royalist resistance in the Vendée and Normandy in 1803, engineered the execution of the Duc d'Enghein in 1804, and lured the Spanish Bourbons to Bayonne in 1808. He continued Fouché's policy of recruiting the police from veterans of the revolutionary armies, and was the right choice to conduct the mass arrests of clergy that the break with the Pope entailed. His replacement of Fouché represents a hardening of the latent Jacobinism of the regime, the Terrorist past of his predecessor notwithstanding.

The lands of the outer empire were almost all ripe for counter-revolution, often on a scale the French had not met before; its acquisition breathed new life into many old problems. Inevitably, the regime became more revolutionary in its policies, in inverse proportion to the number and ferocity of the old demons it met. Many old radicals were retained in local office in the territories of the inner empire – or their re-emergence, as in Italy – and an increasing reliance on that most Jacobin of institutions, the army, side-by-side with the new generation of *auditeurs*. The young *auditeurs* and the die-hard Jacobins came to the fore in the last years of Napoleonic rule. The quarrel with the Pope, coupled with the challenges of the outer empire, meant Napoleon needed men of their outlook more than ever. In its last years, the Napoleonic Empire became more demanding, authoritarian and, all too often, tyrannical but, from an imperial rather than a Francocentric perspective, that tyranny had more to do with the Terror than the *ancien régime*. The Napoleonic order collapsed suddenly, after a brief but fiercely contested struggle fought by ever younger administrators as well as ever younger conscripts. It did not live long enough to ossify; if anything it grew more youthful with every challenge, as well as more revolutionary.

Nevertheless, if the outer empire (the frontier) became the preserve of the newer and more radical elements in the Napoleonic state, the inner empire witnessed the consolidation of those other, very different groups – the provincial notables at local level, the 'immortals' of the Directory at the centre of the state – who had been Napoleon's original bedrock of support. They remained what Napoleon had first christened them, *les masses de granit* – immoveable, ever more secure in wealth and influence – even as he began to distrust them after the disllusionments of 1809, and they began to distrust him as the costs of the blockade and the risks of war increased.

Imperial France, 1807–1814

France was the core of the Napoleonic Empire; with a population of approximately 30 million, it represented two-thirds of the population of the imperial departments. Until 1812, Frenchmen provided the bulk of the Grande Armée; it was always the source of most of its ruling elite. French official culture was the culture of the Empire, French its written – although not spoken – *lingua franca*. From about 1808 onwards, the effects could be felt of the initial reforms carried out by Napoleon in the first years of his rule. Before 1807, the regime had developed and then imposed its agenda. By 1808, as the Empire entered its first crisis, the relative success and failure of the 'Napoleonic Revolution' begins to emerge.

The ethos of these reforms was uniformity and centralization but, even after the efforts of the revolutionaries between 1789 and 1799, France remained a country of vast regional differences. To grasp the true nature of Napoleonic rule in its heartland, the reforms of the regime must be assessed in the context of the French regions, and then in terms of its attempts to mould a governing elite to hold France together from the centre. The history of France in these years is that of the emergence of an important form of the modern state in Europe.

The French regions under Napoleonic rule

The map of imperial France is a study in support or opposition for the regime. Broadly, this was conditioned by three factors: physical geography, which made opposition more or less possible; the influence of the Continental System on the economies of the various regions; and the recent political history of the main regions of France during the 1790s. An examination of the French regions during the later years of the regime reveals that the imperial heartland was far from a Bonapartist monolith, and also that the inner empire, as a whole, was drawing together across pre-Napoleonic boundaries to form a core that did not embrace all of France itself.

NORTHERN FRANCE

The complexity of French political geography emerges in the contrasting responses to imperial rule of the Flemish departments of the north-east and the Norman departments, further west. The hub of the north-east was the department of the Nord, centred on Lille. Throughout the second phase of Napoleonic rule, the economy of the Nord continued to grow, despite short-lived economic slumps. Its varied textile industries survived the general crisis of 1810–11 relatively lightly, and benefited from imperial preference and protection from British competition. This is borne out by the demographic expansion of its cities in these years, which gave the Nord the highest population density of any department in the Empire and, usually, the highest conscription quota, which was met without difficulty until 1813. Its commerce and industry increasingly integrated with those of the equally successful Belgian departments, an example of French expansion enabling a natural economic unit to emerge, within the tariff walls of the Continental System. Even the fall of the Empire did not interrupt the growth of textiles, although the more traditional wool and linen industries gave way to cotton. The picture was not quite as dynamic in the neighbouring departments of the Pas de Calais and the Somme, but it was still one of prosperity. In the Pas de Calais, the deprivations of the blockade in the coastal ports of Calais and Boulogne were partly offset by the intense interest taken by the government in developing agriculture there. The Somme became an important producer of gunpowder for the army, and a centre of flour and paper mills. Until 1813, the north-east remained politically stable. Its urban notables, often drawn from commerce and industry, and large sections of the urban workforce, became increasingly secular in outlook, and benefited greatly from the creation of an extensive network of schools, both primary and secondary, especially after 1806. The countryside, in contrast, tended to remain deeply Catholic and it was here, rather than the towns, that the 'Flemish Vendée' of 1813 exploded.

The Norman departments present a more complex range of experience, for although they shared much in common with the departments of the north-east, their western borders touched the heartland of Chouannerie, and they were not part of the economic renaissance of Flanders – French and Belgian – in these years. Although deep inside France, they benefited little from the Continental System. The economic life of the Norman ports – Le Havre, Dieppe, Honfleur, and Cherbourg – was virtually extinguished by the blockade, and local industries, particularly forges, declined in number, partly through shortages of manpower as a result of conscription.[2] Similar problems faced the agricultural sector, sometimes endangering grain production, but the period also saw the progressive consolidation of farms into larger, more profitable units. However, in these circumstances, official efforts to extend agricultural land made little impact. Larger industrial enterprises tended to collapse, especially during the recession of 1810–11, and Normandy survived as a 'pilot region' of French industry only because it was based mainly on small-scale firms producing for localized markets and so immune to the 'grand strategy' of Napoleonic market design.

Neither the Normans nor the government felt secure, as the economic troubles of the later years were compounded by bad harvests and an increasingly fragile political climate: Normans loyal to the regime had to fear British incursions along the coast and the embers of Chouannerie further west and inland, circumstances that made Normandy almost a frontier of the inner empire, although only three days' march from Paris. In March 1812, the regime responded aggressively to a series of grain riots in Caen and the surrounding countryside, in the department of the Calvados, which appeared to have the potential to link popular, essentially economic discontent to Chouannerie: strong detachments of the Imperial Guard fought a ruthless campaign in western Normandy, prior to its departure for the Russian campaign.[3] Clearly Napoleon regarded it as a sensitive area.

THE WEST

The west of France was the theatre of the Vendéan and Chouan risings during the Revolution and, despite determined efforts to pacify them involving both the carrot and the stick, the western departments always remained one of the weak points of the whole Empire. Napoleon's brutal response to the relatively minor disturbances in the Calvados was conditioned by a lingering lack of confidence in his grip over the countryside of the nine departments comprising the Vendée militaire, the rugged, isolated *bocage*. Here, significant numbers of peasants and clergy continued to defy the Concordat, supporting the Petite Église, in an act of defiance against both the Pope and the Emperor. Conscription quotas remained artificially low as much from fear and resignation as from hope of appeasement. Finally, in 1808, Napoleon initiated a further series of singular concessions to the three departments most tainted by royalism, the Vendée, itself, the Deux-Sèvres and the Loire-Inférieure: they were exempted from taxation for 15 years and an extensive programme of rebuilding was to be subsidized by the state. None of this bore fruit, and only the fall of the Empire in 1814 pre-empted another rising, fuelled by the need to impose more realistic conscription quotas and the breach with the Pope.

Beyond the Vendée militaire lay the five Breton departments. Although a remote region, Brittany had almost 2 500 000 inhabitants; it was also a source of bitter resistance to the regime, until at least 1805, when the martial law imposed during the Revolution was finally lifted. The first years of the Consulat saw determined, often brutal campaigns against the Chouans and, even as late as 1809, small bands of ex-Chouans operating on the borders of the departments of the Côtes-du-Nord and the Morbihan terrorized tax collectors and families who had bought *biens nationaux* during the Revolution. In 1806, Chouans kidnapped the pro-government Bishop of Vannes.[4] The regime and its supporters were always an embattled minority in Brittany: few regions had known more autonomy under the *ancien régime*, and none resented its loss more. Even the Concordat did not really appease these intensely Catholic populations. The loyalty of the Bishop of Vannes was exceptional in the region. In the Côtes-du-Nord, the Bishop of St-Brieuc used the Concordat to re-establish refractory, openly royalist priests throughout the diocese; the bishop of Rennes, in the Ille-et-Vilaine, was in league with the schismatic Petite Église, which refused to recognize the Concordat. The bishops were in almost constant conflict with the prefects throughout the period,[5] and the attitude of the Breton clergy to the Concordat may be likened more to that of newly annnexed regions in Italy or Germany, than to other parts of France. The regime had few supporters outside the towns or the owners of *biens nationaux*; although conscription was eventually enforced and outward calm prevailed, the local administration was never at ease. The prefect of the Côtes-du-Nord remained to the end more a '*commissaire de police supérieur*' than a mere civil servant. Like many future prefects in the departments of the outer empire, after 1808, he had ambitious plans to improve the economic and cultural life of his *administrés*, but his tangible achievements did not stretch far beyond the restoration of order.[6] The besieged character of Napoleonic rule in the western countryside was encarnated in the 'new towns' of Napoléonville, created in the troubled backcountry of southern Brittany, and Napoléon-Vendée, in 1804, made the new capital of the department of the Vendée. Both were built on the sites of villages destroyed in the repression of the rebellion, and stood as symbols of the intention of the regime to master the West. In fact, they were isolated strong-points surrounded by a hostile *bocage*.

The *bocage* was not the whole of the West, but the last years of the Empire are notable for turning former strongholds of loyalty to the revolutionary regimes into centres of surly, sometimes pro-royalist opposition. The great port of Bordeaux suffered a fate comparable to all the maritime centres of the Empire, as the effects of the blockade and the loss of the colonies choked its trade; its population fell from over 120 000 in 1790 to 88 398 in 1809, and it continued to fall into the 1820s. There was a brief revival of commerce between 1802 and 1806, but thereafter trade stagnated, even if the steep decline of the 1790s was slowed. Only smuggling and a series of concessions over neutral shipping after 1811 prevented the total collapse which seemed so imminent in 1808, when the American consul wrote 'The grass is pushing through the pavements of this city. Its splendid port is a desert . . .'[7] Previously a republican bastion, the economic crisis allowed covert royalist groups, masquerading as the Institut Philanthropique, to grow in influence to the point that in 1814 Wellington chose Bordeaux as his target, assured of a sympathetic welcome. Conditions in Nantes, further north, were little better; the blockade reduced the port to local traffic, although its importance as a naval base prevented a complete eclipse. The proximity of the *bocage* – Nantes was the *chef-lieu* of the Loire-Inférieure – restrained political disaffection among its notables, but there was little positive support for the regime after 1808, in a city made famous by its determined resistance to the Vendéan army in 1793. The smaller port of La Rochelle was equally disaffected; even the transfer of the *chef-lieu* of the department – Charente-Inférieure – to the port from Saintes did not win the regime clear support.

Thus, an 'outer layer' of economic – and in Bordeaux, political – disaffection increasingly wrapped a volatile, determinedly royalist countryside. Secure support for the regime had shrunk to the market towns of the interior, the famous 'blue islands in a sea of white', such as Niort, Chinon and Saumur: a narrow base, akin to circumstances in the Kingdom of Naples or Andalusia in the same years.

THE SOUTH AND THE CENTRE

By 1807, considerable progress had been made in restoring normal life to most of the south, although the eastern Pyrenees always remained recalcitrant. The small-scale peasant agriculture of much of the Midi, like that of the west, spared these areas from involvement in the imperial market design, but their periodic inability to achieve self-sufficiency in grain provided an increasingly unstable background to Napoleonic rule, after the relative successes of the early years. This only became dangerous after the failure of the harvest of 1811, however, and the inland areas of the southern countryside enjoyed a period of relative prosperity, as well as security, in the middle years of the Napoleonic period.

This economic prosperity appears all the more real when contrasted with the collapse of the great port of Marseille which, like Bordeaux, saw a steep decline in population from 111 000 in 1799 to 80 000 in 1813, as people sought work in its agrarian hinterland.[8] Its popular classes, never sympathetic to the regime, moved ever closer to overt royalism. Only Toulon, of the Mediterranean ports, enjoyed a degree of prosperity during the blockade, as a naval base and arsenal; thus, it was a bastion of loyalty to the regime.[9] A combination of prosperity and the goodwill of the propertied classes created by the restoration of order enabled the regime to surmount the economic crisis of 1811–12 better in the Provençal countryside than in the cities.

Economic conditions, and even the prevalence of law and order, are not the most influential elements on the political geography of the south, however. Broadly, the grip of the regime loosened, moving from east to west. Provence, although never an area noted for loyalty, was essentially secure. In the central Midi, the Cévennes region, the regime could count on the Protestant minority to maintain the order established under the Consulat; its grip was effective, but based on local fears of a renewed civil war, rather than on any positive reasons. The textile industries of the Gard collapsed between 1809 and 1812, causing considerable hardship in the countryside and sizeable towns like Nîmes and Beaucaire, but the Protestant elite of the area – themselves the victims of the slump – were unswervingly loyal to the regime in the face the latent threat of popular, Catholic royalism, which did, indeed, burst upon them in 1814–15.[10] The regime had a hard core of support, but hardly a secure base.

Further west, the Pyrenean departments might be properly classified as part of the outer, rather than the inner empire, the fact that they were part of pre-revolutionary France notwithstanding. In contrast to the departments of the Massif Central or Provence, they showed few improvements in the enforcement of conscription. While the year 1811 might be described in Provence as the point when the regime was at the apogee of its power,[11] the prefect of the Pyrénées-Orientales, in Perpignan, admitted that conscription was no more effective in 1811 than in 1799.[12] The war with Spain only increased disorder; the creation of a weak satellite state, followed by the civil war, brought havoc to the isolated border areas, and sorely over-stretched the local forces of order. The Gendarmerie remained too busy try-ing to enforce conscription to act as a proper police force, and so became an irrelevance, at best, even to the propertied classes.[13] As in the Gard, the Napoleonic regime could not extend its basis of local support beyond those who had served the previous revolutionary regimes.

A poignant indication of the true nature of French control in this area is that from 1806 onwards the authorities turned to exactly those repressive police tactics that were being abandoned in Provence, the Piedmontese and Rhenish departments, and in the Kingdom of Italy: the occupation of whole villages and the imposition of fines on the extended families of missing con-scripts or known bandits.[14] The numbers of *réfractaires* were reduced in the central Pyrenean department of Hautes-Pyrénées between 1805 and 1810 to levels lower than those of the Pyrénées-Orientales, but only because the same, ruthless methods were applied more effectively, rather than through any real amelioration of public order.[15] In 1808, the government virtually resurrected the *ancien régime* privileges of this region in matters of con-scription: companies of semi-regular troops were to be raised, largely from the *réfractaires*, and were promised they would not be called upon to serve outside the Pyrenees. This amounted to far more than an amnesty; it was an admission by the state that this region would co-operate in the defence of France only on its own, traditional terms. The initial response was excel-lent: 600 out of the 1200 *chasseurs de la montagne* raised in the Hautes-Pyrénées were *réfractaires*, but when these terms were violated in 1809, and they were ordered to Spain, all but 275 deserted.[16] The corps raised in the Pyrénées-Orientales eventually came to consist of bands of smugglers, under their own chiefs, who had virtually made private treaties with the authorities. In every case, their military value proved miniscule.[17] Even the restitution of *ancien régime* provincial privilege failed. More significantly for the place of these departments in the Napoleonic Empire, as a whole, these tactics were replicated in the newly annexed departments of central Italy and in the Illyrian departments, both hardly secure sectors of the Empire. The case of the Pyrenees underlines the real, effective borders of the inner empire. To the east, secure frontiers had been forged by 1807, making not only Piedmont and Lombardy part of the inner empire, but Provence as well. To the west, the relationship between Spain and the Pyrenean departments reversed the process.

It was not only the Spanish border and the proximity of the war that pulled the Pyrenees out of Napoleon's orbit, however, but the failure of the regime to establish itself there before 1808. The Napoleonic regime proved no more able to curb the deep-rooted independence of the region than had those of the 1790s. This went much deeper than opposition to conscription, high taxation or even the Concordat. The regime was singularly unsuccess-ful in its attempt to disarm the region in 1806.[18] However, a deeper sign of estrangement from the state can be detected in the way local people simply ignored the judicial system for regulating their disputes. Even the propertied classes simply ignored the state; they saw that its justice was not respected by the lower classes, who they had to control, and thus justice remained largely in the private sphere, making a mockery of French rule at the most basic level.[19] The government was increasingly resented throughout southern France, not only for the general imposition of conscription or the economic crisis after 1811, but at a cultural level, particularly as regarded the religious reforms of the Concordat. However, only in the Pyrenees did the regime fail to lessen these sources of antagonism from overt resistance to mere discontent by 1807. In most other regions, it is difficult to make a direct link between the popular unrest caused by the economic crisis of 1810–12 and the politically inspired movements of 1814, during the fall of the Empire. Roussillon, however, is an example of continuous rejection of authority, unmatched even by the Vendée.

The departments of the Massif Central, the mountainous core of central France, saw little material change during the Napoleonic period, but against this immobile material background, the Napoleonic regime made determined political and administrative advances, a true example of internal conquest. Poverty remained the hallmark of this region; large sections of its population either migrated for much of the year, to augment local resources, or were dependent on such income. Agricultural self-sufficiency remained the goal of its peasantry, but local methods of cultivation often remained backward, and the region would have endured severe famine without harvests of chestnuts to supplement its fragile levels of grain production. A succession of prefects failed to modernize agriculture or expand industry; the region stood further outside the ambitions of the imperial market design than any other in the Empire. Despite its poverty, the Massif Central was among the few parts of France where the population rose in these years; the first years of the Consulate mark the start of an upward trend that would last into the mid-nineteenth century.[20] During the Napoleonic period, the total population of its nine core departments probably exceeded 2 500 000; that of the Puy de Dôme alone numbered well over half a million.

Thus, the region made up in human resources what it lacked in natural wealth. However, the 1790s had revealed the violent nature of this large population, and the first years of Napoleonic rule witnessed ferocious, widespread resistance to conscription and the Concordat. The regime overcame the powerful combination of cultural antagonism to strong government and forbidding geography, to the extent that the political feuds of the 1790s were squashed, if not completely extinguished. By 1811, these departments had been changed from among the worst suppliers of men for conscription, to among the most reliable: Napoleon had tapped this important source of manpower by a sheer effort of bureaucratic will, persistent policing and ever more ruthless prefects, epitomized by Camille Périer, an *auditeur* under 30 when he became prefect of the Corrèze in 1810. A new generation of professional administrators reduced this isolated region to obedience. This process took longer in the Massif than elsewhere, but its results were complete: even in 1814, much of the Massif was notable for its political passivity. A bastion of resistance had been surrounded, and worn down. The replacement of rebellion with surly resignation was not the ideal outcome of state-building, but it represents a stunning triumph of the relative and the possible, from the vantage point of the regime.

THE EAST

Eastern France – the northern Rhone valley, dominated by Lyon; Burgundy; the Champagne; and Alsace-Lorraine – was the most solidly pro-Napoleonic region in France. The east enjoyed a rising level of economic prosperity which was often directly attributable to the market design of the Continental System: of all the various regions of under Napoleonic hegemony, eastern France benefited most clearly from policies that so often brought ruin in their wake elsewhere. Whereas the north-eastern departments benefited from imperial expansion because it created a natural economic unit with Belgium, these areas derived their prosperity specifically from the privileged position granted them by the imperial tariff boundaries and the wider policy of turning away from Atlantic markets, towards continental trade. Lyon thrived as the manufacturing centre of silk, produced in Italy specifically for its needs, at the direct expense of indigenous Italian industry; Alsatian commerce and industry thrived in great part due to the market design, even absorbing capital and manpower from less privileged parts of the Rhineland, such as Berg; Burgundian wines spread throughout the vast German markets opened for them, as a direct result of French military conquest.[21] When Napoleon spoke of an economic policy of 'France first', these regions were the first among equals.

By and large, they knew when they were well off, and it is reflected in their political outlook. This loyalty, although based on sound economic foundations, had to be worked for by the regime, for its political inheritance from the Revolution was far from uniform. Lyon had been a centre of ferocious resistance to the Jacobin regime in Paris, and had suffered physical devastation as intense as any in the Vendée; the result was that the second largest city in France had a marked penchant for royalism, by the first years of the Consulate. In Burgundy, although the Napoleonic regime enjoyed great support from the outset – for the region contained a large number of purchasers of *biens nationaux* – the administration of its largest city, Dijon, remained in the hands of Jacobins. Returned émigrés and militant clergy were reduced to silence, but Napoleon did not dare purge the Dijonnais Jacobins, many of whom were elected to the electoral college of the department as late as 1810.[22] Both cities became centres of Bonapartism, and remained so after the fall of the Empire. The two

Alsatian departments of Haut- and Bas-Rhin, like Burgundy, had large numbers of purchasers of *biens nationaux* during the Revolution, to the extent that the peasantry came to own two-thirds of rural property by 1800. However, this was balanced by the return of many émigrés, ranging from influential nobles to the 1800 peasants of the countryside near Wissembourg who fled across the border during the wars of the 1790s and returned to find their small farms confiscated.[23]

Lyon stands at the crossroads of north-eastern and south-eastern France, where the valleys of the Rhône and the Saône meet, and its true identity – as a northern or southern entity – remains a lively source of discussion. In the Napoleonic period, its politics and economy link it emphatically to the north-east, whereas in the 1790s it was an epicentre of the factional violence and counter-revolutionary resistance so typical of the Midi.[24] This transformation is no less dramatic for being predictable, in the light of Napoleonic economic policies. Napoleon took a personal interest in the reconstruction of Lyon from the outset, declaring as early as June 1800 that within two years, 'the commerce of this city, once the envy of Europe, will regain its original prosperity'. The silk industry grew apace, literally fuelled by cut-rate Italian raw materials: the number of silk workers rose from 6500 in 1801, to 9500 in 1807, and peaked at 13 146 in 1811; the crisis of that year lowered them by only 150. The urban population also grew apace, from 94 000 in 1810, to over 120 000 by 1812, a rise of over 20 per cent. This prosperity permitted a degree of urban renwal, and some of the major damage of the Federalist revolt of 1793–94 was repaired. The city came as close to flourishing in these years as could be expected at a time of major European war. The regime won back the greatest urban stronghold of counter-revolution in France.

Elsewhere, the regime had firmer foundations to build upon, and it did not fail to capitalize on the loyalty to the Revolution it found in Burgundy and Alsace. Strasbourg, in particular, and the left bank of the Rhine, in general, prospered in these years. The blockade, as opposed to the wider strategy of the Continental System, did hinder some sectors of the economy, particularly the cotton industry, and, as inhabitants of a border region, Alsatians were tempted into the lucrative business of smuggling, possibly as much by greed as necessity. However, in contrast to similar activities in other frontier areas – notably the Dutch, Hanseatic and Pyrenean departments – Alsace offers an example of a region that defied this aspect of imperial policy, without political implications. The Haut- and Bas-Rhin were among the most reliable sources of recruits, despite the proximity of the rugged Vosges mountains. Burgundy, the Ain, and the Jura – the eastern hinterland of Lyon – were equally obedient. Resistance to conscription was small scale, and above all it was never overt or collective, even in mountain communes.

Indifference was probably more typical of the political complexion of the eastern departments than true enthusiasm, but this region proved exceptionally loyal to Napoleon, not only in the last campaigns of 1814, but during the 100 Days. It was no coincidence that he chose to 'emerge' from hiding at Lyon on his march to Paris, in 1815, where he re-proclaimed the Empire. In Dijon, there was genuinely popular support for Napoleon in 1815, as there was throughout Alsace and Lorraine.[25] In no other area of France was support for the regime as solid or as general as here.

PARIS

Paris was the centre of the Empire, and its history encapsulates many of the contradictions of the Napoleonic regime. There was a dispute within its administration over the character of the city itself, which magnifies the paradoxes surrounding the First Empire. Frochot, one of its two prefects, sought to create a Paris fit to be the capital of an empire of the professionals, devoid of an industrial workforce prone to political agitation. Frochot strove to build a city of monuments and vast offices, peopled by bureaucrats, diplomats and service industries – a dream that would embody a particular vision of the Empire and its purpose. Yet, Frochot's vision was propelled less by confidence than by fear. He looked back with unease on the events of the 1790s, and was determined that any risk of mob rule at the centre of power should be averted by the most definitive means conceiveable: by making the mob – the artisan classes – redundant to the life of Paris.

Frochot's dream foundered on all counts. There was never enough money to realize his monumental building plans on a large scale. Above all, he could not stop the growth of industry and commerce at the heart of the Empire. Frochot always argued that this growth was fragile and artificial; it was too dependent on political circumstances – the imperial market design, in particular – to withstand economic realities. There were signs that he had good cause for caution, first in 1801 when a bad harvest threatened disorder, and then in 1805–06 when over-production and saturated markets led to a banking crisis which threatened industrial recession. For most of the period 1801–12, however, Paris witnessed an unheralded industrial boom, as it was sheltered from British competition by the blockade, fed cheap raw materials by the Continental System and provided with a monied clientele by the Imperial Court. Four industrial sectors benefited especially in these circumstances: luxury trades, cotton, chemicals, and mechanical engineering. Most enterprises were on a small scale, few factories employed more than 20 or so workers, but the workforce swelled, especially after 1806. By 1811, over 30 000 people worked in 57 cotton mills, of which there had been only five in 1804.[26]

It proved impossible to limit the natural expansion of Paris in these years. The population rose from 546 856 in 1801 to 714 000 by the end of the Empire. During the good times, seasonal migrants – usually from Normandy, the Alps and the Auvergne – became permanent, and increasingly they were joined by migrants from neighbouring departments, drawn to Paris by the ever higher level of wages. Paris acted as a magnet for the educated and working classes alike in these years. This was an emphatic sign of confidence in the Parisian economy, which reached its zenith in tandem with the political fortunes of the regime, between 1806 and 1809, but it always worried the police. Regulations bent on controlling the activities of the Parisian workforce flooded from the Prefecture de Police, prohibiting clandestine trade unions, monitoring their movements through the imposition of *livrets* (compulsory records of employment that every worker had to carry), breaking the handful of strikes that occurred, and spying on their leisure activities.

Yet Paris was also a favoured, almost pampered city: Napoleon spoiled his capital, just as he did the Imperial Guard, for they both stood close to the levers of power. During the subsistence crisis of 1810–12, he plundered the grain resources of northern France to satisfy the Parisian working classes as thoroughly and ruthlessly as he plundered the regiments of the line for recruits for the Guard. Paris did not starve at the height of the economic crisis, as Napoleon swept the policy of free trade aside, reverting in 1812 to the Jacobin policy of a maximum price fixed on grains. As a result, there were no popular disturbances of a political nature, even when the boom collapsed after 1811. Like the Guards, Parisians grumbled, but the old centres of revolutionary agitation – the artisan quarters, the eastern faubourgs – remained the most dependable parts of the city. It was no coincidence that Napoleon always preferred to enter Paris through them, rather than the more royalist western suburbs. Here, the myth of the 'Jacobin emperor' was not just the invention of Napoleon's memoirs, but a reality forged by deliberate policy from 1800 onwards.[27] The capital, like the Empire itself, had a Jacobin core.

Beyond this core, the goodwill of Paris rested on a combination of prosperity and good order, and Napoleonic policy centred on providing them. Frochot saw clearly that both were brittle, dependent on the success of the Continental System and continued military victory. Neither survived long after 1814; the fate of Paris was bound up even more with that of Napoleon than it had been with the Revolution.

THE SUM OF THE PARTS

It is almost a commonplace to think of France as divided into two parts – almost two countries – by an imaginary line running from north-west to south-east, from St Malo to Lake Geneva. Its academic origins date from the statistical essay of Adolphe d'Angeville in 1836, but it received its seminal form in the work on levels of literacy by Louis Maggiolo in 1879. The more general, impressionistic work of Angeville and the specific enquiries of Maggiolo are deeply imbedded in French self-perceptions, and the 'Maggiolo line' has reappeared frequently in analyses of electoral, social and cultural behaviour in the last century, its applications reaching far beyond their academic origins.[28] The assumption behind the Maggiolo line is of a France of the north and east that is advanced, liberal and urban, more secular, better educated and fed, generally more pro-Revolutionary than the France of the south and west, where the last bastions of royalism and fanatical Catholicism mix with a lower material level of life, based on a more agrarian economy. The Maggiolo line, as it has evolved in the analysis of French culture, has come to symbolize 'enlightened' France from 'traditionalist' France – 'lightness' from 'dark'.[29]

The 'line' has been rejected in favour of geographic analyses that place a dual emphasis on a still more varied sense of regionalism – that of microregions too localized to fit a general line – alongside the view that these regions do fit a wider pattern of France as a coherent, meaningful geographic unit.[30] Yet the Maggiolo line has always exercised a powerful influence on the study of French identity. Within its original sphere (the assessment of literacy – and with it, levels of formal education) the line has been modified, as shifting from north-east/south-west, to a division that is more emphatically east/west by the mid-nineteenth century.[31] The basic premise of a gradual, but continuous trend of 'improvement', on both sides of the line, has also been questioned.[32] The power of the Maggiolo line persists, however, as a method of analysis, as well as a myth.[33]

Many Napoleonic prefects, usually those sent from the north or east to the south, had a vision of France that anticipated that derived from Maggiolo. Napoleon certainly shared it. This is evident in his expressed belief that the prefects of the southern departments should be northerners, exactly because they would be 'men nourished on the Enlightenment', and therefore uninclined to tolerate the backwardness of their *administrés*. The classic case of this was the attitude of Thibaudeau to the people of the Bouches du Rhône, the department of which he was prefect.[34] He described the Provençal as being 'as variable as his climate, he is primitive, brutal, hasty, excitable, indolent or taciturn'. This was as nothing compared to the contempt of the prefect of the Loire-Inférieure, in Brittany, who declared 'we think it superfluous to [give in] detail the diversity of mores, language, beliefs, or customs to be found here; ignorance and superstition shape their general character'.[35] Thus, the concept of the Maggiolo line was a determining element in the policy of the Napoleonic regime, 80 years before it was articulated. Napoleon's own prejudices in this regard are all the more striking because he was a Corsican.

The assumptions on which 'the line' rested were more prejudicial than scientific in the Napoleonic period, underlined by the incomplete and impressionistic nature of most official statistics gathered by the regime.[36] Indeed, the experience of the prefects tended to a belief in a thoroughly atomized France, as they dissected and sub-divided the people and geography of their respective departments.[37] The closer they drew to their *administrés*, the more conscious the prefects became of the complexity of France, and the deeper their determination became to obliterate these differences. Their ideal remained that of a united and uniform society, where differences would not be assimilated but extinguished, to be replaced by modernity, as they understood it: a secularized, French-speaking society, dominated by urban and northern values. What emerges is the sense of cultural estrangement between rulers and ruled, whatever the preferred geographic configuration of France. The concept of a cultural Maggiolo line dominated their thinking, and their policy was always to advance it further south and west, although even in the north and east the prefects of Flemish and Alsatian departments could be as crushing in their attitudes to local culture as their colleagues in the Midi.[38] As the Empire expanded, so their ambition became to push the line back, into the Mediterranean, off the coasts of Calabria and Cadiz, and into the bay of Lisbon, in the west.

The model of a Maggiolo line would seem to have a practical, historical relevance, quite different from the prejudicial judgements of contemporary administrators, however. If the concept is applied to Napoleonic France in political terms, and especially in terms of conscription and brigandage, it acquires a remarkable relevance. The overriding image is of a west and south deeply at odds with the regime, where open rebellion – or the persistent fear of it – prevented the introduction of trial by jury, the continued use of *colonnes mobiles* to police the countryside in place of fixed gendarmerie brigades, and a general tendency among the clergy and laity to regard the Concordat less as a welcome restoration than as a continuation of Jacobinal de-christianization by other means. The line runs through the Norman *bocage*, probably to the mouth of the Rhône. The political heartland of the Napoleonic regime conforms broadly to a north-west/south-east divide, but the pacification of Provence and the Cévennes – however fragile – together with that of the northern Massif Central, probably advance the line further east, along its southern front. The creation and simultaneous pacification of the inner empire in Piedmont and the Rhineland were essential to this shift. It was consolidated by the development of the Continental System, which oriented French commerce and regional prosperity eastwards. Napoleon did not begin with a realm centred on the Saône-Rhône-Rhine arteries, but by 1807, it was increasingly pulled this way.

French society and the Napoleonic state

Regionalism remained the essence of French society under the Napoleonic regime, and for decades to come, but this was far from the intentions of those at its helm. The essence of state policy was centralization and uniformity, and if the life of the people demands a regional approach, the relationship between the regime and the people of its heartland, France, must also be seen in terms of the general policies laid down at the centre of power.

THE WORLD OF WORK

By the middle years of the Empire, it was clear that the broad objective of those at the apex of the Napoleonic state was to create an immobile society, governed by a highly mobile, almost rootless elite of professionals. This was not an abstract concept, but a policy with very real ramifications for *fonctionnaires* and *administrés* alike. The regime sought to curtail and regulate the movements of its citizens and, incongruously for a state so bent on unity, to circumvent the lives of ordinary people within prescribed administrative limits. The department was the limit of free, unregulated travel; beyond its borders, passports were required of the propertied classes, and *livrets du travail* for workers – cards which had to stamped by the police when a workman changed job – that enabled the state not only to monitor the movements of ordinary people, but to keep them in one place, if desired.[39] The department became the basis of all statistical enquiries and the central government came to assume that it was, invariably, a self-contained economic and social unit, despite massive evidence to the contrary.

The determination to anchor French society is equally apparent in the marked preference of the regime to base its own conscious definition of its local elite – notability – mainly on the ownership of landed property. Wealth, as such, was less important than stability,[40] and stability was interpreted in a physical, very literal sense. It was also reflected in the desired organization of religious life, under the terms of the Concordat. Bishoprics were, in so far as possible, synonymous with departments. Everywhere, the parish was the only recognized sub-division of the diocese, and so the centre of religious life; the parish priest, the *curé*, was the sole source of authority here, and the long-established practice of inviting preachers from elsewhere was discouraged. In these ways, it was hoped that the citizen might be more easily taxed, conscripted, ministered to and also protected. Movement was not something the authorities liked among the labouring classes, and Napoleonic legislation on begging and vagabondage is remarkable for its severity.

It proved an impossible task to circumvent French life in such narrow limits, however. Internal, seasonal migrations were traditional and essential parts of working life in many parts of France. They took place on a massive scale in the Massif Central, the Alps and the Pyrenees, where most of the adult male population spent a large part of the year working either in the cities or in other regions, practising itinerant trades. Equally, the labouring populations of wealthy areas, such as Normandy, would migrate at harvest time to the neighbouring regions of the Ile de France or Picardy, or to adjacent departments within their own region, while at the same time receiving itinerant craftsmen from the Massif Central and the Limousin. The regime did not break these patterns, which would only disappear with industrialization later in the century.

Where elements in French society did seek a restoration of more regulated social and economic practices, they met with at least partial disappointment. Many craftsmen hoped that the tighter controls on movement by the *livrets* heralded the restoration of the trade guilds, which had been abolished in 1789. This was generally favoured by the police as a useful means of control; the Parisian police actually created *syndics* for mastercraftsmen in most trades, a step which was technically illegal, but that aroused considerable enthusiasm among skilled workers.[41]

At the other end of the social scale, the regime set great priority on reestablishing the legal profession, and regulating its membership to those trained in the new law schools. This raised hopes within its ranks of the restoration of the *ancien régime* Order of Barristers, with its rights of self-regulation. These hopes were disappointed, in similar fashion to those of the mastercraftsmen who desired the return of the guilds, and for identical reasons. Napoleon was deeply suspicious of the barristers, personally, and this reinforced the wider outlook of the regime: that the purpose of the organization and regulation of any aspect of working life – whether that of an itinerant tinker or a barrister – was to ensure state control in that sphere. The barristers were never accorded any authority over their own profession; the curriculum of the law schools was laid down by the Ministry of Justice and recruitment was decided by the state,[42] just as an Auvergnat stone mason required the permission of his prefect to work ouside his department. After 1811, these controls tightened at every level. As has been seen, they even extended to those the regime called its nobility.

At the heart of these policies lay a fundamental dispute between the regime and large portions of French society. The thwarted hopes of mastercraftsmen and barristers ought not to be equated with political opposition; it was a question of disappointment, not resistance, wholly different from the liberal and reactionary defiance that marked the early years. Nevertheless, the restorative character of many of the initial Napoleonic reforms raised hopes in some quarters of a partial return to the *ancien régime*. Yet, just as the transformation of the Consulate into the Empire did not mean a monarchial restoration, so the reordering of the workplace did not open the way to the return of corporatism. Nor did the introduction of the Concordat allow the restoration of many aspects of popular religion – or of any religious life outside the parish. The popular lay confraternities remained outlawed, alongside the guilds and professional bodies who had once supported them. The intention of the Napoleonic 'restoration' was to strengthen the state and standardize life, not to revive particularism.

These tensions were reflected within the state itself, for the disappointment of these conservative hopes was by no means a foregone conclusion. It was only after about 1806 that the regime decided to blend its authoritarianism with the liberal individualism of the Revolution, rather than the corporatism of the old order. The possibility of restoring the guilds and the Order of Barristers was debated by the Council of State several times, but ultimately the liberal view prevailed: that the freedom of profession established in 1789 should remain, if now subject to certain strictures in the case of medicine, the law and public service. This remained a haven of deregulation – almost an anomaly – in so tightly controlled a society.

THE NOTABLES AND THE STATE: TWO ELITES

Above and outside the immobile, regulated France of the *administrés*, the regime sought to create the basis to perpetuate that 'empire of the professionals' upon which it relied. The Université Impériale and its *lycées* were producing their first generation of pupils by about 1806–07. Drawn from the immobile ranks of the notables, the more promising among them were destined, at least in the eyes of the government, to become the next generation of imperial officers and administrators. The *lycées* were created to give them the appropriate education for this role, but as the sons of the notables confronted this system of education, other signs of reticence emerged between the state and society.

The issue of elite education reveals a clear distinction between the culture of the notables and that of the state. Even within the ranks of those most solicited by Napoleon, a gulf began to emerge between the aspirations of notable families for their sons, and those of the state culture, the 'official France' whose values were taught in the *lycées*. A united, professional, centralized state could not hope to survive without an educated bureaucracy and army, staffed by men who shared a national culture and a distinct set of values, but it was by no means clear that Napoleon was going to get this from the notables. The curriculum was meant to reassure the conservative instincts of the landed classes, by the reintroduction of classics and a degree of religious study, yet this served only to emphasize how unlike the Church-run schools of the *ancien régime* the *lycées* actually were. The general goal of the curriculum was clearly to create professional administrators; great stress was placed on science, mathematics and modern languages. The ethos of school life was military, both in the daily routine and the uniforms themselves. Classes changed to military drum beats; ranks and punishments were replications of military norms.

An educational system of this kind did not appeal to those same notables who spent considerable sums on buying replacements to help their sons avoid conscription. The limited appeal of the *lycées* indicates that the notables resented the militarization of their lives. Imperial victories were crucial to their well-being, but they did not want to be directly involved in creating the Empire, any more than the peasantry. The imperial ethos was alien to them. It is even more striking that this reluctance did not come in the final, beleaguered years of the Empire, but at its zenith, in 1805–07. They detested the creation of the Gardes d'Honneur, the thoroughly elitist corps of national guards, selected from the wealthiest taxpayers of each department, representing as it did an attempt by the government to recoup for service those who had bought replacements.

The cultural divide between the Napoleonic state and its most prized citizens, the French notables, was deep, for when the notables rejected the *lycées* – and the state culture they stood for – they turned, instead, to the more traditional Catholic schools. Fontanes, who became Rector of the Imperial University in 1808, brought the differences between the state and Catholic schools to light, in his unsuccessful attempts to get Napoleon to soften the curriculum of the *lycées* by introducing more formal religion and more traditional humanist studies at the expense of science. He also tried to introduce more clergy to the teaching staff, but with no real success. Fontanes saw the serious nature, and the wider implications, of the rift exposed by the unpopularity of the *lycées*, but was unable to ameliorate it. His sense of unease is reflected in the opening words of the memoirs of Alfred de Musset, who was a schoolboy in these years. They reveal the unease which underlay Napoleonic rule, even at its peak:

> During the wars of the Empire ... worried mothers brought a pale, passionate, nervous generation into the world, conceived between two battles, brought up in colleges to the roll of drums, thousands of children looked around at each other with sombre eyes, flexing their puny muscles ... Every year, France made a present to this man (Napoleon) of 300,000 youths ... Never were there so many sleepless nights as in the time of this man; never were there to be seen, leaning on the ramparts of town walls, such a nation of sorrowing mothers; never did such silence envelop those who spoke of death. And yet, never was there so much joy, so much life, so many warlike fanfares, in every heart. Never was there so much pure sunshine, to dry out the stains of so much blood. It was said that God made it for this man, and it was called the sun of Austerlitz. But he made them, himself, with his never-silent cannons, which left only clouds of smoke the day after his battles.[43]

A glaring contradiction lay at the heart of the state's plan to extract future empire-builders from the ranks of the notables: the Napoleonic regime sought to glorify empire, commitment to service in far-flung wars and departments, while at the same time it deliberately enshrined the ideal of a landed, localized, stable network of family-based elites at the heart of French society. The incongruity of this became clear as the notables shunned the *lycées*. Few outside Paris ever filled the number of places available: that of Bordeaux had only 180 pupils for 350 places in 1809 and only 255 by 1813; most of them were the sons of ex-revolutionaries. Even the politically loyal city of Lyon had only 150 pupils at its *lycée*, in 1810. The vast majority of pupils were drawn from sons of civil servants and officers, for whom Napoleon provided generous scholarships. The revolutionary-Napoleonic state was in danger of becoming hereditary well below the level of the Bonaparte dynasty.

Had the regime lasted longer, there were clear indications that two elites would have emerged: a social and economic elite based on the 600 wealthiest taxpayers in each department, rooted, for the most part, in their localities, inward-looking, politically powerless, with only the departmental electoral colleges as a collective means of expression; beside them, in an almost parallel universe, stood the professional elite of the army and the imperial civil service, composed of men whose lives revolved around their careers, and whose horizons were European, rather than local, ready to serve in the Italian, German or Dutch departments, as required, and who sent their sons, in turn, to the *lycées*. The French elite was united by a common language and the long experience of living under a relatively centralized state long before 1789. There was a true national, literary culture to bind them, but as Napoleonic rule acquired its own identity through the creation of a state culture, that official culture diverged from – and threatened to outweigh – the older sources of cultural unity in France. Some reconciled the two, some did not: the regime increasingly wrapped itself in the trappings of the old monarchy, not only in its iconography, but in new history textbooks describing the Bonapartes as 'the fourth dynasty' in a continuous history of France.[44] Seen in the context of the reticence of the notables to embrace state culture, such efforts become less the expression of unbounded egotism, than another aspect of *ralliement*, a desperate attempt to preserve cultural unity. It did not fail, altogether.

There was another side to the picture of fear and anxiety painted by de Musset, for a generational divide was emerging within the French elite at the height of the Empire. De Musset portrayed the fears of his parents, not of his peers: his classmates rallied to Napoleon in the 100 Days – 'It was the unsullied air of heaven, gleaming with glory and resplendent with so much steel, that children breathed then.'[45] Even within the ranks of the Savoyard nobles, loyal to the House of Savoy, who had refused to serve France since the annexation of their province to France – now the department of Mont Blanc – in 1792, the new generation of nobles increasingly took service in the Grande Armée.[46] For those caught up in the heady creation of the Empire, the prospects seemed endless, but they were only attainable in the service of the state.

The regime was renewing itself from within from 1808 onwards, particularly by purging its ranks of many older men. They were replaced mainly by a new generation aged between 21 and 30 who had known only the Napoleonic order since childhood. These younger administrators brought with them not only the necessary vigour for ruling the new unruly territories acquired after 1808, but also a fresh perspective on the role of the state in society. Above all, they possessed a strong sense of confidence – of superiority – in the whole edifice of contemporary French culture and its single greatest achievement, the Napoleonic state. In bringing these younger men into power and responsibility, Napoleon sought to break with the quarrels of the past but equally to find men he felt he could trust, who, although inevitably from wealthy backgrounds, would conform to Eugène de Beauharnais's vision of the professional bureaucrat, whose interests were wholly at one with those of the state. By the last years of the Empire, Napoleon's initial reforms provided him with the human material to achieve this. The main instrument Napoleon chose for his policy of renewal was the office of *auditeur* to the Council of State, his central policy-making body. There were only 16 *auditeurs* in 1805, but the office grew along with the Empire. By 1808, they had risen to 34, and many of them had seen service as military administrators with the Grande Armée or as intendants of areas temporarily under French control. Following the upheavals of 1809, Napoleon reshaped their role and increased their number considerably. By January 1810, there were 350 of them, by 1813, 452. The *auditeurs* played a role in the life of the Empire out of all proportion even to these numbers. Most were French, usually the sons of the political elite of the Revolution, together with some scions of the old nobility, but from 1809 onwards they were also drawn from the Dutch, Belgian and Italian departments: the office was an instrument of *ralliement*, as well as of renewal. Although many Dutch and Italian recruits were reluctant to serve the French and were not really loyal to the regime, most acquired a profound respect for the Napoleonic system of government; it was a certainty they never abandoned. The *auditeurs* made their most obvious impact in the departments of the outer empire; all the Illyrian intendancies, the two Roman departments and the civil administration of Spain north of the River Ebro all fell to their lot. These young bureaucrats were very conscious of their elite status, and their confidence – often sheer arrogance – lent a real ferocity to the almost traditional rivalries between the civil and military authorities.

The heartland of the French Empire was stable and secure, on the eve of its last phase of expansion in 1808. There was little overt political opposition to the regime and, as a new generation began to take its place within the elite, the signs were that opposition would continue to dwindle. However, on several different levels, divisions of a less obvious, but more fundamental kind were emerging. Geographically, if the 'imaginary line' between a loyal, ordered, prosperous country and a more backward, rebellious France was shifting from north/south to east/west, it continued to exist. Within the ranks of the elite, at the heart of the social groups the regime had chosen as its foundation, two different cultures were taking shape. When the Empire struck out into new territories, it carried with it the official culture of the professional elite and the image of the 'enlightened France' of the north and east.

Ruling the outer empire, 1808–1814

Napoleonic rule was brief in the territories of the outer empire, but although at the level of institutions its influence on the societies of these areas was ephemeral, the impact of annexation was no less profound for being almost wholly negative. They would get their first taste of rule by a modern state when that state was at its most demanding; conscription, the blockade and cultural imperialism would hit them all at once. Bad memories are often more enduring than good ones, and this was largely the case for the peoples of central Italy, Spain, the Illyrian provinces, and the North Sea coast. The experience of the outer empire was, truly, a short, sharp shock.

The North Sea coast: the Dutch and Hanseatic departments

In June 1810, the former Kingdom of Holland became nine French departments. Lebrun was appointed Governor-General, responsible for their integration into the Empire, the same role he had played earlier in Genoa and Parma. A largely decorative council was appointed to advise him from among Louis' leading advisors, but the real power lay with a new bureau for the Dutch departments, in Paris. The Dutch departments were in a unique position: having been under pro-French regimes since 1795, they did not find the administrative reforms difficult to absorb. Indeed, the full introduction of the Civil Code proved remarkably easy and popular, as Dutch magistrates were by now well versed in French law; after the fall of the Empire, it was maintained virtually unaltered by the restored monarchy until 1838. The French made annexation more difficult for themselves by creating new departments instead of working through those already established under Louis, and also by bringing in French and Belgian prefects, who were then moved deliberately from one department to another to prevent them developing that sympathy for the Dutch which had undone Louis. As a result, they were heavily reliant on the local officials of the former kingdom.

All this was nothing compared to the resentment engendered by the full introduction of conscription and a more effective enforcement of the blockade. Louis had protected his subjects from conscription, as had Murat in Naples, by raising forces of his own, but now Napoleon was determined to plunder Dutch reserves of manpower unhindered, especially for the navy. His new prefects sensed Dutch resentment, and moved with circumspection; it was estimated that only 17 300 troops were raised between 1811 and 1812, from a target of 40 000. Nevertheless, riots were frequent at the departure of conscripts. They posed no serious threat to public order and were usually composed of desperate women and children, but in 1813, as the collapse of French rule became more likely, resistance to conscription grew in violence and intensity. At Oud Beierland, in southern Holland, the crowds numbered in thousands and several people were killed in confrontations with the French.[47] The urban middle classes were often able to buy replacements, usually with the connivance of local officials, but lower-class resentment was intense.

The hatred and economic hardship provoked by the enforcement of the blockade was far more serious than the conscription riots; it also showed how slack Louis's regime had actually been about smuggling. While the civil administration, heavily influenced by Dutch politicians, was content to change as little as possible, the police and customs' officials behaved ruthlessly. Under Devilliers Duterrage, the gendarmes, coastguards and excisemen carried out arbitrary nocturnal arrests and house searches often notable for a gratuitous brutality which appalled even the French officials. Widespread corruption and extortion only compounded popular hatred of the French. The losses incurred by the blockade were not offset by annexation, thus disappointing the slender hopes of those Dutch businessmen who had seen some advantages in annexation. The Dutch departments were not allowed to trade on equal terms with France; legitimate markets were not opened up on a scale capable of replacing British or colonial trade. The burning customs' house became the symbol of Dutch resistance. Napoleon's financial policy was equally ruthless, above all his reduction by a third of the Dutch public debt. Large sections of the urban middle classes had invested in the public debt and this entailed a real financial loss to them.

Thus, Napoleon's three key policies intensified Dutch resentment at the loss of independence. Even long-standing supporters of the French were alienated after annexation. Donker Curtius – a leading magistrate – saw his son arrested arbitrarily for refusing to join the Garde d'Honneur, a national guard for the propertied classes. The French officials who presided over this had little confidence in the imperial edifice and their words echo those of their colleagues in Italy and Germany after the revolts of 1809. Lebrun told Napoleon early in 1811:

> I told Your Majesty that tranquillity reigns here. I did not say that there is general contentment... I hope that the enemy will not appear, but should that happen I doubt very much that we could count on the help of the Dutch.[48]

He was right.

The Dutch, at least, had a long acquaintance with the revolutionary-Napoleonic state and its workings. In contrast, the three Hanseatic departments, created in December 1810 from the coastal area between Lübeck and Osnabruck, have been justly described as one of the last and least durable creations of the Napoleonic state system.[49] With the exception of a few areas subtracted from the Kingdom of Westphalia – which deprived the 'model kingdom' of its outlet to the sea – these departments had been under French military occupation and had witnessed attempts to introduce both conscription and the blockade, but they had proved ineffective. Now, their imposition came as a severe blow, compounded by the wholesale introduction of the Napoleonic administrative system.

The Hansa ports had no tradition of centralized government; their political and legal traditions were alien to those of the French. Many local magistrates were horrified by the comparative severity of the French criminal code and had no idea how the new system worked. To overcome this, the French simply imported their own officials into the area *en masse*, thus excluding the indigenous elite from power and influence. The shock was compounded by French corruption. There was no concerted attempt to implement the policies of *ralliement* and *amalgame* among the wealthy merchant oligarchies of these great ports, a clear sign of the makeshift, expedient nature of the annexation. Far from the centres of power, they slipped back into the arbitrary practices of the *ancien régime* and the Revolution. The gendarmerie, 400 strong, was brought straight from France to implement conscription as quickly as possible, which actually led to the breakdown of law and order in an area where disorder had been largely unknown. Between 1811 and 1813, the marshlands along the coast were filled with men fleeing conscription, many of whom soon turned to banditry. Real power soon passed from the civilians to Marshal Davout, who proved an uncompromising military ruler.

Mass unemployment was the major consequence of annexation. The end of legitimate colonial trade led straight to the collapse of sugar refining, and there were over 300 refineries in the Hamburg area alone. The enforcement of the blockade ended large-scale smuggling with Britain, which had flourished under the pre-annexation collaboration between French commandants and the senates. This created so much hardship that even French officials pitied the plight of these coastal communities, among them the prefect of the neighbouring Dutch department of Ems-Oriental, who wrote in 1811: 'The islands ... that live from smuggling will be, and are already, deeply impoverished. A way should be found to employ these unfortunates in some sort of work on the mainland.'[50] There was no such possibility, and not only because of the blockade. As in the Dutch departments, the French denied the Hanseatic ports the right to trade freely with France, which led to the collapse of the textile industry; the numerous artisan classes of the ports were devastated. The ship-building programmes begun by the French did not provide enough work to compensate for dislocation on so vast a scale.

These annexations began in an atmosphere of resignation, but rapidly this was transformed into widespread hostility. Almost every sector of society felt its most vital interests damaged by annexation. The flourishing urban civilization of the North Sea coast had been ruined economically, and its sophisticated culture brutalized. Its economic fate was shared by almost all the coastal areas of the Empire, France not excepted. Bordeaux and Nantes, for example, never recovered from the blockade, unlike the North Sea ports. However, the cultural and political disruption of French rule were their own, and unique.

The Tuscan and Roman departments

The French had high hopes for Tuscany, despite the violence of the counter-revolution there in 1799 and the bitterness surrounding the deposition of the Bourbons in 1808. Yet these hopes were based on the false assumption that the reforms of Peter-Leopold in the 1780s had been popular and that they had fostered a peaceful, well-ordered state which could be easily revived under French rule. They were wrong on both counts: the enlightened reforms had been rejected violently in the 1790s and their originators were too unpopular and too small in number to provide a solid basis of support for the French. Nor did Tuscany have the basis of an orderly society; banditry was endemic over much of the countryside, especially in the inaccessible southern marshlands, the Maremma, and the mountain valleys to the north. There was also Arezzo, the centre of counter-revolution in 1799, which was still restive after annexation. The urban centres of the three Tuscan departments sheltered a mass of paupers, long perceived as dangerous by the authorities and the propertied classes, even if they posed no political threat.

Although these conditions predated the political upheavals of the decade prior to annexation, the succession of weak governments that ruled Tuscany had intensified them. Fear of disorder, rather than any tradition of enlightened reform, provided the French with a source of support rare in the outer empire. The new regime could deploy its most effective tactic, the restoration of order, and, by and large, the Tuscan propertied classes responded favourably, especially in the smaller towns and rural areas. The Tuscan notables respected French effectiveness, at least as far as repressing social disorder was concerned. In turn, this made the enforcement of conscription easier than it might otherwise have been, as the local authorities used it as a way to dispose of a wide spectrum of 'social nuisances', from dangerous bandit chiefs to unfortunate vagabonds, supported by French gendarmes. The willingness of the French to protect their collaborators in local government from the intimidation that went with social disorder brought forward many notables who were not really pro-French. Their way with the landed classes was also smoothed by the almost total absence of seigneurialism in Tuscany, thus sparing the French so many of the tensions that bedevilled them in Naples, Berg and Westphalia.

This pattern corresponds very closely to the successes of 1800–07 in the inner empire, but it should not be exaggerated. Tuscany is an example of how promising signs of *ralliement* and acceptance of imperial rule were compromised by the economic demands of the blockade, the strains of war and the intransigence of French religious policies. Livorno, the major port of the region, suffered greatly from the blockade, as did Prato, the only Tuscan centre with a highly developed textile industry. Tuscan agriculture had a significant commercial sector, centred on the export of olive oil, which was affected very badly by the loss of export markets brought about by the blockade. This, in turn, increased resentment of taxation among the landed classes and led them to oppose costly French improvement projects such as road-building, purely on financial grounds. The burdens of taxation and conscription embittered the popular classes, as they did all over Napoleonic Europe, while the patrician families of Florence resented the loss of their former prestige.

All this was compounded by a general lack of faith in the solidity of French rule. This crucial ingredient, which had been so important in consolidating the inner empire, was not present in the newly annexed territories, but it was not always due to military or diplomatic developments. Tuscany is a clear example of how the Empire was now simply overstretched, within its own borders. Between 1809 and 1812, considerable progress was made in the restoration of order, but although the following years did not see widespread disorder, the drain on military resources led to signs of weakness in the fight against the bandits. Now, instead of defeating them, as they had in the inner empire, the French were often reduced to making truces with the bands, whereby the bandits usually agreed to serve in Spain as irregular troops. It was a difference local officials took note of. They approved of what the French sought to do, but came to doubt their ability to achieve it.

The French had few straws to cling to in the two departments of the ex-Papal States. The intransigent passive resistance initiated by Pius VII did not abate after annexation. Added to this was the total incompatibility of the Papal government with the Napoleonic system. Probably nowhere else in western Europe did rulers and ruled find themselves thrust into such different dimensions as here. The French did not understand what they were dismantling because they were confronted by an administrative structure where not only was there no division between Church and state, but where the Church was the state. The Papal Curia, the highest administrative organ of the Roman Catholic Church, doubled as the civil service of the Papal States. The College of Cardinals was, effectively, the Council of State. Many Cardinals were deported by the French for their loyalty to the Pope, and only a handful of laymen held high posts in the Papal government; neither the nobility nor the middle classes were part of public life. In short, the French had nothing – and almost no one – to work through.

As in Tuscany, the highest posts went to Frenchmen. General Miollis became Governor-General after heading the transitional administration, the Consultà, until 1811. The prefects of the two new departments, Tiber (later Rome) and Trasimeno, were also both French. Among the ranks of the imported administrators in Tuscany and Rome were many magistrates, gendarmes and officials from the Piedmontese departments; many young French-trained Piedmontese magistrates gained quick promotion in the tribunals of the new departments. As with the use of prefects from Lombardy in the new Venetian departments a few years earlier, the inner empire was now colonizing the outer. This was far from a purely French expansion.

Like the Tuscan Giunta under Menou, the Consultà was remarkably successful in creating the institutional framework for French rule, but in much more difficult circumstances. Several noble families accepted office in the Roman departments, but usually only at local level. However, the non-noble professional classes tended to remain hostile to the regime, largely due to their close personal and economic ties to the clergy. Most successful families had clergy in their ranks, the equivalent of political connections in other states. Although reluctance to serve the French was less marked in provincial centres like Perugia and Spoleto than in Rome itself, there were few indications that a new class of secular, largely middle-class administrators would emerge here, in contrast to northern Italy, excluding the Veneto, or as was showing signs of happening in Tuscany. Much of this came from hatred of the new regime, but often it was due to the absence of laymen with adequate administrative backgrounds among those willing to serve.

The introduction of conscription was nothing short of traumatic for the Roman people; banditry increased and the population of Rome fell from 136 268 in 1809 to 112 648 in 1814, largely as a direct result of men fleeing the call-up.[51] Nevertheless, the ruthless determination of the prefects ensured that the two departments usually filled their quotas, while brigandage – although endemic in the mountains and along the border with Naples – was contained by the local police forces and the handful of troops Miollis had at his disposal. Thus, the Roman people were introduced to the modern, secular state, experiencing more wholesale change in the period 1809–14 than any other country in Europe.

Beyond the level of institutions, this experience was wholly negative. In both the Roman and Tuscan departments no pretence was ever made that French rule was popular with the masses. Their resentment found its most coherent expression in passive, widespread resistance to the introduction of the Concordat, the trauma of which was as deeply – and more widely – felt than the introduction of conscription. The dissolution of the regular orders, the abolition of many dioceses and of the lay confraternities had been disruptive enough elsewhere in western Europe. In the Roman departments, at the very heart of the Catholic world, it was interpreted as a savage blow to the whole fabric of society. Throughout the Papal States, the orders given by Pius VII to ignore the French regime were obeyed, especially in religious matters, as far as possible, thus threatening the daily functioning of the Church. Lay support for their clergy amounted to a non-violent movement of national resistance, orchestrated first by the College of Cardinals and then, when they were arrested and deported, by vicars-general of the dioceses and parish priests. Thousands of clergy at all levels were arrested by the French, ostensibly for their refusal to take the oath of allegiance to Napoleon, but really in an attempt to deprive the masses of the leadership they provided. In spite of their original intentions, the French found themselves returning to the anticlericalism of the revolutionary years. Over most of central Italy, the French came to depend heavily on the radicals of the 1790s, especially in the police; in Rome, they were virtually the only loyal support the regime had. If the symbol of popular resistance along the North Sea coast was a burning customs' house, or a guerrilla raid that of Spain, the anger of the Roman and Tuscan masses was expressed in the celebration of banned saints' days, the empty stalls in St Peter's Basilica for official celebrations and, most poignantly of all, the refusal of the entire population of four Roman dioceses to have their children baptized by the few collaborationist bishops of the area between 1809 and 1813. Despite its impressive administrative reforms, as well as the ambitious attempts to restore Rome's architectural and artistic heritage, the French regime remained virtually friendless, still haunted by Fesch's dread prophecy made before annexation: 'what would they not do to them, if they had the power'.

The course of French rule in Tuscany represents the practical problems imposed by over-expansion; in the Roman departments, it exemplifies those created by the radical ideology of reform at the heart of Napoleonic imperialism. It was not just the demands of war these populations rejected, or even the edifice of the modern state, but the world of the Enlightenment itself. French ambitions ran far beyond the imposition of conscription, taxation and the Napoleonic administrative system. Here, they overreached themselves more than territorially. Indeed, there were signs between 1809 and 1812 that they were making more progress in parts of Spain than in central Italy.

The Josephist Kingdom of Spain, 1809–1813

THE HIGH TIDE OF FRENCH RULE, 1809–1812

In the satellite kingdom of Spain, a very clear distinction must be made between basic military control of the country – occupation – and true pacification. The difference between the two had been clear in the minds of the French from the outset. After the end of the Wagram campaign in 1809, it did not take long for the French to drive the *Junta Central* out of Seville and pen its successor, the Cortes, behind the walls of Cadiz, in the far south-west. In the course of 1810 and 1811, with no major wars elsewhere to distract them, the French were able to secure their grip on Andalusia in the south, Asturias in the north, and, after a series of determined sieges, to take Valencia and the southern part of the Catalan coast. Thus, these years represent the apex of French military control in Spain; Joseph's kingdom had been extended from its core around Madrid and in the north-east, to include most of the south and east.

This was also the lowest ebb of large-scale resistance. The juntas and the Cortes now held on only to a few coastal areas: Cadiz itself, most of Galicia in the far north-west, and a few ports in Asturias and Murcia. With the vital exception of Portugal, real control had passed away from most of the juntas. Those of Navarre, Aragon and Catalonia had virtually merged with the guerrilla bands; those of Leon and Old Castille took refuge in Galicia. That of Asturias had been reduced to between two and five men, fleeing from one mountain hamlet to another during the winter and spring of 1811; its members often slept fully clothed, so great was their fear of capture. Their plight applied to most of the Spanish juntas between 1809 and 1812:

> What must be imagined most often, is the image of a small group of men, trudging for hours under the Asturian rain and the rugged peaks of the Cantabrian mountains, while below them, in the valley, the hamlet where they had found shelter the night before, burns.[52]

Even during these years, military occupation could fluctuate. When French troops were temporarily withdrawn from Asturias, for example, its ragged junta briefly found itself restored to the regional capital, Oviedo. Almost simultaneously, Soult and Suchet consolidated the French grip on Andalusia and Valencia, respectively. The sheer size of Spain still thwarted French efforts to establish a consistent grip on the country. When coupled to the determination of the Spanish to resist, the size of Spain made it very difficult to transform military occupation into pacification.

Nevertheless, where a degree of control was established, there were clear signs that the policy of restoring order and normal government was gaining ground. Suchet, in Aragon, Catalonia and then in Valencia, Bouchet in Asturias and, up to a point, Soult in Andalusia, were adept at counter-insurgency tactics and developed policies to secure the support of local populations, often weary of war and unconvinced of the effectiveness of the guerrilla fighters they sustained. In these areas, especially in Andalusia, the French convinced a significant segment of the propertied classes of the usefulness and effectiveness of their rule. It has even been suggested that between 1810 and 1812 a major part of the Spanish propertied classes were 'passive collaborators' in Joseph's regime, if far from sympathetic to it.[53]

THE CHARACTER OF JOSEPH'S RULE

This progress was the work of military commanders, not the civilian administration. All Spain north of the River Ebro, which included Suchet's commands of Aragon and Catalonia, had been placed under the full, direct control of the French army. South of this line, when Suchet took Valencia and Soult took Andalusia, they treated these areas as their own responsibil-

ities, ceding little power to Joseph's Spanish officials. Even where both pacification and a degree of collaboration were achieved, it was often in fla-
grant contradiction to the policies Joseph sought desperately to promote. In
Valencia, the co-operation between Suchet and the upper classes was
achieved at the price of condoning the perpetuation of feudalism. Valencia
was one of the most heavily seigneurial regions in Spain. In the late eighteenth and early nineteenth centuries, its countryside had been rocked by
several serious peasant revolts against the handful of powerful noble landlords of the province. Valencia was also an important rice-producing area
and, as such, an unparalleled source of supplies for Suchet's troops. Thus,
he aided and abetted the perpetuation of the feudal rights of the great landlords in return for provisions: French troops kept order in the Valencian
countryside and even helped to collect feudal dues.[54] Nothing could have
been further from the spirit of the anti-seigneurial legislation Joseph and his
afrancesado ministers were drawing up in Madrid.

Valencia was not unique. Whether in the 31 departments into which the
kingdom was notionally divided in April 1810, or even the administrative
units set up by Paris north of the Ebro, real power lay with the soldiers. If a
sign distinguishing the outer from the inner empire is the prevalence of the
military over the conventional civil administration centred on prefects and
departments, then Spain is an important example of it. The viability of
Joseph's kingdom was compromised by the fact that the most successful
instances of pacification were not really the work of his government.

The extent of pacification must not be exaggerated, even though it was
bearing more fruits than in southern Italy or the Illyrian provinces in these
years. The guerrilla war qualifies any temptation to speak of a pacified
'Josephist' Spain. This aspect of the resistance has become part of historical
myth, and so attracted many emotional, perhaps overrated assessments of
its effectiveness. Great stress is often placed on the contribution made by
the guerrillas in tying down large numbers of French troops, both for the
process of pacification and simply to keep open their lines of communication. There is much truth in this, although ultimately it was probably less
important than the more coherent resistance of Portugal, which provided
the springboard for eventual liberation. The guerrillas were most effective
where they behaved more like regular soldiers on 'irregular duty' than free-
spirited partisans. In Asturias, the only successful guerrilla resistance in
1810–11 came from small detachments of regular troops still acting under
orders, rather than the true irregulars, whose indiscipline and ineffective-
ness engendered support for Bouchet. Guerrilla resistance improved over
time, but usually only when the bands, the *partidas*, became strong enough
to act as regular troops, as in Navarre and Aragon in the last stages of the
war in 1813. All this points to the essential wisdom of the determination of
the provincial juntas, if not the Cortes, to impose a degree of discipline on
the *partidas*. It also lends credence to the view that they were a drain on
efforts to rebuild an effective Spanish army.[55]

The guerrilla war epitomizes the strengths and weaknesses of counter-revolutionary resistance in revolutionary and Napoleonic Europe. Unable and often unwilling to fight outside their own areas, or to take orders from a higher command, the *partidas* could not advance the liberation of the country without help from outside. Nor could they remain undefeated within. Throughout the period 1809–12, if any tide can be detected, it was probably turning against the *partidas*. The real value of the guerrillas to the anti-French struggle was more subtle. Their continued existence, although not a military threat, was a powerful barrier to the process of *ralliement* and any return to normal life for ordinary people. Even when the *partidas* were too weak to ambush French patrols, they could still visit horrors on isolated local officials who collaborated, just as their presence in an area could provide a focal point – a refuge – for those who were determined to resist. These conditions aggravated the divisions within Spain and made the rhetoric of the politicians in Cadiz a fearsome reality in the remotest corners of the peninsula. The ultimate result was the destabilization of Spanish society at a very basic level. When French rule had looked at its most secure in Andalusia, in 1810–12, the guerrillas met their match. A younger generation of liberals and Freemasons flocked to Joseph. Their will probably stiffened by the dire threats coming from the proximity of Cadiz, these *afrancesados* formed irregular units of their own which committed many atrocities. The parallels with southern Italy are very powerful.

This was the background against which Joseph had to work and he tried vigorously to present his regime as the only hope of surmounting these bitter divisions. It was a classic – almost caricatured – statement of Bonapartist policy as it had first emerged in post-revolutionary France in 1799, but Joseph lacked the power and the wide consensus necessary to put it into practice. That it was given any life at all was because soldiers like Suchet happened to agree with him. Suchet's commitment to Joseph's policy of appeasement is very clear in his treatment of the members of the Valencian junta, all of whom he pardoned on taking the city. Where the French generals took a different view, these policies became a mockery, as in Barcelona. For most of the period 1808–10, the city was controlled by Casanova, an *afrancesado* who the French military made Director-General of Police. Casanova ran Barcelona through a network of corrupt spies and his vast powers were only curbed after 1810, when Paris took direct control of Catalonia in preparation for annexation to France. Casanova was a hated figure; he went in constant fear of assassination but obviously made a niche for himself within the imperial service.[56] When his position in Barcelona became untenable, by 1812, he was appointed Chief of Police in Genoa, another city where the ravages of the blockade bred discontent.

Joseph had a small but active core of ideological supporters, such as the young liberals of Seville or Llorente, the ex-secretary of the Inquisition, who became responsible for reforming the Church along the lines of the

French Concordat. Beside them were older, enlightened administrators such as Azanza and O'Farril, whose main purpose in collaborating was to curb the French. Their fear of patriot vengeance and of popular disorder outweighed the severe doubts they harboured about Joseph's ability to act independently of Napoleon. These men were probably typical of the many 'passive collaborators' in the war-torn provinces, and of those civil servants who had stayed at their posts in 1808, in a simple effort to maintain a semblance of order. Casanova was typical of another kind of *afrancesado*, the pure opportunists who joined the French for expedient, often mercenary reasons. If the largest 'ideological' base of collaboration was among the bourgeois youth of Andalusia, the equivalent for the opportunists was probably along the border with France, in the Pyrenees. Ironically, because the French commandants allowed the blockade to be flouted in this area, a huge network of powerful bandit-merchants developed along the border. Most had a vested interest in the perpetuation of French rule, but they also supplied the patriot *partidas*. While the blockade ruined Barcelona, inland centres such as the Cerdanya and Tarragona flourished. Chaos in these border areas, partly fostered by French corruption, spawned a loose but not insignificant bond between occupiers and occupied.

In truth, there was no real national government in Spain between 1808 and 1814. Effective administration existed only in those places where a responsible French general (whether honest like Suchet or corrupt like Soult), guerrilla leaders with pretensions to statesmanship such as Esposa y Mina in Navarre and Palafox in Aragon, or a provincial junta, could achieve some degree of control. Joseph's government in Madrid and the Cortes in Cadiz fought an ideological war of words for the soul of a Spain from which they were both cut off, the *afrancesados* by their treason, the Cortes by its adoption of liberal ideas and physical isolation. Both were swept away when the war reached its conclusion. In the meantime, provincial Spain drifted into lawlessness on a huge scale, its economy exhausted by the raids of the British from Portugal and the usual rigours of French military occupation. Almost everywhere, the French and the guerrillas engaged in an unseemly race for the harvest to deny the other supplies and revenue, as much as to provision themselves.

As long as the military deadlock continued, so would the anarchy Spain had sunk into. An Anglo-Portuguese attempt to invade Spain in 1809 had ended in retreat and only the narrowest of defensive victories for Wellington. Then, Massena failed to break it for the French, when his invasion of Portugal was repulsed in the winter of 1810–11. The final campaigns of 1812–13 would unleash still further destruction, but well before they began, Spain presented a terrifying spectacle of suffering, graphically recorded by the artistic genius of Goya. His paintings are a remarkable window on a collective psyche scarred by violence and deprivation but marked, equally, by a will to resist the French.

There are many qualifications to the idealized view of the Spanish resistance. The junta of Catalonia had great trouble raising taxes; guerrilla indiscipline could drive peasants into the waiting arms of the French, as in parts of Asturias; the patriot leaders could turn on each other with great ferocity, as they did at local level in Asturias and Galicia, or in the Cortes itself. Yet in spite of all this, few ever turned away from the cause. Cold and cowering in the mountains, the provincial juntas and the *partidas* never contemplated surrender, even to a regime which had shown itself fair and friendly to those who accepted it. Large armies and small *partidas* dissolved when defeated, only to regroup. The clergy there had no alternative but resistance, and their influence on the masses was incontrovertible. Whereas in Rome and Tuscany they could only submit to exile, in Spain they could join the guerrillas. Above all, the struggle remained a popular one. The first *afrancesados* had hoped the traditional collective instincts of resignation and Catholic obedience would pave the way for Joseph; instead, they sustained the dangers and privations of the resistance. Ironically, they also helped to undermine authority – all authority save that of the Church – by perpetuating chaos.

THE CORTES OF CADIZ, 1810–1813

The crushing defeats inflicted on the Spanish by Napoleon late in 1808 all but destroyed the tenuous authority of the *Junta Central*. The *Junta Central* and the provincial *juntas supremas* reacted in a curious way to these disasters. They turned in on themselves, began to debate the deeper causes of their plight and turned to the question of fundamental, long-term reform. The ensuing debates produced some of the most profound political thought of the period, but the times were not propitious for detached reflection. By concentrating on the fundamental issues, at a time of crisis, the Spanish resistance exposed the deep ideological divisions in its ranks, and finally tore itself apart. Chased to Seville, the *Junta Central* resolved to call the Cortes, but its members were divided over its character and purpose. Jovellanos and the moderates wanted the Cortes for legalistic reasons: only the Cortes could establish a legitimate regency with the authority to run the war.[57] The radicals, led by Quintana, Blanco-White and Calvo de Rozas, saw the Cortes as a chance to give Spain a new constitution. Calvo, in particular, argued that reforms were needed desperately if support were not to be lost to Joseph. They found a supporter in the British representative, Lord Holland. He became a close friend of Quintana and his circle, and was instrumental in winning them away from French models of reform.

The Junta held together long enough to issue the decree convoking the Cortes on 22 May 1809. Their unity was a lingering fear of despotism, and is reflected in the language of the decree, which spoke of the need 'to reconstruct the august edifice of our ancient laws, in order to place an everlasting barrier between deathly arbitrary rule and our imperceptible rights...'.[58] This reflected both a compromise within the Junta and the views emanating from the provincial juntas, which showed reservations about traditional absolutism and audible calls for constitutional government.

The radicals in the Junta won the struggle over the form of the Cortes and the manner of its election: the Cortes was a single chamber assembly, elected without provision for the traditional, separate estates of the realm. It met in Cadiz in September 1810, after the *Junta Central* had been driven there from Seville, and dissolved itself. Before this, the Junta managed to implement elections for the Cortes that were a true landmark in the development of European politics. The nobles and clergy were invited on an individual basis; they were not elected, but did not have the right to sit as a separate house. Most of the other 302 deputies were elected by a chain of assemblies stretching from parish to provincial level. Their distribution was fixed according to population, based on the 1797 census. At parish level, every male householder over 25 could stand for election to the district assembly. The popular element was gradually filtered out, but it was predominant at the base. The French occupation prevented many northern provinces from holding elections in 1810. Deputies for these areas were chosen by a committee of the Cortes, controlled by Quintana's faction, who packed these seats with radicals. Arguelles, the leading orator of the 'liberals', as they were soon called, was among them. Where elections were held, however, conservative elements proved strong: one-third of the deputies were clergy,[59] and their numbers rose still further, as proper elections were held in the liberated areas.

The clergy and other conservative deputies soon clashed with the liberals, who did well in the large coastal cities. Both proved themselves masters of political propaganda and organization, even if their rivalry was played out within the narrow confines of the besieged port of Cadiz. The city became a cauldron and a political laboratory; the debates of the Cortes increasingly appeared as a dress rehearsal for civil war, rather than the centre of national resistance.

The alliance between liberals and conservatives (*los serviles*) had been fragile from the start. They had been able to work together in the familiar environment of the provincial juntas, when faced with the crisis of the war. However, in the different, very rarified atmosphere of Cadiz, ideological divisions over the reforms proposed by the liberals snapped the alliance forged in 1808. The deep-rooted fear of arbitrary rule, shared by most deputies, poisoned the relations of the Cortes with the series of Regency Councils created to act as an executive to run the war, but even this source of unity was not enough to stem the growing bitterness between liberals and *serviles*. Fear of arbitrary rule created an initial consensus for the drafting of a new constitution. At this stage – but not by 1812 – conservative deputies favoured constitutional checks on royal power. The liberals got their way over administrative and judicial reforms, which sketched out a centralized, standardized state. However, the debates over ecclesiastical reform and the abolition of seigneurialism were ferocious and produced irreconcilable enmities. The *serviles* salvaged a great deal from the assault on seigneurialism. Most property rights of this kind were left intact, to the deep disappointment of liberal deputies from Valencia,[60] where feudal property was extensive, as was collaboration with the French.

The clerical deputies were a powerful force when they stood together. As early as November 1810 they had done so in the debates on censorship, when even enlightened clerics, such as Aguiriano y Gomez, the Bishop of Calahorra, in Rioja, joined the *serviles*.[61] The debate on censorship was important for bringing together conservative opinion. It was hardened further by liberal attempts to legislate the abolition of the regular orders in 1810–11, and finally by their proposal to abolish the Inquisition, tabled in January 1813. These debates brought the ideological divisions to a head. The liberals forced a vote, which they won by 90 votes to 60, but by so doing they shattered any remaining unity within the Cortes. Many *serviles* now recanted their support for earlier reforms and displayed a new, hitherto unexpected support for royal absolutism, once the king was restored. They rejected the constitution they had helped to frame in 1812. As a result, none of the legislation debated or voted in Cadiz became law after the defeat of the French.

The reaction in the provinces to the abolition of the Inquisition should have shown the liberals how little support they had in the country at large. Most bishops simply refused to comply with the decree. The Bishop of Santander, in the French-held north, threatened to excommunicate any of his priests who dared read it to their flocks. Many provincial juntas refused to implement not only the decree on the Inquisition, but almost all the reforms voted at Cadiz, including the constitution of 1812 itself. Those 'on the ground' saw that to do so risked creating a civil war within the civil war.

The Cortes had fallen prey to delusions, in its isolation. Liberals like Quintana and Arguelles imagined they could refashion Spanish society according to the purest liberal ideology. In the constitution of 1812, they produced a political framework imbued with a powerful insistence on the rights of the individual in every sphere of life that excited future generations of Spanish reformers. It raised the hopes of reformers in Italy and Germany that liberalism could flourish without Napoleon and, indeed, in opposition to him. It had no relevance to the Spanish resistance, however.

A romantic, conservative vision of 'the true Spaniard' evolved in opposition to abstract liberal concepts of the citizen and the individual. The historian Capmany expressed it lyrically, when he declared true patriotism as the sole preserve of 'those who hold their land dearest ... [who] are the roughest and most ignorant; the ploughman, the dairyman, the shepherd, the rustic labourer [who] do not lose sight of the spire of the parish church'.[62] This ideal, too, was buffeted in the last years of the war. Only in their hatred for each other did the deputies truly catch the mood of the times.

PORTUGAL, 1808–1814: A PEOPLE TRANSFORMED

When Wellington drove Junot from Portugal in September 1808, the royal administration proved incapable of controlling the popular fury which swept Lisbon in the wake of the French defeat, to say nothing of the violence in the provinces where the Junta of Porto was still the only real power. The ostensible targets of this orgy of popular vengeance were the collaborators – the 'Jacobins' – and social groups who were traditional targets of hatred. This meant Jews, Freemasons and foreign merchants, even though few of them had actually collaborated. Within the political violence and ethnic pogroms, a mass of private vendettas were also being settled amid the anarchy. These circumstances continued over most of Portugal into the spring of 1809, and they always resurfaced when the French threatened to regain the military initiative, as in September 1810 when the Intendant of Police in Lisbon reported on the popular reaction to the fall of Almeida to Soult:

> The populace is still stunned... General optimism sees it very much as the result of treason, so much so that a terrible explosion could result: the cry is for the punishment of many traitors.[63]

The authorities feared this disorder almost as much as those it was directed against. Indeed, the first decrees issued by the Regency, after Junot's withdrawal, asserted categorically the judicial monopoly of the state and the illegality of private vengeance.[64] As late as January 1809, the Intendant of Police pleaded with the Regency that 'It is essential that [the Regency] establish some form of procedure that, without compromising [the views of] public opinion, will establish and preserve good order.'[65] So impotent were the authorities in the autumn of 1808, that they gave in to the popular fury. The magistrates of the Inconfidencia – the highest police tribunal – actually encouraged anonymous denunciations as the easiest way of appeasing public opinion and the only way of finding the guilty. As a flood of denunciations poured in, the Prince Regent – now in Brazil – stood aghast that people had been condemned without due process of law, and that the death penalty had been applied without royal sanction.[66]

Gradually, the Regency reasserted its authority. It was not an easy task, and was done in ways and for ends that had more to do with internal politics than the war with France. Activism at street level was mastered by the Regency in the course of 1809–10, as private vendettas were channelled towards government aims, after seeing the futility of trying to forbid them. They did this by evolving a policy of 'selective repression', aimed at prominent individuals. However, those targeted were not singled out merely for their 'collaboration', but for their liberal, reformist views. 'Selective repression' emerged first in a series of decrees in December 1808. Then came two infamous mass arrests in Lisbon. The first was in March 1809 – 'the Holy Week Arrests' – followed by the more ruthless, definitive *Setembrizada*, at the height of the invasion scare of 1810, when 64 prominent liberals were seized and held until 1814.[67]

From a state of impotence, the Regency skilfully transformed itself into a political and psychological manipulator. It acknowledged popular fears, and so mastered them. Their policy of 'selective repression' allowed the Regents to manipulate a mass national movement while, at the same time, creating a climate of intimidation that extended far beyond the relatively few people it actually touched. 'The actions and policies of the Regency translate not only into an efficient policy of repression, they legitimized and normalized it.'[68] Liberal opposition was stifled until 1814, allowing the Regents to restore the old order. The British often baulked at these policies. The Regents had to appease Wellington – hardly a liberal figure in his own country – more than once. Only abroad, in London and Brazil, did liberal opposition make itself heard.

Everything depended on British protection. Although Wellington and other field commanders expressed disquiet about how the Regency dealt with its critics, Beresford, the viceroy, had no such qualms. He worked closely with the Regents to enforce strict censorship, especially to stifle news of the debates of the Cortes of Cadiz. An 'ideological claustrophobia' was maintained in Portugal in these years.[69] Beresford continued as viceroy after 1814, and his policy of repression did not abate.

Under Beresford, Portugal underwent one of the most rapid and truly profound transformations of any society in revolutionary Europe. Between 1807 and 1809, Portuguese society slipped into anarchy, 'an unleashing of desperate hopes and energies'.[70] However, in the years between his arrival in 1808 and the final rout of the French in 1813, Beresford turned Portugal into a virtual 'barrack-state'. He mobilized Portuguese resources for the war effort successfully and his 'Orders of the Day' reveal the progressive militarization of a populace that had, almost literally, 'run amok' a few years earlier.[71] This remarkable metamorphosis far exceeded the much trumpeted mobilization of France during the Terror in its intensity and universality, if not, inevitably, in the numbers of people involved. The dictatorship of Beresford produced the only army of the period to achieve sustained, consistent victories over the French. This was all done by and for the cause of a counter-revolution rooted in dynastic loyalty and intense popular Catholicism, but its internal dynamics are still little understood.

This awesome effort left Portugal prostrate by 1814; it remained so for many years afterwards. Its population fell by over a quarter of a million, from a total of approximately 3 200 000 in 1807 to 2 960 000 by 1814, reaching its lowest level of 2 875 000 in 1811.[72] Dislocation was less due to the fighting than to the destruction of the economic infrastructure necessitated by Wellington's 'scorched earth' policy against the French. The laying waste of productive land and communications networks on such a scale proved almost impossible to rebuild after 1814. The domestic market for Portuguese industry all but vanished, and the costs of war engendered a financial crisis that took decades to surmount. London imposed disadvantageous trade treaties on Portugal, opening the colony of Brazil to British trade and eventually turning Portugal itself into a British economic colony. The Portuguese economy had boomed between 1800 and 1806; henceforth, she was increasingly dependent on British imports.

Political instability followed the end of the war. The militarization of society and the formation of a more meritocratic army deprived the nobility of a degree of its traditional prestige, and created a large, restive officer corps of middle-class origins. They gave the liberal opposition powerful support after 1814. Until then, Portugal remained a formidable, heroic and remarkable bastion of resistance to Napoleon.

The Illyrian provinces

French intervention in Spain had devastated a previously peaceful, if troubled, country. In the Illyrian provinces, the French were drawn into one of the most volatile areas of Europe, the Balkans. Their rule only intensified existing problems; French rule was disastrous, destabilizing and thoroughly hated by almost every section of the population. It was also unsuccessful from a French point of view. These provinces were occupied for purely strategic and diplomatic reasons: to cut the Austrians off from the sea, so strengthening the blockade, and for use as a bargaining counter in future negotiations with the eastern powers. Thus, in stark contrast to the lands of the inner empire, there was never any guarantee of the permanence of French rule on the part of the regime itself. French priorities make their subsequent conduct appear incongruous. The Illyrian provinces were not intended as permanent acquisitions, yet from 1809 to 1813 they were imperial departments in all but name, ruled directly from Paris. All senior officials, under a military governor-general and a civilian intendant-general were French, as were the provincial intendants (prefects) under them, who were chosen exclusively among the young *auditeurs*, which reproduced the tensions between military and civilian officials so characteristic of the initial phase of imperial rule elsewhere. However, in the Illyrian provinces, as in Spain, French rule never progressed beyond this stage.

While the French expended considerable effort in futile attempts to introduce their system of government, legal code and the Concordat, by 1811 the enforcement of the blockade had failed. Two years after annexation, the Illyrian provinces were removed from the imperial customs' system, which meant that British goods were the only merchandise prohibited in the area. This amounted to an admission that the customs' service was capable of controlling neither the Adriatic coastline, dotted with many inlets and tiny islands, nor the isolated, rugged inland frontiers with Austria and the Ottoman Empire. Smuggling assumed massive proportions in the following years. Instead of concentrating on their limited strategic objectives, the

French imposed their ideology on a part of Europe where it could not have been more out of place. They met unprecedented problems over the introduction of their administrative system. The French Revolution has often been described as primarily an urban revolution, and the Napoleonic Empire as 'the empire of the towns', principally because the French administrative system was based in urban centres, radiating from the towns into the countryside; government corresponded to a nationwide urban network.[73] The basic truth of this was discovered in the interior of the Illyrian provinces, especially in what is now Croatia, where virtually no towns existed. The office of *maire* was not sought after in any rural part of the Empire, nor were the numerous refusals the French received in Illyria anything new. Predictably, the coastal cities of Ragusa, Trieste and Fiume resented their loss of privileges and independence greatly. What they were faced with, away from the coast, was a society without urban centres, for whom their system was not just unpopular, but incongruous. In the provinces of the Military Croatia, the imperial system could not take root; cantons and communes, the basic units of the administrative chain, could not be set up. In its Balkan enclave, the Napoleonic state reached the ultimate limit of its applicability to European society. The experience of Illyria reveals the Napoleonic state as a wholly western European phenomenon, and how limited was its relevance outside it.

The French inherited a very diverse population composed of Slovenes, Croats, Serbs, Italians, and Germans, whose cultural, linguistic and religious divisions had survived under Venetian and Habsburg rule. Literally dozens of legal systems were in use in 'Illyria', some based on Austrian or Venetian law, some on Roman or canon law, and almost all of them heavily qualified by local customs and practices. French legal reforms succeeded only in creating more chaos. As in many parts of Germany and southern Italy, attempts to abolish feudalism served only to disappoint the peasants and unsettle their landlords. This was not helped by French ignorance of the local languages but, even here, the clash of Balkan society with the Napoleonic bureaucracy produced a peculiar twist. French officials had always shown great reluctance to learn foreign languages, but at least in western Europe they knew what the local languages were. In the Illyrian provinces it took them some time to grasp that Slovenian, Croatian and Serbian were distinct languages. Their ambitious plans for a system of *lycées* was partially realized against great odds, but it was fatally compromised, because instruction was offered only in French, Italian and German.

Added to ignorance and incongruity were the introduction of heavy taxation, the blockade, the Concordat, and conscription. The fierce resistance to these policies follows a widespread, truly European pattern. Yet, only in these negative aspects were the western Balkans drawn into the mainstream of the history of western Europe in this period. It is hard to establish if French taxation was actually heavier than that imposed by the Austrians, but it was certainly considered more vexatious. To this day, Slovenian dialect has preserved the word *fronki* as a term for taxes, a revealing folk legacy of this period.[74] Resistance could reach spectacular levels, as in June 1812 when a military expedition had to be sent into the coastal islands of Dalmatia to collect overdue taxes, a costly, impractical method.[75]

The introduction of the Concordat was an act of ideological rigidity by the French. Previous attempts to do so by Italian administrators between 1805 and 1809 had been resented in Dalmatia, the coastal area around Ragusa. Nevertheless, these early signs did not convince Marshal Marmont, the French Governor-General appointed in 1809, to leave such matters alone. He ignored the advice of Italian officials such as Dandolo, who had experience of the area. With the wholesale introduction of the Concordat, the numerous, influential Catholic clergy of Dalmatia, Croatia and Slovenia soon became the leaders of resistance to French rule. The suppression of the regular orders produced a guerrilla leader as redoubtable as any in Spain, the Franciscan friar Dorotich, 'a picturesque, if far from edifying character'. He fled into Austrian territory when his order, devoted to the peaceful ideals of St Francis of Assisi, was abolished. Henceforth Dorotich waged a tenacious partisan war from across the border in Bosnia and Albania until 1813, when he returned to Ragusa in triumph.[76] To convert a Franciscan into a warlord was quite an achievement for French policy, but even more lamentable was the reaction of the people of Lagosta, an island off the Dalmatian coast, when the French closed their confraternity. The women savaged the French officials who came to seize the silver altarpieces, while the men, who had served as coastguards since 1810, withdrew their co-operation and became raiders for the Royal Navy, close by in Corfu.[77] The French could not even play the Orthodox minority off against the Catholics. Despite many improvements in their status, including full tolera-tion and the creation of a bishopric, the Orthodox population remained adamantly anti-French. The secularization of the state, the introduction of compulsory civil marriage in particular, was anathema to so conservative a culture.

The impact of the blockade joined the people of these provinces to the fate of the other coastal regions of the Empire. The maritime trade of the Adriatic coast and the fishing industries of the islands collapsed more as a result of raids by the Royal Navy and the protection it afforded pirates than of French policy, simply because the French did not have the power to enforce it. Many coastal communities were devastated, albeit only for the duration of the war, after which the economy made a quick recovery. The French intendants were acutely aware of this, but their plans to develop the ports of Trieste and Fiume came to nothing in the face of war and shortages of money. Just as in parts of the North Sea coast, even the French came to see smuggling as the only means of survival left to many maritime commu-nities. As one intendant remarked, at least its proceeds helped them pay their taxes.[78] The blockade alienated the commercial classes of the coastal cities as well.

The impact of conscription best reveals the extent to which French rule destabilized the region. On the coasts, many fishermen joined the British, who liked them to operate in their own areas as privateers, far more preferable than risking incorporation into the French Navy and service further afield. In the hinterland of Croatia, the proximity of the Austrian and Ottoman borders, coupled with an economic structure which left most peasants landless, made mass emigration easy. The French feared it had actually reached levels large enough to ruin the local economy. The flight from conscription intensified banditry in a region where it had long existed as a way of life. Most rural areas were in a state of almost permanent revolt, which worsened after 1812 when there were fewer French troops in the area. The border area became easy prey to raids from the Ottoman provinces of Bosnia and Serbia.

Despite their expressed desire to 'civilize' the Illyrian provinces, the general pattern was one of increasing, rather than diminishing disorder. Only in Slovenia were the French able to eradicate the brigandage they found and thereby create a reasonable basis of support for themselves. This was the only positive 'folk memory' they left in the region.[79] Elsewhere, the French had very few supporters – 'a handful of intellectuals, Freemasons and Jews who had suffered discrimination under Austrian rule'.[80] Only in such circles were the French able to recruit for the lower grades of the administration, which came to be dominated by Freemasons, a tiny minority of the urban middle classes, and it was only in their narrow ranks that French rule left a lasting, positive impression. Yet even this was partly false. Later generations of intellectuals saw in Napoleonic rule the genesis of a new national consciousness, but in fact, one of the few aspects of Balkan politics Napoleon understood was the ferocious divisions among the Slavic peoples and that any attempt to evoke nationalist feelings would eventually mean favouring one ethnic group over another.[81] This, at least, both he and his officials steadfastly refused to do; it was anathema to the whole concept of imperial government.[82] Of the mass of mistakes made, perhaps the worst was avoided. However, for the young, idealistic *auditeurs*, who dreamed of 'civilizing' the Balkans, and for their more hard-bitten military colleagues in search of conscripts, the result was resounding failure. The masses remembered only oppression, probably the sole thing uniting so diverse a region.

Cultural imperialism: the quarrel with the Pope and the new Concordat

The arrest of Pius VII was much more than a personal quarrel between the Pope and the Emperor about state control over the Church, or a diplomatic row about the seizure of the Papal States. After 1809, the Concordat – and the compromise it embodied – collapsed. The Pope excommunicated Napoleon, and refused to confirm new bishops in their sees because Napoleon had appointed them. As a result, many dioceses stood vacant, including Paris itself. In reply, Napoleon openly revived the 'Gallican principles' that Louis XIV had used against Rome in the seventeenth century, by which the head of the French state claimed the right not only to propose bishops, but that they did not need to be installed by the Pope. This policy broke with the Concordat, which had required the Pope's agreement to Napoleon's choice of candidates. Napoleon sought to extend the four 'Gallican articles' to Italy and, possibly, Germany. He then set about removing the centre of the Church from Rome to Paris, often by nefarious means, as when the cardinals who were brought to Paris in April 1810 for the marriage of Napoleon and Marie-Louise were then detained and subsequently arrested.

In 1811, Napoleon sought to break the deadlock between Church and state by calling a Council of Bishops to reshape the government of the Church. Most of the higher clergy in France and Italy attended, but they refused to support him against the Pope. Faced with this, Napoleon turned his back on the Concordat, telling Pius VII early in 1812 that he considered it void. In its place, the Ministry of Religion – Cultes – produced a new Concordat by 1813. Although the military collapse of the Empire prevented its implementation, the new Concordat makes interesting reading. It embodies the radical, almost anticlerical spirit at work within the imperial civil service. The Concordat of Fontainebleau, as it came to be known, was more than a neat means of solving a technical, high-level dispute over Church–state relations. It was an assault on the traditional character of Catholic belief and the role of the Church in society of at least the same magnitude as the Civil Constitution of the Clergy of 1791. In its language, as much as in its terms, the new Concordat expressed an unswerving belief in the cultural superiority of the French Enlightenment, the strongly felt need to impose that culture on the common people of western Europe, and, paradoxically, the fear and frustration of those local officials – old Jacobins and young *auditeurs* alike – who were busy carrying 'the torch of French civilization' to the outer empire. If Napoleon was at war with the Church, his state was at war with the culture that sustained it. This struggle had never abated, but in the heightening tension of the final years of the Empire it acquired its old intensity.

Economic imperialism and the Continental System: from blockade to market design

The outer empire had been created because of the policy of blockade, but its most obvious consequence was to swell the extent of Napoleonic hegemony. Alongside political, military and cultural domination, the French also sought to create an economic system commensurate with the position of mastery they held from 1806 onwards.

The blockade was central to the war against Britain, but it was only one component of the regime's economic policies; it was only a means to a greater end. This is clear when the blockade is set in a wider political and economic context. The blockade made its major impact on the coastal areas of western Europe, yet the vast majority of people in Napoleonic Europe neither lived in the great maritime cities, nor earned their livings from large-scale commerce. No major port within Napoleon's orbit escaped the catastrophic consequences of the blockade, yet these areas are an exceptional case, if a very important one.

Napoleonic Europe was predominantly agricultural. Its economic structures were still more early modern than urban or industrial in character, based on very localized markets for limited agricultural surpluses and the products of small industries, usually linked closely to agriculture. Vast sectors of the European economy were still not advanced enough for government policies to alter them in a lasting way, or to take rapid effect, no matter how powerful the regime behind them. This is the essential background to Napoleon's plans for the European economy. The most significant economic development in these years, at least in terms of the number of people affected, were the bad harvests of 1810–11. The harvests did not fail everywhere, however. Northern Italy was able to sustain itself, even if most of France and Germany saw food shortages. In central Italy, the threat of famine to the Roman and Tuscan departments was averted only by large-scale, state-purchased imports of grain but they came from the Kingdom of Naples, which had enjoyed a good harvest. This was 'the end of the luck factor' for Napoleon, in that the poor harvests broke a long sequence of good ones in most of the Empire stretching back to 1803. The end of this run may have done more to unsettle Napoleon's hegemony than any of his deliberate policies.

Nevertheless, his policies made a considerable impact on some parts of the Empire. Their long-term importance is far from clear, but in the last years of the Empire, the emergence of a Napoleonic 'market design' for Europe did much to shape contemporary attitudes to the regime, and even more to push the Empire towards its final military crisis. Just as the rise of the Napoleonic state system redrew the political map of western and central Europe, so the Napoleonic market design meant reshaping the customs' barriers of the Grand Empire. Two massive reorganizations – the Berlin and Milan Decrees of 1806–07 and then the decrees of St Cloud and the Trianon in 1810 – created the commercial borders of Napoleonic Europe. Their terms reveal the aggressively Francocentric nature of this market design. While the blockade was meant to keep British goods out of Europe, the market design – the commercial policy of the Continental System – was intended to let French commerce and industry fill the resultant gap. This is the essence of the 'one-way common market', and it was the core of Napoleon's economic strategy.

The commercial borders of the Grand Empire were devastatingly simple: the territories of the Empire of 1799 – France itself, plus the Rhenish and Belgian departments – could circulate their goods freely throughout the rest of the Grand Empire. However, the states and imperial departments outside this zone were forced to pay high, increasingly prohibitive tariffs on their own exports to France and to each other. The aim was clear: with British and overseas markets closed to them, the non-French manufacturing centres of continental Europe were to be squeezed out, while those within the French tariff zone were protected from all foreign competition. In those few areas where commerce and manufacturing were important parts of the local economy, the results were catastrophic in the short term, although Napoleonic control probably did not last long enough for its tariff policies to do permanent damage to even the worst affected areas.

The selfishness of the market design emerges with stark clarity when the fates are compared of manufacturing regions on either side of the preferential zone. Well-developed manufacturing industries existed within both the Rhenish departments, an area inside the preferential zone, and the Grand Duchy of Berg, outside it. The former German states which composed the Grand Duchy of Berg were among the most industrialized in Europe; mining was the main economic activity of the uplands of the Wupper valley, together with textiles, while the lowlands were important commercial routes, centred on Düsseldorf. The chief market for the manufactured goods of the region, before the Napoleonic occupation, was France, but the market design of the Continental System sealed this off after 1806. In 1807, Berg's outlet to Italian markets was also withdrawn; its products were banned from parts of Italy that were targeted as 'captive markets' for French goods.

This is a major example of another aspect of the Napoleonic market design: that Paris controlled not just its own trade relations with the other states of the Grand Empire, but trading among those states. In Italy, olive oil from the French-ruled Tuscan departments was blocked from entering the Kingdom of Italy, which had been a well-established market before French rule. A series of trade treaties between Bavaria and the Kingdom of Italy imposed by Napoleon gravely disrupted their flourishing well-established trade over the Alps.

In Berg, by 1808, this policy had made redundant almost all of the 10 000 textile workers who supplied the Italian market. By that year, only the biggest firms were still operating, and further French efforts to isolate the Dutch departments from the rest of Europe, because of continued smuggling, worsened the plight of Berg still further. In 1810, the Trianon Tariff put prohibitive duties on all colonial goods entering Berg. Henceforth, local industries could only obtain the raw materials they needed, chiefly cotton, by contraband. Berg was not without influential friends; both Beugnot and especially Roederer fought its case tenaciously in Paris, but French industry was also in deep recession after 1810, and their arguments faltered upon the strength of vested French interests. The general malaise was summed up by Roederer late in 1813:

> in general, manufacturing industry is stagnating; the cotton factories have been wiped out; but the cotton works of Rouen [in northern France] are flourishing... The metallurgical works also suffer from a great lack of orders... I am assured that in Elberfeld and Barmen, one man in seven survives on charity.[83]

Predictably, a serious revolt broke out in January 1813, the first such in the Confederation of the Rhine. It was driven by misery, rather than politics. As Beugnot put it, Berg was now 'a violent country, and this stems from the fact that it is the only manufacturing country for which the hardships demanded by the Continental System have produced no compensation whatsoever'.[84] French economic strategy reduced one of the most skilled workforces in Europe to a horde of beggars and bandits, if only temporarily.

The prosperity of those parts of the Rhineland under direct French rule exposes the artificially induced nature of Berg's demise. Strasbourg became one of the busiest trading centres in Europe, while Aachen, Cologne and Neuss also prospered. The same industries which collapsed in Berg expanded in the French-ruled left bank of the Rhine. They reached levels of production hitherto unknown, a process hastened, at least in part, by the mass emigration of capital and skilled labour from Berg.

Other pockets of commercial or industrial activity outside the preferential zone went the way of Berg. In Neuchâtel, the specialized textile industry, based on a system of cottage production, was decimated by high French tariffs and effective expulsion from the Italian markets. The Prince of Neuchâtel was Berthier, the most loyal of Napoleon's marshals and, as his Chief of Staff, probably the closest to him. As early as 1807, he wrote to the Emperor:

> It is enough to say that [Neuchâtel's] inhabitants are one of your peoples ... Their industries have been destroyed and many industrious men have been forced to go abroad. I beseech Your Majesty...[85]

The failure of even Berthier to get any response shows how determined Paris was to persist with so Francocentric a policy. Ad hoc concessions, in the form of special 'import licences', were granted increasingly as the economic crisis deepened, but they provided no real relief to those areas worst hit by the policy of 'France first'.

Belgian manufacturing industry shows the advantages – and limits – of operating inside the preferential zone. Belgian industry was dynamic. All its major sectors continued to expand, if often fitfully, in the two decades before 1814. Coal-mining became almost a mania once French legislation lifted previous restrictions on this activity, causing one Napoleonic official in Liège to comment that:

> [the law] which allows each proprietor to mine his land [down to a level] of thirty metres... was interpreted in its widest sense by the local administration, the courts and the landowners; there was not a soul with a corner of land who didn't want to dig a hole.[86]

Out of this lunacy emerged a high number of stable, substantial mining companies, well able to withstand the crisis of 1811. Indeed, there were 140 mines in one Belgian department alone, the Ourthe, in 1812. For the first time these firms were assured a large, stable market, safe from British competition and firmly within the preferential zone. The same was true of the metallurgical industry – the Belgian departments produced 25 per cent of the Empire's iron by 1813 – as well as steel, which got important help from the government, turning Liège into a centre of the war industry.

Textiles was the largest sector of Belgian industry and, although its road was a rockier one than steel or coal, the general trend was of growth, most of which came in the last years of the Empire, the crisis of 1810–11 notwithstanding. By 1814, the city of Ghent had been transformed from a market centre into an industrial town based on textiles, as small or medium-sized factories replaced cottage industry. This process had its victims, especially among the traditional trades and crafts formerly protected by powerful guilds which the French had abolished. These men reasserted themselves, briefly, when French rule collapsed in 1814, but neither the present nor the future were with them. The ban on British cotton after 1806 produced a boom in textiles as Belgian manufacturers saw their chance and seized it with both arms, only to face a crisis of over-production in 1808–09. A major factor in the industry's quick recovery after 1809 was the tightening of the blockade, which choked off those British goods still illegally in circulation. By the spring of 1810, Belgian textiles in general, and Ghent cottons especially, were again in full expansion, until by 1812 the industry was larger than in 1808. Growth continued after 1814, and the brief slump of 1813 was solely the result of the war.

Belgian dynamism had its limits. Isolation from Britain led to technological stagnation; most mines and textile mills still used old-fashioned production methods and new machinery was relatively scarce, because the best then being made was British. Over-production was always a latent threat, if not always a problem. Above all, the new circumstances favoured those who could adapt and adjust quickly. It was less important, for example, to use modern machinery than to switch from declining textiles like linen to profitable ones such as cotton, or to get out of cottage industry and into factory production. Napoleonic Belgium produced a generation of resourceful and progressive entrepreneurs, more than capable of meeting the challenges – and opportunities – of the imperial market design. In textiles, they were led by the Lievin family in Ghent, in mining, by the Orban brothers in Liège. Their opportunism, tenacity and willingness to modern-ize their businesses make them worthy equivalents in business of Lannes or Murat on the battlefield, and their loyalty to the regime was probably more assured. Bauwens Lievin opted to serve Napoleon during the 100 Days, and afterwards moved his operations to France.

The textile industries of Switzerland and the lower Rhine followed a pat-tern similar to that of Belgium, as did mining throughout the Rhineland. An important development in the Confederation of the Rhine was an increasing integration of the economies of the various states, as entrepre-neurs and investors shifted their capital from one centre to another, in the search for markets and to work within the preferential zone. In this way, for example, capital originally accumulated in Berg found its way into Aachen and Cologne, while the Rothschilds invested heavily, if discreetly, in Bavarian textiles. Western Germany emerged from Napoleonic rule as a more coherent economic unit than before, although not necessarily a more advanced one. Initially, the renewed political divisions of the restoration period did more to hamper the industrialization of this area than to help it. Only the unified Prussian Rhineland continued its progress uninterrupted.

By 1810–11, the problems created by both the blockade and the tariff system were affecting France as well as the rest of the Empire. French industry probably had the productive capacity to fill the gap created by the expulsion of Britain and the destruction of rivals like Berg. However, nei-ther the French nor the remnants of the manufacturing sector in Italy or Germany could find adequate markets. The main cause of the slump of 1810–11 within France is attributed to over-production, which in turn led to a collapse of prices. The impoverished urban centres of Italy and Germany could no longer afford French goods. This reflected the same problems facing the industrialists of Berg, who desperately sought new markets in central Europe in 1807–08, only to be frustrated by a lack of demand. The textile firms of the Tuscan city of Prato profited at first from the absence of British competition, only to face disappointment and con-traction when their ambitious search for new markets also failed. All of this points towards a basic flaw in the market design itself: the exclusion of overseas trade from the whole system exposed the fact that the European markets could not absorb even French manufacturing output, let alone that of other regions.

It is indicative of the essentially protectionist outlook of most continental manufacturers that they did not seek free trade as a replacement for the French market design, but admission to the preferential zone. The petitions of the commercial representatives of Berg, Neuchâtel and Italy sought inclusion in the protective network, never open competition. As the exam-ple of Prato illustrates, many within the Continental System welcomed pro-tection from British competition. The French disregarded a genuine source of collaboration by persevering with the policy of 'France first', although even a more benign system would still have confronted the lack of markets.

As the Belgian experience shows, even the best protected industries were exposed to the 'boom-bust' economy inevitable where demand is made fragile by the absence of a stable consumer base.

The position of Saxony was probably what most contemporaries aspired to, revealing the commercial possibilities for a friendly state outside the scope of the Napoleonic market design. Here, although the indigenous linen industry almost collapsed after 1806, the Saxon cotton industry grew apace, and even the crisis of 1810–11 checked its expansion only briefly. This was due to the potent combination of the removal of British competition and the well-established fair at Leipzig, the Saxon capital, which handled two-thirds of Lyon's silk exports. Above all, Saxony was not tied formally to the Napoleonic state system, and so escaped its customs' regulations. Its manufacturers could import cotton from the middle east at affordable prices, and export their textiles more freely than the states of the Confederation of the Rhine or the Kingdom of Italy. Polish mining and distilling followed a pattern similar to Saxony for identical, essentially diplomatic reasons. Saxony is an important reminder that many industrialized inland areas derived positive benefits from both the blockade and the wider-ranging policies of the Continental System. Saxon dependence on this combination of circumstances is borne out by the collapse of its textiles boom under the pressure of Prussian competition after 1814.

All these areas, successful and unsuccessful alike under the Continental System, were exceptional in their high levels of industrialization. What mattered to most of the people of the Empire was the impact of the blockade and the imperial market design on agriculture. This vast sector of economic life is still relatively little studied, but it seems that Napoleonic policies were marginally more beneficial than harmful. They did not have the devastating consequences so evident in coastal regions. Within the Empire, the official policy that probably did most to disrupt the world of small, localized economies was the reintroduction of municipal tolls for local markets, the *octrois*, which became increasingly onerous on wine producers, butchers and the grain trade in the last years of the Empire. In agriculture, as with industry, what really mattered in the final analysis was the relationship of a given region or sector of the economy to France. The parts of Napoleonic Europe where this is clearest are northern and central Italy and the Grand Duchy of Warsaw.

The French always saw Italy as a potential economic colony. Its role in the imperial market design was to provide raw materials for French manufacturing and to be the larder of the Empire. This was as true of the nominally independent Kingdom as of the imperial departments. To this end, indigenous industries were crippled. The major casualty of this policy was the silk industry, centred on the Lombard parts of the Kingdom of Italy and the Piedmontese departments. Silk manufacturing all but collapsed in these areas as the raw silk they produced was directed to Lyon, its designated centre, to be turned into finished goods. Silk manufacturing and, indeed, most manufacturing, was on a relatively minor scale in Italy, however. On the whole, the role of an imperial granary suited Italian economic realities. Rice production grew apace in these years in the malarial lowlands of the Po valley, greatly aided by the abolition of *ancien régime* legislation which had restricted its cultivation. Almost the whole of the Italian rice crop was exported to France, while maize sustained the domestic market. In general, the Napoleonic market design profited those parts of Italy where commercial agriculture had developed, as opposed to industries based on agriculture which were important parts of the economy in the Po valley, Tuscany and the Legations. Outside these zones, in most of the peninsula, subsistence agriculture continued much as before, based on the peasant smallholding. In these circumstances, imperial economic policies made little impact on the structures they found. In the same manner as Napoleonic policies only tended to favour industries already in advanced stages of development, such as Belgian or Rhenish textiles, so in Italy it was only areas of well-established commercial agriculture that expanded in this period. Previous trends intensified, but did not spread.

The Grand Duchy of Warsaw, although within the Napoleonic state system, was of no direct importance to the market design. The French did not see Poland as a source of raw materials, but of unearned income from peasant labour and rents. Polish grain production and exports had been healthy in the late eighteenth century, but were noticeably disrupted by the expansion of the Continental System. Indeed, it has been calculated that grain prices fell directly in line with the Polish provinces coming under Napoleonic control. In direct contrast, those parts of Galicia which remained under Austrian rule and never entered the Continental System saw no falls in grain prices before 1815.[87] From 1810 onwards, the blockade began to paralyse agricultural growth, as cereal prices fell to a third below their 1805 levels. The great Polish landowners regarded the economic changes after 1806 as a catastrophe.[88] However, Napoleonic rule did not last long enough to achieve this alleged 'pauperization of the aristocracy', which was undoubtably the last thing the French wanted to happen in Poland, the blockade notwithstanding.

There is often a fairly clear relationship between economic prosperity and loyalty to the regime evident within the industrial sectors of the economy and also in some areas of commercial agriculture. The example of Poland is a clear exception to this, as it is in so many other respects, but it should still serve as a warning not to interpret the economic crisis of 1810–11, or a wider detestation of French economic policies, as signs of a feeling that the end of Napoleonic hegemony was at hand. The territories of the inner empire continued to plead for more integration, not less, as late as 1812, seeing the potential advantages of the absence of British competition. They were still unconvinced that there was any likely alternative to French hegemony.

This confidence, however reluctant, was not shared by the French themselves by 1811. The economic crisis only intensified the regime's belief that success on all fronts depended on the effectiveness of the blockade, in the face of the stark truth that it was not working. In official eyes, this meant that the outer empire had been created for nothing, at least as yet. The North Sea and the Baltic coasts were now perceived as the weakest links in the blockade, and the Russian alliance which supposedly sealed them to the British was seen as worse than useless.

Napoleon did not embark on his last, most ambitious offensive in a spirit of confidence or enthusiasm, but from a feeling of frustration which the economic crisis of 1810–11 was rapidly turning into desperation.

Notes

1 Antonielli, *Prefetti*, pp. 419, 530.
2 J. Vidalenc, 'L'industrie dans les départements normads à la fin du Ier Empire', *Annales de Normandie*, 7 (1957) pp. 281–307, 282–3.
3 Ibid., pp. 179–201, 199.
4 R. Durand, *Le Département des Côtes-du-Nord sous le Consulat et l'Empire (1800–1815)*, 2 vols (Paris, 1926) i, pp. 165, 176–9.
5 Ibid., i, pp. 365–486.
6 Ibid., ii, pp. 457–68.
7 Cited in P. Butel, 'Le port de Bordeaux sous le régime des licences, 1808–1815', *Révue de l'Historie Moderne et Contemporaine*, 19 (1972) pp. 128–48, 129.
8 C. Bonnet, 'L'impact de la Révolution et de l'Empire sur la démographie Provençale. L'exemple des Bouches-du-Rhône', *Annales du Midi*, 101 (1989) pp. 14–28. Agulhon, *La Vie sociale*, p. 438.
9 Agulhon, *La Vie sociale*, pp. 416–17.
10 Lewis, *Second Vendée*, pp. 156–64.
11 Agulhon, *La Vie sociale*, p. 420.
12 Brunet, *Le Roussillon*, p. 307.
13 Ibid., p. 481.
14 Ibid., pp. 363–8.
15 J-F. Soulet, *Les Premiers Préfets des Hautes-Pyrénées (1800–1814)*, (Paris, 1965) pp. 178–83.
16 Soulet, *Les Premiers Préfets*, p. 186.
17 Brunet, *Le Roussillon*, pp. 355–62.
18 Ibid., pp. 476–8.
19 Ibid., pp. 480–4.
20 Jones, *Politics and Rural Society*, pp. 12–18, fig. 2, p. 16.
21 J. Labasse, *Le Commerce des soies à Lyon sous Napoléon et la crise de 1811*, (Paris, 1957). G. Ellis, *Napoleon's Continental Blockade.* pp. 268–72. P. Viard, *L'Aministration Préfectorale dans le département de la Côte d'Or sous le Consulat et le Premier Empire*, (Paris, 1914) pp. 80, 268–70, 283.
22 S. Charléty, 'La vie politique à Lyon sous Napoléon Ier', *Révue de l'Historie de Lyon*, (1905) pp. 371–85, 372. Viard, *L'Administration Préfectorale*, pp. 85–96.

23 R. Marx, 'De la Pré-révolution à la Restauration', in *Historie de l'Alsace*, ed. P. Dollinger, (Toulouse, 1970) pp. 328–76, 330–2.

24 An example of this, destined to be a classic point of departure for the topic: F. Braudel, *The Identity of France*, vol. i, *History and Environment*, (Eng. trans., London, 1988), especially pp. 288–95.

25 P. Gonnet, 'Les Cents Jours à Lyon', *Révue de l'Histoire de Lyon*, (1908) pp. 24–39. R.S. Alexander, *Bonapartism and Revolutionary Tradition in France, The Fédérés of 1815*, (Cambridge, 1991) pp. 156–62.

26 J. Tulard, *Paris et son administration (1800–1830)*, (Paris, 1976) p. 236.

27 Ibid., p. 295.

28 R. Chartier, 'Les deux France. Histoire d'une géographie', *Cahiers d'Histoire*, (1978) pp. 393–415.

29 B. Lepetit, 'Sur les dénivellations de l'espace économique en France, dans les années 1830', *Annales ESC*, (1986) pp. 1243–72.

30 For the seminal expression of this: Braudel, *The Identity of France*. More recently, X. de Planhol, *An Historical Geography of France*, (Eng. trans., Cambridge, 1994).

31 F. Furet and M. Ozouf, *Lire et Écrire, l'alphabétisation des français de Calvin à Jules Ferry*, 2 vols (Paris, 1977).

32 J. Queniart, 'Les apprentissages scolaires élémentaires au xviiie siècle: faut-t-il réformer Maggiolo?', *Revue d'Histoire Moderne et Contemporaine*, (1977) pp. 3–27.

33 Lepetit, 'Sur les dénivellations', p. 1268.

34 Agulhon, *La Vie Sociale*, p. 412.

35 Cited in M-N. Bourguet, 'Race et folklore, L'image officielle de la France en 1800', *Annales ESC*, (1986) pp. 802–23, 808, 815.

36 Bourguet, *Déchiffrer la France*, pp. 238–86.

37 Ibid., pp. 306–8.

38 Bourguet, 'Race et folklore'.

39 S. Kaplan, 'Réflections sur la police du monde du travail, 1700–1815', *Révue Historique*, 261 (1979) pp. 17–77, 76–7.

40 L. Bergeron and G. Chaussinand-Nogaret, *Les Masses de Granit. Cent mille notables du Premier Empire*, (Paris, 1979) pp. 62–4.

41 M.D. Sibalis, 'Corporatism after the corporations: the debate of the restoration of the guilds under Napoleon I and the Restoration', *French Historical Studies*, 15 (1988) pp. 718–30.

42 M. P. Fitzsimmons, *The Parisian Order of Barristers and the French Revolution*, (Cambridge, MA, 1987), pp. 154–87.

43 A. de Musset, *La Confession d'un Enfant du Siècle*, (Paris, 1960 edn) pp. 1–2.

44 J-K. Burton, 'L'enseignement de l'histoire dans les lycées et les écoles primaires sous le Premier Empire', *Annales Historiques de la Révolution Française*, (1972) pp. 98–109.

45 A. de Musset, *La Confession*, p. 2.

46 J. Nicholas, 'Le ralliement des notables au regime impérial dans le département du Mont Blanc', *Révue de l'Histoire Moderne et Contemporaine*, (1972).

47 Schama, *Patriots*, p. 625.

48 De Musset, *La Confession*, p. 622.

49 J. Vidalenc, 'Les departements hanséatiques et l'administration napoleonienne', *Francia*, (1973) pp. 414–50.

50 Cited in Vidalenc, 'Les departements hanséatiques', p. 430.

51 Nardi, *Roma*, p. 47.

52 A. Fugier, *La Junte Supérieure des Asturias et l'Invasion francaise*, (Paris, 1930) p. 40.

53 Jüretschke, *Los Afrancesados*, pp. 198–9.

54 Ardit, *Historia del Pais Valencia*, pp. 213–14.
55 Esdaile, *The Spanish Army in the Peninsula War*, (Manchester, 1988) pp. 63–4.
56 J. Mercader Riba, *Barcelona durante la Occupación Francesa*, (Madrid, 1946) pp. 274–95.
57 G. Gomez de la Serna, *Jovellanos, el español perdido*, 2 vols (Madrid, 1975) ii, p. 225.
58 M. Suarez, *El proceso de la convocatoria a Cortes (1808–1810)*, (Pamplona, 1982) p. 74.
59 Aymes, *La Guerra de Independencia*, p. 77.
60 Ardit, *Historia del Pais Valencia*, iv, pp. 211–12.
61 Ollero de la Torre, *Un riojano en las Cortes de Cadiz: el Obispo de Calahorra, Don Francisco Mateo Aguiriano y Gomez*, (Logroño, 1981) pp. 73–8.
62 Cited in Artola-Gallego, *Los Origenes*, i, p. 379.
63 Cited in Da Silva Dias, *Os Primordios*, vol. I, tom. ii, pp. 552–3, note 1.
64 N. Daupias d'Alcochette, 'La Terreur Blanche à Lisbon', *Annales Historiques de la Révolution française*, 37 (1965) pp. 299–331, 300, note 1.
65 Da Silva Dias, *Os Primordios*, vol. I, tom. ii, p. 534.
66 D'Alcochette, 'La Terreur Blanche', pp. 300–1.
67 Da Silva Dias, *Os Primordios*, vol. I, tom. ii, pp. 553–8.
68 Ibid., p. 568.
69 Ibid., p. 531.
70 Ibid., p. 510.
71 The 'orders of the day' are analysed in Do Carmo Reis, *As Revoltas do Porto*, pp. 138–40.
72 Ibid., p. 124.
73 Woloch, *New Regime*, explores this across the period. On urbanism and the initial organization of the administration: M-V. Ozouf-Marignier, *La Formation des départements: la réprésentation du territoire français à la fin du 18e siecle*, (Paris, 1989). T. Margadant, *Urban Rivalries During the French Revolution*, (Princeton, NJ, 1992). On the Empire: S.J. Woolf, 'L'administration centrale et le développement de l'urbanisme à l'époque napoléonienne', in *Ville et territoires pendant la periode napoléonienne, Collection de l'École Française de Rome*, 96 (Rome, 1987) pp. 25–34.
74 M. Senkowska-Gluck, 'Pouvoir et société en Illyrie napoleonienne', *Révue de l'Institut Napoleon*, 136 (1980) pp. 57–78, 61.
75 P. Pisani, *La Dalmatie de 1797 a 1815*, (Paris, 1893) pp. 359–60.
76 Pisani, *La Dalmatia*, p. 234.
77 Ibid., p. 373.
78 Ibid., p. 385.
79 Senkowska-Gluck, 'Pouvoir et société', p. 61.
80 M. Senkowska-Gluck, 'Illyrie sous la domination napoléonienne, 1809–1813', *Acta Polonia Historica*, 41 (1980) pp. 99–121, 116.
81 G. Cassi, 'Les populations Juliennes-Illyriennes pendant la domination napoleonienne, (1806–1814)', *Révue des Études Napoléon*, xix (1930) pp. 193–212, 202–4.
82 Even the name given to these provinces, the classical name for the area, Illyria, was chosen simply because no adequate contemporary term existed to comprise all the different ethnic groups of the region. Illyria was simply a term of convenience, but indicative of French awareness of the complex character of the region. See Cassi, 'Les populations Juliennes-Illyrian', p. 197.
83 Schmidt, *Berg*, p. 407.
84 Ibid., p. 408.

85 Courvoisier, *Le Maréchal Berthier et sa principauté de Neuchâtel (1806–1814)*, (Neuchâtel, 1959) p. 321.
86 Cited in P. Lebrun, M. Bruwier and J. Dhondt, *Essai sur la révolution industrielle en Belgique 1770–1847*, (Brussels, 1979) p. 317.
87 B. Grochalska, 'L'économie polonaise et le renversement de la conjuncture (1805–1815)', *Révue de l'Historie Moderne et Contemporaine*, (1970) pp. 620–30, 624.
88 Ibid., pp. 628–9.

|6|

Collapse: the fall of the Empire, 1812–1814

From the Russian campaign to the Battle of the Nations: the collapse of central Europe

The war with Russia

By 1810–11, Napoleon had reduced the terms of Tilsit to the enforcement of the blockade, for which he needed Alexander's co-operation in closing the Baltic. When this waivered, and Anglo-Russian relations improved, his course of action was clear. Alexander was even readier to fight than Napoleon. He felt Russia was in a good position to deal with Napoleon by late 1811. Despite the recent war over Finland, Sweden had been converted, if not into an ally, then at least into a useful, benevolent neutral; peace was made with both Persia and the Ottomans. By 1812, for the first time in several years, Alexander was free to concentrate on Napoleon. He released over 200 000 experienced troops for service in the west, almost exactly the number Napoleon still had tied down in Spain. With the French so deeply advanced in central Europe, any war the Tsar might now choose to fight could be a defensive one. Poland was probably the single issue most troubling Alexander. It was a lingering threat to his security that made any hope of a stable accommodation impossible with Napoleonic Europe. This sense of inevitability strengthened Alexander's will to fight on to an extent Napoleon, with his more limited objectives, failed to grasp until it was too late. Above all, whatever Alexander chose to do, by 1810, he was free to do it. Gradually, almost without it being noticed, Alexander had also freed himself from the grip of the great Court families. His ministers and their subordinates – first the reforming Speransky, then the reactionary Arakcheev – were his own men, and the bureaucracy, if still inefficient, was in the grasp of the autocrat more fully than at any time since Peter the Great.

Napoleon was well aware of the scale of the task he had set himself, 'the most difficult enterprise I have ever undertaken', in his own parting words. Although it is obvious, the Grande Armée was to be provisioned by a carefully organized series of supply lines and depots, set up in the course of its advance – a necessary concession to the hostile terrain, whatever its cost in mobility, as he had learnt in the Eylau and Friedland campaigns of 1807. The numerical strength of the Grande Armée was awe-inspiring; with upwards of 650 000 combatants, it was the largest army yet seen in Europe. However, Napoleon's acknowledged need for allies more powerful than any he had previously called upon was ultimately a sign of weakness. Austria and Prussia were pressured into contributing troops for the campaign, a sign that the invasion of Russia was too big an undertaking for the states of the inner empire to tackle alone.

Whereas Napoleon had clear political reasons for invading Russia, never before had he gone into war with such ill-defined military goals. In truth, the defined objectives of the campaign of 1812 did not extend much beyond catching a Russian army and defeating it in the field. Napoleon risked an interminable war in 1812, whether or not he succeeded in combat. Never before had he commanded so large a force over so vast an area and, at many crucial moments, it proved beyond him to adapt to these new demands. Large Russian forces were allowed to slip away from the French at crucial junctures, first at Vilna and then with the failure of the 'manoeuvre of Vitebsk', in July. It would be wrong to think that the Russians avoided major battles, however. They merely wanted one on what they hoped would be their own terms. First at Smolensk in mid-August, and then further east at Borodino on 7 September 1812, they gave battle behind well-prepared defences. Yet the Russian army won few major engagements with the mainly French main body of the Grande Armée. Smolensk and Borodino were the ghastliest battles of the Napoleonic wars. The carnage on both sides may properly be described as obscene; at Borodino alone, almost 30 per cent of all combatants were killed or wounded.[1] The Russians withdrew, still with a large force of 90 000 intact, but the road to Moscow was now open to the French, who occupied it a few days later. The Russian army had undergone considerable reorganization in the years since Tilsit, but it was still unable to defeat the French in open battle, nor was it able to deal Napoleon a fatal blow during his horrific retreat from Moscow in October–November 1812. The Grande Armée was not destroyed in battle, nor by the Russian winter, which only began in earnest in the very last stages of the French retreat. The Grande Armée suffered very serious losses on its advance into Russia, largely through sickness caused by heat, and the staggering casualties of Smolensk and Borodino; the army that withdrew from Moscow was already exhausted and greatly depleted. Napoleon remained in Moscow for almost seven weeks, in an attempt to bring Alexander, who remained in St Petersburg, to terms, but eventually it became obvious that the Russians held numerical superiority, thus making Napoleon's advanced position untenable.

Of the 650 000 troops who began the invasion, only 93 000 returned. However, even these figures disguise the most serious, long-term damage to the Napoleonic war machine. The majority of those troops lost were the best, for while the Austrian and Prussian commanders had managed to keep their forces out of the worst disasters, the mainly French central army group was decimated: only 25 000 of an original force of 450 000 struggled back to Poland in early December 1812.[2] Equally serious for the future was the loss of good cavalry and artillery horses; probably over 200 000 perished in Russia, and never again would the French have an advantage in this sector, thus compromising their ability to follow up otherwise successful engagements.

On the face of it, the Russian catastrophe should have been the end of Napoleonic hegemony, but it was only the beginning of the process and, for contemporaries, even a victory of these proportions did not signal a return of confidence. The campaign of 1812 had all but exhausted Russia both financially and militarily, and the Russians themselves were divided over whether to pursue Napoleon over their own borders. Metternich kept Austria neutral, still afraid to fight even a shattered Grande Armée, but tried to arrange peace between Napoleon and Alexander, which Napoleon saw as an incentive to fight on.

Both these factors bought Napoleon enough time to bring the administrative machine of the inner empire to his temporary rescue. Without its system of conscription, Napoleon would have had to capitulate in the autumn of 1812, but now the well-oiled administrative machine came to the rescue of the prostrate military one. In the course of early 1813, a new – if markedly inferior – army was created, in its own way an achievement as spectacular as the heroic retreat from Moscow. It was the last rallying of the whole inner empire to the Napoleonic cause. The work of consolidation between 1800 and 1807 now bore its last fruit, and its harvest was not inconsiderable. The levy of 1813 had been called up early, thus there were already 137 000 fresh conscripts in the depots when Napoleon returned to Paris in December 1812. Together with 80 000 national guards and four Imperial Guard regiments withdrawn from Spain, the core of a new force was created for the front in central Europe, but the real triumph of the administration – seconded by the Gendarmerie, which itself had 3000 men withdrawn for active service – was the capture of almost 100 000 deserters and *réfractaires* from the levies of 1808, 1809 and 1810. Added to this effort by the imperial departments was the continued loyalty of the princes of the Confederation of the Rhine. Although many wavered temporarily after the first shock of the news from Russia – notably Max-Joseph in Bavaria and Frederick of Württemberg – most remained unconvinced that Austria was strong enough to protect a German league of neutrality from either side. Fearful of losing the territories they had gained from the

Imperial Knights and the prince-bishops, they rallied to Napoleon. Denmark, too fought on with the French. None of them wanted to see Germany dominated by Russia.

Set against this was the determination of the British to capitalize on the results of the Russian campaign and the defection of Prussia from Napoleon's camp. This at last convinced Alexander to march into Germany, and so to accept British help; it tipped the military scales against Napoleon decisively. Prussia's willingness to fight was in marked contrast to the hesistancy of Russia and Austria.

The revival of Prussia

Whereas the other two eastern powers had failed to reform sufficiently their armies and bureaucracies to pursue the war effectively, the Prussians had thoroughly rebuilt their army by 1812. Between 1806 and 1812, the Prussian state was greatly weakened first by Tilsit, and then by a series of challenges to the authority of central government by the junkers, in their provincial assemblies.[3] A short-lived ministry led by vom Stein began the process in 1808 and, although it failed in its more ambitious, long-term aims, centred on curbing seigneurialism, vom Stein's ministry instituted much-needed changes in central government, particularly the adoption of the principle of collective cabinet government. Driven from office in 1809 because of his pro-Austrian attitude, vom Stein eventually went into the service of the Tsar, but he left behind an enduring system of government: henceforth, specialist bureaucrats controlled the Prussian state. Vom Stein himself sought to bring the Prussian nobility into partnership with the central government. He was of an ancient noble family of Imperial Knights, whose lands had been swallowed up by Nassau. His struggle to rebuild the shattered Prussian state led him away from his ideological roots – a belief in local self-government by the propertied classes and a free peasantry – but he would return to them by 1812, when he re-emerged as the Tsar's advisor on German affairs.

Vom Stein was succeeded by two weak ministries, when little was done beyond the reform of the army. In 1810, another reformer, von Hardenberg, came to office. He differed from vom Stein, in that his higher objective was to claw back the absolutist authority of the Prussian state from the provincial assemblies of the nobility, rather than to seek a new form of government through partnership. Centralization was his watch-word; as a product of the Prussian enlightenment, von Hardenberg drew on the same intellectual sources as Napoleonic administrators, and strove for similar results. He did so, however, in a desire to free Prussia from her position as a French client state. Von Hardenberg proved as unsuccessful in his wider ambitions as had vom Stein. His attempts to curb seigneurial power through a series of legal and financial reforms led to 'tax strikes' among the junkers and a well-organized political campaign against him. By 1812, von Hardenberg largely abandoned these projects.

Yet he was not seriously opposed over army reform. This allowed Scharnhorst, Yorck and Clauswitz to refashion the army into a formidable force; tactics and training were brought up to date and the modern military academies revived. It was a remarkable achievement, not only because it took place in so short a time, but because the Prussian High Command had to circumvent the military restrictions placed on them by the terms of Tilsit. Records were kept of the thousands of troops forcibly demobilized in 1807, who then returned to active service on a rota basis, temporarily relieving each other until, by August 1811, there were 74 000 trained troops available for service.[4] By contrast, although the Austrians put large numbers into the field in 1813–14, these troops were usually poorly armed and supplied, and had to be kept out of most of the serious fighting, so limited had been reforming efforts after 1809. British subsidies were essential throughout the campaigns of 1812–14. Thanks to them, Alexander put 110 000 men into the field and Bernadotte brought Sweden firmly into the war against his former patron.

The nobility stemmed the tide of reform in Prussia, but its loyalty to the dynasty, and to the anti-French cause, forged a strong bond between the crown and the junkers, although not of the sort wanted by either vom Stein or von Hardenberg. The junkers made a clear, deliberately archaic distinction between their traditional, unswerving devotion to the King, and the more abstract, modern concepts of the state expounded by von Hardenberg and the bureaucracy. Tradition won and, as was so often the case in this era, it led to stability and success. It was also a potent partnership, allowing Prussia to renew herself to a degree unmatched by the other eastern powers.

The war in Germany

The campaigning opened in April 1813. Two French victories at Lutzen on 2 May, and Bauzen, three weeks later, convinced the allies of the need for an armistice, even though his lack of cavalry prevented Napoleon from pressing home his advantage. During this pause in the fighting, Metternich now saw the futility of bringing Napoleon to a negotiated peace and on 12 August 1813 he brought Austria into the coalition. At Dresden, in late August the rival armies fought a costly, but inconclusive engagement; by now, however, the numerical balance was greatly in favour of the allies. When they next clashed, at Leipzig on 16 October – 'the Battle of the Nations' – the carnage rivalled that of Borodino, but Napoleon found his losses harder to repair than did the allies. This, rather than the Russian campaign, was the battle Napoleon could not afford to lose. The subsequent French withdrawal, first to the Elbe and then to the Rhine, was brilliantly conducted, but their military grip on Germany was broken.

After Leipzig, the princes of the Confederation of the Rhine deserted Napoleon; Berg and Westphalia collapsed. The inner empire north of the Alps was no more, but there is much to be learned from the manner of its passing.

'The war of liberation' and the nationalist myth: 1813–1814 in central Europe

Their decisive victory at Leipzig posed as many problems as it solved for the allies. It soon removed the French from the politics of central Europe, thus allowing a political void to open up between the advancing armies of the allies and the retreating French, into which all concerned poured their hopes and from which they awaited the re-emergence of their old fears.

The princes of the Confederation of the Rhine feared at worst for their thrones and at best hoped to preserve the lands Napoleon had granted them, while the deposed princes, great and small, sought the return of their lands and titles which, in effect, led them to support a wholesale restoration of the old Holy Roman Empire, and there were signs of strong popular support for this too. In the north, a wave of nostalgia for the old order fuelled the anti-French risings that swept the Hansa ports and parts of Berg and Westphalia, where Beugnot and Jerome now lamented the presence of so many ex-Prussian officials in the administration, but it also effected an orderly transition of power in these areas. The native German officials remained loyal to the Napoleonic ethos of order and efficiency, even as they betrayed the regime itself. It was a singular exercise in collaboration and continuity. In the Hansa ports, hopes of a restoration were easily fulfilled because they suited the allies, but the fate of Westphalia and Berg was more complicated.

The end of Napoleonic rule in Westphalia was as poignant as it is illustrative. At the same moment as Jerome pleaded in vain with Napoleon to spare his subjects further sacrifices for the defence of the Empire, a revolt in favour of the deposed Grand Elector broke out in Kassel, the Westphalian capital, and his native regiments deserted in droves to the allies. Restored to Kassel after a French counter-attack, Jerome abandoned his policy of conciliation and reverted to pure military despotism, until definitively driven out in October. Even in its death throes, the Napoleonic Empire was still playing out its initial dilemmas and seeing its paradoxes ruthlessly exposed.

Several princes deposed by Napoleon were reinstated, most notably the Duke of Hanover and Brunswick – George III of Great Britain – and the Dukes of Oldenburg and Mecklenburg, thanks to their family ties with the

Tsar. The defiantly counter-revolutionary ruler of Hesse-Kassel was also restored following the collapse of Jerome's Kingdom of Westphalia. His tenacious loyalty to 'the cause' was unanimously regarded as worthy of reward.

Although there were men involved in these events, mainly grouped around vom Stein, who espoused nationalist aspirations for a more unified Germany, their position was isolated and weak. That vom Stein was able to play a prominent part at all was due only to the divisions among the Russian, Prussian and Austrian leaders. His efforts to create a unified 'third Germany', alongside Austria and Prussia, came to nothing, not only because the allies and the entrenched princes of the Confederation opposed his plans, but through a lack of popular support for such ideas. There was a popular war of liberation in Germany in 1813 – although it did not spread to the southern states or the western bank of the Rhine – but it was not the 'nationalist' war envisaged by vom Stein or imagined by future generations.

In the course of 1812, the counter-revolutionary intelligentsia who had played so prominent a role in the Austrian war effort of 1809, regrouped in St Petersburg when Alexander resumed the struggle against Napoleon. The Tsar asked vom Stein to serve him as an unofficial advisor on foreign affairs, especially in Germany. In the years 1809–13 vom Stein reappraised many of the errors of the propaganda campaign of 1809, but it brought him no closer to the realities of Napoleonic Germany. The military circumstances of 1812 gave him an advantage he had lacked in 1809, in that the fighting took place in those parts of Germany where French rule was the most detested, along the North Sea coast, rather than in the pro-Napoleonic states of the south. Yet, vom Stein did not see his hopes for a Spanish-style revolt fulfilled; there were few mass risings ahead of the advancing armies, and little spontaneous guerrilla activity. Discipline and prudence marked the response of these populations, until the French defeat was assured.

On another level, vom Stein and his collaborators had shed the elitist outlook which had marked their propaganda in 1809. Their collective mind's eye had transformed the German popular classes, and the peasantry in particular, from 'pariah to patriot'.[5] In 1812–13, they strove to incite a truly popular rising. Alexander was often constrained to rewrite vom Stein's more overt incitements to arms against the 'collaborationist princes' of the Confederation of the Rhine.[6] Where vom Stein and his circle missed the point completely was in their belief that the German masses would respond to their specifically nationalist message. When vom Stein abandoned his attachment to the old Reich, he turned to a very specific commitment to the creation of a German nation-state, soon limited by force of circumstances to a 'third Germany' between Austria and Prussia. It was a considerable intellectual evolution and set a clear example – and a stirring challenge – for future generations, but this 'conversion' actually led vom Stein, Arndt and the others even further away from contemporary realities than in 1809. It all showed how little they understood the people they thought they loved with such fervour.

Vom Stein was inspired by the resistance in Russia and, especially, Portugal and Spain, but they were 'old nations', where the state had become identified with popular culture,[7] and where dynastic loyalty was the bridge between local interests and wider allegiances. In Germany, the reverse was the case, and no amount of myth-making can refute this. Far more typical than vom Stein of the aspirations circulating in 'liberated' Germany, was Count Munster, the representative of the Hanoverian court-in-exile. Munster sought, first and foremost, the restoration of his own state and, in the context of 1813, this meant avoiding absorption into either Prussia or vom Stein's 'third Germany'. This he achieved by virtue of his state's peculiar link with Britain. In the longer term, Munster sought to reconcile the re-establishment of the traditions of relatively weak internal government, dominated by the nobility, with a greater degree of co-operation among the German states over foreign and defence policy, particularly against France. This vision of a restored Reich set him in direct opposition to vom Stein, but Metternich made concerted efforts to convince Munster of Austrian goodwill because he probably sensed Munster spoke for a wide spectrum of opinion throughout the propertied classes of Germany.[8] Vom Stein's hopes were based on nothing more than his ability to influence allied diplomacy, but his usefulness to Alexander was based on his determination to continue the war and his proven administrative ability, rather than his patriotic vision of a new Germany. Nevertheless, the Tsar's patronage was the most powerful in central Europe, and until vom Stein reached the limit of Alexander's goodwill, it was more through fear than mockery that other German diplomats nicknamed vom Stein 'the Emperor of Germany' in the last months of 1813.

Vom Stein's instrument was the Central Administrative Council, which the Tsar had allowed him to create for the administration of the 'liberated' German lands. The Central Administration was where the hopes of idealistic, nationalist intellectuals and mediatized, reactionary nobles joined forces against the Napoleonic settlements of 1803 and 1806. Vom Stein himself was a mediatized noble, and he encouraged others of his kind, including the ex-Imperial Knights, to rally to his cause. He compromised his ideals, but it was his only real chance to influence the territorial settlement of Germany. An association of mediatized nobles, linked to the Central Administration, was formed in Frankfurt in 1813, and declared it was preparing 'the hounding of the minor German princes that will make their hairs stand on end', by the imposition of heavy war contributions on the princes. By the terms laid down by the allies, failure to meet these obligations could result in their virtual deposition. Vom Stein also put mediatized nobles in command of his new popular militia, in an attempt to create a military force independent of both the allies and the princes. The states that felt the brunt of these tactics were Nassau, Hesse-Darmstädt and Baden. When they made a stand together, however, vom Stein was forced to back down, especially over the central issue of the level of contributions to the war effort.[9] Soon, vom Stein's unholy alliance of reactionary petty nobles and salon nationalists was stopped in its tracks. Fearing, with some justification, that they would be deposed should their territories fall into the hands of the Central Administrative Council, the princes changed sides on terms that guaranteed most of the lands Napoleon had given them since 1805 and also largely exempted them from vom Stein's authority.

An even more emphatic rejection of vom Stein's ambitions for Germany came from the popular resentment his administration provoked in those areas it controlled briefly: Saxony, whose prince stayed loyal to Napoleon just that little too long, and the now leaderless satellite states of Westphalia and Berg. These areas saw popular risings against Napoleonic rule, but they had been driven by hatred of taxation, conscription and economic recession. Where political goals had been voiced, they had been for the restoration of the *ancien régime*. When vom Stein attempted to impose war taxation and perpetuate conscription – this time in the service of 'the war of national liberation' – he met with the same resentment. What was sought most fervently in 1813 was a return to a political world that did not conscript and did not involve itself in great causes. Mindful of their own interests, the returning princes sided with their subjects.

The events of 1813 were the antithesis of a 'national war', but they were an anti-French revolt. The Central Administrative Council alienated, rather than rallied, the populations it governed. By the last weeks of 1813, von Hardenberg and Metternich outmanoeuvred vom Stein with the Tsar and installed Prussian civil servants as the provisional governors of these areas. With Napoleon thrown back behind the Rhine, the German princes reverted to an introverted concentration on the reconstruction of Germany, to settle their own affairs in their own way, rather than the struggle against Napoleon.

With the eyes of both Russia and Britain fixed on wider horizons, Austria emerged as the determining influence in Germany exactly because, cautious to a fault, Metternich chose to use persuasion rather than force to exploit this position. Prussian policy, based on a desire to partition Germany into Prussian and Austrian spheres of influence, was thwarted by Metternich's judicious wish to maintain the status quo. He sought to influence and direct – even to control – the foreign and military policies of the middle-sized German states, but not to expand Austrian territory at their direct expense. However, Metternich faced opposition from within his own Court, where Stadion and Archduke John, in particular, still advocated the same policy of revenge against the 'collaborators' of the Confederation as they had in 1809. Here Metternich was sustained by the support of the Austrian military commander, Prince Schwarzenberg, and the Tsar, who wanted the princes detached from Napoleon in the interests of a quick victory. Ironically, the need to continue the war helped to ensure that the

Napoleonic state order in southern Germany survived the fall of the Empire.

In the last months of 1813, Alexander led an increasingly reluctant coalition across the Rhine and into the heartland of the inner empire. The struggle here was far from over, for the imperial administration had worked one last miracle, and raised yet another army. The numerical advantage the coalition had enjoyed since the battle of Dresden was no guarantee of success and, with Napoleon now able to fight on his own ground, the hesitancy of many allied commanders became apparent. At this point, 'the Spanish ulcer' tipped the scales in favour of the allies.

The war in Spain, 1812–1814

The military circumstances

The only real benefit Napoleon derived from the Spanish war was that it produced battle-hardened veterans for service in the more pressing sectors in central Europe. Every branch of the Grande Armée, even the Imperial Guard, had come to rely heavily on the experience of combat-ready troops drawn from the Spanish front and, in this particular respect, Napoleon owed the *partidas* a backhanded compliment he could never repay them. Spain became so regular a drain on French manpower between 1809 and 1812, that a singular system of recruitment evolved to cope with the continuous, if seldom spectacular losses of the Spanish front. Following each *tirage*, officers from units based in Spain toured depots in France and competed among themselves for the best conscripts. In 1812, Napoleon drew heavily on this heritage to bolster his elite corps for the Russian campaign, and was able to do so again in 1813 in the early phases of the German campaign. In so doing, however, he gave both the scattered Spanish forces and Wellington's besieged Anglo-Portuguese army a better opportunity to break the military deadlock than they probably realized at first.

It was only as the quantity and the quality of French effectives were reduced simultaneously in the Iberian sector, after 1812, that the *partidas* were able to act as proper military formations, and it was from this point onwards that they scored their biggest successes over the French, especially in northern Spain, where the French grip had been tightest. This starkly contradicted both the contemporary image of the peasant-in-arms so beloved of vom Stein and the myth bequeathed to posterity of the guerrilla triumphant over regular troops. More importantly, the altered state of the French army in Spain allowed Wellington the chance to break out of his Portuguese stronghold. It proved a fortunate coincidence for the allies that the debilitation of the calibre of the French forces in Spain virtually coincided with the evolution of Wellington's Anglo-Portuguese army into a truly formidable fighting force, for Wellington had transformed Portugal into his own vast Camp de Boulogne.

Until 1812, the French had been able to contain Wellington and the Spanish resistance, but only because they had no major distractions elsewhere. Henceforth, inevitably, this changed; Napoleon kept 200 000 men in Spain throughout 1812–13, but even they could not contain the *partidas* and the allied forces at the same time. Nevertheless, the Grande Armée's moment of weakness did not come quite as soon as Wellington assumed it would, when he advanced beyond his Portuguese defences in January 1812. The two undermanned fortresses of Ciudad Rodrigo and Badajoz fell to him. When the French played into his hands, dangerously overstretching their manpower by a futile invasion of northern Portugal, Wellington took Madrid from Joseph's troops on 12 August 1812, following a brilliant victory over Marmont at Salamanca on 22 July.

This sequence of allied victories galvanized the French marshals into a rare – and very effective – period of co-operation. Salamanca and the fall of Madrid at last convinced Soult he had to obey Joseph's order to withdraw from Andalusia to help him against Wellington. As a result, the French abandoned one of their best strongholds, but they were able to concentrate a formidable army in central Spain, a force of 110 000 men, the bulk of which made for Madrid and swept the British garrison aside, while another force, gathered in northern Spain, drove Wellington from Burgos. His retreat turned into a rout; on 17 November 1812 Wellington had fallen back to the safety of Portugal, his army badly mauled by Soult and weakened by hunger and sickness; a tenth of the army deserted during the retreat. Wellington was saved only by Joseph's refusal to pursue him; had Marmont and Soult had the good sense to disobey Joseph on this occasion – as was their usual habit – and had Wellington been made to fight again as the marshals wanted, it would be difficult to see how he could have taken the offensive again, whatever the result of the Russian campaign.

As it was, the Anglo-Portuguese army survived, recuperated and reemerged to fight again a few months later. The task of rebuilding it was not easy, but it was at least feasible. London sent 5000 fresh troops and increased the monthly subsidy to Portugal. In stark contrast, Joseph saw four Imperial Guard regiments and a large number of experienced NCOs withdrawn for service in Germany. Within Spain, the initial successes of the Anglo-Portuguese army in 1812 led to heavier fighting in the north-east by the *partidas* led by Mina and Palafox. Joseph was forced to divert large numbers of troops to contain the fighting, which did not cease after Wellington's defeat at Burgos. The French never really recovered their grip on these areas, and effectively Joseph now faced a war on two fronts. The 1812 campaign had also definitively freed Andalusia in the south, Asturias in the north and Estremadura in the west from French control.

Joseph's blunder was as critical as any committed by Napoleon in 1813, as an effective end to major campaigning in Spain at this point would have had a crucial bearing on the German campaigns. Henceforth, the tide turned in Wellington's favour. As many of the problems facing Wellington and the Spanish were as much of their own making as anything else, it is indicative of the decline in French capabilities that Joseph could do nothing to exploit them.

Wellington spent the winter of 1812–13 wrangling with the Spanish, as well as rebuilding his forces. On 2 October 1812, the Cortes made Wellington commander-in-chief of the Spanish armies, following the victory of Salamanca, but his more direct involvement with the Spanish army became more a source of friction than one of unity, the roots of which were the distrust of their own officer corps felt by the liberal deputies who controlled the Cortes, together with a more widespread distrust of British motives in Spain once the war was over. Most Spaniards suspected London of supporting the revolt of the American colonies, and harboured the same fears as most continental states that British economic imperialism would replace French military hegemony. Fearful of absolutists in their own army, and in love with the same vision of a 'people's war' that so enraptured vom Stein, the Spanish liberals sought to turn the army into a civilian-controlled popular militia just as Wellington demanded its professionalization. With good reason, Wellington did not think the Spanish army fit to take a major part in the final campaign, its large numbers notwithstanding. The brunt of the fighting was born by the Anglo-Portuguese and the irregular units in the north. This dictated the pattern of the campaign of 1813.

In late May 1813, the northern *partidas* intensified their campaigns, thus preventing the release of troops to oppose Wellington's advance. Joseph abandoned central Spain, falling back north of the River Ebro, much as he had done in 1808 after Bailen. This time, however, he had better reason to panic. Wellington moved across northern Spain at great speed, a clear sign in itself that the Anglo-Portuguese had reached the fighting standards once set by the Grande Armée. In an effort to defend the main highway to France and to cover his inevitable retreat, Joseph concentrated his troops at Vitoria where his army was cut to pieces by Wellington on 21 June 1813. The remains of Joseph's army retreated into France and Napoleon stripped him of his throne on 1 July 1813 – an all but empty reaction – and ordered Soult back to the Pyrenees to salvage what he could.

Vitoria was one of the most crucial battles of the last phase of the war. It had ramifications far beyond the Spanish front, where it virtually settled the military issues. Wellington scored this decisive victory just as Napoleon was regaining the initiative in central Europe. With the French driven over the Pyrenees, the next phase of the war would be in France, whatever the result in Germany.

For the 'liberated' Spaniards, however, it was only the beginning of a new nightmare, with the most war-ravaged countryside in Napoleonic Europe as its 'dreamscape', immortalized in the paintings of Goya. He did not have to look far for his material.

Post-liberation Spain: anarchy and reaction, 1813–1814

As the allied armies swept forward, Spain slipped further into anarchy, for however slender a grip on law and order the French may have had, it was stronger than anything the Cortes could put in its place. Its attempts to create a volunteer militia to police the countryside in November 1813 proved virtually useless.[10] Effectively, the country was rudderless, but worse was to come.

During its advance in 1813, the Anglo-Portuguese army, particularly its British elements, had matched the Grande Armée not only as combat troops, but in brutality against Spanish civilians. The sack of San Sebastian – its rape would be more appropriate – rivalled the deeds of the French armies at their worst. British troops laced these atrocities with a strong dose of contempt for the Spanish which is strikingly similar to that displayed by the French. Both armies despised the deeply Catholic culture they encountered, and the British desecrated churches with a Protestant fervour worthy of Cromwell's Roundheads, just as the French had done in the name of Reason. An abhorrence of bullfighting did not, it seemed, preclude visiting far worse horrors on humans.

However dreadful, these atrocities were transient. They soon ended when the campaigning moved on; this had been the pattern since the wars began in 1792. However, Spain had been devastated constantly since 1808 and the campaigns of 1813 burst upon a society and economy already exhausted by war. Behind the armies came the *partidas*. If most *partidas* had hovered on the fine line between bandit and freedom-fighter before 1813, many crossed it now. There had always been a marked reluctance among many guerrillas to join regular units, although this was less true in the north. Elsewhere, however, the *partidas* kept their distance from the front, especially in central and western Spain. When they turned to outright pillage, there was no effective civil power to oppose them. As the people it claimed to embody fell prey to anarchy, all the shortcomings of the Cortes stood revealed. The foolishness of its refusal to discipline the *partidas* was now glaringly obvious.

Into this chaos, Napoleon released Ferdinand VII, in a desperate effort to make a separate peace with Spain and abort a war on two fronts. *El Desiderado* arrived in Spain in late April 1814, a few weeks after Napoleon's abdication, and his presence soon brought the bitter divisions of the last six years to a head. It was now the turn of the politicians to endure anarchy and terror. Ferdinand had no intention of honouring the constitution of 1812 or any of the other reforms enacted by the Cortes, not to mention the Cortes itself. His goal was to return the monarchy to its absolutist foundations. Ferdinand found this much easier to achieve than he had ever dared dream in exile. Wellington had left most of the Spanish army behind when he invaded southern France, fearing it would seek revenge on the French for the ravages of the Grande Armée. Thus, Ferdinand found an army disaffected from the liberals in the Cortes, who had failed to pay or supply it adequately. The liberals were now made to pay the price for their refusal to allow Wellington to reform the army. Their continued fear of the officer corps was based on a largely outmoded view of it as a haven for privileged, reactionary nobles, whereas in reality some of the liberals' own reforms had created a large number of officers who were themselves opposed to privilege.[11] When the Cortes attacked the essence of the army itself, through its plans for a national militia, it alienated even this group. With this army at his back, Ferdinand entered Madrid, while the Cortes remained stranded in Cadiz. Thereafter, he moved quickly. On 10–11 May, he ordered the dissolution of the Cortes and the first of many arrests of the liberal leaders. The 'white terror' had begun.

When Joseph retreated into France it is estimated that as many as 13 000 *afrancesados* went with him. Similar, sad columns of collaborators made their way over the Alps and across the Rhine in these months, perhaps the clearest human testimony to the isolation felt by those non-French people who had served the Empire. This phenomenon is also a poignant reminder of the role of Napoleon as a bulwark against true reaction.

What made the Spanish case unique, however, was that the liberal patriots were soon to share the fate of the collaborators. The persecution visited upon the *afrancesados* was predictable enough; it had been put into practice by the *partidas* at every available opportunity. The ferocity with which the patriots now turned on each other needs some explanation however. The *serviles* were able to carry the day not only through the backing of the King and most of the army, but because they could draw on massive levels of support, indeed, on fanatical loyalty, that the avowedly popular governments of revolutionary France could only dream about, and now they demonized the liberal patriots as they had the *afrancesados*. The Spanish were traumatized by 1813, and in this atmosphere the *serviles*' appeal for a return to the past, based on the certainties of absolute monarchy and absolute faith in Catholic orthodoxy, met a populace only too ready to embrace them. The immobile social and political order preached by the *serviles* was reassuring to a nation trapped between anarchy and destitution exactly because it offered – or seemed to offer – stability. Their political programme was expressed in the traditional language and imagery of the counter-revolution, through religious festivals and pageantry centred on an idealized vision of the King as the saviour of his people. The *serviles* equated royal absolutism with the miraculous salvation of Spain from its present ravages;[12] thus, the restored absolute monarchy became sacred and the political became indistinguishable from the religious. To oppose a specifically absolutist restoration became tantamount to heresy and blasphemy. The leading *servile* journals began preaching this message early in 1814 in language so bloodthirsty that its historian has described it as criminal.[13] This evolved into a systematic campaign, borne on a wave of popular fury, that lasted into the 1820s. The *serviles* were, simply closer to the people than the liberals. The lower clergy were their most powerful arm in what a contemporary newspaper described as 'philosophical disputes [which] open up interpretations of human and divine truths which will engender a war that will cause more changes than the present fighting'.[14] When the *serviles* spoke, it was in the tried and tested terms that had raised the masses against the French in 1808, to stir the last embers of the passions of resistance, for the *serviles* and the masses saw their struggle with the liberals as the continuation of that against Napoleon. They had risen not only to eject the French but to restore 'Church and King'.

The fall of the inner empire, 1813–1814

There were wider lessons to be learned from the aftermath of the Spanish War of Independence. If Spain had indeed been the fount of popular resistance to Napoleon, that resistance now showed itself to be as deeply reactionary as it was truly popular. It was the final betrayal of the liberal vision of the 'national war of liberation' and the first nail in many a liberal's coffin. The most plausibly popular and nationalist revolt in Napoleonic Europe was also the most thoroughly traditionalist. Throughout the lands of the outer empire, and in those parts of the inner empire adversely affected by the Continental System, the collapse of French hegemony was welcomed where it had not actually been fought for. It was very important for the future history of these areas that the collapse of Napoleonic rule was accompanied by widespread support for the restoration of the old order. When the lands of the inner empire were faced with the same fate, however, their responses were far more equivocal. The inner empire proved remarkably tenacious in its resistance during Napoleon's last stand, from December 1813 to his abdication in April 1814. The last months of Napoleonic rule in these areas illustrate all the strengths and weaknesses of the regime in stark clarity; in its last hours, the true 'heartland' of Napoleonic Europe is seen most clearly.

The end of the Empire in Italy

By 1813, the surviving territories of the Empire in Italy were a microcosm of the outer and inner empires. The Piedmontese and Ligurian departments, together with the Kingdom of Italy, belonged firmly to the inner empire, while the Roman and Tuscan departments belonged to the outer empire. The Kingdom of Naples, always problematic before 1807, continued to the end to hold an intermediate position between absorption and tenuous occupation. By late 1813, the French had been driven from the Illyrian provinces and moved into the valley of the Po, while British ships full of Russian troops swarmed along the coastlines of Italy. Napoleonic rule then collapsed in the regions of the outer empire, but held remarkably firm in those of the inner empire. To grasp why, it is necessary to turn first to Murat's Kingdom of Naples.

The tide of banditry had been rising against Murat in his southern provinces since at least 1810; this worsened after 1812 when large numbers of troops were withdrawn for service in Russia. By the autumn of 1813 brigandage was also rampant further north, along the border with Rome and in the countryside around the capital, and the Kingdom of Naples showed every sign of going the way of the Illyrian provinces, Josephist Spain and the Hanseatic departments – of gleefully caving in. Yet this was not what happened.

The duplicitous, skilful diplomatic game played by Murat and even more by his wife, Queen Caroline, was resolved only after the decisive defeat of Napoleon at Dresden. Murat then followed a path from passive support for Napoleon to cautious alliance with the Coalition, although he kept this covert. A formal alliance with the Coalition was not concluded until January 1814 and as late as April the prefects of the Roman and Tuscan departments still believed him their ally.

Murat was able to maintain this balancing act for so long because the British and the Austrians saw that his regime was stronger and more efficient than anything the Bourbons could hope to put in its place. However riven with banditry or thwarted by the local power of the baronage, Murat had shaped a loyal, well-educated bureaucracy at the higher levels of the state and – a crucial factor in the turbulent conditions of 1813–14 – a very formidable army of 30 000 men, officered by veterans of the Grande Armée. To this the Bourbons could counter only with a motley force of deserters. In these respects the Kingdom of Naples bore the traces of nine years of Napoleonic rule. When Murat joined the Coalition, it was enough to change the course of the war in Italy. It also revealed the fragility of Napoleonic rule in those parts of Italy where it was truly weak.

The collapse of Napoleonic rule proceeded apace in central Italy. In the countryside the heavy conscription quotas of 1813 led to the virtual collapse of law and order: brigandage reached massive proportions and armed bands pillaged the treasuries of the small mountain towns almost at will. Napoleon exempted these departments from the last conscription levies of 1813 and 1814, the clearest admission by the imperial government that all hope was lost here. In January 1814 Pius VII was allowed to return to Rome from his prison in Fontainebleau. By the end of February the French administration had fled both Rome and Florence. Unlike most of northern Italy, or even Naples, most of the administration was staffed with Frenchmen and Piedmontese. When the end came they simply withdrew, leaving few traces behind them. Murat knew this would happen and acted accordingly until stopped by Britain and Austria.

The Napoleonic Kingdom of Naples was certainly strong enough to absorb the debris of the outer empire. Growing disorder made the arrival of Murat's disciplined, capable troops very welcome in Tuscany and Rome. They were perceived as saviours by the propertied classes, who felt themselves engulfed by a rising tide of anarchy, who had looked to the French in this role, at least until 1812, and now turned to Murat in the same spirit, indifferent to which side he took in the war. By basing his popularity on the restoration of order, Murat turned Napoleon's favoured tactics against him. His decree abolishing the blockade rallied the commercial classes to him at a stroke.[15]

In northern Italy, there were also contrasting regional reactions to the collapse of Napoleonic rule. Eugène had created a formidable army in the Kingdom of Italy, as well-trained and battle-hardened as Murat's, and sustained by a better system of conscription. Despite its enormous losses in Russia, from where only 1000 of its original contingent of 27 000 returned,[16] under native commanders and stiffened by French troops Eugène's army was a powerful obstacle in the path of the allies.

The Austrians attacked northern Italy in August 1813. Supported by the British navy, they drove the French out of the Illyrian provinces. However, it took over four months to drive Eugène out of the Veneto and even then his decision to abandon it in February 1814 came only when Murat changed sides. Murat avoided confrontation, enabling Eugène to continue his defence of north-western Italy into April. Only when news of Napoleon's abdication reached him did Eugène conclude an armistice. When the end came, Eugène still had a loyal army of 45 000.

As Eugène withdrew from the Veneto into Lombardy, events behind the front showed he was crossing from the outer to the inner empire. In the Veneto his rule collapsed in a renewal of widespread revolts in the countryside, while on Eugène's own orders the Lombard prefects of the Venetian departments withdrew along with the army, much as the French had done in central Italy. Only the prefect of Venice remained at his post. The Austrians sought to keep Napoleonic officials in place, at least provisionally, but they could do little to restrain the outpourings of violence which had been fermenting since the repression of the rebellions of 1809. The Austrian Governor, Reuss-Planten, was powerless against this tide, particularly in the most easterly areas around Trieste where the rampant anarchy of the Illyrian provinces spilled over and all administration collapsed.

In Lombardy, the civil administration stood firmly behind Eugène and public order was maintained almost to the end. Not one prefect deserted his post in Lombardy – even those in the Veneto had done so only when ordered to – and their support of the war effort went far beyond purely professional commitment. In Brescia the prefect himself led the garrison against the Austrian troops in November 1813, and held the town until

January 1814. They all accepted reductions in salary, and many subscribed funds for the war out of their own pockets.[17] The same loyalty and professionalism prevailed in the administration of the neighbouring Piedmontese departments, where conscription continued to be enforced and taxes raised into April 1814. In these last months the institutions of the Napoleonic state were put to a severe test in north-western Italy, and they were not found wanting. Piedmont and Lombardy emerged as part of the heartland of the empire in its time of crisis.

Nevertheless, this loyalty was largely confined to the ranks of the administration and, until the final weeks, to parts of the propertied classes. The administrators had no illusions left about the unpopularity of the regime and when news of the abdication of Napoleon reached these areas, popular discontent erupted, but not until it was clear that Eugène's rule was also over. Melzi, who Eugène had recalled to act as his deputy in 1812, tried to rally the Senate with a proposal that the allied leaders be asked to confirm Eugène in power. When this was rejected, riots broke out in Milan orchestrated by the nobility in which one of the leading ministers of state, Prina, was lynched by a mob. The old rivalries between the landed aristocracy and the professional bureaucrats resurfaced. Melzi was undone by his own creation, the Senate he had filled with landed notables, and Aldini's fears about their loyalty were justified. Revolts followed in Brescia and in Bergamo, where the nobility turned the populace on the prefect when he tried to raise local support for Eugène.[18] By 26 April, Eugène and the French troops had gone, collecting their compatriots in the Piedmontese departments as they went.

The final withdrawal was very orderly. There were no further outbreaks of violence on a large scale in Lombardy and virtually none in the Piedmontese departments. This was in great part due to the professionalism of the Napoleonic prefects and the good sense of the Austrian commander, Bellegarde, who asked them to stay at their posts on a provisional basis until the transition of power was over. More significantly in the long term, it is clear that although there was great tension within the propertied classes between pro- and anti-Napoleonic factions in Lombardy and Piedmont, there was also a shared will to avoid the anarchy and bloodshed of the late 1790s. This is especially evident in Piedmont, which was almost without a police force in these months because the gendarmes, as French soldiers, withdrew with Eugène. The riots in Milan, Brescia and Bergamo were isolated incidents. More to the point, they were urban, for no one on either side wanted to risk inciting the peasantry. The combination of the Austrian army, headed by the moderate Bellegarde, and the Napoleonic prefects, ensured the peasants did not act on their own initiative.

Genoa and the Ligurian departments were exceptions to this ordered pattern. Their coastal position had made them victims of the blockade, while it also made them easy prey for raids by the British fleet. As in southern Italy but on a much smaller scale, the British had been able to revive banditry in this area, where it had been endemic until the Napoleonic period. Bentinck, the British commander, took Genoa from the French in the name of the old Republic. This proved very popular locally, winning the support of the nobles, merchants and the popular classes, but it also led to a collapse of the administration and public order as the French withdrew *en masse*. Bentinck's desire to revive the old Republic was quashed by the allies. By the time the restored King of Piedmont-Savoy landed in Genoa, barely a month after Bentinck had liberated the city, it was clear the Republic was stillborn and that Liguria would be ruled by the Piedmontese. At this point, even in Genoa, a degree of support emerged for the Napoleonic state. The House of Savoy quickly showed itself to be as reactionary as Ferdinand VII in Spain, if nothing like as bloodthirsty. The restored Court in Turin abruptly dismissed all those officials who had served the French and reintroduced most of the ordinances of the *ancien régime*. Faced with the prospect of being ruled by a regime that was rapidly proving itself incompetent as well as reactionary, in 1815 the Genoese petitioned the Congress of Vienna, in vain, to be allowed to return to French rule.

In the Venetian departments of the Kingdom of Italy hopes ran high for the restoration of the old Republic, abolished by Napoleon in 1797, but the region was returned to Austrian rule. Here, unlike Genoa, Napoleonic rule had been shorter and harsher. Consequently, nostalgia for the old order prevailed alongside resentment of Austrian rule, rather than a desire to preserve the Napoleonic reforms. Elsewhere in Italy, a relatively benign Austrian occupation directed by Bellegarde paved the way for peaceful restorations in Tuscany, Parma, Modena, and the Papal States.

There is little evidence of incipient pan-Italian nationalism in these events. Where the masses were able to assert themselves, they sought the restoration of the old order; many did not look much beyond the expulsion of the French. The propertied classes backed whoever seemed best able to preserve order, priorities which favoured first Murat and Eugène and then the Austrians. Only the Piedmontese elite swerved from this path, guided in part by dynastic loyalties rooted deeply in the past. The nationalist conspiracies of tiny groups such as the Carbonari were barely audible in all this. Italian nationalism was the exclusive property of powerless sects while the real conflict was between a nostalgia for the old order and the increasingly appreciated benefits of Napoleonic rule.

The fall of the Rhineland and the Low Countries, 1813–1814

Almost 100 000 French troops escaped the allies and retired behind the 'natural frontiers' of France in December 1813, where a new army was waiting, drawn from the conscripts of 1815 – boys of seventeen – and from reservists, gendarmes and the national guard. On the face of things, this miracle was purely administrative, but these unlikely troops performed wonders in the coming months. The resilience of this raw army fully justified the initial reticence of many allied commanders about carrying the war into France.

The allies concentrated 300 000 troops along the Rhine and decided on a winter campaign on a wide front. Their initial problems were eased greatly by a declaration of neutrality by the Swiss Confederation and its subsequent occupation by Austrian troops in the last days of 1813. Yet the coalition became increasingly overstretched both militarily and diplomatically as the campaign went on. Their slow advance and internal suspicions let Napoleon concentrate his forces for a tenacious defensive action. Initially, however, the decision to fight in winter found him unprepared; the Low Countries and the west bank of the Rhine quickly fell to the allies.

The competing diplomatic interests among the allies were too sensitive for them to concentrate on decisions about the future of Europe at this stage. Even so seemingly straightforward an option as the restoration of the House of Orange in the Netherlands was not actually taken until the end of the fighting, in late May 1814, although the country was in allied hands by the end of 1813 and the Prince had returned to Amsterdam. His position remained ambiguous for several months, for the allies considered putting a Habsburg on the throne or even of restoring Louis Bonaparte. Although all were agreed that Holland would remain an independent country, it was still not clear who would rule it.

Within Holland, the allies feared that after almost 20 years of French domination there would be considerable support for a republic modelled on French lines. They greatly overestimated this political current, for as in much of the rest of the crumbling Napoleonic Empire, the overwhelming popular feeling was one of dynastic loyalty. Lightly defended by the French, the Dutch departments saw a host of spontaneous localized assaults on customs' houses and French officials. By November 1813, 'authority fell away from the French Empire in the Netherlands like dead flesh from a skeleton'.[19] These outbursts against the depredations of the blockade and conscription were wholly predictable, but the tenacity of dynastic loyalty to the House of Orange among the popular classes, urban and rural alike, was much in evidence. As in the Piedmontese departments, it had survived almost two decades of foreign or republican rule. As in Spain, Piedmont, Rome, Genoa, and Venice there was no doubt that a restoration of the old order was what the masses desired.

Nevertheless, caution guided the actions of both the Prince of Orange and the hastily assembled 'General Administration' which attempted to fill the gap left by the hasty withdrawal of the French. The Prince promised to grant a constitution; the self-appointed General Administration saw its main task as trying to curb the popular tumult. It took its time about endorsing the Prince until the French had been driven out of the country, and it also actively recruited many men who had served Louis Bonaparte and even several who had been in the French administration. This was done with the twin aims of achieving political reconciliation and ensuring continuity in the administration of justice and finance.[20] Discussions on the new constitution went on throughout early 1814, and it emerged that even the most committed republicans of the 1795–1805 period were now reconciled to an Orangist restoration, so disillusioned were they by the brutality of French rule in its final years. It was also clear that even the most intransigent royalists recognized the need for some form of constitutional monarchy. More important still, there emerged a shared desire to avoid violence both in terms of public order and political animosity. The Prince of Orange and the Dutch politicians readily found common ground in their wish to retain most of the Napoleonic administrative system. The men of the General Administration knew its merits well enough as well as its potential for exploitation by an authoritarian ruler. To the die-hard Orangists, it offered an end to federalism and a more secure future for the dynasty. The Prince, now William VI, was a firm admirer of Napoleonic centralization and of the Emperor; his autocratic tendencies soon emerged. English-style cabinet government was rejected and William's preference for a Napoleonic-style Council of State was incorporated into the new constitution. He now exercised a very tight control over his ministers. This met with the approval of his chief backers, the British and the Prussians, who regarded centralization as the surest way of strengthening a state they saw as a bulwark against any future French aggression.[21] It found acceptance among a relieved but politically apathetic populace and a political elite favourable to many aspects of Napoleonic rule. By the time the allied diplomats finally settled the fate of the Netherlands, the Dutch political elite had already mapped out a workable system for the country which owed its success in equal measure to the practical experience of Napoleonic reform, dynastic loyalty and the deeper legacy of a sophisticated political culture.

The Belgian and Rhenish departments lacked the strong dynastic and political traditions of the Netherlands, and had also been parts of metropolitan France for a very long time. The diplomatic fate of these areas was even less clear to the allies than that of Holland. There were no large-scale popular risings against the French, nor did the local elites organize their own government as the Dutch had. This is not to say there were no signs of popular discontent with Napoleonic rule. In Belgium, the breach with the Pope created widespread anger, especially when Napoleon attempted to dismiss the Bishop of Ghent in April 1813 for his refusal to support Napoleon's attempts to circumvent Papal authority over the appointment of clergy. The Bishop got powerful support from both his cathedral chapter and from all but 30 of his 1200 parish priests, who refused to recognize his replacement. This was but the most overt of many signs that the religious policies of the last years of the Empire had alienated many people in these intensely Catholic departments.[22]

Set beside this, however, was the full integration of Belgian commerce and industry into the French economy and the solidity of its administration right up to the arrival of the allied troops. On the whole, the deeply Catholic peasantry of Flanders – who were a major source of conscripts – welcomed the allies,[23] while the French-speaking Walloons of the industrial areas around Liège and their Flemish counterparts in Ghent looked with fear towards an uncertain future. Although the Belgian departments had no tradition of independence they had a collective sense of unity based mainly on their integrated economy. The great rivers which allied diplomats tended to see only as boundaries for potential partitions of the region were, in fact, the arteries of its commercial life-blood. The political classes were united in their determination to keep the region together and by a shared will to preserve law and order. There was a wave of riots against the retreating French and then – in some cases in the space of a week – against the rigours of allied occupation. Urban guards sprang up all over Belgium in the winter and spring of 1814 to protect persons and property from popular disorder and to ensure continuity with the French administration.[24]

However, there were still deep political divisions within the ranks of the elite. The nobility and the clergy, together with many urban artisans, sought a return to Habsburg rule. They hoped this would entail a restoration of their urban and provincial privileges under the old estates and the guilds. Popular support for these hopes emerged in Ghent where the old trade guilds, banned since 1795, were resurrected as soon as the French withdrew.[25] Much to the surprise of the allied leaders, the conservative elements of the Belgian elite found a collective voice very quickly. Soon after the French left Brussels a well-attended meeting of nobles and clergy sent a delegation to allied headquarters in France with a petition requesting a return to Habsburg rule. They were too late, for Metternich had already renounced Austrian claims to the region. Emperor Francis received them but advised the delegation to work for union with the Dutch. Henceforth, however, at least the allies were aware of this influential section of Belgian opinion and advised the Dutch to take it into consideration.[26]

In contrast to the nobles and clergy, there was still strong support for the French among the burgeoning commercial classes, especially among the owners of *biens nationaux*. This faction was cultivated by the Dutch throughout 1814, who were encouraged by the British in their ambition to annex Belgium. Many leaders of the commercial classes were converted to this as the prospect of remaining French receded. Chief among them were the two great business magnates, Lievin Bautwens and Huytens, who saw the new Dutch constitution as their best hope of preserving the liberal social and commercial policies of the French period.[27] The brutality of a long occupation by the Prussians, while the fate of the country remained undecided, won many Belgians over to the prospect of union with the Dutch.

London had no intention of allowing France to continue to dominate the Channel coast, and Castlereagh reached the view that the Dutch needed the whole of Belgium to check any further aggression by France. He had only now learnt the lesson Napoleon had in 1805–06 when dealing with the dissolution of the Holy Roman Empire: small weak states were useless as allies or clients; only those of a middling size could serve this purpose and where they did not exist they had to be created. This was the view that finally prevailed among the allies. However, the Belgian elite was disappointed under Dutch rule. For conservatives the new Dutch constitution erased all hopes of a return to the political world of the old order, while the liberal middle classes continued to look to France, and would almost get their way in 1830 when Belgium finally broke free of Dutch rule.

The ex-French departments on the west bank of the Rhine showed considerable loyalty to Napoleon during the last crisis of the Empire. The countryside was reluctant to supply the retreating French army and in some places conscription proved difficult, but not impossible, to enforce. However, the business communities of Crefeld, Cologne and Aachen were open in their support for the French. They continued to raise money for the French war effort and taxes were collected until the French withdrew in February 1814. As in Piedmont and the Kingdom of Italy, virtually every administrator, French and Rhenish alike, stayed at his post until relieved by the Prussians. In August 1814, six months after the end of French rule and four after the abdication, the city of Crefeld celebrated Napoleon's birthday.[28] The future of the Rhineland raised a host of potential problems for the allies. They had been a patchwork of small states with a few enclaves of Prussian territory before the Revolution and under French rule since 1798. After complex negotiations, these ex-French departments were given to Prussia; the old rulers were not restored. The transition to Prussian rule was remarkably smooth because the provisional administration that ran the area from March 1814 to April 1815 was in the hands of an able, reform-minded Prussian, Johann August Sack, a protege of vom Stein. Sack admired much of what he found, which made it easy for him to work with the local elites. He did not hesitate to employ those who had served the French.[29] It was very fortuitous that a region so thoroughly a part of the inner empire was absorbed by Prussia, a state itself on the path of reform since 1807.

Wellington's invasion of south-western France

France was far from a monolith in the last months of the First Empire. As Turin, Cologne and Brussels stood firm for 'the cause', Bordeaux opened its gates to Wellington's army, its trade ravaged by the blockade. Toulouse also welcomed the British, an event all the more poignant because on 10 April 1814, Soult fought ferociously to deny Wellington the city. Soult's heroism was not appreciated in Toulouse, however. He withdrew eastward, not only because of his heavy losses, but in the knowledge that Toulouse had reasserted its counter-revolutionary traditions to the point that he did not feel secure there. The welcome Wellington received proved Soult right.[30]

Wellington had feared a French version of the Spanish guerrilla war in the south-west when he crossed the Pyrenees but he found quite the reverse. Most of the region had been counter-revolutionary in the 1790s and in many frontier areas such as Roussillon conscription and taxation had always been difficult to enforce. In the course of 1813, they collapsed altogether, in stark contrast to the Rhineland or north-western Italy. While the administrators of the Kingdom of Italy remained loyal to Eugène, there was talk in Toulouse of a secessionist 'Kingdom of the Midi' under the Bourbons should the allies make peace with Napoleon. Bitter denominational rivalries resurfaced throughout southern France, particularly in the Cévennes. In the west, civil war again threatened the Vendée and fears of renewed fighting persisted there well into 1815. When contrasted to events in many of the non-French departments, it would seem that the revolutionary-Napoleonic state had put down firmer foundations 'abroad' than in much of the south and west of France. In the final analysis – or the last ditch to be more precise – there was an inner empire, a truly Napoleonic Europe, but it was not always synonymous with France.

The final stages of the war, January–May 1814: the fall of northern France

The campaign fought by Napoleon between January and March 1814 is regarded as a masterpiece by most military historians, even those who are generally critical of him.[31] For the first time in several years Napoleon really did have direct control of operations and he soon proved his technical superiority over the allied commanders. This is all the more apparent because the troops under his command were not only fewer in number but now also of an indisputably inferior quality to those of the coalition. The Young Guard now counted as veterans those who had served in only the campaigns of 1813. It was now composed of promising conscripts and for the first time there were desertions from its ranks. The Old Guard numbered only a few hundred men by 1814, and Napoleon had to use it continuously to turn the tide in crucial engagements. 'His ultimate reserve had become a corps of regular shock troops'.[32] Nevertheless, the miracle performed by the administration was almost matched by Napoleon, as well as by Soult and Eugène on the secondary fronts. Led by their Emperor the conscripts worked wonders.

Napoleon knew that his only hope was to get between the two main allied armies under Blucher and Schwartzenberg, which he did, but he soon found he could do far more against them than he had imagined. Blucher's troops were advancing on Paris in a disorderly fashion, which allowed Napoleon to use his weaker forces to best advantage: he struck quickly with his full force at isolated enemy detachments and then moved on. 'The rapier was to replace the bludgeon of 1812.'[33] Then, Napoleon led a mere 31 000 troops on a rampage through the Prussian columns that produced a string of victories in mid-February, the 'Six Days Campaign'. Blucher's army now faced a complete rout but Napoleon had to switch his meagre resources to counter Schwarzenberg's more cautious advance. He moved faster than Schwarzenberg thought possible and found the Austrian forces at Montereau, inflicting a heavy defeat on them. Napoleon defeated the Austrians again at Troyes, and Schwarzenberg continued to retreat. For the only time in the history of the revolutionary wars, there were now a series of popular rural risings in favour of the French government, as the peasants of the Champagne and the Ile de France harassed the allied troops.

Blucher, however, regrouped and resumed the offensive, matching Napoleon's audacity with his own. He headed not for Napoleon but for Paris. Napoleon caught up with him at Laon on 7 March and was defeated in a three-day battle. The tide had turned for the last time. Although Napoleon was still able to rout the allies at Rheims in a surprise attack, he could not prevent their entry into Paris on 30 March. He defeated Schwarzenberg again to the south of Paris but in the first days of April the marshals finally deserted him. Napoleon abdicated on 4 April.

Although military historians point to the inevitability of Napoleon's defeat, this was not the view from the allied trenches in the winter of 1814. As with Eugène in Milan a few weeks later, Napoleon's fall was political more than military. It was engineered from within. Those closest to Napoleon – Fouché, Talleyrand, the marshals, and the Senate – knew it was impossible to make him accept reasonable terms. To most of the allied commanders, however, the French guns seemed perilously close at times. Seen in this context – of Napoleon rampant rather than at bay – the allied declaration made at Chaumont to fight on for another nine years if necessary appears as an act of nervous defiance. When this is coupled with the willingness they showed – in virtually the same breath – to offer Napoleon peace, his throne and the borders of 1792, their unease is clear to see.

When Napoleon escaped from Elba on 1 March 1815 and began his last desperate bid for power, it was undertaken within a purely French context. The allied leaders in Vienna regarded his return as an attempt to renew the whole process of imperial expansion, and they may have been correct. Nevertheless, that was not how Napoleon announced his intentions. He declared himself ready to fight only to keep his throne, not to regain non-French territories. That he was able to gain any support at all in France, never mind to reassume control of the state so quickly, is a remarkable tribute to the legacy of his regime. Once again, his administrative machine gave him an army of 100 000 almost from thin air. As in 1814, the provinces did not respond as one to the change of regime, beyond the needs of conscription. The pattern was traditional, nonetheless. Burgundy, in the east, proved itself loyal to the regime, as it always had been. Its peasants had been among the few to benefit from the sale of *biens nationaux* in 1790, and its attachment to the Revolution was never in doubt since. In the west, the countryside showed signs of renewing the Vendéan revolt; the towns reacted to this as they had since 1793, by rallying to a non-royalist central government for protection.[34] There was similar unease throughout the Midi.

The only serious attempt to help Napoleon outside France came from Murat in Naples, but his advance on Rome was halted by the Austrians. His troops were easily scattered and he lost his throne. Outside the borders of France, the restoration of the Bourbons to Naples, in place of Murat, was probably the only important result of the 100 Days. Napoleon's defeat at Waterloo did not so much seal his fate as underline it. The allied forces in Belgium, under Wellington, were finally able to confront Napoleon's army in one place, at one time, and so defeat it. Even had Napoleon won at Waterloo in what Wellington himself admitted was 'the nearest run damned thing you ever saw in your life', defeat would have come later. The allied armies had not yet been demobilized and were on the march.

France stood alone in 1815. From the moment the process of French expansion began, with the invasion of Belgium in 1792, there had never been a pro-French popular rising of any significance anywhere in Europe except Poland and Ireland. So it stayed to the end. Liberated Polish prisoners of war flocked to Napoleon's colours – 325 fought at Waterloo and 260 more were raised *after* the battle[35] – while in Ireland the republican secret societies planned an insurrection that was stillborn at the news of Waterloo. These are poignant, but derisory, exceptions to prove the rule that the Grand Empire had left no abiding loyalties to its founder. This is far from the real legacy of Napoleonic hegemony, however. The system outlived the man, and the experience of Napoleonic rule, for better or worse, left a far more profound imprint on Europe than the legendary aura surrounding the ruler himself.

Notes

1 These figures drawn from Chandler, *Campaigns*, p. 807, by general consensus among historians, are the most reliable set of figures offered.
2 Chandler, *Campaigns*, pp. 852–3.
3 Berdhal, *Prussian Nobility*, pp. 107–38.
4 P. Paret, *Yorck and the Era of Prussian Reform, 1807–1815*, (Princeton, NJ, 1966) p. 139, note 58.
5 The title of a recent book by John Gagliardo, which traces the development of

this change throughout the late eighteenth century.

6 J.R. Seeley, *The Life and Times of Stein*, 3 vols (Cambridge, 1878) 2, pp. 519, 527.

7 H. Seton-Watson, *Nations and States*, (London, 1977) pp. 15–88.

8 Kraehe, *Metternich*, i, pp. 213–16.

9 Anderson, 'State-building in nineteenth century Nassau', pp. 241–4.

10 Esdaile, *Spanish Army*, pp. 166–7.

11 Ibid., pp. 176–8.

12 J. Herrero, *Los Origenes del pensamiento reaccionario español*, (Madrid, 1971) p. 385.

13 Ibid., pp. 393–4.

14 Ibid., p. 377.

15 R.P. Coppini, *Il Granducato di Toscano dagli 'anni francesi' all'Unita, Storia d'Italia*, (Turin, 1993) xiii, p. 165.

16 F. Della Peruta, 'War and society in Napoleonic Italy', in *Society and Politics in the Age of the Risorgimento*, eds. J.A. Davis and P. Ginsborg, (Cambridge, 1991) p. 48.

17 Antonielli, *Prefetti*, pp. 517–19.

18 Ibid., pp. 523–4.

19 Schama, *Patriots*, p. 636.

20 Ibid., pp. 642–3.

21 G.J. Renier, *Great Britain and the Establishment of the Kingdom of the Netherlands, 1813–1815*, (London and the Hague, 1930) pp. 132–53.

22 Verhaesen, *La Domination française*, iv, pp. 57–70.

23 Ibid., pp. 96–8.

24 Ibid., pp. 148–51.

25 Ibid., p. 152.

26 Renier, *Great Britain and the Netherlands*, pp. 236–8.

27 Ibid., p. 232.

28 M. Diefendorff, *Businessmen and Politics in the Rhineland, 1789–1834*, (Princeton, NJ, 1980) pp. 202–3.

29 Ibid., pp. 215–42.

30 D. Gates, *Spanish Ulcer: a History of the Peninsular War*, (London, 1986) pp. 459–67.

31 Chandler, *Campaigns*, pp. 955–6, 1003–4, for the accepted view. Even the usually critical Connelly praises this campaign: *Blundering*, pp. 195–8.

32 Connelly, *Blundering*, p. 197.

33 Chandler, *Campaigns*, p. 955.

34 See R.S. Alexander, *Bonapartism and Revolutionary Tradition in France: the Fedérés of 1815*, (Cambridge, 1991).

35 Biecki, 'L'effort militarie polonais', p. 163.

Conclusion

Europe at the fall of Napoleon: the nature of power

The leaders of the last coalition had learnt many hard lessons along the road to Paris. First among them, that the military value of 'the nation-in-arms' had nothing to do with the romanticized peasant risings envisaged by vom Stein and Stadion, nor with the Spanish guerrilla. Rather, the future lay with Napoleonic conscription, and with states able to create the sort of army which was still defying the allies even as the abdication was signed at Fontainebleau. The campaign of 1814 was a final reminder of the power of the revolutionary-Napoleonic state. It proved, if proof were still needed, that the old order simply could not be restored, because it could not hope to survive. The campaigns in northern France, Italy and the Pyrenees were not mere Pyrrhic victories for the Grande Armée, they were a tribute to the new state and a warning to any who rejected reform along Napoleonic lines. Henceforth, governments would have to take this course at whatever the cost in terms of proven popular resentment of the new state. After 1815, Europe enjoyed a century of relative peace, singular in its history, but it was ushered in with a clear realization that power rested, literally, with the big battalions. The trick was how to acquire them, as Napoleon had shown.

The last phase of the war foreshadowed the emergence of Britain as the only European state able to fill the void left by the fall of the Napoleonic Empire. Her modern, highly sophisticated economy had been harnessed by the state for the war effort through the tax reforms of Pitt and Addison until, by 1814, Britain was capable of fielding armies as large as those of her continental allies as well as financing another half a million coalition troops and maintaining the Royal Navy which, at its height in 1810, was a juggernaut of 144 000 men and nearly 150 warships in northern Europe alone.[1] The Royal Navy had successfully blockaded the great ports of western Europe; it ferried arms, munitions and gold to the allies from the Baltic to the Aegean; it linked together all the disparate centres of resistance to Napoleon. Its warships raided the coasts of Italy and Croatia incessantly. Its Royal Marines were everywhere and nowhere, their under-sung exploits at least a match for those of Murat's hussars or the Old Guard. British naval power had a long history prior to the Napoleonic wars, but the emergence of Britain as a conventional military power was unprecedented. In the course of the Peninsular War, an army was forged which proved itself to be the only force in Europe truly capable of outfighting first-class French troops. By 1814, the British army had expanded in quantity as well as quality.

The magnitude of her power allowed Britain to get her way over virtually every issue she felt strongly about: the annexation of Belgium by the Dutch; the restoration of the Bourbons in France; her retention of most of the colonies captured from the French and the Dutch. However, British interests, although intense where they existed, were very limited in continental Europe. By 1822 she had virtually withdrawn from European affairs.

The Congress of Vienna created a state system that was meant first and foremost to contain France, thereby protecting the rest of Europe from future military aggression and revolutionary upheaval. The peacemakers saw Napoleon as the heir of the French Revolution. His suppression of parliamentary life, the imposition of stifling censorship and his dynastic trappings were all lost on them. To the powerbrokers of Vienna, the Napoleonic Empire was the most formidable of the revolutionary regimes, driving its doctrines forward with maximum force. Understanding the revoltionary decade in its own terms was simply incongruous to them.

Based on the assumption that Napoleon incarnated the Revolution, allied policy entailed dismantling his satellite states. However, the new state system could not really resemble the old order, with it mass of small weak states which the French had found so easy to overrun. In 1814, Metternich might possibly have realized the dream he had cherished until 1809 when, together with Stadion, he had risked so much to restore the small German states. Instead, he turned to the models and lessons Napoleon had unwittingly taught him in the intervening years. The Congress expanded the Kingdom of the Netherlands, which received Belgium, and Piedmont-Sardinia which annexed Genoa. In contrast to Napoleon's approach to territorial readjustments, no new thrones were created in 1814–15. Yet this difference with the Napoleonic state system should not obscure the deeper reality. The principle of his state system was continued after his fall. The power vacuum of the old order – literally the geographic space in western and central Germany between France and the three eastern powers – was filled with states similar in size and strength to those Napoleon had created between 1803 and 1807 as buffers against Austria and Russia. In diplomatic and military terms the crucial differences with the Napoleonic order were that these states were no longer controlled by one superpower, but were under the influence of two relatively effective regional powers: Austria, alone, in Italy and in partnership with Prussia in Germany. In the new order of things these states remained satellites, but were now meant to point west to contain France, rather than east. To this end, the states of the Confederation of the Rhine survived more or less as Napoleon had shaped them.

Napoleonic imperialism: the legacy of French cultural nationalism

The imperial bureaucracy rarely showed respect for indigenous cultures. It never questioned the necessity or desirability of replacing what it found with French culture and Napoleonic government. Napoleonic administrators spoke of their *administrés* as 'primitive', 'barbaric' or, at the very least, 'rustic'. The reports of the *auditeurs* in Illyria refer openly and repeatedly to the 'ignorance' and 'stupidity' of the local clergy, Catholic and Orthodox alike, sentiments also expressed by officials in the Italian departments. They felt this ignorance had also infected the mass of the people for, however much the imperial officials loathed the clergy, they were too exposed to its power – and in real danger from its wrath – ever to doubt the central place of the Church in society. They needed the help of the Church everywhere, and life was easier when this happened. Those bishops and priests who preached obedience, especially to conscription, were highly prized. The Bishop of Vannes, in Brittany, was notable among them.[2] When set in an imperial context, such examples appear as tiny islands of co-operation in the stormy sea of relations between the Church and the Empire. In the convulsed conditions of Josephist Spain, the Church came very close to being 'demonized' by the regime and its collaborators. It is no coincidence that it was an *afrancesado*, Joseph's minister J.A. Llorente, who wrote a history of the Spanish Inquisition that defined its image for generations to come as a fanatical, bloodthirsty instrument of intolerance and superstition.

Many of these views, rooted as they are in an innate sense of superiority, often were shared by British officers serving in these same areas. They, too, took a disdainful view of their Spanish, Portuguese and Sicilian allies, and of the Dutch. Perhaps one of the greatest ironies of the long struggle between Britain and Napoleonic France is that both saw themselves as the sole champions of a common civilization. Whatever their perceptions of each other, the two arch-enemies shared a contempt for the rest of Europe.

For the French who, unlike the British, actually ruled large parts of the continent, the backwardness fostered by the Church had to be confronted by more than institutional reforms. It is a remarkable sign of how deeply the values of the Revolution had penetrated the young *auditeurs* that even those of noble origins became ferocious opponents of seigneurialism and, therefore, champions of peasant emancipation. To find such views flowing constantly from the pens of young nobles is a powerful indication that a new generation of truly 'Napoleonic' administrators was being forged, especially on the embattled fringes of the Empire.

Their arrogance, energy and enthusiasm did not blind the *auditeurs* to the scale of the task before them and this, too, is an important difference with earlier generations of enlightened reformers of the *ancien régime* and the revolutionaries of the 1790s. Hardened by the violence they often faced, as well as by their constant conflicts with the military, the *auditeurs* knew how isolated and detested French rule was. They put their ultimate faith in education. The *auditeurs* were buried under the demands of conscription, harassed by the brigandage it provoked and constantly starved of money by the demands of the war, but they struggled to create local schools and *lycées* and, above all, to remove education from the hands of the clergy. Behind the battalions of the Grande Armée another, truly epic battle was fought, between the parish clergy and the new secular state. It was not over territory, but for the minds of the people of western Europe. Usually, their ambitious plans came to nothing. In most of rural Europe, France included, there were too few educated laymen or 'enlightened' clergy to staff a mass education system and too little funding to support such projects.

A poignant example of all the problems facing the *auditeurs* is that of de Viefville des Essars, in the department of the Serge, in the Pyrenean mountains of Catalonia in northern Spain. Viefville was not even able to occupy Puigcerda, his prefecture, for eight months, because of guerrilla activity. Once there, he suffered a nervous breakdown but recovered, remained at his post and was able to carry out some useful, if limited reforms within the narrow confines of the few small towns he controlled. Streets were paved, dykes and canals were reinforced, public health improved by the introduction of regular refuse collection and better sewage, but his ambitions for a better hospital for Puigcerda came to little for lack of money. Outside his prefecture, the French administration hardly existed and was greatly compromised by the demands of war. He called the effects of military occupation 'a vicious circle that ruins the inhabitants, provokes complaints and charged emotions, and discredits the civil authorities in the eyes of the people'.[3] There was much that was well intentioned in French imperialism, and posterity must admire these aspirations. Nevertheless, the whole enterprise was inspired by cultural arrogance and its ultimate result was to confirm – indeed, to strengthen – reciprocal prejudices.

The policy of 'Frenchification' was not confined to the masses. The French were determined to create a European elite in their own image, but many of those 'targeted' for assimilation regarded it as conscription applied to the intelligentsia. *Auditeurs* from the Roman departments had to be pressed into service, and even in areas long part of the Empire, such as Piedmont, young nobles like Cesare Balbo bitterly resented being 'called up' to the Council of State, although Balbo, in particular, went on to serve his

French masters well. Resentment was felt even more deeply among many Italian, Rhenish and Dutch notables, whose sons were taken to select *lycées* in France at an even younger age than the *auditeurs*, with the express purpose of imbuing them with French culture. This was all perceived by those affected as a particularly tyrannical form of cultural imperialism. Their reluctance to serve was shared by the majority of the old French nobility. They were put under considerably less pressure to enter public life than non-French aristocracies, and responded, in the main, by 'opting out'.[4] Within France, the regime felt secure enough to ignore such elements, but it could not afford to do so elsewhere.

For the peoples of the Napoleonic Empire, the French and their local supporters were still Godless murderers; for the imperial bureaucrats and soldiers, the European masses remained savages or bumpkins. These were not attitudes born of ignorance, but of the closest association. Familiarity often bred contempt. The officers and men of the Grande Armée travelled widely and constantly across western and central Europe, but this did nothing to dampen their sense of superiority; rather, it sharpened their prejudices. In his memoirs, General de Rocca recounts his own impressions of the German and Spanish peasantries, both of which he saw at close hand:

> As regards learning and the improvement of social customs, Spain was a century behind the rest of Europe ... the Spaniards were much given to indolence and their government was corrupt and disorderly, the inevitable results of a long lived despotism: their government, although arbitrary, had none of the militaristic, absolutist power which existed in Germany, where the constant submission of one and all to the orders of one man incessantly compromised individuality.[5]

His disdain for both the Germans and the Spaniards is obvious: he saw the former as little more than downtrodden, mindless robots, the victims of reactionary – if efficient – despotism; the latter were lazy, superstitious and backward, but ferocious when roused. Implicit here is a French sense of being superior to both, based on the French image of themselves as the heirs and interpreters of the Enlightenment at its best. Their better grasp of logic and reason, they felt, made them better organized and less religious than the Spanish, but freer and more individualistic than the Germans.

De Rocca's views are important because they are typical. Contact with the other peoples of Europe only reinforced the conviction that the Enlightenment and the Revolution had made France a beacon of civilization in a dark world. This sense of superiority and isolation come together in the words of the wife of an *auditeur*, Madame Pierre Roederer, whose husband was the prefect of the Trasimeno, one of the departments of the ex-Papal States. While expecting her second child, she wrote to her father-in-law, 'I swear to you that Spoleto [the prefecture] is not where I want to have him, more than anything, I want my son to be utterly French.'[6] Unlike her husband, Madame Roederer spoke Italian well and had many friends in the area, but France was still the centre of the universe, the only place fit to bring up a child.

When such attitudes are set beside the reciprocal reluctance of Italian or Dutch families to send their sons to France as students or *auditeurs*, imperial integration had made no progress at a human level. The most enduring legacy of the Napoleonic Empire was the divisions it reinforced and in some cases created in European society. The Revolution drove a wedge through the mosaic of animosities of the *ancien régime*. The Empire perpetuated them, despite its best efforts.

Napoleonic rule: the legacy of institutions

The key to understanding the relative importance of the Napoleonic legacy in Europe, is the concept of the Empire as divided into an inner and an outer fringe. In this respect, Napoleonic rule created two Europes, with a third, vast, utterly non-Napoleonic Europe beyond them.

Beyond the inner and outer empires were vast regions of Europe where the Napoleonic adventure was of only marginal importance and often none at all. Even at its height, the Napoleonic Empire was not synomymous with the whole of Europe. Although it contained 80 million at its zenith, over 100 million Europeans escaped its influence almost entirely. For a brief period, between 1800 and 1812, France dominated western and central Europe, although even this only became clear to contemporaries by 1805. It must never be forgotten that the Peace of Tilist was a compromise, a recognition by Napoleon and Alexander that Europe was to be shared by them, and then only after – and if – Britain could be humbled. The Napoleonic Empire always shared the field with Russia and Britain. It was never the sole arbiter of Europe.

In the outer empire, Napoleonic rule was traumatic and destabilizing. It was ephemeral, in that it left few institutional traces, yet profound in the aversion to the Napoleonic state it implanted at so many levels of society. The duration of French rule in any given part of Europe can be a useful indication of the degree to which it influenced political and administrative structures. However, a short but brutal experience of Napoleonic hegemony could produce influences equally profound and enduring, if of a different, more subjective character. Spain is the classic example of this process, but other cases can be set beside it, notably the Illyrian provinces. Nor were such reactions confined to socially and economically backward areas. The Hansa ports emerged from the Napoleonic period with a deep aversion to the Napoleonic code and the whole concept of strong, centralized government. Significantly, in the 1840s, the Senate of Hamburg chose to model its new police force on the London Metropolitans, not the French Gendarmerie. The outer empire was a disastrous blend of regions whose social, economic and political structures were retarded in comparison with those of France, and those which were well ahead of the imperial power in these respects.

Within the inner empire – France, western Germany, northern Italy and the Low Countries – the Napoleonic system left a powerful institutional heritage. It became the breeding ground of the professional administrators, just as the lands of the outer empire became their proving ground. The defeat and exile of Napoleon did not spell the end of his system, far from it. A whole generation of administrators, foes as well as friends, had grown up in awe of his bureaucracy, just as a generation of soldiers marvelled at the prowess of the Grande Armée. The aura of military invincibility was fading even before 1812 but that of administrative perfection lives on to this day in continental western Europe. Standards of efficiency were set by the imperial administration which the successor states of the inner empire were expected to meet.

The maintenance of civil order and the protection of property were the most basic of these expectations. Competent, effective policing had won the French co-operation – if not always friendship – even in soil as unpromising as Portugal, Spain and Calabria. Where good order had become a way of life by 1814 – as it had over most of the inner empire – restored governments were expected to meet French standards. Where they failed to do so, as in those parts of the Papal States formerly attached to the Kingdom of Italy, the restored regimes lost support.[7] Where such expectations were met, the restoration could endure many other tensions and still prove stable, as in the Prussian Rhineland.[8] Here, the French Criminal Code, retained by the Prussians, was regarded as a guarantee of civil equality by propertied Rhinelanders, to the point that it was seen as a feasible substitute for a constitution. By the 1840s, Prussian jurists were assimilating it into their own Code; in 1851, Prussia adopted it in full, finally translating it into German.[9] The Code had only been in force since 1810, but its impact went far deeper than the period of French rule, a reminder that time is not always the surest guide to assessing the influence of French rule. It also serves as a reminder of the profound differences within European regions, as they are now perceived: just as the Code was embraced in some parts of the Rhineland, it was abhorred in others, such as Mainz – previously the preserve of an enlightened prince-bishop – and in the Hansa ports.

Nevertheless, the true test of the strength and depth of the Napoleonic legacy was justice and policing. Good policing was the means to a end, not the end itself, however. Within the framework it provided, governments were now expected to raise revenue by an equitable system of taxation, and to administer justice through a professional magistracy, in a cheap, accessible, unified hierarchy of courts, through codified law, based on the concept of judicial equality. By 1814, a generation of legists had been formed within the inner empire, whose whole experience was with the Code Napoleon. The contours of the 'inner' and 'outer' empires acquired their lasting importance in this sphere: the division was between those core areas –

stretching from eastern France to west-central Germany, and from northern Italy to the Dutch coast – which became habituated to Napoleonic centralization, and another Europe, less influenced by these norms. It is a division that reasserts itself whenever the role of administrative and legal institutions assumes a central place in European politics. The true heart of Napoleon's Empire was a version of a 'middle kingdom', at the crossroads of Europe, more than a pure extension of France itself. His realm resembled the original inheritance of Charles V, more than of Louis XI, of Lothar, more than Charlemagne, when reduced to the effectiveness of his rule or the durability of its legacy.

The bitter legacy: an elitist empire

The Congress of Vienna could not restore the essence of the old order where the Napoleonic regime had been efficient, rather than destablizing, and it is here that its lasting influence is most immediately clear. States not only had to be viable in diplomatic and military terms; internally, governments also had to be strong enough, financially, to provide effective policing and administration if they hoped to be popular. Thus, the world of the small, weak but undemanding states of the Holy Roman Empire did not reappear: a world was lost in Germany. In Italy, the restored states remained weak for the most part, and fell prey to internal unrest. There were crucial exceptions in northern Italy, however, where Austria reabsorbed not only Lombardy but also Venetia, and in the expanded territories of the House of Savoy. The Austrians maintained much of the powerful administrative machinery Eugène had left them. In Piedmont-Sardinia, as in Spain, the newly restored rulers initiated a fierce, regressive policy of integral restoration. Yet even in these bastions of reaction the practices, institutions and in many cases even the men of the Napoleonic period reasserted their usefulness in the course of the 1820s and 1830s.

Although many liberals were alienated by the restorations of 1814, they were few in number outside France: their attempted revolutions almost always failed but even when they did not, liberal demands were increasingly of a purely political, rather than an administrative nature. Only the first of these revolutions, those of 1820 in Naples, Piedmont and Spain, sought administrative reform as well as constitutions based on that of 1812 in Cadiz. Thereafter the more practical demands of the rebels were met, if gradually, as the experience of the inner empire reasserted itself. Behind the sound and fury of the political revolutions of the early nineteenth century an unspoken and therefore often underrated consensus had developed among radicals, liberals and reactionaries alike all over western Europe about the nature of the state. Whatever their political complexion, the regimes of western Europe after 1814 were dominated by a new increasingly powerful caste of professional bureaucrats. Within their separate states they went on to create strikingly similar administrative and judicial structures.

Even the most popular aspects of Napoleonic rule were the preserve of an elite, however. It must never be forgotten that, in so far as their voices can be heard at all, the common people of Europe had different priorities and preoccupations from those of the propertied classes. Theirs had not been 'the empire of the professionals', but of the recruiting sergeant and the cancelled Holy Day. Napoleonic rule left very deep scars in the body of Europe, all the more profound for being less tangible than the ideological divisions within the educated, propertied elites. The Napoleonic state embodied all those things the common people of western Europe resented and resisted when the occasion presented itself. Their antipathy reached beyond material burdens such as mass conscription and heavy taxation which were eased in the long years of peace after 1814. Until more long-term, structural changes such as industrialization and urbanization altered the nature of west European society almost beyond recognition, the modern state was distrusted and detested for its secular character, its remoteness and its very professionalism. The restoration which occurred in 1814 was not what the counter-revolution had struggled for. Neither the Spanish *partidas* nor the *shutzen* of the Tyrol fought for centralization, but this was what their adored, now restored rulers pressed upon them. The Roman clergy and conservative German intellectuals had not endured exile in the name of the modern secular state, but their cherished moral and political order never returned.

The state was the practical expression of an alien, elite culture. Writing of the enlightened absolutists of the generation immediately preceding the Napoleonic era, one historian has pointed directly to the way in which the Enlightenment widened the gap between the culture of the educated classes and that of the common people.[10] Napoleonic rule made the educated into the administrative classes and helped to turn cultural estrangement into a yawning chasm between the state and the citizen.

Nations and states

Napoleonic rule was not conducive to the evolution of nationalism, at least as it is now understood. Resistance to French imperialism was strongest in exactly those states where a sense of national identity was irrevocably bound up with the ideologies and institutions of the old order – Britain, Spain and Portugal – just as it strengthened it within France itself. Only in the very exceptional cases of Poland and Ireland did nationalist aspirations help the French cause.

Elsewhere much has been made of the experience of the Kingdoms of Westphalia and Italy for the development of German and Italian nationalism, respectively. For the masses, the truth is probably the exact reverse.

The nation-state had become inseparable from the centralized state and, as such, a living nightmare. It was the very fact that most nationalists within the political classes also linked the two together that made nationalism appalling to so many of those who had resisted – or sullenly resented – Napoleon. Where modern nationalism was perceived at all, it was generally abhorred by the masses as well as their more conservative rulers. Nor was the 'nationalism' of conservative thinkers such as Fichte or Gentz even aimed at political unification. They had older, far subtler goals than those of modern nationalists, which were sophisticated enough to absorb political diversity into a wider and looser sense of cultural identity. The richness of the political culture they upheld – and the sad fact that it is so elusive to the contemporary mind – stands as a stinging condemnation of the cruder political culture of modern Europe in the twentieth century.

The struggle against Napoleon was one of diversity against standardization, of tradition against innovation, of dynastic loyalty against usurpation. It was a popular struggle, uniting every level of society, but it was about preserving the past, a past in which the 'nation-state' had no part. Conversely, the fall of the Empire revealed the supra-national character of the 'empire of the professionals'. The 'inner empire' was more secure on the Rhine than in Roussillon; it had more support in Brussels than in Bordeaux. As the Vendée prepared to rise again, the Piedmontese departments submitted to conscription. Clearly, the heartland of the Empire was not synonymous with France or the French people, but with where and among whom the Napoleonic system of government was accepted. This system rested on a sense of French cultural superiority, but it was open to all, and hoped to draw all to it. Napoleon worked outwards, from the basis of a national culture, but it was an elite culture, alien to most French people, and it was not meant to remain the sole preserve of the French. By the standards of later generations, Napoleon was not a nationalist. He was far too realistic.

Napoleon: the paradoxes of success

Napoleon has cast a shadow over these pages, but his personality has been absent, and this is fitting, in the search for the contemporary reality of his Empire. The cult of his personality was reserved for the Grande Armée and the Council of State. His manner of ruling was quite the reverse of the Romantic image that grew up around the defeated radicals of the nineteenth century. It sought to embody the impersonal, tightly regulated 'well-ordered police state' so idealized in the eighteenth century.

Napoleon stamped his will and his name on his political world, but he chose to be known by his deeds, rather than by his personality. Among his contemporaries, he succeeded to a degree more than he wanted to. On the night of 22–23 October 1812, General Malet spread the rumour in Paris that Napoleon had died in Russia. Malet then proclaimed himself the leader of a provisional government. He was arrested within hours. The plot was farcical in itself, but it is revealing of the true nature of the regime, as those who dealt with Malet – Savary, the Minister of Police-Générale and the Councillors of State, under the chairmanship of Cambacérès – had no way of knowing if the rumour was true. They continued at their posts, loyal to the regime and unruffled by the prospect that Napoleon might, indeed, be dead. Yet they did not proclaim the King of Rome as Emperor. They just carried on; the ultimate leadership of the state had become an irrelevance, as the Empire could 'fly on auto pilot'.

Napoleon suddenly sensed his own and his dynasty's irrelevance to the imperial system. On his return to Paris, he tried to set the apex of government on a more personal and dynastic basis: in February 1813, an official regency was proclaimed under Marie-Louise, to control the central government during his absence on campaign; her advisory council was composed of the Princes of the Blood and the dignitaries of the Court. In its last months, Napoleon intended the Empire to be ruled in a wholly different manner than hitherto. It was a retreat from professionalism, into the world of *ancien régime* personal monarchy, and it came too late: when the marshals and the Senate betrayed him, the system marched on, without him. The veterans of the Imperial Guard wept at Fontainebleau as he took his leave of them, but the prefects, ministers and magistrates carried on. This was the true extent of Napoleon's personal power, and the victory of his administrative policy: he sought solidity, and he got it.

Napoleon had already proved that the Empire and its goals were more important than his extended family, if not his own son. His brothers were made kings only as a last resort, and sacked with little ceremony: Louis was ejected from his throne in 1810; Joseph followed him in 1813. In 1814, it was his turn. Napoleon need not have divorced Josephine to produce an heir; he already had one in the Council of State. The force of a mind and a personality as strong as Napoleon's could not, in the final analysis, destroy the powerful governing edifice he helped to create. Overt opposition could be crushed, the personnel of the state could be purged, but the system itself proved intractable.

War is rightly regarded as the cardinal influence on the history of Napoleonic Europe; wars created and fuelled the Empire. Yet, paradoxically, the ceaseless campaigning made Napoleon an absentee monarch. If few decisions could be taken without him, the formation of policy and, above all, its implementation, were left to the administrative machine. Foreign war made the Empire into a more thoroughly 'civilian state' than it might otherwise have been. To shift the historical emphasis from the military to the administrative aspects of the Napoleonic Empire, is to reduce the presence of the man himself. Ironically, if predictably, his direct influence was strongest in the years of comparative peace before 1805, when the foundations of the regime were laid. Its initial framework bore his mark, although, because he was seldom a true innovator, the Napoleonic state cannot be said to incarnate the man to the same degree as the army. After 1805, circumstances forced Napoleon to let the state run itself most of the time. It did exactly that, and went on doing so after 1814. Chateaubriand, ever the sharpest thorn in Napoleon's side during his rule, felt himself hounded by the Napoleonic state after the fall the Napoleon. In his pamphlet, *De la Monarchie selon la Charte*, in 1816, Chateaubriand warned of the dangers and incompatibilities of retaining the professional bureaucracy of the Empire under a constitutional regime. He also discerned how the professional bureaucrats had convinced the new regime to let them carry on by making Louis XVIII and the allies believe 'there must be no purges; the royalists are incompetents'.[11] Chateaubriand held this to be another manifestation of Napoleonic myth-making. Were it so, it has proved the most durable and important part of the myth. The Bourbons – and, eventually, most of the other restored regimes – did not listen to advice of the type offered by Chateaubriand. The bureaucrats stayed, and their descendants remain at the heart of Europe to this day.

None of this detracts from the authoritarian nature of the regime, nor from the remarkable genius of the man himself, yet the nature of both has often been misunderstood. Napoleon did not run the Empire alone, nor was it run capriciously: quite the reverse. The imperial bureaucracy was rigid, chauvinistic and often ruthless, but it was determinedly civilian in character and dedicated to high, well-defined professional standards. The Empire was certainly not meant to be a 'family enterprise', nor did it really become so. Chateaubriand was right in claiming, in the immediate aftermath of the wars, that 'our present plight is the result of Napoleonic slavery: it left us only an aptitude for the yoke'.[12] Yet he did not invent the yoke, nor administer its use.

Napoleon has been derided as a destroyer by his critics, from Chateaubriand to the present day, his genius portrayed as essentially impulsive. The results of his rule give credence to this, certainly in the outer Empire. Nevertheless, the creation of the Empire reveals a more nuanced mind. Napoleon respected legitimacy; he knew its power. Old ruling houses were deposed or degraded only with great reluctance: Savoy, the Spanish and Neapolitan Bourbons were deposed only after all else had failed; the Hohenzollerns were humbled after gross treachery. Napoleon was not alone in breaking his word, although he often took longer to take ultimate revenge than his rivals. Caution gave way to panic, and then to action, sometimes brilliantly judged, as in 1800 or 1805; at other times, with great tactical skill but muddled thinking in the long term, as in 1808–09; finally, with grave error, after 1812. Only after 1812 did Napoleon truly abandon caution and reject all offers of accommodation.

Perhaps the gravest legacy of the Revolution that Napoleon carried with him was its diplomacy. The ideological madness of the Girondins and the crude cynicism of the Directory blinded the courts of Europe to many of the changes wrought by Talleyrand, and approved by Napoleon. Napoleon's regard for legitimacy was not believed by many. Had it been, Francis II would not have been misled into a war in 1809, which ended, not in the destruction and dismemberment of the Habsburg monarchy, but by Napoleon's marriage to Marie-Louise.

This is a long way from the concept of the empire as an autocracy. It is further still from the Romantic image of the 'man of destiny'. Napoleon's response to the Malet affair reveals the reality of Empire to have been anything but an autocracy. His image as the Romantic hero came after the reality of his rule: until he wrote his memoirs on St Helena, Napoleon never sought to portray himself in so anti-establishment a light. The Court paintings reflect more reality than Napoleon knew, depicting him as a remote figure, surrounded either by the formal trappings of authority, or at the head of his troops – on remote foreign fields. This was, indeed, an accurate image of his place in the regime.

There was a strong element of revolutionary radicalism in the regime, but not of the kind conjured by Stendhal after 1814. Napoleon feared the old demons of counter-revolution within his realm, and fought them with as much determination as the Jacobins. If he was less ruthless, it was only because he was in a stronger position than the Committee of Public Safety. The police and the Gendarmerie remained the preserve of ex-Terrorists; most ex-nobles were confined to *mairies*, the army or the diplomatic corps. Monasteries and convents were closed, clergy hounded and gaoled, a Pope imprisoned. Napoleon died an excommunicate: to Catholic Europe – most of Europe – he was but another Robespierre. The Napoleonic Empire showed just how close enlightened absolutism and the Terror actually were. Much of Napoleon's genius lay in blending the two.

In exile, Napoleon soon evolved into the Prester John of revolutionary radicalism. He reinvented himself in his memoirs and these, perhaps, are the real triumph of his personal talents. The official style of the Empire had been neo-classical, formalist and studied. Yet, as his meetings with Goethe show, Napoleon was very sensitive to the cultural currents of Romanticism, so at odds with the official culture he promoted. On St Helena, this shrewd cultural awareness led to the *volte face* of the memoirs. Their style, in itself, signifies a remarkable awareness by the author, of the tastes and sensibilities of the audience he had targeted. Napoleon revamped his career to appeal to a new age in a triumph of creative cynicism. Napoleon did not extinguish the Revolution, but saved it from stagnating and pushed it forward into Europe. Napoleon portrayed himself as the 'natural arbiter between kings and peoples', as the purveyor, as well as the heir, of the Revolution. There is more than an element of truth in his assertion that the Empire fought privilege in the cause of equality, but it was repackaged for a new generation in the language of liberalism. The ultimate goal of the Napoleonic state had been to extend liberty: the Code enshrined personal liberty; political liberty would grow from it, in time.

Napoleon was believed by many; his life and deeds became accessible to post-1814 malcontents. He was venerated by a younger generation who had not known the Empire at first hand, as well as by the ageing veterans of the Guard, and, as Napoleon well knew, the former were more valuable recruits than the latter, for this particular campaign. As Jean Tulard has said, 'the greatest of Napoleon's victories was over his detractors. It was won at St Helena, where the ogre became God.'[13] When his remains were returned to France in 1840, the crowds behind the official cortege were a coalition of the Old Guard and students. Napoleon was injecting younger blood into his system, to the end. This was his final transfusion, and it gave him prolonged life. Beyond the myth, another heritage survived throughout Europe, greyer, but stronger than the heroic legend, hated and admired: the modern state.

Notes

1 P. Mackesy, 'Strategic problems of the British war effort', in H.T. Dickinson, *Britain and the French Revolution*, (London, 1979) pp. 152–3.

2 Forrest, *Conscripts*, pp. 220–3.

3 J. Mercader-Riba, *Puigcerda, capital del department del Serge*, (Barcelona, 1971) pp. 18–19.

4 Ellis, 'Napoleonic elites', pp. 240–1.

5 M. de Rocca, *Mémoires sur la guerre des français en Espagne*, (Paris, 1814) p. 43.

6 ANP, Archives Privées, Fonds Roederer, 29–AP–15, Mme. P. Roederer to Louis Roederer, undated, (*c*.Dec 1812–Jan 1814).

7 S.C. Hughes, *Crime, Disorder and the Risorgimento. The Politics of Policing in Bologna*, (Cambridge, 1994).

8 Diefendorff, *Businessmen and Politics*.

9 J. Engelbrecht, 'The French Model and German Society: the impact of the Code Pénal on the Rhineland', paper given to Coloque International: Révolutions et Justice pénale en Europe, (1780–1830), Louvain-la-Neuve/Namur, Belgium, 23–25 November 1995.

10 D. Beales, 'Social forces and enlightened policies', in *Enlightened Absolutism. Reform and Reformers in Later Eighteenth Century Europe*, ed. H.M. Scott (London, 1990) pp. 37–53.

11 'De la Monarchie selon la Charte', in *Chateaubriand, Grands écrits politiques*, ed. J–P. Clément, 2 vols (1993, Paris) ii, pp. 386–7.

12 Chateaubriand, *Napoléon*, p. 412.

13 *Napoléon à Sainte-Hélène*, ed. J. Tulard (Paris, 1981) p. 6.

Select bibliography

The following bibliography makes no pretence to comprehensiveness. It covers only those areas which fell within the sphere of Napoleonic influence, and so takes no account of the rich literature of the British Isles, Russia, Scandinavia or the Balkans for the Napoleonic period. It concentrates on three categories of contribution to the subject: literature in English, recent literature and enduring works of a seminal character. It should be noted that truly irreplaceable works [*] have been included in French. This, in itself, might serve as a reminder to the serious student of how important is the knowledge of foreign languages for the study of Napoleonic Europe. The notes to the text make clear that *Europe under Napoleon* rests, of necessity, almost entirely on non-anglophone scholarship, despite the growth of anglophone studies of the period, many of the highest quality.

Works of reference

D. Chandler, *Dictionary of the Napoleonic Wars*, (London, 1979).
O. Connelly, ed., *Historical Dictionary of Napoleonic France*, (Westport, CT, 1985).
C. Emsley, *The Longman Companion to Napoleonic Europe*, (London and New York, 1993).
*J. Tulard, ed., *Dictionnaire Napoleon*, (Paris, 1987).

General works on Napoleonic Europe

O. Connelly, *The Epoch of Napoleon*, (New York, 1972).
O. Connelly, *French Revolution/Napoleonic Era*, (New York, 1979).
O. Connelly, *Napoleon's Satellite Kingdoms*, (New York, 1965).
F. Crouzet, 'Wars, blockade and economic change in Europe, 1792–1815',

Journal of Economic History, 24 (1964).

G. Ellis, *The Napoleonic Empire*, (London, 1991).

C.J. Esdaile, *The Wars of Napoleon*, (London, 1995).

C.J. Esdaile, 'The Napoleonic period: some thoughts on recent historiography', *European History Quarterly*, 23 (1993).

P. Geyl, ed., *Napoleon: For and Against*, (Eng. trans., London, 1949).

R.B. Jones, *Napoleon. Man and Myth*, (London, 1977).

F. Markham, *Napoleon*, (London, 1963).

G. Lefebvre, *Napoleon*, 2 vols (Eng. trans., London, 1969 and 1974).

P.W. Schroeder, *The Transformation of European Politics, 1763–1848*, (Oxford, 1994).

J. Tulard, *Napoleon: the Myth of the Saviour*, (Eng. trans., London, 1984) – Readers should note that this translation is unreliable, and are advised to use the original *French edition, (Paris, 1977).

S.J. Woolf, *Napoleon's Integration of Europe*, (London, 1991).

D.G. Wright, *Napoleon and Europe*, (London, 1984).

The Napoleonic wars: general works

J-P. Bertaud, 'Napoleon's officers', *Past and Present*, 112 (1986).

G. Best, *War and Society in Revolutionary Europe, 1770–1830*, (London, 1982).

T.C.W. Blanning, *The Origins of the French Revolutionary Wars*, (London, 1986).

A.S.K. Brown, *The Anatomy of Glory: Napoleon and his Guard*, (London, 1962).

D. Chandler, *The Campaigns of Napoleon: the Mind and Method of History's Greatest Soldier*, (London, 1966).

D. Chandler, *Dictionary of the Napoleonic Wars*, (London, 1979).

D. Chandler, ed., *Napoleon's Marshals*, (New York, 1987).

O. Connelly, *Blundering to Glory: Napoleon's Military Campaigns*, (Wilmington, DE, 1988).

J.R. Elting, *Swords Around a Throne: Napoleon's Grande Armée*, (New York, 1988).

M. Glover, *Warfare in the Age of Bonaparte*, (London, 1980).

G. Jeffrey, *Tactics and Grand Tactics of the Napoleonic Wars*, (New York, 1982).

*H. Lachouque, *Napoléon et la Garde Impériale*, (Paris, 1957).

J.A. Lynn, 'Toward an army of honour: the moral evolution of the French army, 1789–1815', *French Historical Studies*, 16 (1989).

*J. Morvan, *Le Soldat impérial*, 2 vols (Paris, 1904).

G. Rothenberg, *The Art of Warfare in the Age of Napoleon*, (London, 1977).

Napoleonic France

R.S. Alexander, *Bonapartism and the Revolutionary Tradition in France. The Fédérés of 1815*, (Cambridge, 1991).

R.S. Alexander, 'The Fédérés of Dijon in 1815', *Historical Journal*, 30 (1987).

E.A. Arnold, *Fouché, Napoleon and the General Police*, (Washington, DC, 1979).

E.A. Arnold, 'Some observations on the French opposition to Napoleonic conscription, 1804–1806', *French Historical Studies*, 4 (1966).

L. Bergeron, *France under Napoleon*, (Eng. trans., Princeton, NJ, 1981).

*J-P. Bertaud, *Bonaparte Prend le Pouvoir*, (Paris, 1987).

*F. Bluche, *Le Bonapartism. Aux origines de la droite autoritaire, 1800–1850*, (Paris, 1980).

C.H. Church, *Revolution and Red Tape: the French ministerial bureaucracy, 1770–1850*, (Oxford, 1981).

I. Collins, *Napoleon and his Parliaments*, 1800–1815, (London, 1979).

I. Collins, *Napoleon, First Consul and Emperor of the French*, (Historical Association pamphlet, 1986).

G. Ellis, *Napoleon's Continental Blockade: the Case of Alsace*, (Oxford, 1981).

G. Ellis, 'Rhine and Loire: Napoleonic elites and social order', in *Beyond the Terror*, eds. G. Lewis and C.M. Lucas, (Cambridge, 1983).

C. Emsley, 'Policing the streets of early nineteenth century Paris', *French Historical Studies*, 1 (1987).

M.P. Fitzsimmons, *The Parisian Order of Barristers and the French Revolution*, (Cambridge, MA, 1987).

A. Forrest, *Conscripts and Deserters: the French army and society during the Revolution and Empire*, (Oxford, 1989).

F. Furet, *Revolutionary France, 1770–1880*, (Oxford, 1988).

R.B. Holtman, *Napoleonic Propaganda*, (Baton Rouge, 1950).

R.B. Holtman, *The Napoleonic Revolution*, (Philadelphia, PA, 1967).

L. Hunt, D. Lansky and P. Hanson, 'The failure of the liberal Republic in France, 1795–1799. The road to Brumaire', *Journal of Modern History*, 51 (1979).

P.M. Jones, *Politics and Rural Society. The Southern Massif Central, 1750–1880*, (Cambridge, 1985).

G. Lewis, *The Second Vendée. The Continuity of Counter-Revolution in the Department of the Gard, 1789–1815*, (Oxford, 1978).

M. Lyons, *Napoleon and the Legacy of the French Revolution*, (London, 1994).

P. Sahlins, *Boundaries. The Making of France and Spain in the Pyrenees*, (Berkeley, CA, 1989).

M.D. Sibalis, 'Corporatism after the corporations: the debate on the restoration of the guilds under Napoleon I and the Restoration', *French Historical Studies*, 15 (1988).

D.M.G. Sutherland, *France 1789–1815, Revolution and Counter revolution*, (London, 1985).

E.A. Whitcomb, *Napoleon's Diplomatic Service*, (Durham, NC, 1979).

E.A. Whitcomb, 'Napoleon's prefects', *American Historical Review*, 69 (1974).

I. Woloch, 'Napoleonic conscription: state power and civil society', *Past and Present*, 111 (1986).

I. Woloch, *The New Regime. Transformations of the French Civic Order, 1789–1820s*, (New York, 1994).

Napoleonic Europe

The German states and the Habsburg Empire

The entire issue of *Central European History*, 24, No. 3 (1991) is devoted to the German states in the revolutionary/Napoleonic/early Restoration period, and contains valuable articles on Baden, Nassau, Saxony, and Prussia.

R. Berdahl, *The Politics of the Prussian Nobility: the Development of a Conservative Ideology, 1770–1848*, (Princeton, NJ, 1988).

T.C.W. Blanning, 'The French Revolution and the modernization of Germany', *Central European History*, 22 (1989).

T.C.W. Blanning, *Germany and the French Revolution: Occupation and Resistance in the Rhineland 1792–1802*, (Oxford, 1983).

J. Breuilly, 'State-building, modernization and liberalism from the late eighteenth century to unification: German peculiarities', *European History Quarterly*, 22 (1992).

W. Carr, *The Origins of the German Wars of Unification*, (London, 1991).

M. Diefendorff, *Businessmen and Politics in the Rhineland 1789–1834*, (Princeton, NJ, 1980).

F.G. Eyck, *Loyal Rebels. Andreas Hofer and the Tyrolean Uprising of 1809*, (New York, 1986).

H.A.L. Fisher, *Studies in Napoleonic Statesmanship: Germany*, (Oxford, 1903).

J. Gagliardo, *From Pariah to Patriot. The Changing Image of the German Peasant, 1770–1840*, (Lexington, 1969).

J. Gagliardo, *Reich and Nation: the Holy Roman Empire as Idea and Reality, 1763–1806*, (Bloomington, 1980).

M. Gray, *Prussia in Transition: Society and Politics under the Stein Reform Ministry of 1808*, (Philadelphia, PA, 1986).

M. Gray, 'Schroetter, Schon and society: aristocratic liberalism versus middle-class liberalism in Prussia, 1808', *Central European History*, 6 (1973).

C. Ingaro, *The Habsburg Monarchy, 1618–1815*, (Cambridge, 1994).

D. Klang, 'Bavaria and the War of Liberation, 1813–1814', *French Historical Studies*, 4 (1965).

E. Kraehe, *Metternich's German Policy*, 2 vols (Princeton, NJ, 1963 and 1983).

L.E. Lee, *The Politics of Harmony. Civil Service, Liberalism and Social Reform in Baden, 1800–1850*, (Newark, NJ, 1980).

C.A. Macartney, *The Habsburg Empire, 1790–1918*, (London, 1968).

P. Paret, *Yorck and the Era of Prussian Reform 1807–1815*, (Princeton, NJ, 1966).

G. Pedlow, *The Survival of the Hessian Nobility, 1770–1870*, (Princeton, NJ, 1988).

K. Roider, 'The Habsburg Foreign Ministry and the political reform of 1800–1805', *Central European History*, 22 (1989).

G. Rothenberg, *Napoleon's Great Adversaries: Archduke Charles and the Austrian Army 1792–1814*, (London, 1982).

H. Schmitt, 'Germany without Prussia: a closer look at the Confederation of the Rhine', *German Studies Review*, 6 (1983).

J.J. Sheehan, *German History, 1770–1866*, (Oxford, 1989).

W.M. Simon, *The Failure of the Prussian Reform Movement, 1807–1819*, (Princeton, NJ, 1966).

J.A. Vann, 'Habsburg policy and the Austrian War of 1809', *Central European History*, 7 (1974).

J. Whaley, *Religious Toleration and Social Change in Hamburg, 1529–1819*, (Cambridge, 1985).

C.E. White, *The Enlightened Solidier: Scharnhorst and the Miltarische Gellschaft in Berlin, 1800–1805*, (New York, 1989).

Italy

M. Broers, 'Italy and the modern state: the experience of Napoleonic rule', in *The French Revolution and the Creation of Modern Political Culture*, vol. iii, *The Transformation of Political Culture, 1789–1848*, eds. F. Furet and M. Ozouf, (Oxford, 1989).

M. Broers, 'The parochial revolution: 1799 and the counterrevolution in Italy', *Renaissance and Modern Studies*, 33 (1989).

M. Broers, 'The police and the *padroni*: Italian *notabli*, French gendarmes and the centralized state in Napoleonic Italy', *European History Quarterly*, 26 (1996).

M. Broers, 'Policing Piedmont, 1789–1821', *Criminal Justice History*, 17 (1994).

M. Broers, 'Revolution as vendetta: Napoleonic Piedmont, 1800–1814',

Historical Journal, 33 (1990).

M. Broers, 'War and Crime in Napoleonic Italy', *Criminal Justice History*, 18 (1995).

O. Chadwick, *The Popes and the European Revolutions*, (Oxford, 1979).

J.A. Davis, *Conflict and Control. Law and Order in Nineteenth Century Italy*, (London, 1988).

J.A. Davis, 'The impact of French rule on the Kingdom of Naples, 1806–1815', *Ricerche Storiche*, 20 (1990).

A. Grab, 'Army, state and society: conscription and desertion in Napoleonic Italy (1802–1814)', *Journal of Modern History*, 67 (1995).

A. Grab, 'State power, brigandage and rural resistance in Napoleonic Italy', *European History Quarterly*, 25 (1995).

H. Hearder, *Italy in the Age of the Risorgimento, 1790–1870*, (London, 1983).

R. Johnston, *The Napoleonic Empire in Southern Italy and the Rise of the Secret Societies*, (London, 1904).

D. Outram, 'Education and politics in Piedmont, 1796–1814', *Historical Journal*, 19 (1976).

F. Della Peruta, 'War and society in Napoleonic Italy: the armies of the Kingdom of Italy at home and abroad', in *Society and Politics in Italy in the Age of the Resorgimento*, eds. J.A. Davis and P. Ginsborg, (Cambridge, 1991).

R.J. Rath, *The Fall of the Napoleonic Kingdom of Italy (1814)*, (New York, 1941).

J.H. Roselli, *Lord William Bentinck and the British Occupation of Sicily, 1811–1814*, (Cambridge, 1956).

S.J. Woolf, *A History of Italy, 1700–1860: the Social Constraints of Political Change*, (London, 1979).

The Low Countries

J. Drhondt, 'The cotton industry at Ghent during the French Revolution', in *Essays in European Economic History, 1789–1914*, eds. F. Crouzet, W. Chalnor and W. Stern, (London, 1969).

E.H. Kossman, 'The crisis of the Dutch state, 1780–1813: nationalism, feudalism, unitarism', in *Britain and the Netherlands*, eds. J.S. Bromely and E.H. Kossman, vol. iv (The Hague, 1971).

E.H. Kossman, *The Low Countries, 1780–1940*, (Oxford, 1978).

J. Mokyr, 'The industrial revolution in the Low Countries in the first half of the nineteenth century: a comparative case study', *Journal of Economic History*, 34 (1974).

S. Schama, *Patriots and Liberators. Revolution in the Netherlands 1780–1813*, (New York, 1977).

Spain

D.W. Alexander, *Rod of Iron: French counterinsurgency Policy in Aragon during the Peninsular War*, (Wilmington, DE, 1985).

*J.R. Aymes, *La Guerre d'Indépendence Espagnole, (1808–1814)*, (Paris, 1973). For those with French, but not Spanish, this is an excellent synthesis of the classic literature.

W. Callahan, *Church, Politics and Society in Spain, 1750–1854*, (London, 1985).

W. Callahan, 'The origins of the conservative Church in Spain', *European Studies Review*, 10 (1980).

O. Connelly, *The Gentle Bonaparte: a Biography of Joseph, Napoleon's Elder Brother*, (New York, 1968).

C.J. Esdaile, *The Duke of Wellington and the Command of the Spanish Army*, (Manchester, 1990).

C.J. Esdaile, 'The Duke of Wellington and the military eclipse of Spain', *International History Review*, 11 (1989).

C.J. Esdaile, 'The Duke of Wellington and the command of the Spanish army', in *Wellington: Studies in the Military and Political Career of the First Duke of Wellington*, ed. N. Gash, (Manchester, 1990).

C.J. Esdaile, 'Heroes or villains? The Spanish guerrillas and the Peninsular War', *History Today*, 38 (1988).

C.J. Esdaile, *The Spanish Army in the Peninsular War*, (Manchester, 1988).

C.J. Esdaile, 'War and Politics in Spain, 1808–1814', *Historical Journal*, 31 (1988).

D. Gates, *The Spanish Ulcer: a History of the Peninsular War*, (London, 1986).

B. Hamnett, 'Constitutional theory and political reality: liberalism, traditionalism and the Spanish *Cortes*, 1810–1814', *Journal of Modern History*, 50 (1977).

B. Hamnett, 'Spanish constitutionalism and the impact of the French Revolution, 1808–1814', in *The Impact of the French Revolution on European Consciousness*, eds. H. Mason and W. Doyle, (Gloucester, 1989).

R. Herr, 'Good, evil and Spain's uprising against Napoleon', in *Ideas in History*, eds. R. Herr and H. Parker, (Durham, NC, 1965).

D. Hilt, *The Troubled Trinity: Godoy and the Spanish Monarchs*, (Tuscaloosa, AL, 1987).

G. Lovett, *Napoleon and the Birth of Modern Spain*, 2 vols (New York, 1965).

J. Polt, *Gaspar Melchor de Jovellanos*, (New York, 1971).

Portugal

D. Francis, *Portugal, 1715–1808*, (London, 1985).
D.D. Howard, 'Wellington and the defence of Portugal', *International History Review*, 11 (1989).
H.V. Livermore, *A New History of Portugal*, (Cambridge, 1966).

The Illyrian provinces

There is no accessible study in English of the Illyrian provinces under French rule. For a comprehensive study, in French:

*M. Senkowska-Gluck, 'Pouvoir et société en Illyrie napoléonienne', *Révue de l'Institut Napoléon*, 136 (1980).

Much can be learned about Illyria in:

S.J. Woolf, 'Civilization and ethnicity in the Napoleonic Empire', *Past and Present*, 124 (1989).

The Grand Duchy of Warsaw

N. Davies, *Poland, God's Playground*, vol. i (London, 1979).
J. Hartley, *Alexander I*, (London, 1994).
M. Kukiel, *Czartoyski and European Unity (1770–1861)*, (Princeton, NJ, 1955).
P. Wandycz, *The Lands of Partitioned Poland, 1795–1918*, (Seattle, 1974).
W.H. Zawadzki, *A Man of Honour. Adam Czartoyski as a Statesman of Russia and Poland, 1795–1831*, (Oxford, 1993).

Index

Page references to maps are shown in *italics*.
France and Napoleon are largely omitted from this index as references are ubiquitous.

●

Printed in the United States
6784